A CENTURY OF PIONEERING

A HISTORY OF

THE URSULINE NUNS IN NEW ORLEANS

(1727-1827)

SISTER JANE FRANCES HEANEY, O.S.U., PH.D

EDITED BY MARY ETHEL BOOKER SIEFKEN

URSULINE SISTERS OF NEW ORLEANS, LOUISIANA

LIBRARY OF CONGRESS CATALOG CARD NUMBER: 92-85519

INTERNATIONAL STANDARD BOOK NUMBER 0-9635044-0-1

ORIGINALLY WRITTEN AS A DISSERTATION PRESENTED TO
THE FACULTY OF THE GRADUATE SCHOOL OF ST. LOUIS UNI-
VERSITY IN PARTIAL FULFILLMENT OF THE REQUIREMENTS
FOR THE DEGREE OF DOCTOR OF PHILOSOPHY, 1949.

COMMITTEE IN CHARGE OF CANDIDACY,
PROFESSOR JOHN FRANCIS BANNON, S.J.,
CHAIRMAN AND ADVISER,
PROFESSOR BERNARD WILLIAM DEMPSEY, S.J.,
ASSOCIATE PROFESSOR,
JOSEPH PETER DONNELLEY, S.J.,
PROFESSOR LAURENCE J. KENNY, S.J.,
ASSOCIATE PROFESSOR,
THOMAS PATRICK NEILL

JACKET AND BOOK DESIGN BY SALLY LIGHTFOOT KOCH

*Cover photo, "View of the River from Ursuline Bell Tower",
courtesy of Historic New Orleans Collection, 1960.28.*

PUBLISHED BY THE URSULINE SISTERS OF NEW ORLEANS, LOUISIANA

PRINTED BY BOOKCRAFTERS, CHELSEA, MICHIGAN.

TABLE OF CONTENTS

PREFACE

IT IS THE PURPOSE OF THIS BOOK TO DESCRIBE THE COMING OF THE URSULINES TO NEW ORLEANS IN 1727, TOGETHER WITH THEIR WORK AS NURSES AND EDUCATORS AND THE VARIOUS PROBLEMS THAT THEY FACED DURING ONE HUNDRED YEARS. THIS HISTORY OF THE URSULINES TERMINATES IN 1827, FOR WITH THE COMING OF THE RELIGIOUS OF THE SACRED HEART TO LOUISIANA IN 1821 THE WORK OF THE URSULINES CEASED TO BE UNIQUE. BY ARDENT PRAYER, PATIENT LABOR, AND HEROIC SUFFERING THEY HAD PREPARED THE SOIL SO THAT OTHERS MIGHT REAP A RICHER HARVEST.

THE HISTORY OF THE URSULINES IN NEW ORLEANS HAS BEEN TOLD, IN PART, BEFORE. MOTHER THÉRÈSE WOLFE BASED HER *URSULINES IN NEW ORLEANS, 1727-1925*, ALMOST EXCLUSIVELY ON MATERIALS FOUND IN THE CONVENT ARCHIVES. FATHER JEAN DELANGLEZ, S.J., IN *THE FRENCH JESUITS IN LOWER LOUISIANA, 1700-1763*, UTILIZED MATERIALS IN THE FRENCH ARCHIVES AND RELATED THE STORY OF THE EARLY YEARS OF THE URSULINES IN NEW ORLEANS IN SO FAR AS THEIR STORY IMPINGED ON THAT OF THE JESUITS. MR. SAMUEL WILSON, JR., IN HIS ARTICLE, "AN ARCHITECTURAL HISTORY OF THE ROYAL HOSPITAL AND THE URSULINE CONVENT OF NEW ORLEANS," IN THE *LOUISIANA HISTORICAL QUARTERLY* WOVE INTO THE NARRATIVE MANY FACTS NOT INDICATED BY THE TITLE. THE ANONYMOUS WORK THE *URSULINES IN LOUISIANA, 1727-1824* IS OF LITTLE HISTORICAL VALUE. NEARLY ALL THE PERIODICAL LITERATURE REPEATS THE ERRONEOUS TRADITIONS THAT HAVE BECOME A PART OF THE "HISTORY" OF THE URSULINES IN NEW ORLEANS.

IT SEEMED, THEREFORE, TO THE PRESENT WRITER THAT BY EXPLORING ARCHIVAL REPOSITORIES IN THIS COUNTRY, IN CANADA, AND IN CUBA, AND BY CONSULTING DOCUMENTS IN THE FRENCH AND SPANISH ARCHIVES, A FULLER ACCOUNT MIGHT BE WRITTEN AND A RE-TELLING OF THIS PHASE OF URSULINE HISTORY BE JUSTIFIED. EVEN AFTER LONG RESEARCH, HOWEVER, THIS NARRATIVE HAS MANY MISSING PARTS. WHAT RECORDS ONCE EXISTED HAVE LONG SINCE DISAPPEARED. FATHER CHARLES BOURNIGALLE COMPLAINED OF THIS FACT SOME EIGHTY YEARS AGO WHEN HE THOROUGHLY EXPLORED THE CONVENT ARCHIVES WITH A VIEW TO COMPILING THE ANNALS.

IT IS A PLEASURE TO EXPRESS GRATEFUL ACKNOWLEDGEMENT AND SINCERE APPRECIATION TO THE MANY PEOPLE TO WHOM THE WRITER IS

OBLIGATED FOR ASSISTANCE OF VARIOUS KINDS. TO NAME ALL WOULD UN-
DULY LENGTHEN THIS ACCOUNT. SOME HOWEVER, SHOULD NOT BE PASSED
OVER WITHOUT MENTION. TO FATHER JEAN-MARIE BEAUCHEMIN FOR
VALUABLE ASSISTANCE WHILE WORKING IN THE ARCHIVES OF THE ARCH-
DIOCESE OF QUEBEC, AND TO FATHER THOMAS T. MCAVOY, C.S.C., CUSTODIAN
OF THE CATHOLIC ARCHIVES OF AMERICA, THE WRITER EXPRESSES HER GRATI-
TUDE. A WORD OF APPRECIATION IS DUE TO THE STAFF OF THE DIVISION
OF MANUSCRIPTS OF THE LIBRARY OF CONGRESS FOR UNFAILING COURTESY
AND ASSISTANCE. TO THE COMMUNITY OF THE MONASTÈRE DES URSULINES
OF QUEBEC FOR GRACIOUS HOSPITALITY AND THE PRIVILEGE OF WORKING
IN THE ARCHIVES UNDER THE ABLE DIRECTION OF THE ARCHIVIST, THE
WRITER IS GRATEFUL. SINCERE THANKS IS ALSO DUE TO THE ARCHIVIST
OF THE URSULINE CONVENT OF NEW ORLEANS FOR HOSPITALITY AND GEN-
EROUS ASSISTANCE DURING THE MONTHS THE WRITER SPENT ON ARCHIVAL
RESEARCH IN NEW ORLEANS. FINALLY THE WRITER IS PROFOUNDLY INDEBTED
TO HER COMMUNITY, THE URSULINE SISTERS OF DECATUR, ILLINOIS, FOR
THE OPPORTUNITY AND FREEDOM TO ACCOMPLISH THIS WORK.

SPECIAL ACKNOWLEDGEMENT AND GRATITUDE ARE DUE TO FATHER
BANNON, S.J. FOR HIS COMPETENT DIRECTION, SUSTAINED INTEREST, AND
HELPFUL ADVICE IN THE PREPARATION OF THIS BOOK.

Sister Jane Frances Heaney, O.S.U.

Decatur, Illinois
June 20, 19986

FOREWARD

THE STORY YOU ARE ABOUT TO READ IS ONE OF REMARKABLE BRAVERY. IT CHRONICLES THE EXPERIENCES OF A SMALL GROUP OF WOMEN WHO ACCEPTED A CHALLENGE TO COME TO A "NEW WORLD" IN ORDER TO SPREAD THE GOSPEL THROUGH THEIR EDUCATIONAL EFFORTS. IN MAKING THIS COMMITMENT, THEY HAD ONLY A VAGUE IDEA OF THE CONDITIONS THEY WOULD FACE: HEAT, RAIN, MOSQUITOES, POVERTY, INADEQUATE LIVING CONDITIONS, OVERWORK, EMOTIONAL PAIN, POLITICAL DILEMMA, AND LENGTHY MESSAGES FROM FRANCE AS TO WHAT THEY SHOULD BE DOING. YET THEIR RECORDS REFLECT AN ACCEPTANCE OF CIRCUMSTANCES THAT IS HARD TO IMAGINE IN OUR TWENTIETH-CENTURY WORLD OF MATERIAL LARGESS.

DURING THE 1940'S SISTER JANE FRANCES HEANEY, O.S.U. RELENT-LESSLY PURSUED DOCUMENTS RELATING TO THE HISTORY OF THE FIRST HUNDRED YEARS OF THE URSULINE NUNS IN THE UNITED STATES. THE ORIGINAL MANUSCRIPT FOR HER 1949 PH.D. DISSERTATION WAS CONSIDERED FOR PUBLICATION SEVERAL TIMES, BUT DELAYS ENSUED. THE URSULINE SISTERS OF NEW ORLEANS AS PUBLISHERS, THROUGH THE GENEROSITY OF THE PATRONS LISTED IN THE APPENDIX OF THIS BOOK, NOW OFFER TO READERS THE WONDERFUL DETAILS OF THE NUNS' EXPERIENCES DURING THE EARLY PERIOD OF THEIR ESTABLISHMENT IN NEW ORLEANS.

THE EDITOR HAS TRIED TO RETAIN THE FLAVOR OF SR. JANE FRANCES' ORIGINAL MANUSCRIPT. THE READER MUST KEEP IN MIND THAT IN 1949 A ROMAN CATHOLIC NUN WOULD HAVE BEEN RELUCTANT TO CRITICIZE THE CLERGY IN HER DISSERTATION. TODAY, ADDITIONAL RESEARCH HAS SHOWN THAT POLITICS PLAYED A LARGE ROLE IN THE DIRECTIONS THE CLERGY GAVE TO THE RELIGIOUS, UNDER BOTH THE FRENCH AND SPANISH REGIMES, AND EVEN DURING THE PERIOD OF UNITED STATES GOVERNANCE. IT WILL BE OBVIOUS TO THE READER THAT SISTER JANE FRANCES HAS HER "FAVORITES" AMONG THE HISTORICAL CLERGY, AS WELL AS AMONG THE POLITICAL FIGURES. DURING CERTAIN PERIODS THERE ARE GAPS IN THE ORIGINAL RECORDS AS WRITTEN BY THE URSULINES, WHO MAY HAVE BEEN

AFRAID TO RECORD POLITICAL HAPPENINGS THAT RELATED TO THEIR VERY EXISTENCE, LEST THEY BE CALLED TO TASK BY THE CLERGY. THE RECORDS DO SHOW THAT THE URSULINES WERE NOT AFRAID TO STAND UP FOR THEIR RIGHTS OR TO EXPRESS OPINIONS WHEN THE WELFARE OF THE COMMUNITY, THE STUDENTS OR ORPHANS WAS IN JEOPARDY.

WE HAVE INCLUDED THE FOOTNOTES AND BIBLIOGRAPHICAL MATERIALS THAT SISTER JANE FRANCES METICULOUSLY COMPILED. WE ALSO INCLUDE A SUPPLEMENTARY LIST OF BOOKS THAT HAVE APPEARED SINCE 1949, WHICH WERE GENERALLY HELPFUL TO THE EDITOR IN RESEARCHING PERTINENT DATA. FOR AN UPDATED, COMPREHENSIVE BIBLIOGRAPHY OF LITERATURE REGARDING THE ROMAN CATHOLIC CHURCH IN LOUISIANA, CONSULT THE ESSAY ENTITLED "LOUISIANA CATHOLIC HISTORIOGRAPHY" BY DR. CHARLES E. NOLAN, ARCHIVIST OF THE ARCHDIOCESE OF NEW ORLEANS, IN *CROSS, CROZIER, AND CRUCIBLE*, (NEW ORLEANS, 1993), A PUBLICATION FOR THE BICENTENNIAL OF THE ARCHDIOCESE OF NEW ORLEANS.

SISTER JANE FRANCES HEANEY DIED ON DECEMBER 8, 1992, JUST AS WE WERE MAKING ARRANGEMENTS FOR THE PRINTING OF THE BOOK. I KNOW SHE JOINS ME IN THANKING THOSE WHO WERE SO IMPORTANT IN ARRANGING THE PUBLICATION OF THIS WORK. SPECIAL THANKS MUST GO TO SISTER DAMIAN AYCOCK, O.S.U., PRESIDENT OF URSULINE ACADEMY AND FORMER SUPERIOR, FOR SAYING "YES, LET'S DO IT!", TO SISTER MARY JACQUELINE PRATT, O.S.U., FORMER SUPERIOR, WHO BROUGHT THE MANUSCRIPT TO THE ATTENTION OF A PUBLISHER AND TO ALUMNAE, AND TO SISTER SUSAN KIENZLER, O.S.U., CURRENT SUPERIOR, WHO HAS CONTINUED TO SUPPORT PUBLICATION OF THE BOOK. SISTER JOAN MARIE AYCOCK, O.S.U., URSULINE ARCHIVIST, HAS SPENT HUNDREDS OF HOURS GATHERING ADDITIONAL ARCHIVAL INFORMATION AS WELL AS PICTURES, KEEPING RECORDS ON OUR PATRONS, AND HAS BEEN A SOURCE OF ENCOURAGEMENT AND SUPPORT TO THE EDITOR. SISTER JACQUELINE TOPPINO, O.S.U. PHOTOGRAPHED MANY OF THE PICTURES IN THE BOOK AND HELPED TO GIVE DIRECTION WITH REGARD TO THE RULE OF THE URSULINES. SISTER GERTRUDE BECKER, O.S.U. TYPED THE ORIGINAL MANUSCRIPT FOR THE PH.D. PRESENTATION IN 1949, AND SR. PIERRE LANDRY, O.S.U. AND SR. LOYOLA WEILBAECHER, O.S.U. BOTH ASSISTED IN CORRECTING THE USAGE OF FRENCH WORDS. URSULINE ALUMNA SALLY LIGHTFOOT KOCH GAVE US THE BENEFIT OF HER ARTISTIC TALENT FOR THE COVER AND BOOK DESIGN. FINALLY I MUST GIVE A TREMENDOUS ROUND OF THANKS TO SALLY KITTREDGE REEVES, A DAUGHTER OF THE SACRED HEART AND AN ACCOMPLISHED AUTHOR AND HISTORIAN, FOR THE TIME AND EFFORT SHE GAVE IN HELPING TO PUT TOGETHER THE MESSAGE OF THIS BOOK. SALLY AND I SHARE A LOVE FOR BOTH THE URSULINES AND THE RELIGIOUS OF THE SACRED HEART IN THAT WE HAVE BOTH BEEN BENEFICIARIES OF A HERITAGE IN WHICH WE AS WOMEN COULD GROW AND

LOVE GOD AS WOMEN. THE WOMEN CHRONICLED IN THIS BOOK SHOULD INSPIRE ANYONE TODAY THROUGH THEIR UNPARALLELED SPIRIT AND DETERMINATION TO PERSEVERE IN THE FACE OF SEEMINGLY ENDLESS OBSTACLES.

Mary Ethel Booker Siefken
December 14, 1992
New Orleans, Louisiana

INTRODUCTION

BY SAMUEL WILSON, JR., F.A.I.A.

FOR MORE THAN TWO AND A HALF CENTURIES THE URSULINE NUNS OF NEW ORLEANS HAVE BEEN A VITAL PART OF THE HISTORY OF THE CITY, CONTRIBUTING TREMENDOUSLY TO ITS RELIGIOUS, EDUCATIONAL AND CULTURAL PROGRESS. FROM ITS FOUNDING IN THE EARLY SIXTEENTH CENTURY IN NORTHERN ITALY, THIS TEACHING ORDER SPREAD TO FRANCE AND THEN TO CANADA. FINALLY IN 1726 THE URSULINES OF ROUEN, ON THE URGING OF FATHER NICHOLAS IGNATIUS DE BEAUBOIS, SUPERIOR OF THE JESUIT MISSION OF THE ILLINOIS, AGREED TO COME TO LOUISIANA. A TREATY WAS THEN SIGNED IN PARIS ON SEPTEMBER 13, 1726 BETWEEN THE COMPANY OF THE INDIES AND THE URSULINES FOR "A NEW ESTABLISHMENT... TO RELIEVE THE POOR SICK AND PROVIDE AT THE SAME TIME FOR THE EDUCATION OF YOUNG GIRLS."

NUMEROUS BOOKS AND ARTICLES HAVE BEEN WRITTEN ABOUT THE URSULINES OF NEW ORLEANS, ONE OF THE EARLIEST BEING THE SERIES OF FIVE LETTERS WRITTEN BY MARIE MADELEINE HACHARD, SISTER SAINT STANISLAUS, TO HER FATHER IN ROUEN, DESCRIBING THEIR JOURNEY TO NEW ORLEANS IN 1727 AND THEIR FIRST YEAR IN THE TINY COLONIAL TOWN. THESE LETTERS WERE FIRST PUBLISHED IN ROUEN IN 1728 AND REPRINTED FROM ONE OF THE RARE ORIGINAL COPIES IN 1865 WITH AN INTRODUCTORY NOTICE BY PAUL BAUDRY. THE LETTERS WERE AGAIN PUBLISHED IN 1872 WITH AN INTRODUCTION AND NOTES BY GABRIEL GRAVIER. THESE FIRST THREE PUBLICATIONS WERE IN THE ORIGINAL FRENCH. IN 1925 AN ENGLISH TRANSLATION OF THE LETTERS WAS INCLUDED IN THE SUPPLEMENT TO A VOLUME ENTITLED *THE URSULINES IN NEW ORLEANS AND OUR LADY OF PROMPT SUCCOR*, EDITED BY THE REV. HENRY CHURCHILL SEMPLE, S.J. AND PUBLISHED IN NEW YORK. THIS INTERESTING AND WELL ILLUSTRATED VOLUME CONTAINS MUCH INTERESTING INFORMATION ABOUT THE URSULINES IN NEW ORLEANS FROM 1727 TO 1925 AND QUOTES NUMEROUS HISTORICAL DOCUMENTS. IT IS NOT, HOWEVER, A COMPREHENSIVE, DOCUMENTED HISTORY OF THE ORDER IN LOUISIANA. THEN IN 1974 ANOTHER ENGLISH TRANSLATION BY MYLDRED MASSON COSTA WAS PUBLISHED IN NEW ORLEANS. THESE FASCINATING LETTERS CONTAIN ONE OF THE EARLIEST ACCOUNTS

OF LIFE IN THE FRENCH COLONIAL CAPITAL OF LOUISIANA.

MY OWN INTEREST IN THE URSULINES AND THEIR OLD CONVENT BUILDING ON CHARTRES STREET, THEN THE RECTORY OF ST. MARY'S ITALIAN CHURCH, BEGAN AS A STUDENT PROJECT AT TULANE UNIVERSITY'S SCHOOL OF ARCHITECTURE IN 1929 WHEN CLASSMATE WILLIAM C. GILMER AND I SUBMITTED MEASURED AND RENDERED PLANS AND A PERSPECTIVE DRAWING OF THE CONVENT IN THE ANNUAL COMPETITION IN LOUISIANA ARCHITECTURE FOR THE S.S. LABOUISSE PRIZE. ALTHOUGH OUR SUBMISSION WAS NOT AWARDED THE PRIZE, THE PROJECT AROUSED MY INTEREST IN THE ARCHITECTURAL HISTORY OF THIS VENERABLE BUILDING, THE ONLY BUILDING THAT HAS SURVIVED ALMOST INTACT FROM THE PERIOD OF THE FRENCH REGIME IN LOUISIANA.

IN 1934, WITH THE BEGINNING OF THE HISTORIC AMERICAN BUILDINGS SURVEY, I HAD THE OPPORTUNITY TO AGAIN STUDY THIS OLD BUILDING. WORKING WITH OTHERS UNDER THE DIRECTION OF RICHARD KOCH, ARCHITECT AND DISTRICT OFFICER OF THE SURVEY IN LOUISIANA, WE PRODUCED A COMPLETE SET OF MEASURED DRAWINGS, WITH PLANS, ELEVATIONS AND DETAILS, AND DEPOSITED THEM WITH OTHER RECORDS OF THE SURVEY IN THE LIBRARY OF CONGRESS. THE SURVEY HAD BEEN ESTABLISHED DURING THE DEPRESSION YEARS OF THE 1930'S AS A WORKS PROGRESS ADMINISTRATION PROJECT TO PROVIDE WORK FOR UNEMPLOYED ARCHITECTS AND DRAFTSMEN. THE PROJECT WAS JOINTLY SPONSORED BY THE NATIONAL PARK SERVICE TO RECORD IN MEASURED DRAWINGS, PHOTOGRAPHS AND HISTORICAL RESEARCH, BUILDINGS SIGNIFICANT IN THE ARCHITECTURAL HISTORY OF THE UNITED STATES. THE OLD URSULINE CONVENT WAS ONE OF THE FIRST TO BE SO RECORDED.

IN 1938 THE AMERICAN INSTITUTE OF ARCHITECTS AWARDED ME AN EDWARD LANGLEY SCHOLARSHIP FOR STUDY AND TRAVEL IN EUROPE TO INVESTIGATE THE ORIGINS OF LOUISIANA ARCHITECTURE. DURING THE COURSE OF MY RESEARCH IN THE *ARCHIVES NATIONALES* IN PARIS, I MADE THE SURPRISING DISCOVERY THAT THE OLD CONVENT ON CHARTRES STREET WAS NOT THE BUILDING THAT HAD BEEN ERECTED FOR THE URSULINES BY THE COMPANY OF THE INDIES ON THEIR ARRIVAL IN NEW ORLEANS IN 1727, BUT A SECOND BUILDING REPLACING THE DETERIORATED FIRST STRUCTURE OF BRICKS BETWEEN POSTS CONSTRUCTION. THIS SECOND BUILDING OF SUBSTANTIAL BRICK CONSTRUCTION WAS AUTHORIZED BY THE KING, LOUIS XV, AND DESIGNED IN 1745 BY THE FRENCH MILITARY ENGINEER AND ARCHITECT, IGNACE FRANÇOIS BROUTIN, AND COMPLETED ABOUT 1750. PLANS OF BOTH THE FIRST AND SECOND CONVENT BUILDINGS WERE FOUND IN THE PARIS ARCHIVES, AND CORRESPONDENCE OF THE GOVERNOR, BIENVILLE, AND THE ENGINEERS WITH THE MINISTER OF THE MARINE CONFIRMED THIS IRREFUTABLY, ALTHOUGH IT HAD BEEN BELIEVED OTH-

ERWISE SINCE AT LEAST AS EARLY AS 1817 WHEN JACQUES TANESSE, CITY SURVEYOR, PUBLISHED HIS WELL-KNOWN "PLAN OF THE CITY AND SUBURBS OF NEW ORLEANS FROM AN ACTUAL SURVEY MADE IN 1815". IN MARGINAL DRAWINGS THE MAP ILLUSTRATES AND IDENTIFIES THE LATER BUILDING AS *"CONVENT DES RELIGIEUSES CONSTRUIT EN 1733"*.

THE RESULTS OF MY 1938 RESEARCH WERE PUBLISHED IN AN ILLUS-TRATED ARTICLE ENTITLED "AN ARCHITECTURAL HISTORY OF THE ROYAL HOSPITAL AND THE URSULINE CONVENT OF NEW ORLEANS". THIS APPEARED IN THE *LOUISIANA HISTORICAL QUARTERLY* IN JULY 1946. THE URSULINES AT FIRST HAD DIFFICULTY IN ACCEPTING THE FACT THAT THE OLD CONVENT ON CHARTRES STREET WAS NOT THE ONE BUILT FOR THEM BETWEEN 1727 AND 1734, FOR NO RECORD OF THE CONSTRUCTION OF A SECOND BUILDING COULD BE FOUND IN THE CONVENT ARCHIVES. THE RESEARCH OF SISTER JANE FRANCES HEANEY FOR HER DISSERTATION AT ST. LOUIS UNIVERSITY IN 1949, HOWEVER, CONFIRMED THIS FACT.

A STUDY OF THE DRAWINGS FOR THE FIRST AND SECOND CONVENT BUILDINGS INDICATED A REMARKABLE SIMILARITY IN THE GREAT STAIRWAY IN BOTH BUILDINGS AND LED TO THE SURMISE THAT THE STAIRWAY FROM THE FIRST BUILDING HAD BEEN REUSED IN THE SECOND STRUCTURE, WHERE IT REMAINS TODAY. MY LATER RESEARCH IN THE MANUSCRIPTS DIVISION OF THE LIBRARY OF CONGRESS PROVED THAT THIS WAS INDEED THE CASE. IN THE *TOISE' DE BATIMENT*, A QUANTITY SURVEY OF THE WORKS OF CARPEN-TRY, MASONRY, IRONWORK, ETC. USED IN BUILDING THE SECOND CONVENT, THE ARCHITECT-ENGINEER BERNARD DEVERGES RECORDED:

> THE LABOR FOR THE DEMOLITION OF THE STAIRCASE OF THE OLD HOUSE WITH ITS RE-ESTABLISHMENT IN THE NEW HOUSE AT WHICH THERE HAS BEEN SET UP ANEW THE SEVEN FIRST STEPS FROM THE BOTTOM, THE BALL VOLUTE OF THE STRINGER OF THE FIRST RAMP AS WELL AS THE STRINGERS OF THE ATTIC RAMPS, REDUCING THEM TO TWO INSTEAD OF THREE WHICH IT HAD, THE SAME AS THEIR RAMPS, THOSE WHICH HAVE BEEN NARROWED ACCORDING TO THE ARRANGEMENT OF THESE NEW RAMPS TO THE TREADS, THE LENGTH OF WHICH HAVE BEEN DIMINISHED BY FOUR INCHES. ESTIMATED THE WHOLE TOGETHER AT THE SUM OF NINE HUNDRED FIFTY LIVRES, THUS...950.

IN A LATER ENTRY DATED DECEMBER 31, 1753 FOR WORK "AT THE NEW HOUSE OF THE NUNS," THERE WAS LISTED "THE FURNISHING OF A MILLER'S LADDER, PLACED WHERE FORMERLY WAS THE STAIRWAY IN THE OLD HOUSE," INDICATING THAT THE OLD CONVENT CONTINUED TO BE USED AT LEAST FOR SEVERAL YEARS AFTER THE NEW CONVENT WAS COM-PLETED. THIS LENGTHY AND DETAILED *TOISE'* ALSO EXPLAINED THE CHANGE

IN DESIGN OF THE TWO FACADES OF THE BUILDING FROM BROUTIN'S DRAWING OF 1745. THE CENTRAL ELEMENT OR FRONTISPIECE WAS ENLARGED FROM THE ONE BAY OF THE ORIGINAL DESIGN TO THE THREE BAY, PEDIMENTED FRONTISPIECE OF THE BUILDING AS IT EXISTS. DEVERGES, WHO HAD BECOME ENGINEER-IN-CHIEF OF LOUISIANA AFTER THE DEATH OF BROUTIN IN 1751, WROTE THAT "THE ENTRANCE FORE BAYS ON THE TWO FACADES OF THE BUILDING [HAVE] BEEN ENLARGED IN THE EXECUTION BY SEVENTEEN FEET MORE IN WIDTH EACH, THAN WAS SHOWN ON THE PLAN OF THE PROJECT."

THIS *TOISE'*, DATED DECEMBER 31, 1749, WITH CONTINUATIONS DATED FEBRUARY 9, 1751, DECEMBER 31, 1752, DECEMBER 31, 1753 AND APRIL 10, 1754, WAS THE BASIS FOR PAYMENTS TO THE CONTRACTOR JOSEPH DUBREUIL FOR "THE WORKS OF THE HOUSE OF THE URSULINE NUNS...ACCORDING TO THE CONTRACT MADE WITH HIM BY MONSIEUR MICHEL, COMMISSIONER OF THE MARINE, *ORDONNATEUR* IN THIS PROVINCE, THE THIRD OF JANUARY, ONE THOUSAND, SEVEN HUNDRED FORTY-NINE."

THE FIRST HUNDRED YEARS OF SERVICE OF THE URSULINES IN NEW ORLEANS WAS A PERIOD OF MOMENTOUS EVENTS AND GREAT CHANGES THAT HAD A GREAT IMPACT ON THESE DEDICATED NUNS. ONLY TWO YEARS AFTER THEIR ARRIVAL, THE MASSACRE OF THE FRENCH BY THE NATCHEZ INDIANS OCCURRED, LEAVING NUMEROUS ORPHANS WHOM THE URSULINES CARED FOR. IN 1734 THEIR FIRST CONVENT WAS FINALLY OCCUPIED, AND LESS THAN TWENTY YEARS LATER IT HAD TO BE REPLACED. IN 1762 LOUIS XV GAVE LOUISIANA TO HIS COUSIN, CARLOS III OF SPAIN. THE URSULINES WITNESSED THE EVENTS OF THE REVOLT OF THE COLONISTS AGAINST THE SPANISH GOVERNOR ANTONIO DE ULLOA IN 1768 AND HEARD THE SHOTS FIRED IN THE EXECUTION OF THE REVOLT'S LEADERS. IN 1788 THE CONFLAGRATION OF MARCH 21 THAT DESTROYED MUCH OF THE CITY THREATENED THE CONVENT. THE RELIGIOUS SAW THE EFFECTS OF A SECOND DISASTROUS FIRE ON DECEMBER 8, 1794. IN 1803 SPAIN RETROCEDED LOUISIANA TO NAPOLEON'S FRANCE, AND ON DECEMBER 20 OF THAT YEAR FRANCE TRANSFERRED IT TO THE UNITED STATES. IN SPITE OF THEIR FEARS OF LIVING UNDER A NEW AND ESSENTIALLY PROTESTANT GOVERNMENT, THE URSULINES REMAINED AND CONTINUED TO CARRY OUT THEIR CHARITABLE AND EDUCATIONAL WORK, ASSURED BY PRESIDENT THOMAS JEFFERSON THAT "THE PROPERTY VESTED IN YOUR INSTITUTION BY THE FORMER GOVERNMENT OF LOUISIANA...WILL BE PRESERVED TO YOU, SACRED AND INVIOLATE." THEY HEARD THE SOUNDS OF THE BATTLE OF NEW ORLEANS IN 1814-15 AND PRAYED FOR THE AMERICAN VICTORY. AS THEY NEARED THE END OF THEIR FIRST CENTURY OF SERVICE IN NEW ORLEANS, THEY BUILT A NEW CONVENT DOWN THE RIVER AND GENEROUSLY DONATED THEIR VENERABLE OLD BUILDING TO THE BISHOP OF NEW ORLEANS. IT NOW HOUSES THE ARCHIVES OF THE ARCHDIOCESE OF NEW ORLEANS.

THE URSULINES CONTINUED THEIR SERVICES IN THEIR NEW CONVENT BELOW THE CITY FOR MOST OF THEIR SECOND CENTURY IN NEW ORLEANS UNTIL THEIR REMOVAL IN 1911 TO THEIR PRESENT CONVENT ON STATE STREET, WHERE THEY STILL CARRY ON THE WORK BEGUN IN THIS CITY TWO AND A HALF CENTURIES AGO.

Samuel Wilson, Jr., F.A.I.A.
25 December 1986
New Orleans, Louisiana

STA ANGELA MERICI

Statue depicting St. Angela with children, Hachinohe, Japan. Photo by Sr. Jacqueline Toppino, O.S.U.

CHAPTER 1

Old World Beginnings

Angela Merici

The lofty foothills of the Alps enclose a series of beautiful lakes, the largest of which is Lake Garda located in the eastern area of the region. Sheltered and protected by the mountains from the rigors and changes of an Alpine climate, olive groves and vineyards have flourished for centuries on the fertile slopes and low-lands. Nestling in the southwestern corner of the area is the hamlet of Desenzano, Italy. With a history that reaches back to ancient Rome, Desenzano was of greater importance in the late fifteenth century than it is today.

John Merici, inscribed in the registers of the time as a citizen of Brescia and Desenzano,[1] and his wife, a daughter of the highly respected Biancosi family of the neighboring town of Salo, lived about two miles outside of Desenzano. During their marriage it is generally thought that the Mericis had five children, three boys and two girls.[2] The youngest child, Angela, born March 21, 1474,[3] was destined to leave her influence on succeeding centuries. Her biographers do not even tell us her mother's name, or those of her brothers and sister. Whatever may have been the social position or financial status of the Merici family, it is certain that both father and mother were fervent Christians intent on guiding the footsteps of their children along the path that leads to God. Biographers of Angela place emphasis on the part which John Merici had in the spiritual and intellectual formation of his children. They relate how he gathered his children together each evening and read from the Scriptures, the Lives of the Saints, or the Fathers of the Desert. The seeds of God's message were thus planted in Angela's mind at an early age.

Angela's quiet girlhood, passed amid the routine of simple household tasks, differed from that of other girls only in its serious piety, love of prayer, and unobtrusive spirit of self-denial. If Angela inclined to asceticism, it was not to the exclusion of natural joys. She must have participated in the lively old games, the vintage merrymaking, the guild festivities, and undoubtedly she passed many a joyous, carefree day with her Biancosi cousins at Salo just fourteen miles away.

The tranquil life of Angela's happy home was rudely shaken by the death of her father while he was still in the prime of life, and the subsequent death of her mother within a year. Angela then probably assumed the care of the household, as well as of the grounds. In those circumstances she would have had ample opportunity to develop both that sense of the practical and the executive ability which so strikingly characterized her mature years.

Despite early maturity, Angela and her sister were too young to live alone in the Merici home.[4] Fortunately their maternal uncle, Bartolomeo Biancosi, was glad to welcome the two orphans to his home in Salo. To domestic duties in the Biancosi household the young girls added prayer and service to the needy and poor. Biographers state that Angela's cherished sister, the companion so intimately associated with her in all her activities, had died at the home of their uncle, leaving Angela the sole surviving member of her immediate family. When Angela was of age, probably about 18, she returned to Desenzano to her family home.

The return to Desenzano marked the opening of a twenty year

"Casa Angela", St. Angela's home, Desenzano, Italy. Photo by Sr. Barbara Becnel, O.S.U.

Chair and loom used by St. Angela, Desenzano, Italy. Photo by Sr. Barbara Becnel, O.S.U.

period in Angela's life of which almost no details are known. It is known that owing to the political circumstances of the times there were many persons in the community in need of assistance. The Brescia provinces were besieged by military and political strife. The riviera along Lake Garda, as well as the three valleys that meet at Brescia, formed the point of entrance and egress for many of the foreign soldiers that streamed over the Alps into Italy during the period of the Italian wars.

During this period Angela joined her companions one day in a walk along the road that skirts the lake between Desenzano and Salo, perhaps to carry lunch to the workers in the harvest field. They stopped in a beautiful spot near Brudazzo, where Angela separated from the group to pray. The uncertainties of the future oppressed her, and she implored God to give her direction. Little did she suspect the part she was to take in the vast work of reorganization and reform that would mark the sixteenth century. As she prayed, Angela received some indication of her future work. The exact nature of this supernatural manifestation is not known,[5] but from that time she had a realization that she was to found a "company of virgins."[6] She took no action at the time of the experience, leaving plans for her "company" for the future. It is known that during this period she joined the Franciscan Tertiaries, the Third Order of St. Francis, which was a source of serious spiritual de-

A Fireplace, St. Angela's home, Desenzano, Italy. Photo by Sr. Barbara Becnel, O.S.U.

velopment in her life.

Angela witnessed a decline in faith and Christian morals among the citizenry, and often must have asked herself why error had gained such headway. From the line of action that she pursued, one may infer that she deemed ignorance a major contributing factor in the decline in faith. She realized that this ignorance stemmed in part from the lack of education given to Italian girls. To expect the girls, who knew little besides their prayers, to train their children in faith and morals was presumptuous.[7] Her mission became more clearly defined. The company she was to found must be one devoted to teaching. Her time in Desenzano had been spent in assisting both young and old, but children were the special object of her love and care.

One noble family, the Patengolas of Brescia, developed a warm and lasting affection for Angela during the summer months, which they spent

Brescia, Italy. Photo by Sr. Jacqueline Toppino, O.S.U.

on their country estate not far from Desenzano. In 1516 Jerome and Catherine Patengola had lost both of their sons within a few months and were in need of help and counseling. They turned to Angela, begging her to come and live with them in Brescia. Angela responded to their appeal and moved to Brescia, which would become her permanent home.

At the beginning of the Christian era, Brescia had been famous, powerful, and prosperous. In the late fifteenth century it was the capital of one of the most beautiful of the provinces of the Venetian Republic, but by 1512 Brescia had been subjected to a long siege by the troops of Louis XII under the command of Gaston de Foix and the Chevalier Bayard. The city soon fell into the hands of the French, who sacked and ruthlessly despoiled it. During the next four years, Brescia changed hands six times, until finally on May 26, 1516, it again passed under the dominion of the Republic of Venice. Despite the peace the town was never to recover fully from the terrible depredation inflicted upon it. There was not a family within the walls of the city that did not mourn the loss of at least one member, as well as the destruction of property. Here at a time when charity, comfort, and devotion were sorely needed, Angela showed a great deal of leadership in organizing relief for the people.

Northern Italy continued to be a focal point of the struggle between the French and the Imperial armies. Conditions continued to grow worse, poverty became extreme, and the country was filled with people reduced to begging. While everyone suffered from lawlessness, Angela realized that the young Brescian girls were the most hapless victims. Confronted with the terrible social and political conditions of Brescia, and unsure of her influence, Angela saw no immediate prospect of realizing the formation of a company of virgins as foreshadowed by the vision of Brudazzo. Nevertheless, she felt instinctively that she was doing preparatory work by devoting herself to the welfare of Brescian girls and women.

Urged on by her spiritual guide Father Serafino, Angela began to lay the foundations of her institute in 1532. She first called together twelve young women from the Brescian community to discuss her ideas.[10] Her plan was a simple one which would abandon the old monastic form of living adopted for women. Her associates would continue to live with their families, but would have their company as a source of spiritual and intellectual development. Well instructed and strengthened in their faith, her associates would devote their lives to the teaching of girls and women, who would subsequently carry on the faith in their own homes. Angela envisioned not only the formation of strong, individual Christians, but also the long term reformation of society. Her goal was to train young women in mind, heart, and will to reform the home, the fundamental unit of society. Development of Christian values and morals in the home would eventually have an effect on society in general.

That a foundress would dispense with the monastic life for her

Hills of Desenzano, Italy. Photo by Sr. Barbara Becnel, O.S.U.

institute may not seem unusual today, but in 1530 it was a radical departure from all known standards. With rare exceptions there were two recognized courses open to a woman: either she must enter a monastery where she would be protected by cloistered walls, or she could marry and be content with what happiness her husband saw fit to give her. For young women to enroll themselves under the standard of virginity and devote their lives to God outside the cloister was a truly novel idea. But it was more than that. It was a laudable defiance of the devotees of the reformation, and especially of the monks and priests who considered virginal life for women outside of cloister contrary to the law of God and of nature.

The twelve young women chosen by Angela accepted her standard and began their training under her careful guidance. During two years the first recruits participated in a novitiate of sorts, the family spirit growing among them as they worked together. As the month of November, 1535, approached, it was agreed that Angela, her first twelve associates, and fifteen other young women would bind themselves by the obligation of religious profession. On the morning of November 25, 1535, they assisted at Holy Mass and received Holy Communion in the church

Lake Garda, near the Merici home in Desenzano, Italy. Photo by Sr. Barbara Becnel, O.S.U.

of St. Afra. Afterwards in their oratory, they consecrated themselves to God in obedience and mortification. All signed an act by which they bound themselves to each other and to a full observance of the Rules of the Company of St. Ursula.[11]

The dominant objective of Angela's life was realized. This work of God, the Company of St. Ursula, would become a great order, global in extent. It lacked at its foundation only the seal of ecclesiastical authority which was given August 8, 1536, by Cardinal Francesco Conaro, Bishop of Brescia. The number of Angela's associates continued to grow. The first general chapter was held March 18, 1537, to elect the officers designated in the rule. Although the Primitive Rule makes no mention of a superior general,[12] Angela was unanimously chosen "Mother General for the remainder of her natural life."[13] The assembly proceeded to fill the minor offices provided for by the Rule, and the organization of the Company was complete.

The Primitive Rule does not treat of the work of the institute; but from other sources it is evident that the principal end was the education of young girls. The Rule as amplified by St. Charles Borromeo[14] states:

The Lady Governors will see that all are exercising themselves in teaching Christian Doctrine, in which each should strive particularly to produce fruit.[15]

And again:

> Remember that...all must carry on some charitable work, especially that of Christian instruction. In this let them be prompt in obeying superiors, and so conduct themselves that they will not fail to teach good conduct as well as good doctrine.[16]

The obligation to teach could hardly have been expressed more clearly or with greater emphasis. No one is exempt from teaching, while other charitable work is vague and unspecified. The rule required that the members of the company not only teach, but also be examples of what

Statue depicting St. Angela, Ursuline Generalate, Rome, Italy. Photo by Sr. Jacqueline Toppino, O.S.U.

Statue depicting St. Angela, Sendai, Japan. Photo by Sr. Jacqueline Toppino, O.S.U.

they taught; that the pupils not only learn correct doctrine, but also live their lives according to it. Angela felt that the immediate need of the society of her day was the instruction of the young in principles of the Christian religion, upon which the foundations of morality were based. She put no emphasis on secular education, as the trend of the time was to stress classic studies.

The approval of the Holy See was essential if the company was to grow outside the Diocese of Brescia. Several adverse circumstances, however, delayed the sanctioning of Angela's work by the highest authority of the church. As indicated, the Company of St. Ursula deviated widely from the traditional and consecrated forms of monastic life and rule for women. Its plan, as well as all novel ideas, was viewed unfavorably in 1536. The progress of the Protestant Revolt in Germany and in Switzerland, as well as schism in England, compelled churchmen to be on their guard against innovations. In addition, some of the most influential men in the church were opposed to the establishment of any new religious orders.[17] Angela had not intended her institute to be a local or diocesan society and was not content with the approval of the ordinary of the diocese. Her horizon was worldwide.[18] Angela petitioned Rome for approval.

Although Angela Merici died in 1540 without having received the Papal bull of approval, she had established her company on a solid foundation. With an untroubled mind she could confide the work of her genius to those whom she had so carefully trained and to their

St. Angela's tomb. Photo by Sr. Jacqueline Toppino, O.S.U.

successors. She had given future centuries an original, living gift. The company was original as an institute of women who pledged themselves to a life of virginity, but who sought neither the limitations nor the safeguards of monasticism. It was new in having for its principal aim the religious and moral training of young girls. It was vibrant with a spirit which envisioned expansion and adaptation: a spirit which could fearlessly say, "If according to times and needs, you should be obliged to make fresh rules and change certain things, do it with prudence and

Statue depicting St. Angela in Town Square, Desenzano, Italy. Photo by Sr. Barbara Becnel, O.S.U.

good advice."[19] The gradual unfolding of this idea after Angela's death clearly demonstrates the flexibility of the rule, as well as the ability of her daughters to make changes that were warranted by different times.

At the time of Angela's death the company, numbering about one hundred fifty members, was confined to Brescia and its vicinity. After Pope Paul III granted the bull of approbation for the company on June 9, 1544, rapid expansion of the order throughout Italy began. The towns of Desenzano and Salo were fittingly among the first to petition the mother general, Countess Ladrone, for colonies of Ursulines shortly after the papal bull. The city of Cremona opened a new field to the Ursulines in 1565, and two years later they were working in Bergamo. Meanwhile, the background was being prepared for a significant manifestation of the law of change under the guidance of Charles Borromeo, Archbishop of Milan.

The Company of St. Ursula at Milan

In the mid-sixteenth century Milan was going through a sad period in its history. It had lost its political autonomy, and in 1535 had become a dependency of the Spanish crown under Charles I. Foreign domination left its disgraceful mark on the whole of upper Italy, but Milan, because it was the seat of the Spanish governors, suffered more than any other city from this unwanted oppression. Political misgovernment also brought religious disorders into Lombardy. Milan had not seen its archbishops for more than a half century. These prelates, once they were appointed, were content to collect their revenues and to delegate the immediate government of the archdiocese to others. There was no shortage of priests, but the clergy lacked knowledge and spiritual enrichment. As a result religion languished among the people. Reception of the sacraments was infrequent, and religious instruction rare.[20] There was a need for reform not only in Milan, but in the whole of Christendom.

The Council of Trent provided the means necessary for the achievement of this colossal work. To carry out the decrees of the Council of Trent an indefatigable, enlightened, zealous apostle was needed, and Charles Borromeo was such a person. Named archbishop of Milan in 1560 by Pope Pius IV, Charles decided to go to Milan to personally oversee the archdiocese. However, it was five years before he was free to leave Rome to begin his work there.

One of Borromeo's most cherished enterprises was the establishment of schools for the teaching of Christian doctrine. He had heard of the Company of St. Ursula and was quick to perceive the effectiveness of the new congregation. They could be the persons to achieve his designs. Cardinal Borromeo wrote to Father Landini, one of the directors of the company at the time, asking for further information about the young society. Father Landini's reply, dated December 21, 1566, summed up the activities of the Ursulines:

> This Company has given sisters to all the hospitals of Brescia. It directs schools for little girls to give them Christian instruction. God makes use of it for the conversion of souls and to attract to His service many families, among whom these sisters live.

It would be hard to say, hard to make you understand, all the good which the Lord derives from this holy Company in every sort of work of piety and mercy. The Company frequent the Sacraments, cultivate prayer, spread the Divine worship. The evangelical virtues of poverty and obedience shine within it. Truly, it is this spectacle of delicate young girls, who, reviving the Spirit of Agnes and Agatha, dwell intact amid perils and scandals.[21]

Happy to find the rule of the Company of St. Ursula suited to his purpose, Cardinal Borromeo introduced the principles of the Brescia company into Milan. Through private initiative a group of pious women

Vision Cross, commemorating the vison of St. Angela, Brudazzo, Italy. Photo by Sr. Jacqueline Toppino, O.S.U.

in Milan bound themselves together.[22] Recruited from all classes of society, the first Ursulines of Milan continued for some years to live with their families, exactly as did their sisters at Brescia. They assembled on certain days, and at such times Cardinal Borromeo frequently gave them instructions. It may have been on one such occasion that the prelate manifested his desire that they live in community and practice certain uniform observances. To substantiate this mode of life, the archbishop obtained a bull from Pope Gregory XIII in 1582,[23] which authorized the Ursulines to form congregations, to live in communities, and to adopt this modified form of the company everywhere. Cardinal Borromeo did not cloister the Ursulines as has often been erroneously stated. The bull authorized them to live in community without cloister, devoted to the education of children. At the time of Cardinal Bor- romeo's death, six years after the establishment of the Ursulines in his archdiocese, there were already eighteen houses and six hundred Ursulines in Milan.[24]

Milan is thus considered the second primitive province, or congregation, of the Company of St. Ursula. From the two centers, Brescia and Milan, numerous foundations were formed in the sixteenth century. Those from Brescia kept the Primitive Rule of St. Angela,[25] while those from Milan adopted the modifications of Cardinal Borromeo. Bologna, Modena, Parma, Ferrara, Venice, Genoa, Foligno, Piacenze, and other large cities of northern and central Italy all had Ursulines by the end of the sixteenth century.

The Company of St. Ursula was not to be confined to Italy. In her Testament Angela had said that her institute would endure.[26] Cardinal Bor- romeo predicted that it would spread through the whole world.[27] At the end of the sixteenth century, the company of St. Ursula was established in southern France, and with that expansion the law of change became operative once more.

The Ursulines in France

The Protestant Revolt made itself felt in France at a very early date. During the first half of the sixteenth century, between twenty and thirty per cent of the total population embraced French Protestantism. The Protestant recruits were primarily from the prosperous middle class *(bourgeoisie)*, to whom preceding French kings had entrusted many important offices, and their authority was out of proportion to their number. This influential group was eager to curb the royal power. The French kings, having gained practical control of church property through the disposition of benefices, were opposed to revolution withing their own domains. Furthermore, they considered religious unity essential to political solidarity and to their own personal rule. In consequence, a series of so-called religious wars, which were as much political as religious, embroiled the whole of France from 1562 to 1593.

While this struggle was at its height Françoise de Bermond was born at Avignon in 1572. She was destined to be the foundress of the first Ursulines of France, a second Angela of the order. Françoise was a bright and enthusiastic student and was given an education which surpassed in breadth and solidity that given to girls of her rank. As a young woman she would be guided by Father Jean-Baptiste Romillon to take up the work of Christian instruction in Avignon.

Father César de Bus founded a society in Avignon, the Fathers of Christian Doctrine, who devoted themselves to the teaching of children of the lower classes. Having read the life of St. Charles Borromeo, he proposed to establish, after the model of the Ursulines of Milan, some religious catechists for the young of both sexes. The first Sister of Christian Doctrine, as the religious were called, was his niece, Cassandre de Bus. With three other young girls, Cassandre commenced her work in 1592 at l'Isle-sur-Sorgue, a small city not far from Avignon. Father de Bus, who was already blind, handed over the direction of the new society to his close friend, Father Jean-Baptiste Romillon, who had given guidance to Françoise de Bermond.

The enterprise was scarcely under way when opposition arose to the work of the Sisters of Christian Doctrine. Opponents alleged that it was related to Lutheranism, as the head of that movement had insisted that education was as necessary for girls as for boys. Just when opposition seemed about to engulf the young society, Father Romillon received a copy of Angela Merici's Rule as revised by Charles Borromeo for the Ursulines of Milan. Here was the solution to a knotty problem. The type of foundation Father de Bus envisioned was not new; it already existed in Italy. St. Charles Borromeo had recognized its effectiveness, even its necessity. What a striking justification, given the praise of St. Charles Borromeo, for the French religious.

Father Romillon offered the Rule of St. Ursula to Cassandre de Bus, as well as to Françoise de Bermond and the women who had been working with her in Christian formation. After an assiduous study of the rule, Françoise de Bermond and her companions decided they wished to enroll under the banner of St. Ursula. They joined Mlle de Bus, who also accepted the rule, and the foundation of the first Ursuline Community in France was laid in 1596. Françoise de Bermond,[28] although only twenty-four, became the first superior of the l'Isle community. She immediately wrote in the name of her associates to Pope Clement VIII, asking permission to teach Christian doctrine publicly. The pope granted the request and blessed the work which was recognized as an extension of that of Milan. From the small convent of l'Isle-sur-Sorgue emanated several foundations: Aix, Marseille, Avignon, Valence, Pont-St. Esprit, Arles, Salon, and many others. After the foundation at Aix, which was the capital of Provence, that city became the center of government of the congregation established by Françoise de Bermond.

In 1605, shortly after the Ursulines opened their schools in Avignon, the cardinal-archbishop of Bordeaux, François de Sourdis, passed through Avignon on his way to Rome to assist at the conclave after the death of Pope Leo XI. Cardinal Sourdis had heard of the excellent work being done by the Ursulines, and he visited them and observed the instructions which they gave to the young girls. The prelate decided he would establish a similar congregation at Bordeaux, but the project was delayed until after the conclave in Rome. Upon his return Cardinal Sourdis found three young ladies ready to take up the work of Angela. They were Françoise and Marie de Cazères, cousins, and Jeanne de la Mercerie. They spent six months in retirement in the study of the Rule of the Ursulines of Milan as a preparation for the reception of the habit and the making of the simple vows prescribed by the rule.[29] The congregation of Bordeaux was solemnly established November 30, 1606. No less than six houses were founded from Bordeaux between 1606 and 1618: Libourne, Bourg-sur-Mer, St. Macaire, Laval, Potiers, and Angers. Only a lack of well-trained teachers prevented a further extention in the south and west of France. While these developments were taking place in the south of France, Paris was coming under the influence of the Ursulines.

Two of the most illustrious Catholic women of that epoch, Madame Acarie[30] and her cousin, Madame de Sainte-Beuve, were instrumental

Depiction of St. Angela. Stained glass window, Ursuline Academy.
Photo by Sr. Jacqueline Toppino, O.S.U.

in establishing the Ursulines in Paris. Madame Acarie had introduced the Reform Carmelites into France. She also had under her protection a group of virtuous young women who were evidently not called to the Carmelite order. For them she dreamed of organizing some educational work similar to that of Françoise de Bermond in Provence. Madame Acarie proposed to Madame de Sainte-Beuve that she become the foundress of an Ursuline convent in Paris. She considered the matter seriously and prayerfully and consulted her director, Father Contery, S.J., who approved the plan of Madame Acarie.

Father Contery pointed out certain practical details which were of great importance for the Company of St. Ursula. He explained to Madame de Sainte-Beuve the difference between congregations and religious orders. He showed her that a religious order recognized by the church and the state would offer much greater security for the future. He advised her to propose as a condition that the congregation would petition Rome to be raised to a religious order, and that it would accept the obligations attached thereto, especially that of cloister.[31] Madame Sainte-Beuve readily acquiesced in the views of Father Contery. Meanwhile, Madame Acarie sent for Françoise de Bermond, who was not able to come immediately, as she was occupied with a foundation at Marseilles. Madame Acarie utilized the ensuing months to get everything in readiness. When Françoise de Bermond arrived at Paris in March 1606, future Ursulines, a convent, pupils, and a school were all waiting for her direction. Mother de Bermond trained her young associates in the spirit of St. Angela and instructed them in her own methods of teaching Christian doctrine.[32]

At the end of two years those in authority had to decide definitively whether the institute of Paris would continue to be a simple congregation

Depiction of St. Ursula. Stained glass window, Ursuline Academy. Photo by Sr. Jacqueline Toppino, O.S.U.

or would become a religious order. In 1610 Madame de Sainte-Beuve assembled a council of learned men, as well as personal friends of herself and Madame Acarie to solve this unique problem. This group drew up a plan and submitted it to Rome with a petition to erect a monastery.[33] Despite the energy with which Madame de Sainte-Beuve pushed matters in Paris and in Rome, the bull of approbation was not signed by Paul V until June 13, 1612. It ordained the observance of the Rule of St. Augustine, and the closest accord with the decrees of the Council of Trent. It emphasized Angela's original conception of the education of girls. To the ordinary three solemn vows was added a fourth: that of instructing young girls. The vow of instruction was to have preference over monastic observance.[34]

The Company of St. Ursula in its historical development had again yielded to the law of change. The Company of St. Ursula had become the Order of St. Ursula without sacrificing any of its original intentions. Angela's idea of the Ursulines as educators had been emphasized by the vow of instruction. Paris set the mode. Within twenty years seven large monasteries were inaugurated: Bordeaux, 1618, Toulouse, 1615, Lyons, 1619, Dijon, 1619, Tulle, 1621, Arles, 1642, and Avignon, 1637. Each of these monasteries in turn became a mother-house with numerous off-spring. Not content with the ever-widening network of educational establishments in Europe, the Ursulines began to turn their gaze toward the New World. The Jesuits were working among the native tribes of North America. The Ursulines dreamed of rendering their work more fruitful by educational work among the Indian children of Canada.

Ursulines in Canada

As early as 1632, Father Paul Le Jeune, S.J.,[35] wrote in the *Relation:* "We owe a great deal to . . .the Ursulines."[36] Mother Mary of the Incarnation (Marie Guyart-Martin) of the community of Tours corresponded with some of the Jesuit missionaries. In 1636 Father Poncet, S.J.[37] sent her a pilgrim staff and wrote: "I am sending you this little staff to invite you to serve God in New France." This seemed a good omen to Mother Mary who desired to go to work in the Canadian mission.[39] In the *Relation* of 1636 Father Le Jeune wrote of Mother Mary of the Incarnation: "Here is the heart of a real Ursuline who tells me how her Order may one day reach these immense forests." He added that he had the names of thirteen Ursulines who were anxious to devote themselves to the mission.[40]

Madame de la Peltrie was a wealthy widow living at Caen at the time of the above correspondence. During a serious illness, she made a vow that, if she were cured, she would go to Canada and devote herself to the instruction of Indian girls. The Jesuits advised Madame de la Peltrie to go to Tours for an interview with Mother Mary of the Incarnation. Agreements were made for Madame de la Peltrie to accompany the Ursulines, and arrangements were made for departure from France. The Ursuline Community of Tours gave as a companion the young Sister Marie Joseph de la Troche. At Dieppe, where they were to embark, an Ursuline of that community, Mother Cécile de Ste-Croix, joined the small group. Three Augustinian nuns, Marie Guenet de Saint Ignace, Anne Lecointre de Saint Bernard, and Marie Forrestier de Saint Bonaventure, who were to found the Hotel-Dieu at Quebec, embarked on the same ship. Thus through the generosity of two religious orders Christian charity and education were implanted in New France.

After a tedious and painful voyage of three months, they arrived at Quebec, August 1, 1639. Madame de la Peltrie rented a two-room house for the Ursulines[41] situated on the shore of the St. Lawrence River, where the missionaries immediately began their apostolate. With some inconvenience they succeeded in lodging from six to eighteen Indian girls of all ages the very first year. Day classes were opened for the French children of the neighborhood. The study of the Indian languages was a necessity. Mother Mary of the Incarnation and Mother Sainte-Croix applied themselves to the Algonquin; Mother St. Joseph, to the Huron language. Under the capable direction of Father Le Jeune, within two months they were able to teach catechism. While these pioneering women went about their daily duties "trying to follow the rule of a large monastery,[42] in the corner of a small house," their convent was slowly rising. They took possession of it November 21, 1642. It was the largest and finest building in New France, made of stone and three stories high.

New members came from France, and the work advanced successfully. In 1644 the complex contained the "seminary"[43] (the boarding school), the day school, and an orphanage. Mother Mary looked forward to recruiting new members of the community from the colony, and in

1646 the Ursulines opened the novitiate to Charlotte Barre and Catherine Lezeau.[44] Despite sickness and extreme poverty, the burning of the first monastery on December 30, 1650, and incursions of the Iroquois, the Ursulines courageously fulfilled their duties as Christian educators. When the loved Mother Mary of the Incarnation died in 1672, the monastery of Quebec was firmly established, and the Ursuline spirit was deeply rooted in New France.

At the request of Bishop Jean-Baptiste de Saint Vallier, the Ursulines of Quebec founded a monastery at Trois-Rivières in 1697.[45] To the duties of teaching, they added the care of the sick in an adjoining hospital. Here in the New World, Angela's idea of adaptability, the law of change as understood and applied by the Ursulines of Canada, is again evident. This principle of elasticity allowed them to take up the work of hospital sisters until such time as a nursing community could replace them. And it is in this two-fold vocation of nurses and Christian educators that the Ursulines made their next foundation in New Orleans in the colony of Louisiana.

Beginnings of Christianity in Louisiana

Spanish explorers in the early part of the sixteenth century first brought Christianity to the southern part of what is now the United States. Enthusiastic missionaries sailed with every fleet of caravels that set out from the shores of Spain. With the discovery of Florida in 1513 Juan Ponce de Leon opened the way along which so many others were to follow and advance. Some members of the ill-fated Narvaez expedition passed the mouth of the Mississippi River in 1528 without knowing it. Several secular priests and five Franciscan priests accompanied them, among whom was the first bishop-designate of Florida,[46] Father Juan Suarez.[47] The great expedition of Hernando de Soto from 1539-1542 definitively marks the coming of missionaries into the Mississippi Valley and the first conversions among the natives. Included in the personnel of the expedition were twelve priests, eight belonging to religious orders and four secular priests.

But despite costly attempts made by Spain to colonize north of the Gulf of Mexico, "on the first of January 1562, there was not a Spaniard—there was not a white man of any race—on the soil of the

René-Robert Cavelier, Sieur de la Salle, 1643-1687, takes possession of Louisiana in the name of Louis XIV, 1682. Courtesy Historic New Orleans Collection, 1970.1.

mainland of what is now the United States."[48] Over the years Franciscans, Dominicans, and Jesuits braved the wilderness of other regions, but the lower Mississippi Valley remained buried in oblivion for more than a century longer. In 1682 the French trader and explorer, Rene Robert Cavelier, Sieur de la Salle, organized an expedition which explored the Mississippi River from its northern origins to the mouth of the river at the Gulf of Mexico. He claimed the entire region, including those who lived there, as the property and subjects of Louis, King of France, naming the territory Louisiana. La Salle returned to France and urged that a colony be established at the mouth of the river. An expedition was dispatched from France in 1684 for that purpose, but it missed the Mississippi delta and eventually ended in disaster for LaSalle in 1687, when he was assassinated by his men. Sieur de LaSalle's claiming of Louisiana in the name of France affected the whole future of Catholicism in Louisiana. When later exploration was followed by colonization, the faith was established by priests from France, and the vast region was placed under the jurisdiction of the bishop of Quebec.

After the Treaty of Ryswick was signed in 1697, Louis XIV was persuaded to make the exploration of Louisiana an official undertaking

*Jean Baptiste Le Moyne, Sieur De Bienville, 1680-1768. Comman-
dant, 1716-1717, and Governor, 1733-1743, of Louisiana. Courtesy
Historic New Orleans Collection, 1990.49.*

and agreed to underwrite the effort. The men chosen to execute this
ambitious project were two sons of Charles le Moyne of Quebec: Pierre
Le Moyne, sieur de Iberville and Jean Baptiste Le Moyne, sieur de Bienville.
Iberville and Bienville sailed from Brest, France in October, 1698, with
a company of two hundred soldiers and colonists. The story of the early
years of the colony of Louisiana is an unbroken record of adversity,
contention, and physical hardship for the settlers. The fur trade did not
prove as profitable as had been expected, and for many years the food
supply was inadequate. During the War of the Spanish Succession, 1702-
1713, Louisiana was, to all intent and purpose, abandoned by France.

In 1712, King Louis XIV granted the trade of Louisiana to Sieur
Antoine Crozat, a wealthy merchant. For a period of fifteen years, Louisiana
was a proprietary colony. Crozat infused some new life into the undertaking,

but when he realized that profits would be small, if any, he lost interest and transferred his patent to the crown in 1717. The Duke of Orleans serving as regent for the young Louis XV, conferred upon the Company of the West[49] the commercial rights which Crozat had surrendered, giving proprietorship to the Company. This in effect allowed it to work immediately to secure colonist by any and every means. Soon there was a steady flow of immigration, with most of the colonists debarking at the posts of Biloxi, Mobile and Dauphin Island.

The colony did not and could not prosper as long as it was limited to the sandy land on the Gulf of Mexico. For some time Bienville had desired to establish a capitol at a "dry spot" which he had seen in 1699 on the banks of the Mississippi, and in 1717 Bienville sent plans to France for a proposed town to be built on the site. Approval came from Paris from the Company of the West commissioning him to carry out the project, which was to be called "Nouvelle Orleans" in honor of the Duke of Orleans. In early 1718 New Orleans was founded when a detachment of men was sent to clear a site for the proposed town.[50] Four years later the official headquarters of the colony was transferred to New Orleans.

In the early beginnings of the various settlements in the Louisiana territory the areas settled were primarily military outposts. Still the work of Catholic religious was much in evidence. Father Anastase Douay came to lower Louisiana with Iberville in 1699. The priests of the Seminary of Quebec petitioned Bishop St. Vallier in 1696 for authority to establish missions on both banks of the Mississippi and its tributaries. Three of these priests left Quebec for the Mississippi Valley in July, 1698. In addition the Jesuits had been in the Illinois Country for some years.

By its charter the Company was obligated to build churches in its settlements and to provide priests for them. In 1722 the colony was divided into three ecclesiastical districts, with the Capuchins, the Carmelites and the Jesuits each administering a district.[51] That same year the Capuchins and the Jesuits took possession of their districts. The Carmelites were at Mobile when the arrangement was made, but in December 1722, a new ordinance was issued recalling them and adding their district to that of the Capuchins.[52] Less than a year later the Company decided that the Capuchins could not furnish sufficient subjects, curtailed their district, and extended that of the Jesuits. Even this division was not final, as a further abridgement was made in the Capuchin territory in February, 1726. The Capuchins evidently had more zeal than men to fill the posts under their jurisdiction. The Company also judged that they were less fitted for the missions with the Indians than were the Jesuits. The Capuchins were placed in all the French posts, and the Jesuits were charged with the spiritual care of the natives.[53]

According to the settlement of 1726, the Jesuit superior was permitted to maintain a house in New Orleans as a reception center for missionaries coming from or returning to France, a depot to receive mission supplies from France, and a point of contact between the Jesuit mission superior and officials of the colony. The Company conceded this residence in New Orleans with the stipulation that the Jesuits should not perform any ecclesiastical functions there without the consent of the Capuchin superior. This clause led to a controversy involving not only the Jesuits and the Capuchins, but also the Ursulines, who arrived in New Orleans the following year.

After the ecclesiastical reapportionment of the territory in 1723, the Louisiana Mission was made independent of the Illinois Mission, and Father Nicolas Ignatius de Beaubois[54] was appointed superior of the lower Mississippi region. Father de Beaubois, who had been superior of the Illinois mission, was intimately acquainted with the situation of the Jesuits in the upper valley. He decided to go to Europe to arrange for a new agreement between the Company of the Indies and the Jesuits. When Father de Beaubois arrived in New Orleans, the city was divided into two factions: that of Jacques de La Chaise, ordonnateur, who was appointed by the Company as commissioner of the colony, exercising the financial and economic affairs of the colony, and that of Bienville, who had been named by the king to rule the colony as Commandant from 1718 to 1725. The two men had initially cooperated but difficulties arose between them owing to conflicts in jurisdiction. Out of a natural inclination for Bienville—a staunch friend of the Jesuits—Father de Beaubois threw in his lot with the Bienvillists. Informers and newsmongers seized upon this imprudence to injure him in the estimation of the Company, which had persuaded the king and his advisors to recall Bienville to France.[55]

Father de Beaubois left for Mobile to embark for France and just missed drowning when the ship he was to sail on sank on Easter

Sunday, April 1, 1725. When the Jesuit finally reached France, he found Company officials very interested in the effective control of the Indian tribes. Thwarting the influence and infiltration of the English from the Atlantic seaboard among the Indians of the eastern part of the colony was another concern. In addition the Company wished to secure religious women to take charge of the military hospital of New Orleans, as well as of the education of young women and girls in the colony. Father de Beaubois contributed substantially to the realization of the first and the last of these objectives. By a new contract with the Jesuit missionaries, he secured a promise of better conditions for the Jesuit missionaries, who were exercising the most effective control over the Indians through Christian instruction. He brought to fruition the last objective by recruiting a group of Ursuline missionaries for Louisiana.

CHAPTER 2

The New World Mission Begins

The establishment of the first educational institution for women in the United States was almost simultaneous with the foundation of New Orleans. By a strange coincidence the founders of this first school for women, although members of a teaching order, came primarily to take charge of the military hospital. As early as 1701 Iberville had asked for Grey Sisters to direct the hospital[1], but sisters for Louisiana were difficult to secure. During the years 1723 to 1726, the Council of Louisiana wrote continually to the officials in France requesting Brothers of Charity, Hospital Sisters, or Grey Sisters.[2] The Council pointed out that until sisters or brothers took charge of the hospital, the sick would always be badly cared for, and the hospital would be an onerous expense to the Company. When Monsieur Jacques de la Chaise came to New Orleans in 1723 as *ordonnateur,* he wrote to the officials in France:

> If you could, gentlemen, induce four good Grey Sisters to come and settle here and take care of the sick, it would be much better. They (the sick) would get more assistance from these nurses, than from the male nurses who steal the ration.... Those people keep no record of things consumed, whereas a good sister who will take charge of the medicines will not deliver any except on receipts which will be explained. I do not know, gentlemen, whether my idea will be so fortunate as to be approved by you.[3]

The note of economy struck by de la Chaise appealed to the directors, but as they could induce neither Brothers of Charity nor Grey Sisters to go to Louisiana[4], they resorted to another expedient. The directors decided:

> We can in imitation of Canada take another means which appears as advantageous to the Company as useful to the Colony; and this expedient would be to establish

in this hospital some Ursulines, who will charge themselves with the care of the sick that the Company will send them. They will receive the inhabitants, who think they would be better cared for there than at home, by paying so much per day and they will keep a school for young girls according to their institute. Their economy together with legacies, donations and compensations, will diminish in a few years the greater part of the expenses the Company is obliged to incur for the maintenance of the hospital.[5]

Le Commerce que les Indiens du Mexique font avec les François au Port de Mississippi, ca. 1720, François Gerard Jollain, Jr. Courtesy Historic New Orleans Collection, 1952.3.

Father de Beaubois had suggested the Ursulines to the directors of the Company. They approved his plan and commissioned him to carry it out.[6]

What led Father de Beaubois to propose Ursulines,[7] and what assurance had he that he could secure an adequate number of religious for the work? These questions cannot be answered with absolute assurance, but certain facts are revealing. As indicated, the board of directors said they were acting "in imitation of Canada." Abbé Raguet[8], the ecclesiastical director of the Company, clarified this statement in a letter to Bishop de Mornay on May 8, 1726.[9]

> The Ursulines having succeeded in the care which they have of the sick in Canada, I have thought that they would succeed also at New Orleans. I have, therefore, brought my project to a satisfactory conclusion. I believe that I have procured two benefits, the one for the sick, the other for the education of girls.[10]

The annals of the Ursuline Convent of New Orleans tell of a conversation between Father de Beaubois and Bienville during which they decided to ask the Ursulines to come to Louisiana.[11] Some writers have conjectured that this supposed conference may not have occurred, but Bienville certainly must have known that his mother, Catherine Primot, had been educated by the Ursuline nuns of Quebec. Bienville may have known that a band of Ursulines from Quebec had taken charge of the hospital in Trois–Rivières. His elder brother, Charles Le Moyne de Longeuil, with whom he corresponded,[12] was governor of Trois–Rivières from 1720 to 1724.[13] Father de Beaubois, who spent two years in Canada before going to the Illinois Mission, could have been familiar with the work of the Ursulines at the hospital of Trois-Rivières. Both of these men knew that sisters were needed for the military hospital and for a girls' school in New Orleans. They may have discussed the matter during the long voyage that they made together from Mobile to France in the summer of 1725.

It is well-known that, from the time of the first Ursuline foundations in France, the Jesuits assisted them in various capacities. Thus many members of the two orders were well acquainted. Father de Lamberville, who at an earlier date filled the office of procurator for the Jesuit North American Missions, had a sister in the Ursuline Convent of Rouen,[14] which gave three religious for the foundation in New Orleans. Among the first group of Ursulines to come to Louisiana was Sister Ste. Angélique, a sister of Father Le Boullenger, a Jesuit Illinois missionary.[15] For many years Sister Ste. Angélique had desired to be a missionary like her brother. Did Father de Beaubois, who had been superior of the Illinois Mission, know in some way of this sister's desire? In any case, it is quite certain that the Jesuits were instrumental in obtaining the Ursulines[16] for the military hospital and for the school for girls in New Orleans.

Extant records do not tell us how Father de Beaubois set about recruiting the Ursuline missionaries for Louisiana. Perhaps the Jesuit addressed himself directly to the superior of the Ursuline Community of Rouen of which Sister Ste. Angélique was a member.[17] At any rate, he learned that there was another religious at Rouen who had cherished a desire for many years to go to the American missions.[18] This potential missionary was Mother Marie St. Augustin Tranchepain. Mother St. André, her contemporary and the second superior of the Ursuline Convent of New Orleans, wrote of Mother St. Augustin:

> She entered the novitiate in 1699...and from that

Map of France showing the origins of the first Ursulines to come to Louisiana. Courtesy Ursuline Archives & Museum.

time had a singular attraction for the missions.... Our Lord made her understand that she would have much to suffer before going there and after her arrival.... Though she made many attempts to fulfill the designs of Providence in her regard, she was not successful. Then God made known to her that a Jesuit, whom she did not know and who did not know her, but who was then in France, was to be her guide and leader in a foreign land where He wished her to serve Him by establishing an Ursuline Convent.[19]

The foundation at New Orleans demanded a superior of rare ability, and Father de Beaubois found just such a person in Mother St. Augustin. The Community of Rouen gave two other religious, Sister St. Jean Judde, and Sister Ste. Angélique.[20] Around this nucleus the community of New Orleans was formed. With the permission of the archbishop of Rouen,[21] Mother St. Augustin and her companions went to Paris to make the necessary arrangements with the Company of the Indies.[22] They were assisted by Mother St. Amand Bruscoly, superior of the Ursulines of the Rue St. Jacques. The board of directors of the Company in their meeting of March 20, 1726, declared that the foundation could not be made too soon.[23] Nevertheless, six months elapsed before a contract similar to that made with the Jesuits[24] was drawn up and signed on September 13, 1726.[25]

The contract is prosaically practical. There is no romantic declaration of intentions, no picturesque vagueness about future obligations or recompense. It reveals only a businesslike determination on the part of the Company to get a good deal for its money. All duties and privileges are clearly defined in twenty-eight articles. The first three articles of the contract treat of the religious. The Company agreed to maintain six religious at the hospital and to grant each one five hundred francs to help defray the expenses of her journey. They were also to have free passage for themselves and four servants on the vessels of the Company. When they arrived in the colony, they were to take over the management of the hospital in the condition in which it was on their arrival. The religious were to establish their living quarters in the existing buildings as best they could, until the Company could erect a suitable convent.[26]

Officials in the colony were to have an inventory made of the Negroes, Negresses, cattle, furniture, beds, linen, and utensils of the hospital before putting the Ursulines in charge.[27] Article Six, which apportioned the work is of special interest:

> The Superior will appoint a religious as housekeeper, who in this capacity will be charged with the effects of the hospital, and with all that will be furnished there for the sustenance of the sick: she will appoint two other Religious to be continually occupied in the service of the patients, another to keep the school of the young girls, and the sixth will serve as aid to those who find themselves overburdened in their functions and she shall always be ready to fill the place of those of her sisters who, through illness, may be unable to perform their duties.[28]

In other words, four religious with the help of a fifth were expected to care for sixty to eighty patients, as well as a ward for the convalescent. The religious were given no place on the administrative board of the hospital. The governor of the colony, the first Councillor of the Superior Council, the procurator general, the parish priest of New Orleans, the superior of the Jesuits,[29] two notable inhabitants elected by the Superior Council, and the royal physician were to constitute this board. The Ursuline superior could attend the meetings and could propose measures which she deemed suitable or necessary, but she could not participate in the voting.[30]

To help provide for the subsistence of the religious, the Company of the Indies agreed to grant them a plantation of eight *arpents*[31] frontage on the Mississippi River. The Company also assumed the obligation of paying the overseer an annual salary of three hundred francs for the first five years. Until this plantation produced sufficient income for the religious, the Company contracted to pay each of the six religious six hundred francs a year. The Company promised to provide Negroes to cultivate the plantation for a period of five years, but the Ursulines were responsible for their wages.[32]

The Company was to supply what was necessary for the sick, but the superior and the head nurse were to render a strict account of all persons and provisions received at the hospital. The poor were required to present a statement signed by their parish priest and the procurator general confirming their penury before they received gratis treatment. Hospital rates for all other persons were left to the discretion of the administrators, although persons in the service of the Company were to receive preference.[33] There were also directives concerning food: "The Religious who will have care of the sick, shall not permit any of them, even the convalescent, to receive any food but that furnished by the house."[34]

It is evident from the contract that the Company placed the education of young girls second to the care of the sick.

> When the Religious can do so conveniently, they will take, if they judge proper, girls-boarders at the rate which the Superioress will regulate, and the payment for room and board will be remitted into the hands of the treasurer of the Religious, but none of those who will be charged with the sick will be taken away from them, or applied to the education of the boarders.[35]

When the income from the plantation became sufficient to support more than six religious, the community could increase its number in proportion to its revenue, but the community was not to increase its membership at the cost of potential wives for the settlers. Girls born in Louisiana were not to be received as religious without the permission of the Council.[36] Additional religious from France were entitled to free passage. Any religious obliged to return to France because of health or other reasons was to have free passage for herself and a servant. However, if a religious became incapacitated, she would no longer be counted in the number of six that the Company agreed to maintain. She could be treated at the expense of the hospital during the remainder of her life.[37]

To protect the spirit of the order, Article XV was specified.

> But as it is proper that the Religious have the liberty to live according to their own way of life, they will have for themselves in particular a treasurer...who will

be accountable to her Superior to provide for the needs of the Sisters from their own funds such as their salaries and the revenues from their plantation, and they will govern themselves as to the interior of the house according to their rule and the spirit of their Institute, in such a way that the service of the hospital will not suffer from it in the least.[37]

The Contract was not signed at the time it was drawn up. The departure of the Ursulines depended upon two essential conditions; the authorization of Bishop de Mornay to make a foundation in Louisiana, and the consent of the archbishop of Rouen for the religious to withdraw from their communities in France.[38] Bishop de Mornay was piqued because the Company had made arrangements with the Ursulines without first consulting him. This was not the first instance of the Company's independent action. It had also dealt with the Carmelites and Jesuits and had referred to the coadjutor only after matters had been arranged.[39] The bishop manifested great surprise when he received a letter from Mother St. Augustin Tranchepain requesting permission to open a convent in New Orleans with Father de Beaubois as superior.[40] This was the first that the prelate had heard of the matter, and he was reluctant to consent. Bishop de Mornay did not oppose the Ursulines' going to New Orleans,[41] but he objected to Father de Beaubois as their superior. He preferred that they be under the direction of his colleagues, the Capuchins.[42]

Bishop de Mornay forwarded Mother St. Augustin's letter to Abbé Raguet, asking his opinion.[43] Raguet replied that he favored the proposed foundation, and that he thought it natural that the Ursulines should place confidence in Father de Beaubois, since he would be the only one they would know in the colony when they arrived. As to the choice of their superior, the Company could not make any decision in that regard; that decision was one for the ecclesiastical authorities. The abbé suggested that the jurisdiction of the superior might be restricted "to a merely charitable and friendly overseeing, to a giving of advice and consolation in the trials of the spiritual life."[44] After considering the matter for some time, Bishop de Mornay told Abbé Raguet that he would not consent to the Jesuit being the superior of the Ursulines. He would write to Father de Beaubois and to Mother St. Augustin and inform them of his decision. He was convinced that the Ursulines would do much good in the colony, but "they must be under the jurisdiction of the Ordinary."[45] This was tantamount to saying that the Ursulines must have a Capuchin for superior, for both Bishop de Mornay and his vicar general, Father Raphaël de Luxembourg, were Capuchins.

Abbé Raguet responded that the jurisdiction of the Ordinary would be exercised everywhere, and the religious would be subject to it. As if to emphasize that the Capuchins were not being ignored, he pointed out that the *curé* of New Orleans, a Capuchin, was a member of the board of the hospital which the Ursulines would manage. Since Father de Beaubois had done the Company the favor of securing the Ursulines, he could advise them as a friend. However, for anything concerning his ecclesiastical ministry, he must look to Father Raphaël.[46]

A glance at the Paris Rule, which the Ursulines of New Orleans observed, would readily have clarified any uncertainty regarding the powers of the superior.

> The first and principal Superior of the Ursuline Religious is the Bishop of the Diocese.... Nevertheless, because ordinarily he is occupied by the important affairs of his diocese, and as he is not able to attend to the affairs which arise daily in the monasteries.... It is necessary that the Ursulines have another Superior who will be elected by the Religious every three years.... The power of the Superior will extend as much to the spiritual as to the temporal affairs of the monastery, and principally to have observed and kept the Rules and Constitutions, without changing, or altering anything, and also to maintain union and good understanding between the inferiors and Superiors...and nothing of consequence or importance will be done in the monastery without his consent and permission.
>
> The Superior will officiate at the clothing and professions of the young ladies, or he will delegate someone to do it. He will appoint the confessors and chaplains after having consulted with the Superior and the Councillor.
>
> He will provide preachers and no one will preach without his consent, and no young lady will enter the

monastery to be a religious without his permission and no one will be sent away without informing him of it.

He will sign the registers of the professions of the Religious and all contracts and all leases of land, and also the annual receipts and expenditures of the monastery.[47]

It is evident that the Rule gave the superior broader powers than those suggested by Abbé Raguet. This is significant since the Rule had papal approval. Abbé Raguet knew that Mother St. Augustin was opposed to having a Capuchin for superior. She had been very emphatic on that point, declaring "that the Capuchins would never enter her house."[48] What grievance Mother St. Augustin had against the Capuchins is not known; nor what answer Abbé Raguet gave her. Probably he assured her that the Ursulines would be free to choose whom they wished. Otherwise, we may be certain that Mother St. Augustin, the staunch defender of the rights conferred by the constitutions, would not have concluded arrangements to go to Louisiana. Unless the Ursulines could live according to their Rule, the Company could look elsewhere for "thrifty Sisters" to take charge of the hospital.

Mother St. Augustin appealed directly to the bishop of Quebec, Bishop St. Vallier, asking him to approve Father de Beaubois as the Ursulines' superior, as well as spiritual advisor to the hospital.[49] Bishop St. Vallier found this request "just and reasonable,"[50] and replied to Mother St. Augustin to that effect.[51] About the same time the bishop wrote to Bishop de Mornay. After this correspondence Bishop de Mornay seemed more or less reconciled to the Ursulines' and Jesuits' going to Louisiana, as long as Father de Beaubois was not to be vicar general.[52] Making a distinction between confessor and superior, Bishop de Mornay wrote to Father Raphaël de Luxembourg:

> Since the last letter that I wrote you, I have seen Father de Beaubois, who is returning to Louisiana with some Sisters who are to take care of the hospital and of the instruction of children. Reverend Father de Beaubois promised me that he would do nothing but in agreement with you, and I am exhorting you to live in harmony with him. Although the Sisters asked for him as their

confessor, all the more since going with them to Louisiana, he will gain their confidence, I am leaving everything in your hands, in order that, receiving his powers from you, he will have more liaison with you. He could then be their confessor and you the superior, or vice versa, just as you will think fit. Although I strongly resented this at first, I did not wish to take any decision without knowing what you thought about it.[52]

Mother St. Augustin, relying on Bishop St. Vallier's approval of their choice of a superior and on whatever promises Abbé Raguet made, thought that the issue was closed. Little did she realize that the problem would rise again after she and her companions reached Louisiana. Meanwhile the archbishop of Rouen was being "incessantly importuned" by the directors of the Company and the Ursulines to issue letters of obedience to the volunteers for Louisiana. Although he had given permission to the sisters to go to Paris to settle arrangements with the Company, the archbishop delayed his consent, wanting assurance from the king that the settlement would be permanent. In the early days of September 1726, he wrote:

> I cannot give this consent {to go to Louisiana} until I am assured not only that the King approves of it but that the King by his authority will render this establishment secure and permanent, whatever events come to pass, and that these women will be assured a livelihood the remainder of their days and that after having worked a long time in Louisiana, they will not become a care to their house of profession. I am writing that I may know from you the intentions of his Majesty. As soon as you have informed me of them and have assured me that His Majesty will ratify all that has been done for the said establishment, I will give my letter of obedience and my consent. I have the honor of writing to you in the presence of M. the coadjutor of Quebec {Bishop de Mornay} who seems to me to desire this establishment exceedingly.[54]

A few days later Father de Beaubois learned that the archbishop was more favorably disposed toward the project. After an interview with the archbishop, the Jesuit told Abbé Raguet that the archbishop had finally consented to everything.[55] Father de Beaubois recounted that he was no longer that "unmanageable bishop," whom they had previously interviewed, and that all that remained was to give him the names of the religious so that the "obediences" could be drawn up.[56] Father de Beaubois was anxious to get the matter of the contract settled "*sur le champ*," so that he could leave for Louisiana. After almost six months of opposition and delay, the contract was duly signed by the directors of the Company[57] and by the Ursulines on September 13, 1726.[58] The Ursulines asked that the contract be approved by royal warrant (*brevet*), and the directors of the Company also sent a petition to this effect to

Louis XV, King of France 1715-1774. Courtesy Ursuline Archives & Museum, Photo by Sr. Jacqueline Toppino, O.S.U.

the king.[59] Louis XV, "wishing to favor all that could contribute to the relief of the poor and sick and the education of youth," approved the contract by royal warrant September 18, 1726, and placed the religious "under his protection and safeguard."[60]

As soon as the contract was signed Father de Beaubois departed for Hennebont, the port from which they would sail. Mother St. Augustin and her two companions also left Paris for the Ursuline Convent in Hennebont to wait for the additional sisters, who would join them there. She wrote to Abbé Raguet on October 31:

> Permit me to hope that you will be well pleased, or at least not displeased, to know that we have arrived at Hennebont in perfect health and with more good will than ever to sacrifice our lives for the instruction of children and the care of the sick of New Orleans. We do not feel at all the fatigue of the journey that we have already made and we are impatient to be on the sea, exposed to its blows and abandoned to the Providence of Him for the love of Whom we give ourselves without reserve. What displeases us is that we are threatened with remaining here a long time. Would there be no means of advancing that happy day for which I have yearned for 26 years and which has not yet arrived? I have yet one more favor to ask of you. It is to be kind enough to see to it, by your recommendation, that we be lodged on the vessel as is becoming to Religious, that is to say, that we have a room where we can be at liberty. I hope that you will be kind enough to procure this little comfort for us by writing or having someone write to the captain of our ship....
>
> We have been very much embarrassed by the great number of small packages that they have made of our clothing and furniture. It is entirely the fault of the packer to whom we have confided all, persuaded that he would be more acquainted with that than a Religious. We can assure you that the whole could easily be reduced by a fourth and besides there are some bedsteads that we do

not need at all and that we would gladly leave behind....

The Archbishop of Rouen has finally given the obediences of our two Religious of le Havre and Elboeuf and they are already on the way to join us. We shall not have any difficulty in finding more. I have already found more than twelve who wish to come with us. It is the spirit of our Institute that inspires them with this zeal.[61]

The two Ursulines from le Havre and Elboeuf, Sister St. François Xavier Mahieu and Sister St. Joseph Cavelier[62] left Rouen for Paris on October 24, with a young lady, Miss Madeleine Hachard.[63] The missionaries had expected to remain in Paris for only a few days. Father d'Avaugour, Jesuit Procurator of the North American Missions, informed them that the ship was not ready, and that they would be delayed in Paris for one month. It was not until December 8, that they left Paris with Father Doutreleau and Brother Crucy, Jesuit missionaries destined for Louisiana. From Paris they went to Versailles where they were delighted by a visit to the magnificent palace of the king. Some of their experiences were decidedly less enjoyable. On the fourth day of the fatiguing trip, they left Alençon by coach at three in the morning. Madeleine Hachard recounted this incident:

> The roads were so impassable that we had hardly made half a league when we were obliged to alight, our coach being stuck deep in the mud. The drivers added twenty-two oxen to the twelve horses that we had, to draw our equipage out of the dangerous place. We did not wait for it. We went along and walked about a league. We were very cold, and as we found no house in which to seek shelter, we were obliged to sit down on the ground. Father Doutreleau stood on a small elevation in a nearby wood and there, like another St. John the Baptist, he exhorted us to penance. In reality, we had great need of patience.
>
> After having rested a little, we resumed our walk, and at last we had the good fortune to come to a little

cottage where a poor old woman lived alone. She was still in bed, and it was only after many supplications and promises that she did us the favor of opening her door. She had neither wood nor candles. We were obliged to make a fire with furze by the light of which Reverend Father read his breviary while awaiting daylight. We did not fail to reward the charity of the poor woman. Our coach did not join us until about ten o'clock. We advanced that day only four leagues, almost all on foot. In spite of the fatigue we laughed often. From time to time there happened little adventures which amused us. We were covered with mud up to our ears. The veils of our two Mothers were speckled with whitish spots. This produced one of the queerest effects. We arrived at night at Mayenne. . .We went to the inn and were soon in bed, for we were very tired.[64]

The travelers spent the next night at Lavalle, "a pretty town," where their presence stimulated the curiosity of the residents.

Father Doutreleau said Mass for us at the parish church which is opposite the inn where we lodged. Before leaving, we took a cup of chocolate for our breakfast. The whole town was at the door of the inn to see us get up into the coach. Although it was raining very hard, that did not prevent the people from being in the street from five o'clock in the morning until eight waiting for us. I remarked, on this occasion, that the inhabitants of this town are as curious as those of Rouen to see nothing unusual.[65]

After a journey of ten days, the missionaries reached the Ursuline Convent of Hennebont the morning of December 18. They were welcomed by Mother St. Augustin with "open arms" and a "thousand kind attentions." The following day two Ursulines, Sister Ste. Thèrése Salaun and Sister St. Michel Marion, arrived from Ploërmel, accompanied by Father Tartarin, another Jesuit missionary destined for Louisiana. Sister Ste. Marthe Dain of Hennebont would also join them on the voyage. The contract called for six religious, but at this point the community consisted of eight professed sisters and three postulants.[66] Before the end of the year Sister Ste. Marie Yuiquel of Vannes came to join them.

The unexpected delays put a heavy drain on the resources of the sisters, and Mother St. Augustin was beginning to worry about their financial stability. She shared her anxiety with Abbé Raguet in a Christmas Eve letter of thanks for his sending her nine hundred livres.

> I assure you, Sir, that it could not have arrived here more opportunely. We have no more money and we owe much. The delay of our embarkation occasions us much expense that we did not expect to incur. We are assembled here to the number of twelve[67] in a house where we pay our board at the rate of 300 livres. Along with that, it has been necessary to defray the expense for all of us to come here.[68]

New Year's Day, 1727, was the date set for the formal inauguration of the New Orleans community. The annalist recorded this event in a few simple words.

> The first day of January of the year 1727, all the Religious of the Monastery of St. Ursula of Louisiana assembled in the infirmary of the Ursuline Religious of Hennebont to acknowledge as their first superior Mother Marie Tranchepain de St. Augustin, whom the Bishop of Quebec had confirmed in this charge by two letters, the one written to Reverend Father de Beaubois, and the other written to her. All the professed Religious, and two seculars, came one after the other to make their submission and recognition the day and year as above and signed the above according to their rank of profession.[69]

Who were these courageous women who were forming this new community, sacrificing their well-appointed and time-honored monasteries

"Mystical Marriage of St. Catherine", Gift of Louis XV to the Ursulines before the voyage to Louisiana. His seal is affixed to the back of the picture. Courtesy Ursuline Archives & Museum, Photo by Sr. Jacqueline Toppino, O.S.U.

to launch an enterprise that "many persons in France looked upon as mad"?[70] All the professed religious were members of the Congregation of Paris except Sister Ste. Marie Yuiquel[71], who was of the Congregation of Bordeaux. She was united to the others on the condition that she make the Vow of Instruction.[72] Mother St. Augustin, Marie Tranchepain, was raised by her family as a Protestant, but she became very interested in the Catholic religion and sought instruction at the Ursuline Convent in Rouen.[73] She became a Roman Catholic under the guidance of the vicar general and continued to pursue religious studies. Her family remained Huguenots and sought to change her mind. Despite threats, promises and disagreeable episodes created by her brother, she remained firm in her commitment to her new faith. Attracted by the virtuous lives of the religious and the intellectual challenge of Catholicism, she asked to be admitted and was accepted by the Ursulines of Rouen in 1699. Her dream of pursuing missionary work dated from the time of her entrance into the novitiate, the same year that Iberville and Bienville landed with colonists for the settlement of Louisiana. Some two hundred years later Henry Renshaw, at a meeting of the Louisiana Historical Society, commented on how well-suited her name was to her mission.

> Tranchepain means Cut-Bread or Slice-Bread. Uncouth as the name may appear to casual attention, it has a rich significance and a latent grace of appropriateness. It may be deemed the equivalent of what has been considered to be the etymological significance of the word lady.... Lady means bread-giver or loaf-giver.... A Lady has legal claim to her title only in so far as she communicates... help to the poor, representative of her Master .... Thus the name of the Superior was not an unsuitable one. Her life was to be consumed in benevolent usefulness. She was to divide a divine bread, to dispense a heavenly manna, to distribute intellectual and moral and spiritual nourishment to the multitude.[74]

The assistant superior, Mother St. Jean Judde, was a woman of rare virtue and sterling character who enthusiastically volunteered to go to Louisiana. The members of her large Rouen family strenuously opposed her plan, but none of their entreaties shook her determination.[75] Sister Ste. Angélique Le Boullenger, treasurer of the nascent community, had shown piety and sincerity since early childhood. Like her brother, Father Le Boullenger of the Jesuit Illinois Mission, she was eager to respond to the call of a missionary vocation, even though her health was quite delicate.[76] Sister Ste. Thérése Salaun, a native of Ploërmel and a student of the Ursulines, had entered the novitiate upon completion of her studies. Her life in religion demanded continual self-control, as she had an ardent and imperious nature. Learning that there were Ursulines at Hennebont who were going to Louisiana, she asked to join them. When her only brother learned of her plan, he placed every conceivable obstacle in her way. Mother St. Augustin accepted her in preference to several other volunteers, and with great joy she joined the sisters at Hennebont.[76] Sister Ste. Marie Yuiquel was a member of the community of Vannes, when she volunteered for Louisiana. She was "incredibly active, profoundly humble, and always animated by a spirit of lively faith."[78]

Sister St. François Xavier Mahieu, due to her mother's opposition to her entering religion, was obliged to wait until her death before being professed at le Havre. For over ten years, before any discussion of a mission to Louisiana, she had wanted to dedicate herself to mission work and prayed to St. Francis Xavier to assist her. Informed that Father de Beaubois was trying to arrange for a community of Ursulines at New Orleans and had procured three Ursulines from Rouen, she wrote to him asking to join them. Father de Beaubois and the three sisters easily agreed to her request. It was more difficult to win the consent of her community, especially her superior, who knew the solid virtue of Sister St. François Xavier and did not want to lose her. The Mother Superior wrote to Father de Beaubois and to Mother St. Augustin to prevent their accepting Sister St. François Xavier, pleading her poor health. But the prayers, perseverance, and ardent desire of the would-be missionary finally disarmed the superior, and she gave her approval. The archbishop of Rouen was so opposed to the enterprise that he flatly refused to give a letter of obedience. Mother St. Augustin then appealed to Cardinal de Fleury, but attributed the successful conclusion to the prayers of Sister St. François Xavier.[79]

> While we treated with the powerful of earth, she did it with more efficacy before the Almighty by her prayers and supplications. We were, however, obliged to depart for l' Orient and to leave this fervent missionary still uncertain of being able to join us. Finally, Our Lord having sufficiently tried her, she received her obedience and left immediately to come to join us at the Ursulines of Hennebont, accompanied by a young religious from Elboeuf and a postulant.[80]

The religious from Elboeuf was Sister St. Joseph Cavelier. Like Mother St. Augustin she had desired since first becoming an Ursuline to devote her life to missionary work, and she had prayed for such a challenge. She offered herself to Father de Beaubois, and she was accepted as a member of the group.[81] The postulant who accompanied Sister St. François Xavier to Hennebont was Marie Madeleine Hachard. She belonged to one of the best families of Normandy, distinguished by its social position as well as by its profoundly religious character. Madeleine counted among her relatives three Capuchin priests and a cousin who was Mother Vicar of the Religious of St. Francis. One brother was a religious and another was preparing for the priesthood. Of her four sisters, the eldest was a Franciscan, Elizabeth was asking admission to the same order, and Louise had been admitted to the Val-de-Grace.[82] The parents of this family had a spirit of faith that was very deep. Although relatives and friends discouraged them from giving Madeleine permission, these generous parents gave their much loved and youngest daughter to the service of God.[83] Madeleine appreciated the cost of the sacrifice, and from New Orleans she wrote to her father:

> I lose no opportunity of showing you my perfect gratitude for all the kindness that you have had for me, especially for the blessed consent which you gave for my departure, against the advice of so many persons who were opposed to the designs of God. Of all the favors which I owe you, I regard this last as the greatest and most agreeable to God.[84]

In all her writings Madeleine showed herself joyous and affectionate, intellectually gifted, and better educated than was usual for females at the time. At the age of eighteen she had thought of becoming a Poor Clare, but her spiritual director dissuaded her, assuring her that this was not the religious order to which God called her. Some time afterward, she learned of the plans of the Ursuline group to go to New Orleans, and she begged to join the mission. Because of Madeleine's young age, Mother St. Augustin gave serious consideration to her character and talents, acceding in Madeleine's wishes after three months.[85] Mother St. Augustin promised Madeleine that her novitiate would begin on the day she departed Rouen for Paris, and that she could receive the religious habit at Hennebont. This ceremony took place with great solemnity on January 19,1727.[86] She received the name of Sister St. Stanislaus, and the following day the novice was given the black veil[87] which she kept throughout the voyage.

Mother St. Augustin and her companions[88] had no romantic ideas about the country to which they were going. Friends and relatives, who wished to prevent their leaving France, had painted Louisiana as black as possible. But warnings of hardships to be endured could not cool their ardor for the spreading of Christ's kingdom in the Louisiana colony.

CHAPTER 3

The Voyage and Arrival in Louisiana

All of the missionaries had reached Hennebont by late December, 1726, but by mid-January the prospects of sailing were still dim. The Jesuit Fathers Tartarin and Doutreleau had gone to Lorient just before Christmas to speed up the loading of the ship. The Ursulines had also journeyed to Lorient, thinking the ship was ready to sail. Because of further delays they were lodged in the home of a Mr. Morin, "a man of great refinement and real merit." In his residence they had a room which served as an oratory, another as a dining room, and several bedrooms.[1] On February 22 they were notified to be ready to embark in one hour.[2] Sister St. Stanislaus and perhaps some of the others wondered how they would board the vessel, since it was very high on the side. Father Tartarin, who retained his sense of humor in spite of postponement and difficulties, enjoyed a joke at her expense, as she related to her father.

> Father Tartarin says he will have us put two by two in a sack, and that they will hoist us up with a pulley as they do a bale. But our Captain, although little experienced in the charge of such merchandise, assures us that he will have us carried up more commodiously; that is, seated in an armchair, one after the other.[3]

Whatever the manner of boarding the *Gironde*, they were all on deck ready for sailing when the wind suddenly changed, delaying the departure another day. The delay gave the Ursulines time to arrange their small room, which was a compartment, eighteen feet long and seven or eight feet wide, constructed between the decks. Six beds were set up on each side of the compartment, making it necessary for the thirteenth sister to sleep in the passage.[4] Two port holes twice the size of a hand provided ventilation, and frequently these had to be kept closed to prevent the water from drenching the occupants and the beds. Such cramped quarters constrained the sisters to occupy the room by turns. The Jesuits were even worse off. "They had a wretched little hole without any opening." They preferred to sleep on the top deck "at the mercy of the wind and rain," their heads sheltered by a "clothes-basket".

By two o'clock on the afternoon of February 23, the weather was fine and the *Gironde* sailed from the harbor, only to hit a rock within a half league of port. But assistance from shore sent them on their way again. Then the wind became their next adversary, tossing the vessel continuously and causing all aboard to pay "tribute to the sea." No one escaped the malady, but Sisters Ste. Angélique and St. Stanislaus seemed to suffer less than the others. During the first fifteen days the ship's progress was exceptionally slow, and by March 12 they had gone only as far as the Madeira Islands, where they stopped to take on fresh water. They remained there three days, visiting with some Jesuits who had a college in the city and who brought the travelers a plentiful supply of preserves, lemons and other fruits. Mother St. Augustin recorded that the one French speaking priest acted as an interpreter and said a "thousand kind things" in the name of all. The Lady Abbess of the Poor Clare monastery on the island also invited the Ursulines to visit her monastery. They declined because they understood that women on the island never went out except to go to Mass. At such times they covered their faces with long veils and went in procession, walking in silence or saying their beads. Under such circumstances Mother St. Augustin thought the Ursulines should edify the "public" by remaining attached to their cloister on the *Gironde* rather than appear in a city "where even the secular women did not show themselves."[5]

His ship provisioned, the captain again turned the *Gironde* toward Louisiana. The wind continued unfavorable, and to add to the distress, they encountered a pirate ship. The men armed themselves, cannons were loaded, and combat posts assumed. The Ursulines sheltered themselves in the passage between the decks. The corsairs circled the ship a number of times, but apparently believing that they would be overpowered, sailed away. A few days later another hostile vessel pursued their ship for several hours but did not attack. The unfavorable weather made the voyage unusually long and fatiguing. Sister St. Stanislaus recorded that the one bright feature of the seemingly endless days was the joy derived from religious observances.

If we had any consolation it was the advantage we had of assisting at the Holy Sacrifice of the Mass, which was celebrated every day. Often, we had the happiness of fortifying ourselves with the Sacred Body of Jesus Christ. We had some sermons from the Chaplain of the vessel and from our Reverend Fathers. Prayers were said four times a day, at four and eight in the morning and at five and eight in the evening. Every Sunday and Holy Day, High Mass and Vespers were sung. On Good Friday the adoration of the Cross was devoutly made. We were the first to advance barefoot to venerate the Cross. Then followed the Reverend Fathers, the officers, the passengers, and the crew, all in a respectful manner. On the feast of the Blessed Sacrament, the procession was made around the capstan. In a vessel, it suffices for the officers to give the example, in order to inspire the whole crew with devotion. They never failed to ring and recite the Angelus three times a day.[6]

The *Gironde* anchored in Quay St. Louis, a port in the French part of the island of Hispaniola, in the first week of May. There the missionaries made the acquaintance of "Messieurs the mosquitoes." They flitted about the nuns from sunset to sunrise, never failing to leave their traces. As there was no religious community of women on the island, the officers of the Company offered the Ursulines the use of the Company's warehouse, but meals were eaten in the homes of the officers. The governor came to visit them and twice entertained them at his home "with French magnificence." The officials of the island were anxious to have an Ursuline establishment in their colony and inquired as to how to proceed at the French court. The sisters gave them written instructions and assured them that there would be many who would volunteer for such a foundation.[7]

The *Gironde* sailed from Quay St. Louis on May 19 loaded with provisions, presents, and a three hundred pound barrel of sugar. Weather conditions continued to plague the voyage. Contrary winds alternated with becalmed seas, slowing the progress of the ship. Pirate ships again put in appearances. One of them let down a number of "evil-looking men" who came to the side of the ship, ostensibly to buy wine but in reality to reconnoitre the condition of the vessel and the crew. The captain vacillated between wanting to take the men as prisoners or fire a cannon into their boat "to send them to drink in the bottom of the sea." Prudently he commanded them to retire, which they did, much to the relief of the passengers.

The current of the Gulf of Mexico along with adverse winds drove the *Gironde* toward Blanche Island, where it grounded on a sand bar. The sounding-line indicated that the vessel had sunk more than five feet in the sands, and after trying various maneuvers, the captain decided to unload the vessel. The cannons, tied on wooden rafts were let down into the sea, and the ballast was thrown overboard. When that did not sufficiently lighten the ship, the passengers' chests were selected to go next, with those of the Ursulines being the easiest to reach. As the religious considered the consequences of their trunks awash in the sea, the captain changed his mind and selected the sugar for disposal.[8] The ship still remained grounded. Again the captain considered the sisters' chests, and once again found something else. Sixty-one barrels of brandy and a great number of bales of merchandise belonging to the Company were then sacrificed.[9] The *Gironde* remained in a precarious situation for almost twenty-four hours before the crew succeeded in drawing it out of the sand bar. Scarcely had they gone a quarter of a league, when the ship grounded a second time with great violence. When an extended struggle had once more set the vessel afloat, the captain was unwilling to take further chances. He sent the ship's boat ahead with an officer handling the sounding-line.

Several days passed without further misadventures, and just as Dauphin Island appeared on the horizon, a brigantine was sighted sailing in the direction of the *Gironde*. It proved to be a friendly ship, bringing word to the Ursulines that Father de Beaubois was anxiously awaiting their arrival, and that a temporary residence was available for them until their monastery could be finished. The brigantine accompanied the *Gironde* to Dauphin Island, where the captain intended to take on a supply of fresh water. But before this could be done a favorable wind arose, and the *Gironde* sailed immediately. Exactly five months[10] after embarkation, the ship entered the roadstead at the Balize, which was what the mouth of the Mississippi River was called by the colonists.[11]

M. de Verges, commandant of the post, received Mother St. Augustin

The Mouth of the Mississippi River near the Balize, by John H.B. Labtrobe. The Ursulines left the Gironde at this point and continued upriver in smaller boats. Courtesy Historic New Orleans Collection, 1973.40.

and her companions graciously and offered them the use of his house while they awaited the arrival of boats to take them upriver to New Orleans.[12] In the meantime Father Tartarin hastened to New Orleans to announce the missionaries' arrival. Father de Beaubois, although ill and unable to personally go to the Balize, dispatched a sloop and some pirogues to convey the Ursulines and the Jesuits upriver. M. Massy, a brother of one of the postulants, was in charge of transporting the group. He carried letters of welcome from Governor Étienne de Périer and Jacques de la Chaise, *ordonnateur* (commissioner general) of the colony.

The sloop was too small to accommodate all the missionaries, so they were obliged to separate. Mother St. Augustin and the youngest sisters, accompanied by Father Doutreleau and Brother Crucy, travelled by pirogue. The remaining sisters and their two servants boarded the sloop with M. Massy, while the servants and workmen of the Jesuits used another small pirogue.[13] The entire party intended to keep together when leaving the Balize, but the sloop was so slow that the pirogue pushed on ahead. Ordinarily the trip took six days, but the sloop required an additional day. Sister St. Stanislaus wrote of this most trying part of the long journey:

> It must be acknowledged that all the fatigues of the *Gironde* were not comparable to those which we had in this short passage.... What renders this journey so wearisome is that it is necessary to erect every night some sort of cabin and this must be done one hour before sunset, in order to have time to make some pallets and eat supper. For as soon as the sun sets there come mosquitoes, with which one is assailed, like those which we first saw at the Quay St. Louis.... They sting without mercy and their sting is very annoying . . . Our sailors, to make our pallets, stuck canes in the ground in the form of a cradle around a mattress and shut us up two by two in our cradle, where we lay down without undressing. Then they covered the cradle with a large cloth, so that the mosquitoes...could not find any little opening to come to visit us. This was a most uncomfortable bed as we were drenched with rain and our mattresses nearly swam in the water.... Some of our Mothers were very much inconvenienced. Some caught colds and inflammations, others developed swollen faces and limbs, and one contracted a more serious malady.[14]

The travelers were not much more comfortable during the day, "not being able to sit down, to stand, to kneel or even to stir." The crew and the chests filled the pirogue so full that the religious were obliged to huddle on top of the baggage in a "little bunch" and could change positions only when the pirogue stopped. Their sustenance was biscuit and salt meat from the ship which the master of the pirogue cooked each evening in his pot. About eight or ten leagues from New Orleans they entered a more populated area. There the inhabitants vied with one another in offering hospitality. They were delighted to see the Ursulines and promised to send them pupils. The last evening was spent at the plantation of M. Massy, where they had intended to rest for several days. But Father Tartarin returned from New Orleans with the message that Father de Beaubois expected them the next morning. Very early on August 6, Mother St. Augustin and her companions re-embarked and arrived at New Orleans at five o'clock in the morning.[15] Because of the early hour there were few persons on the wharf. As they started for the house of Father de Beaubois the sisters saw him coming to greet them with unrestrained joy. It was an occasion of great rejoicing, both for the Ursulines who had finally reached the site of their future labor, and for Father de Beaubois who had spent many anxious weeks of waiting.

The *Gironde* had been expected months earlier. Knowing nothing of the various delays that had occurred on the passage, Father de Beaubois

"Landing of the Ursulines" Paul Poincy, 1892, is an often used painting which errs in that the Ursulines arrived on two separate days. Courtesy Ursuline Archives & Museum. Photo by Sr. Jacqueline Toppino, O.S.U.

and the Company officials must surely have worried for their safety. On May 11, Father de Beaubois had written to the secretary of the Company of the Indies:

> We await it [the *Gironde*] with great impatience,
> and I am very anxious for those poor Nuns, whose arrival
> here is looked forward to like that of the Messiah.[16]

Two weeks later Father Du Poisson wrote:

...as they were every day expecting the arrival of the pirogue which was to bring Fathers Tartarin and Doutreleau, our Brethren, and the Nuns, this made us hasten our departure, so as to spare Rev. Father de Beaubois additional inconvenience, although it was a bad season for traveling on the Mississippi... We[17] embarked then, May 25, 1727.[18]

About the same time Father de Beaubois manifested his anxiety to Abbé Raguet, the ecclesiastical director of the Company of the Indies. The abbé managed the religious affairs of the Company and from France acted as a liaison officer between the Company and the Church. In his letter Father de Beaubois struck a note which presaged troubled days ahead for himself and the Ursulines.

The *Gironde* has not arrived and I am commencing to be apprehensive for our poor Religious. They are awaited with impatience and Reverend Father Raphaël is the only one who deems this establishment ridiculous as he himself told me.[19]

Father de Beaubois thought otherwise.

They [the Ursulines] will certainly do very much good here. They will be a great help for the families whose children are deprived of all education.[20]

Now that the Ursulines had actually arrived Father de Beaubois could put aside his anxieties. Many of his friends came to welcome the missionaries as they breakfasted in his home. Then at about ten or eleven o'clock a group of them accompanied the nuns to their provisional convent.[21]

By some accounts the first house inhabited by the Ursulines in New Orleans was the home of Governor Bienville.[22] The 1726 general census of the colony of Louisiana however lists this dwelling as a "large house belonging to the Ste. Reine Concession,"[23] occupied by M. de la Chaise, his two children, and a clerk."[24] Mother St. Augustin[25] and Sister St. Stanislaus[26] simply stated that "it is a house which the Company is renting" for them until their monastery can be built. Governor Périer and M. de la Chaise, *ordonnateur*, in a joint letter of April 22, 1727, had indicated that they intended "to lodge them [the Ursulines] in Mr. Kolly's house in which is the office of the accounts of the former administration.[27] Mother St. André Melotte, second superior of the Ursulines of New Orleans, sketching the early years of the community, recorded that on arriving "they were lodged in a house belonging to Mr. de Coly, that the Company of the Indies rented for them."[28] Less than a year after the coming of the Ursulines the royal engineer drew a plan of New Orleans.[29] This plan shows the square bounded by Bienville, Chartres, Conti, and Royal as "belonging to the Ste. Reine Concession," and indicates that the Ursuline Religious were living there at the time.[30] From all this and more,[31] it is evident that the first residence of the Ursulines was not the home of Bienville.[32]

The Kolly house with two stories and a garret was considered "the finest in the city." Six doors gave entrance into the lower rooms, and large windows covered with fine linen cloth admitted light as well as air to the rooms.[33] A poultry yard and a garden were bounded on

(Illus. 7)
Sketch of Kolly Townhouse, created from an old pencil drawing.

This sketch depicts the Kolly House, the first home of the Ursulines. Courtesy Ursuline Archives and Museum, Photo by Sr. Jacqueline Toppino, O.S.U.

one side and end by "great forest trees of prodigious height and girth."[34] Converting one of the rooms into a chapel was a major priority of the sisters. Beginning the day after their arrival, Father de Beaubois said daily Mass at the residence, and by October 5, a tabernacle for the Blessed Sacrament was completed.[35] The nuns expected to remain in the Kolly house about six months or at most a year.[36] They looked forward to the erection of their monastery across the street from the hospital, but it would be seven years before it was completed. Those seven years were extremely difficult for the nuns, but despite the hardships they suffered, they lost no time in beginning their missionary work. Because of their rule of cloister the sisters could not begin their medical service, as the hospital was across town. But they did fulfill their fourth vow by undertaking the pursuit of Christian education of women.

The families of New Orleans and its environs were anxious to confide their daughters to the nuns.[37] Parents hoped that the education given by the Ursulines would produce great benefits in the colony where religion was "little known and still less practiced."[38] The Kolly house was not large enough to accommodate the students desiring education, and Mother St. Augustin explained the state of affairs to Abbé Raguet in her first letter from New Orleans.

> All the inhabitants try very hard to make us realize the joy they feel in having us for the education of their children. Nevertheless, we have very little means of proving to them our zeal, since we do not have sufficient lodging space to receive either boarders or day pupils, a situation which is very embarrassing and most trying for us. They promise, however, to build for us, in a short time, whatever will satisfy our needs.[39]

A short time after this correspondence workmen began constructing a small house adjacent to the Kolly house which would provide quarters for the boarders and classrooms for the day students. The owner of the house furnished the wood, and the Ursulines paid the carpenters.[40] On November 17, 1727, the first boarders[41] arrived, with day classes opening a few days later.[42] Students were predominately French, but special classes for Negro and Indian girls were held every afternoon from one to two-thirty or later.[43] Mother St. Augustin's letters make clear that the nuns deeply loved the Negro and Indian girls.[44]

Father de Beaubois challenged the Ursulines to an additional service not mentioned in their contract with the Company. He asked them to assume the care of an orphan girl whom he found "serving in a house where she did not have very good example." He sought protection for this girl and suggested that the Ursulines would do a great service if they could provide refuge for other orphan girls. He promised that he and Governor Périer would care for orphan boys.[45] Mother St. Augustin and her sisters generously cooperated and reported to Abbé Raguet:

> We have also charged ourselves with the care of the orphans to provide them with a suitable education which will enable them to earn their living according to their condition. We have at present (April 20, 1728) only three in our house but we are expecting others.[46]

Although Mother St. Augustin gave no hint of the sacrifices entailed, Father de Beaubois recognized the strenuous efforts they were making.

> They are overburdened with work, and, although they are going very much beyond their resources, they shelter gratuitously in their house some orphans who were either wholly abandoned or in very bad hands. The poor girls are entirely under their charge. They have even taken from them the ration that they had from the Company when they were with the wretched persons from whom I have taken them. Nothing could be more unjust....[47]

In accepting the care of the orphans the Ursulines were relying on Divine Providence, for they had no means of supporting them. Providence supplied the need in the fall of 1728 when the Superior Council of Louisiana granted a subsidy of 150 livres for each orphan girl[48] assigned to the Ursulines by order of the commandant and the Superior Council.[49] "I do not expect that amount to make us rich as they come to us entirely destitute, and we have to furnish them with everything. But our recompense is in heaven," wrote Mother St. Augustin to Abbé Raguet.[50]

As more young women came under their care, the influence of the Ursulines spread. Their aim through working with the young women was to revive the spirit of Christianity in the home life of the early settlers. Soon Sister St. Stanislaus could write:

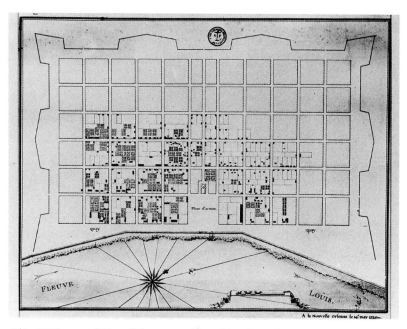

This 1727 map of New Orleans was drawn by Adrien de Pauger, French engineer. Courtesy Historic New Orleans Collection, 1974.25.18.92

Our little community is increasing from day to day. We have twenty boarders, of whom eight have today made their First Communion, three are lady boarders, and three are orphans whom we take through charity. We have, also, seven slave boarders to teach and prepare for baptism and First Communion. Besides, we have a large number of day pupils and Negresses and Indians who come two hours every day to be instructed.

The custom here is to marry girls at the age of twelve, or fourteen years. Before our arrival many had been married without even knowing how many gods there are. You may judge of the rest. But since we have come here, none are married unless they have attended our instructions.... I cannot express to you the pleasure we find in instructing all these young people. It suffices for us to consider the need which they have of instruction. Some boarders of twelve, or fifteen years, have never been to confession or even to Mass. Brought up on a plantation, at a distance of four or five leagues from the city, without any spiritual help, they had never heard of God.... We have the consolation of finding them very docile and ardently desirous of being instructed.[51]

The letters and records of the Ursulines indicate that they were happy in their work of Christian education, but, as noted earlier, their principal assignment in the colony was caring for the military sick.[52] Construction of a monastery near the hospital was essential for the nursing assignment, but many complications delayed its completion. Governor Périer and M. de la Chaise had written to the directors of the Company as early as April 22, 1727: "We are having the last two lots that are above the hospital cleared in order to place in one of them the Ursuline Nuns who are coming."[53] These lots or squares had originally been destined for another purpose. The royal engineer Ignace Broutin explained the change:

> We have altered the plan of M. de Pauger, which was to place the arsenal at the end of the city, while there is a place to put it at the center. I wish to say, in the heart of the place, and they will put the Ursuline Religious, where they had planned the arsenal, and the hospital after that, which will be at the end of the city and adjoining the religious, as is fitting.[54]

These plans had been made while the Ursulines were still on the high seas, but little had been done by the time they arrived. On New Year's Day, 1728, Sister St. Stanislaus wrote to her father that the Company was working hard on the convent and the engineer had come to show them the plans.[55] Apparently the hard work was on the plans, or possibly the building materials, as a week later Mother St. Augustin wrote: "...they are beginning to think of building our house."[56]

Governor Périer gave the nuns reason to hope that the monastery would be finished by the end of 1728.[57] But workmen were scarce, officials were engrossed in other business, and the date for completion was moved to Easter, 1729.[58] In March of 1729 construction had still not even begun. Sister St. Stanislaus wrote:

> M. Mickel, who has undertaken the building of the Ursuline Convent, has his timber all ready and is going to bring it here some day soon in order to put up these buildings at once. The casement doors and the rest of the joiners work will also be ready since it has been a year since they were begun. In spite of that we do not think that it is possible to provide them lodgings in it before nine or ten months, no matter how diligent we may be.[59]

Delay followed delay, and the laying of the cornerstone did not take place until 1730. On one side of the plate enclosed in it was engraved the following inscription [in French]:

> In the reign of Louis XV, King of France and Navarre, the cornerstone of this monastery was laid by the most eminent and most illustrious Lady Catherine de Chibelier, wife of M. Étienne de Périer, Knight of the Order of St. Louis, Captain of the frigates of His Most Christian Majesty, Commandant of the Province and of the Colony of Louisiana. In the year of our Lord 1730.[60]

On the opposite side were engraved the names of the religious who composed the community at that time, along with names of the royal engineer and the architects.[61] Whatever hope the laying of the cornerstone may have stirred in the hearts of the religious, they were to wait four more years before taking possession of the building.

The procrastination in providing a building for the sisters was not only prejudicial to the interests of the Company, but also left the wretched condition of the sick unalleviated. As the sisters were expected to take charge of the sick as soon as they arrived in New Orleans, Mother St. Augustin had inspected the hospital in the fall of 1727. She was appalled by what she saw.

> As for the hospital, I have been there once. They say that they have everything prepared for us; nevertheless, I confess to you, Sir, that I was dismayed by such great misery. There is no stable nor cattle shed of which the lodging is not more agreeable or more commodious. They say there is scarcely any sickness that would force one to this miserable shelter. In short, I had my heart pierced with compassion and I expect often to have recourse to you, Sir, in favor of these poor unfortunate ones who lack the most necessary things.[62]

In her next letter of January 5, 1728, Mother St. Augustin again brought up the matter of the hospital:

> I desire that we may soon be in a position to take possession of the hospital. I have been there once, and I have seen with astonishment the pitiful state of the sick and the absence of the most necessary things. While we wait, we are careful to acquit ourselves well of the duties of our institute.[63]

From France Abbé Raguet, far from the scene and with little understanding of the situation, apparently failed to realize who was responsible for these conditions. He replied by lecturing Mother St. Augustin on her duty, as though she lacked generosity.

> You had been to the hospital only once when you did me the honor of writing me, that is to say, October 25. I would have thought that you would have run more rapidly towards this cross, for from the manner in which you have depicted it, you do not expect to find anything agreeable there, if it is not God alone. Thus you ought

to have only Him and the alleviation of your neighbor in view. As for the conveniences, the niceties, the comforts of this life, they ordinarily follow from rude beginnings; but then one has great reason to doubt if one is better off as to salvation when he merits infinitely less. Your work is, as you know, divided between the care of the sick and the education of young girls. They will combine with that, I think yet another care[64] of which M. Périer and M. de la Chaise will speak to you. But, of all that, the care of the sick is the principal object. Reflect well on that.[65]

Perhaps Abbé Raguet had not counted on dealing with a woman of Mother St. Augustin's forthright character. In her reply, she left not the slightest doubt as to her interpretation of her duty.

> You appear surprised, Sir, that I had been to the hospital only once when I wrote to you. The Company has promised us to have a convent built for us near the hospital. When it will have kept its word, we shall think about carrying out ours. For it is not fitting that we should walk, every day, from one end of the city to the other. Our duty does not oblige us to do that.[66]

The Ursulines wanted to begin their work at the hospital, but until the Company erected the necessary buildings it was impossible for the sisters to do so.

Shortly after arriving in New Orleans Mother St. Augustin took steps to ensure the temporal welfare of the community. On September 20, 1727, she presented a petition to the Superior Council for a plantation of eight *arpents* frontage on the Mississippi River in fulfillment of Article IX of their contract. She asked that the strip be located at Pointe St. Antoine, which is in the present day area of Chalmette.[67] This would be the most convenient site because it was on the eastern bank of the river and not far from the city. Mother St. Augustin also asked for eight Negroes to cultivate the plantation. On November 29, 1727, the petition was returned to the Ursuline Superior with the notation: "The Council grants to the said Lady Religious the eight *arpents* of frontage by forty of depth at the said place, Pointe de Saint Antoine, adjoining that of M. St. Martin."[68] The plantation was given to the Ursulines to supply them with provisions and to recompense them for their services in the hospital. In October the nuns received eight Negroes, two of whom ran away "to the woods or elsewhere."[69] One of the Negroes remained at the convent as a servant, and the others were sent to the plantation where a manager and his wife supervised the daily operations. But while these temporal necessities were being provided for and the educational efforts developing, a cloud of uncertainty was beginning to overshadow the future of the Ursulines in Louisiana. For a time it seemed that the gathering storm might destroy the new establishment.

CHAPTER 4

The Politics Of The New World

When the Ursuline nuns arrived in New Orleans in 1727 Bienville was no longer Commandant and had returned to France. Still, the remnants of the political factionalism that had split citizens into supporters of either Bienville or Jacques de la Chaise still remained. In addition to political divisions in the community, ecclesiastical conflicts between the Jesuits and the Capuchins over areas of jurisdiction persisted. Father de Beaubois, who had been an ardent admirer and friend of Bienville, returned to New Orleans to find de la Chaise and his supporters decidedly hostile. For their part the Capuchins had sided with de la Chaise during the earlier political conflict. As already noted, Capuchin Superior Father Raphaël de Luxembourg looked upon the Ursuline establishment as ridiculous. This attitude, with the political/religious factional disputes going on, boded poorly for the Ursulines and Father de Beaubois. Fortunately, Étienne

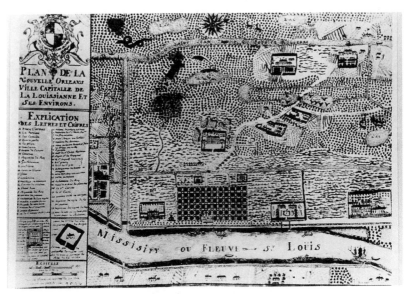

This 1730 Map of New Orleans shows the existing inhabitated area and surrounding areas. Courtesy Historic New Orleans Collection, 1974.25.18.96.

de Périer arrived in 1727 with a commission as governor, and a new policy of impartiality. A shaky truce developed between the political factions.

Father de Beaubois in his role as superior of the Ursulines was very conscientious about caring for both their spiritual and their temporal needs,[1] but his disagreements with political and religious leaders in New Orleans also affected them. He acknowledged this in a letter to Abbé Raguet: "our ladies [the Ursulines] have the misfortune of being in my charge and they become by that fact unworthy of every favor."[2] In her first letter to Abbé Raguet from New Orleans, Mother St. Augustin made no mention of the political factionalism: "we have found in the person of M. Périer all the support and protection that we could desire...M. de la Chaise assures us, also, that he is devoted to us."[3] Abbé Raguet was aware of the factionalism in the colony as well as of the dispute over ecclesiastical jurisdiction.[4] Governor Périer and M. de la Chaise soon informed him of a new controversy occasioned by the arrival of the Ursulines.

> The arrival of the Ursulines here has almost caused a division in the Church. Father de Beaubois claimed to be their superior in the capacity of vicar general and wished to direct them which was contrary to the conditions of his agreement with the Company,[5] but he had himself authorized by the Bishop of Quebec. Father Raphaël, on his side, although very good and very prudent, could not tolerate that Father de Beaubois should perform the function of the office of superior without being stirred by it. We have obliged them to let the matter rest there until M. de Mornay has decided their question.[6]

Two weeks later Father de Beaubois gave his version of the disagreement.

> I have the honor of telling you that I have received by the *Gironde* letters from the Bishop of Quebec.[7] After reproaching me because I had consented not to perform here any of my ecclesiastical functions without the consent of the Reverend Capuchin Fathers, his Grace orders[8] me to perform even in New Orleans, my functions of vicar

general as in all the rest of the colony.... Then he formally constitutes me superior of the [Ursuline] Religious and of the hospital which they are going to serve. This news spread quickly in the city and caused many little scenes. I requested the consent required in order to keep within the limits of the contract and at the same time to obey the Bishop.... As for the Religious, I was charged with them in France. The Reverend Capuchin Fathers have not seemed to trouble themselves with them. Besides they are too overburdened with work to charge themselves still further with the spiritual direction of a community of women; and they would soon be tired of having them on their hands for temporal matters as I have had them for the last four months. However, I know that there are protests and writings with regard to what concerns the Ursulines.[9]

These writings and protests together with certain rumors circulating in the colony, caused the Sisters grave anxiety. Mother St. Augustin expressed her concern in early January, 1728:

They claim that the Capuchin Fathers wish to dispute the right of Reverend Father de Beaubois to be our Superior, even though His Lordship the Bishop of Quebec, full of esteem for this Father, ordered[10] him to take care of us after having reproached him for having consented to live here in idleness, which did not become him. They ought to believe us sufficiently submissive to the Bishop of Quebec to abide by his orders, delighted to find in them our inclination satisfied. Can they imagine that after having chosen Reverend Father de Beaubois for our superior, as we had the right to do, having given him all our confidence, after all the services that he has rendered us, and that he still renders us every day, that we would have so little gratitude as not to recognize it, to withdraw from him our confidence and place ourselves under the direction of persons whom we do not know at all and who would have neither the time nor the means of providing for the spiritual and temporal cares of this house? Once more, if these rumors are well founded and if, in the position where we are, they should wish to restrain us on this point, we who by our constitutions are perfectly free in the choice of our superiors, Father Raphaël would never be the person to whom we would look, whatever desire he might have for it.[11]

Mother St. Augustin was straightforward yet respectful in treating with any official of the church or Company, but she was uncompromising when a major point of the Rule was involved. Patiently she reviewed the position of the Ursulines on the important matter of a superior. She also requested Abbé Raguet to be prepared to support them in this matter if the coadjutor should attempt to constrain them to accept a Capuchin as superior.[12]

Three and a half months slipped by before the sisters had another opportunity to send mail to France. Mother St. Augustin gave Abbé Raguet an account of the work accomplished by the community and told of the evident blessing of God on their tasks. The number of boarders had increased, and the day school was very promising. The results of the instruction of the Negresses were most gratifying. During Holy Week of 1728, Father de Beaubois had given a retreat to the community and to those preparing for First Communion. When the ladies of New Orleans heard of the retreat, they had asked to assist at the exercises.[13]

But despite the satisfaction of seeing young girls and women of the colony appreciate their efforts, there were also stressful times for the sisters. As Mother St. Augustin remarked, "Charity which ought to unite all the servants of God, to form one heart and one soul, here seems to be on its last legs."[14] She was referring to a misunderstanding that had arisen over a woman who had taken refuge in the convent. Madame Louis Jousset La Loire, the wife of a surgeon, Pierre de Manade, was weary of the violent cruelty of her husband and filed a complaint before the Superior Council, asking for legal separation and permission to retire to the convent. Until a decision could be reached Governor Périer placed her at the convent to protect her from her husband.[15]

While at the convent Madame La Loire requested that Father

Theodore, a Capuchin, come to the convent to hear her confession.[16] By chance Mother St. Augustin heard of it a few minutes before the priest arrived. The Ursuline superior was in an embarrassing position. According to the Rule she could not let any *étranger* priest hear confessions in her house without the permission of the father superior.[17] Mother St. Augustin felt obliged to tell Father Theodore of this point of the Rule. But rather than request the necessary permission from Father de Beaubois, he left and reported the incident to his superior. The next day Mother St. Augustin received a very urgent letter from Father Raphaël asking if Father de Beaubois was implicated in the matter. Mother St. Augustin took full responsibility for her actions, replying that she alone was accountable for the refusal made to Father Theodore. Her action

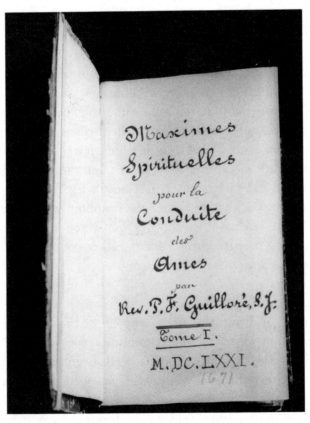

Maximes Spirituelles pout le Conduit des Ames, 1671, was brought from France by the Ursuline missionaires. Courtesy Ursuline Archives & Museum.Photo by Sr. Jacqueline Toppino, O.S.U.

was based on her Rule which forbade the admission of a *confesseur étranger* without the express permission of the father superior.[18] Father Raphaël discredited the validity of this answer, as "some persons worthy of belief assured" him "that the Superior never did anything except in concert with Reverend Father de Beaubois."[19]

The religious infighting was distressful to the Ursulines, and they feared that attitudes in the colony were endangering the work they had so enthusiastically begun. Mother St. Augustin wrote a very explicit letter to Abbé Raguet exposing the growing opposition that was rendering their position almost intolerable. With a keen intellect she evaluated the interplay of forces:

> I perceived clearly on our arrival in this country that M. de la Chaise was the mortal enemy of Reverend Father de Beaubois and of the Jesuit missionaries. I felt sure that we would feel the repercussions of this hatred, especially since Father Raphaël, the counselor of M. de la Chaise, had despaired of winning our confidence. But as this gentleman, at the same time that he profited by all the occasions that presented themselves to embarrass Father de Beaubois and to injure him, feigned very much kindness for us, I have kept from mentioning it.... It is not at all for me to enter into detail; but what I wish to come to is that if Father de Beaubois withdraws as he appears to wish to do, and for which he seems to be making preparation, I have no other course to follow than that which he takes.[20]

Mother St. Augustin knew this decision would come as a shock to the ecclesiastical director of the Company of the Indies. But she felt that the resolution taken by the community was justified, for it had been through the care and devotion of Father de Beaubois that the Ursulines had been established in New Orleans. If he were forced to leave the colony, on whom could they rely for spiritual and temporal assistance? His assistance in finding food and supplies during their early bleak months in the colony had been invaluable.[21] The Capuchins were evidently not able to provide for the Ursulines, nor did they seem to wish to do so.

M. de la Chaise had moreover dropped his mask of benevolence and revealed his true feelings toward the religious.[22] Having stated her case, Mother St. Augustin apprised the Abbé of their good fortune in having another place to go. Already the Ursulines had been offered an "advantageous establishment at Cap Français" which awaited their acceptance.[23] She concluded:

> It would be unfortunate, if we should be reduced to this extremity. Nevertheless, we may have to come to that. While awaiting the decision of all this we shall regard ourselves as unsettled.[24]

At the same time the *ordonnateur* was writing to the Abbé and did not refer to the controversy.

> I have for the [Ursuline] Religious the greatest possible attention. They have at present 18 to 20 boarders which ought to procure for them a very comfortable living. I have induced a part of the inhabitants in the best circumstances to place their daughters in their convent. Regarding that which concerns the hospital, these religious can give their care there only when they will be established there.[25]

De la Chaise did mention the return to France of two sisters, noting that although he did not have any information on "their differences",[26] he was sure Father de Beaubois and Mother St. Augustin had given an explanation to the Abbé.

In fact, both Mother St. Augustin and Father de Beaubois had mentioned the return of the sisters in their letter to Abbé Raguet. The Ursuline superior wrote regretfully:

> I have the sorrow of seeing two of Our Sisters return. Back there they had not been sufficiently tried in their vocation and being found little suited for this establishment, we are sending them back to France, each one to her own community.[27]

Father de Beaubois briefly mentioned the return of the two sisters to France, saying "there was absolutely nothing of scandal on their account."[28] Although the Ursuline missionaries must have been very disappointed to see two of their number return so soon after their arrival in New Orleans, the community records are succinct.

> November 25, 1727, Sister Jeanne Marion de St. Michel professed religious of the community of Ploërmel, and Sister Marie Anne Daen de Ste. Marthe, coadjutrix sister of Hennebon [sic], not being at all suited to the country or to the community returned to their communities by order and obedience of Reverend Father de Beaubois, our Superior.[29]

Even though de la Chaise wrote that he knew nothing "of their differences," he was fully cognizant of what had taken place on the long voyage, and in the first weeks after the arrival of the Ursulines in America. Did he find it convenient to simulate ignorance since his own son and daughter were implicated? Besides the Ursulines there were only three other women on the *Gironde,* two women with their husbands and the daughter of the *ordonnateur,* Mlle de la Chaise. She insisted on staying with the religious even though they would have preferred being alone.[30] Father Tartarin had been instrumental in securing passage for Mlle de la Chaise. Father de Beaubois blamed him for this, but at the same time tried to excuse him.

> The Rev. Father Tartarin did not realize at all the consequences of the passage of Mlle de la Chaise whose dangerous spirit has nearly destroyed our new community of religious. He himself has been punished[31] much for it, and he would never have considered obliging Mlle de la Chaise under such circumstances.[32]

Mlle de la Chaise had exerted all her ingenuity to bring about a division in the little community and to cause it to rebel against Mother St. Augustin and Father de Beaubois. Her brother had meddled in the affairs of the community and even had the crass effrontery to attempt to carry on an intrigue with one of the sisters. His machinations were foiled and his offensive advances repulsed.[33] The senior de la Chaise was informed of this, but "far from doing justice, he only laughed at it. It was from that time on that he gave us unequivocal proof of his ill-will."[34] Governor Périer testified that "the father did all he could on his part to place them [the Ursulines] in the dire necessity of leaving."[35] This interference, together with the difficult voyage of five months, the hardships of the new foundation, and the inability to adapt to the climate of the new country, had chilled the enthusiasm of the two sisters. De la Chaise knew that one of the most weighty factors was the trouble caused by his own son and daughter.

Governor Périer defended and protected the Ursulines, and added his word of disapproval of the treatment meted out to the nuns.

The Reverend Father Raphaël is still very cold toward Father de Beaubois who has done everything that he ought

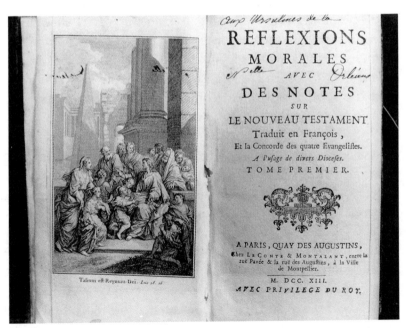

Reflexions is a book which belongs to Sr. St. Angélique Le Boullenger who came to New Orleans in 1727 and died in 1766. Courtesy Ursuline Archives & Museum. Photo by Sr. Jacqueline Toppino, O.S.U.

to have done in order to be on good terms with the Superior of the Capuchins. I doubt that they will ever become good friends. What pains me most in this misunderstanding is that the Ursuline Nuns suffer from it. As they are directed by Father de Beaubois, M. de la Chaise, who does not like him, deflects upon them the trouble that he would like to make that priest experience. Father de Beaubois, on his part, does not think that he has great cause to be pleased with M. de la Chaise.[36]

A short time later Périer wrote:

> I have found them [the Ursulines] very reasonable. They have painted them for us in false colors. They have tried to sow the spirit of division in this community as soon as they arrived. They have done them all the harm that they could because they had a grudge against Father de Beaubois. The only thing lacking was that I should crush them and cause the establishment to fail. By joining myself to their enemies I would have been the most gallant man of the Journal de la Louisiane.[37] I did not desire that title as I wished to maintain that of an honorable man.[38]

Governor Périer's letter, dated August 14, 1728, was scarcely written when the *Beleine* arrived in New Orleans with a pack of letters from Abbé Raguet. In a letter dated April 3, 1728, he took up the question of the Father Superior of the Ursulines. This letter no doubt came as a surprise to Mother St. Augustin. It showed a complete *volte-face*[39] from the attitude exhibited when Bishop de Mornay was so reluctant to give his consent to the Ursulines to leave France, and even more averse to allowing Father de Beaubois to be their superior.

Mother St. Augustin's reply demonstrated that the Abbé was dealing with a woman of conviction. She took up Raguet's letter point by point. He had said that according to the order of the Company and of the Church that a Capuchin should be the Father Superior of the Ursulines.[40] On that score, Mother St. Augustin replied:

I confess, Sir, that I do not understand at all these expressions: according to the order of the Church and of the Company, you are not free to withdraw yourself from his jurisdiction.

1. I have never understood that it was the intention of the Company that we should depend on its orders for our conduct; that it believed itself the mistress to subject us to whomever would seem good to it. I am even persuaded, Sir, that such a thought could never have entered into your mind. You are too intelligent, and I would have had to be a mad-woman to accept such a condition.

2. It matters little to us whether or not Father Raphaël is vicar-general. That does not give him any more right over us. We are entirely free to choose such superior as seems good to us provided he be approved by the bishop. That is what is called for us the order of the Church. We shall not renounce our right and no one will force us to receive a superior against our will. We are all very determined on that point.[41]

Mother St. Augustin reminded the Abbé that they were ready to leave the colony and to go to Cap Français rather than yield this right. They would be able to do as much good there as in Louisiana. Furthermore,

We have not sufficiently great obligations to the Company to abandon ourselves to its designs. The little care that it has to send us the remainder of what belongs to us, and which has remained at Lorient during the 18 months since we have left, and the refusal that they made just recently at the Cap to forward to us some gifts that they wished to send us and opposition to Father de Beaubois show us clearly what we can expect in the future. Far from M. de la Chaise protecting us, as you said, Sir, he has refused us several very necessary things under pretext that he did not have them at the store-house. A few hours later, he found very much more than we had requested, for his friends. You are too intelligent, Sir, to expect, after that, that we should count on the favor of M. de la Chaise. It is not for honest men, and I do not aspire to it. I speak, as you see, Sir, very frankly.[42]

Returning to the question of the supposed union between Périer and de la Chaise, Mother St. Augustin suggested an explanation for Raguet's statement that probably startled him. She suggested that perhaps letters to him had been "purloined", for he obviously did not have a true picture of events in Louisiana. Governor Périer and Father De Beaubois would always have her support as they were "judicious and upright characters and do not know how to resort to trickery and lying."[43] Then, as if to clinch all that she had said before, the Ursuline superior concluded:

> What protection would there be if they withdrew from us that one who has enabled us to live since we are here and in whom alone we place all our confidence. It would be vain for them to wish to enslave us. We have not given up the liberty of conscience we enjoyed in France to come to place ourselves in slavery. All the endeavors that they make for that will be useless.[44]

Mother St. Augustin's frank reply to Abbé Raguet, indicating her determination to preserve the rights of the religious, was unprecedented. Jean Delanglez in *The French Jesuits in Lower Louisiana* commented on her letters:

> ...the energetic letters of Mother St. Augustin Tranchepain...shocked the Abbé enormously. He had not been accustomed to be given plain truths in letters coming from Louisiana; nothing but praise of the magnanimity, wisdom, disinterestedness of the Company of the Indies in general and of Raguet in particular was acceptable or should be sent. [45]

Rather than agree with interpretations issued from someone who had no first hand knowledge of the situation, Mother St. Augustin's reply set the record straight. The Company had not only failed to keep its agreement with the Ursulines, but had also treated them abominably.

The *Beleine* also brought a letter recalling Father de Beaubois to France. His Provincial had been displeased with fallacious reports he had received from Abbé Raguet regarding the priest's private life.[46] The Provincial's decision, however, was made with extreme haste.[47] Abbé Raguet, in his letter informing the Jesuit that he was to leave Louisiana, recommended that he say that he was departing of his own accord. Aside from the ethical character of this recommendation, it would fail to convince anyone, as those on the ship already knew of the recall. The Capuchins on the *Beleine* had apprised the crew and passengers of the letter's message. And on the very day the ship arrived (August 16, 1728), M. de la Chaise gave a dinner in his home during which he remarked, "So, Father de Beaubois is being removed from here."[48] The priest had certainly not decided to leave of his own accord.

But Father de Beaubois remained in the colony until April, 1729.[49] Needless to say, during the intervening months the return order added to the friction. Father Raphaël, probably to counteract the bad impression that the Capuchins had created by broadcasting the news of the recall, threw the blame for the disturbance on the Ursulines. He said they could have been more reserved in showing their discontent about Father de Beaubois' recall.[50]

Father de Beaubois did not personally regret returning to France,[51] for he had written to Raguet several months before saying he was seriously considering a return. He had asked Father d'Avaugour to take the necessary steps with his provincial and with Abbé Raguet to send a successor.[52] He explained that neither cowardice nor fickleness had brought him to this decision. He felt that the animosity Father Raphael and de la Chaise had for him extended to the Ursulines and other missionaries associated with him.[53] He was particularly concerned about how the Ursulines would be treated once he departed.

> As for the Ursuline Religious...he [Father Raphaël] told me himself that he did not wish to have anything to do with them, and Monsieur Périer that they did not concern him. If he speaks otherwise, he deceives.... It has always seemed to me that it was the intention of the Company

that I should have care of them. Nothing was more natural in every way. Their [the Capuchins] triumph is complete, and they will make the most of it. I am waiting until they make some advances to hand over to them the care of the Religious. I am not accountable for the consequences this affair will have.[54]

When the Ursulines said they would go to St. Dominque if their superior was recalled, they were making no idle threat. Governor Périer[55] and Father de Beaubois[56] had both made it quite clear to Abbé Raguet that if the Jesuit left the Ursulines would also leave. When the superior's recall and the letter stipulating that the Ursulines would be under the direction of the Capuchins arrived simultaneously, the Ursulines comprehended fully what they could expect from the Company. It seemed better to them to go where they could do more good without being thwarted and where they could have liberty of conscience.[57] After thoughtful deliberation the Ursulines appealed to the minister of the colonies for permission to depart from Louisiana.[58] Let others save the livres, sous, and deniers for the Company of the Indies. The Ursulines had more important work to do. Count de Maurepas, the minister of the colonies, feeling that this was a drastic step which could prove harmful to the colony, asked Abbé Raguet for an explanation.[59] Raguet responded with a dispatch replete with errors and half truths.

Their house near the hospital not being ready to receive them, they were given a private house, where they started teaching the young girls with such success that great satisfaction resulted in the colony. But some dissensions, mainly due to the fact that they were from different provinces forced the Superioress to send three back to France. The three others who remain are not yet very quiet on account of their devotedness to Father de Beaubois, and the amazing aversion they seem to have for the Capuchins. Father de Beaubois has been begged to do his best to rid them of these prejudices, as well as of their exaggerated gratitude toward him. A letter is being sent telling them that if the aversion they have toward being directed by the Capuchins and their attachment to the Jesuits are the real reasons of their concern, they may calm themselves, because they will always be free to elect as their superior and director, the successor of Father de Beaubois, and that to this Jesuit, strictly faithful to his contract, Father Raphaël and his successors will gladly give the necessary jurisdiction to exercise his functions.[60]

In the letter the Abbé failed to mention that, after an interval of more than a year, construction of a convent near the hospital had not begun. Nor did he note that in order to instruct the girls the nuns had to erect an area for the classes and pay workmen's wages out of their resources. That an abbé residing in France would comment on "dissensions" among the sisters seems somewhat ludicrous. His only communication with them was through letters, which contained no references to "dissensions". Nor was there any difficulty with being from different provinces. The Ursulines of France were divided into various congregations[61], differentiated by their constitutions and without any reference to territorial distribution. Of the nine professed missionaries, eight were of the Congregation of Paris and one of the Bordeaux Congregation. Sister St. Michel Marion and Sister Ste. Marthe Dain, who returned to France, both belonged to the Congregation of Paris,[62] and there had been no disagreement about their return. The third member to return, Sister Anne de St. François had originally come as a postulant. According to the custom of the community, at regular intervals during the novitiate each novice was proposed to the community for retention or dismissal. Apparently Sister Anne de St. François was found unsuited to the religious life, for after seven and a half months as a novice, she was unanimously rejected and sent back to France.[63]

Abbé Raguet spoke of "the three others who remain". Where did that number come from? In deriving the number he must have simply deducted three from the six for whom the Company had agreed to pay. Yet, Mother St. Augustin had given him in her letter of December 24, 1726, the names of the Sisters who were going to Louisiana, nine professed sisters and three postulants.[64] Father de Beaubois had written November 17, 1727:[65] "There remain with us seven professed and three novices,[66] all very content and very well disposed."[67] Sister St. François Xavier Mahieu died July 6, 1728,[68] but probably the Abbé had not yet received word of her death. In short, there were six professed religious and two novices at the time Raguet was writing, November 18, 1728.[69]

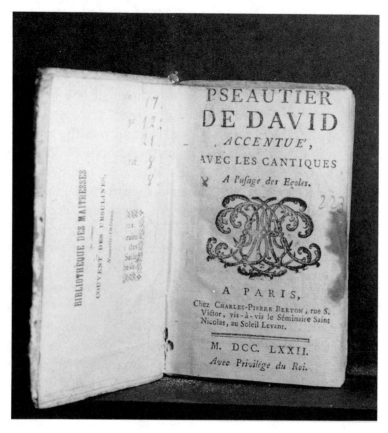

Pseutier De David was brought from France by the first Ursulines. Courtesy Ursuline Archives & Museum. Photo by Sr. Jacqueline Toppino, O.S.U.

Loyalty and gratefulness alone did not motivate the Ursulines' insistence on retaining Father de Beaubois as their director and superior. He had given them spiritual direction and had decisive influence on the spirit and strength of the New Orleans community. The Ursulines had turned to the Jesuits for leadership and spirituality in a superior and had definitely found those qualities in Father de Beaubois. Mother St. Augustin had spoken very frankly with the Abbé about the Capuchins when she had an interview with him in Paris. He knew her attitude and the reason for it. Her "amazing aversion" (*aversion étonnante*) was no surprise to him. In addition during the voyage to Louisiana the maid of Mme Périer had taunted the Capuchin Father Theodore. Seeking revenge against the young woman, he accused de Beaubois of taking liberties with the maid. Father Theodore and his friends talked and joked about it and "...from the joking the foulest calumnies[70] followed, a calumny which also involved the Ursulines, who are virtue personified. Since the Sisters know the character of these Capuchins,[71] are they wrong in not wanting them to be their superiors?"[72]

In his final sentence, Raguet again did an about face. Now the Ursulines are "free to elect as their superior and director the successor of Father de Beaubois. . . Father Raphaël and his successors will gladly give the necessary jurisdiction." In Raguet's letter to the Ursulines he had indicated that the Capuchins should govern them "according to the order of the Company and the Church." Jean Delanglez S.J., in commenting on this complete change of position, says that "it was easier to lecture and upbraid the sisters than to browbeat the Minister of the Colonies."[73] This is precisely what Raguet did in the letter which he told the Count de Maurepas he was writing to the Ursulines. The Abbé censured Mother St. Augustin severely and, Camille de Rochemonteix said, wrote to her "as if he were her Bishop."[74]

> I have read all the letters with which you have honored me and there is not one of them which has not pained me very much.... What makes me fear, Madame, is that I see in all your letters only purely human motives, such as persons the least perfect would have; attachment to a man who, you say, is indispensable to you; aversion for another who sometimes is lacking in kindness; dislike, very blamable in the Christian, for others whose state the Church honors; deliberate contempt with regard to the Company; fickle desire for a new situation. I see in your letters only these motives for your intended transfer. They would not be able to justify your departure; they expressed by the word of God in St. Luke, IX, 62.[75]... Father de Beaubois, having received jurisdiction from Father Raphaël, became by your election and the consent of the vicar-

general of the Bishop, I say, your superior, your director, and in case of the death or change of this Father another Jesuit would succeed to his office.[76] Your astonishing fears with regard to the Capuchins should cease. The Bishop and the Company maintain their authority there; you should be content and all should be in peace. And it would still be so after the removal of Father de Beaubois without your impetuosity. But constancy is rare and without it all is imprudence, turmoil, ruin in establishments, especially in religion.

Abbé Raguet concluded his letter on a note of self-pity and self-righteousness.

> With confusion, I regard my words as wasted. They will be as far as you are concerned. But I have confidence that the Lord, who knows my intentions, will be thankful to me for them.[77]

It is evident that Abbé Raguet twisted and distorted the facts so as to place Mother St. Augustin in the worst possible light. She was no longer the "judicious" and "capable" superior of a few months before.[78] Her "virtue and spirit" and that of her community, "completely esteemed"[79] a short time before, now seemed to be non-existent. Still, Mother St. Augustin, supported by her community, made a firm and dignified reply. They were deeply pained that Abbé Raguet considered their motives "so worldly" and that he "should be scandalized by them." They had acted "only according to duty and to forestall much evil." If the Abbé wanted further proof, they would furnish it, "to the shame and confusion of those concerned."[80]

When Raguet saw that he could not break the determination of Mother St. Augustin with his domineering letters, he directed his shafts toward Father de Beaubois.

> Truly, I shall blame you and you alone, if these good religious cowardly abandon the field of battle.[81] Do not speak to them any more of the would-be rich[82] establishment at the Cap. Tell them on the contrary that

in the Christian Religion all beginnings are strewn with crosses, and how unfortunate that one is who does not carry his.[83]

The ecclesiastical director next leveled his barbs at Father Raphaël. He told him pointedly that however much the Company might esteem him, it was not to him personally that the Company had "sacrificed Father de Beaubois." He also reprimanded the Capuchin superior for having expressed a wish to leave Louisiana.[84] Raguet acknowledged that he was aware of the ill-will that de la Chaise had exhibited toward the Ursulines. He wrote to Father Raphaël:

> I shall not speak to you at length of M. de la Chaise, as I would if I could express my feelings; but I assure you that there will remain scarcely any regard for him if he does not encourage in a marked and evident manner the Jesuit missionaries and their new superior, and if it happens that he has contributed by evil treatment and pretended misunderstanding to the desertion of the Ursuline Religious. That he has been badly disposed at heart and mind in their regard, a single extract from his journal[85] would suffice to prove. Was it necessary in speaking of the waste of the drugs to say that even the Sisters had asked for the panacea? What a twist of words! Did he hope to make us laugh with this wretched jest?... Be persuaded that if the Capuchins treat them badly, I shall be neither silent nor idle.[86]

Abbé Raguet was making every effort to keep the nuns in Louisiana. Undoubtedly, he expected the Company to blame him if they left.

The Abbé had assured Count de Maurepas that if the Ursulines wished a Jesuit superior, they were free to elect him, and Father Raphaël would approve him.[87] Such an election was to take place sooner than Raguet thought, as Bishop St. Vallier of Quebec died December 26, 1727.[88] Bishop de Mornay, his coadjutor with right of succession, automatically became Bishop of Quebec. In accordance with the usual custom, letters renewing their powers were sent to the various vicars-general. Father de Beaubois, however, was deprived of all his faculties, and Father Raphaël became sole vicar-general at New Orleans for the whole colony including the Indian missions.[89] The Capuchin notified Father de Beaubois that he could no longer act as superior of the Ursulines.[90] Father de Beaubois signified his agreement that Father Raphaël would become superior of the Ursulines and indicated that he would do all he could to encourage the sisters to accept the change. The Jesuit ceased saying Mass at the Ursulines' chapel and asked that his sacred vessels be returned to him.[91]

Meanwhile Father Raphaël paid the Ursulines a visit. Changes would be made because of Bishop St. Vallier's death, he informed them, and Father de Beaubois would no longer be their superior. The old arguments were repeated.[92] After Father Raphaël left, Mother St. Augustin sent for Governor Périer to assist her with his counsel. The most prudent procedure seemed to be a new election, and Father Raphaël agreed to this solution. The community of the six professed members was assembled. In the presence of Governor Périer and M. de la Chaise, the election proceeded by secret ballot. In accordance with the Constitutions,[93] Mother St. Augustin proposed four persons: Father Raphaël, Father de Beaubois, Father Souel, a Jesuit who was then in New Orleans, and Abbé Berthelon,[94] a chaplain who had come with Governor Périer.[95] From these two were to be chosen to be presented to the vicar-general for approval. Father Raphaël did not receive any votes, Father de Beaubois received six, Father Souel received five, and Abbé Berthelon one. The act was drawn up and signed by the two officials who took it to Father Raphaël, who confirmed the election of Father de Beaubois, subject to the approval of the bishop[96] on September 25, 1728. The Jesuit did not wish to accept the office again and did so "only at the repeated request of the Capuchin superior himself."[97] After this, affairs moved along much more smoothly, and relationships were more congenial. On the feast of St. Ursula Father de Beaubois invited Father Raphaël to officiate at Mass in the sisters' chapel. Later Mother St. Augustin and her nuns entertained them as dinner guests along with Governor and Mme Périer and M. and Mlle de la Chaise.[98] They continued to cooperate until the departure of Father de Beaubois.[99]

When Bishop de Mornay was notified of the results of the Ursulines' election in September, 1728, he at first refused to approve the selection.

Recueif de Musique a de Chant, music book used by the first Ursulines. Courtesy Ursuline Archives & Museum. Photo by Sr. Jacqueline Toppino, O.S.U.

Recueif de Musique a de Chant, frontispiece, music book used by first Ursulines. Courtesy Ursuline Archives & Museum. Photo by Sr. Jacqueline Toppino, O.S.U.

But in April, 1729, he sent new orders with instructions for Father Raphaël.[100] Father Raphaël told Mother St. Augustin that he would be only too glad to grant the community as confessor a priest in whom they had confidence. He was willing to grant them any director they might desire. He would allow this director freedom in the exercise of his functions, provided he be informed of the most important events in the house, since he must report to the bishop.[101] What subsequent action Bishop de Mornay took is not known. But the Jesuits remained the superiors and confessors of the Ursulines of New Orleans[102] until their expulsion from the colony, except during the period March, 1733[103] to February, 1734,[104] when all the Jesuits in New Orleans and its vicinity were under interdict.[105]

Even before the Jesuits were officially informed of the interdict, Father Raphaël, in compliance with the orders received from Bishop de Mornay, notified the Ursulines that they were to have no relations whatsoever with the Jesuits.[106] Bishop de Mornay had spoken, and the Ursulines had no choice but to obey. The religious submitted as Governor Bienville and Edme Gratien de Salmon, *ordonnateur*,[107] testified in the briefest of statements: "The [Ursuline] Religious have obeyed."[108]

Some historians, using transcripts prepared by Pierre Margry, have depicted the Ursulines as unwilling to submit to the orders of their bishop,[109] but this is an unfair assessment of these women who had given up so much to come to Louisiana. Bienville and Salmon wrote clearly: "...these Sisters, although ready to submit to the orders of the Bishop, say they have essential and specific reasons for not wishing the Capuchins to have entrance to their convent."[110] They were careful to add that these "reasons do not concern Father Raphaël who is respected because of his morals and his learning, but rather Father Hyacinthe whose conduct is so irregular that he is the shame even of the most dissolute."[111]

Father Raphaël had at last attained one of his goals—becoming confessor and director of the Ursulines. A septuagenarian, infirm,[112] and of an age to rest rather than work, he nevertheless had to supervise the religious functions of the parish, the hospital, and the Ursuline community.[113] For nearly a year he continued in this capacity, but in February, 1734, just a few days before his death Father Raphaël gave back "the powers to the Jesuits", and the Ursulines again came under the direction of the Jesuits.[114] Mother St. Augustin did not live to see the ending of the controversy which had almost resulted in the withdrawal of the Ursulines from Louisiana.

Despite the controversy, which was complicated by poor communication between France and Louisiana, daily life for the nuns during this period consisted of spiritual development as well as expansion of their educational efforts with boarders, day pupils, and orphans, whose number increased considerably after the Natchez massacre.

CHAPTER 5

New Responsibilities and a Permanent Convent

⁻On December 2, 1729, citizens of New Orleans awoke to the news that the Natchez Indians, rebelling at Fort Rosalie, had massacred all but a few of the settlers there.[1] The peace that had prevailed in the area for several years between the Natchez and settlers had evaporated when Governor Périer sent a new commandant, Lieutenant D'Echepare, to Fort Rosalie to secure some of the Natchez lands for a plantation. D'Echepare selected an area that included the town of White Apple and demanded that the Indians vacate their land. The Natchez protested, but D'Echepare, who had a reputation as an uncompromising commander, would not negotiate with them. On November 26 the Natchez attacked, using weapons given them by the French for hunting purposes. Estimates are that three hundred settlers were killed and many of the wives and children taken prisoner. Among the victims were two Jesuit priests. Father Paul Du Poisson, a missionary from the Arkansas post, had stopped at the Natchez post in route to New Orleans. Father John Souel, a missionary among the Yazoo Indians was shot by members of the Yazoo tribe returning from a visit to the Natchez tribe.[2]

Although the Seminary priests had opened a mission among the Natchez at the beginning of the eighteenth century, it had survived less than ten years.[3] The missionaries stationed subsequently at the Natchez post served only the French. When Abbé Raguet heard the news of the massacre, he lamented to the minister of the colonies:

> Would to God that a missionary of this Order [Jesuit] had been among these Indians! We would not now be grieving over the loss of our main colonial products, mourning over our compatriots, nor would we have to punish those barbarians at great expense.[4]

Whether or not missionaries among the Natchez could have prevented the killing must always remain a matter of conjecture. But various historians do blame Lieutenant D'Echepare for enraging the Indians through his extremely poor relations with them.

The Natchez spared the lives of most of the young women and children, but took them captive. Governor Périer then sent an expedition of almost seven hundred men to lay siege to White Apple, and after two attempts they liberated the captives. The women and children were brought to New Orleans, where officials faced the problem of providing a home for those who had been orphaned. The officials turned to the Ursulines, asking them to shelter the orphan girls. Mother St. Augustin and her sisters generously accepted this responsibility and welcomed the children into their home and hearts.[4] Father de Beaubois had originally persuaded the Ursulines to accept some homeless children and the number of orphans had gradually increased.[6] The young victims of the massacre greatly augmented their number. Father Le Petit, S.J., then superior of the Louisiana Mission, wrote of these children and the Ursulines who received them:

> The little girls, whom none of the inhabitants wished to adopt, have greatly enlarged the interesting company of orphans whom the Ursulines are bringing up. The great number of these children serves but to augment their charity and attentions. They have formed them into a separate class, of which two teachers have charge.
>
> There is not one of this holy community that would not be delighted to have crossed the ocean, were she to do no other good save that of preserving these children in their innocence, and of giving a polished and Christian education to the young French girls who were in danger of being little better bred than slaves. The hope is held out to these holy religious that ere the end of the year 1730, they will occupy the new house which is destined for them and which they have waited for so long.[7]

The number of children who arrived after the massacre is not known, but in 1731 there were forty-nine orphans at the convent.[8] If the sisters hoped that the sight of their cramped living quarters would spur the officials to finish their building, they were to be deeply disappointed. The Company consented to only pay 150 livres annually for the lodging, food, clothing, and education of each orphan.[9]

Repercussions of the Natchez massacre were long felt throughout the colony. The period following the catastrophe was marked by change in both civil and ecclesiastical circles, as colonists in the outlying districts, fearing attack by roaming bands of Indians, abandoned their plantations and sought refuge in New Orleans or near the forts.[10] A great terror "seized almost everybody, especially the women" even within the limits of New Orleans itself.[11] When the news of the massacre reached France, the Company of the Indies was gravely concerned. It had already expended large sums of money on the colony and instead of the anticipated dividends, losses were high. The massacre had destroyed what was considered the most flourishing post, while Governor Périer persistently urged the Company to send more troops for punitive action. Such a venture, however, would have required a considerable financial outlay, which the Company was unwilling to make. It chose instead to relinquish its monopoly of the trade of the colony and retrocede Louisiana to the French crown.

When the Ursulines learned that the Company intended to return the King's Charter, they must have wondered how it would affect their status. It was the Company that had made the contract with them in 1726 and had brought them to Louisiana, and the retrocession practically nullified the contract.[12] The Company had promised to build a convent for them, but at the date of the formal retrocession, July 1, 1731, the sisters had been in New Orleans almost four years, and their convent was still far from habitable. Would the convent be completed? Would the Ursulines still be expected to take charge of the hospital? Answers to these two major questions would take some months.

There was now a change in political leadership, as Jacques de la Chaise died February 6, 1730, and was buried the following day by Father Raphaël in the "parochial church" of New Orleans.[13] The second councillor, M. Bruslé, took charge of affairs for a short time, followed by another *ordonnateur*, M. McMahon. He was succeeded by Edme Gratien de Salmon, who reached New Orleans on October 4, 1731,[14]to begin a long period of energetic and unselfish service as *ordonnateur*.[15]

At the time of Salmon's arrival the Ursulines did not know how the retrocession would affect them. Through Father d'Avaugour they had presented to the French court accounts of their establishment, of the former assistance from the Company, and of the work they had accomplished. They asked for the protection of the crown, for the confirmation in freehold of the land granted to them in New Orleans, and for a guarantee of the rights and privileges of their institute as they had enjoyed them in France.[16] The nuns also explained that if they were to staff a proposed house of correction, more religious would be needed.[17] They asked the French government for five or six additional sisters and an increase of 1000 livres in their annual allotment. Free passage for sisters traveling to or from France and free shipment on the king's vessels of a ton of freight per year were also requested.[18]

Count de Maurepas, Minister of the Navy and of the Colonies, responded to the nuns' account by requesting a report from Governor Périer and M. Salmon on the work of the sisters.[19] He noted that His Majesty wished to discontinue the allowance for the orphans "since that might be subject to abuse". Nor did an increase in salary for the Ursulines seem necessary, as no house of correction was planned. The King wished to reduce all expenditures. The royal treasury would pay the Ursulines in silver rather than the bills of exchange used by the Company, which should be advantageous to them. With those stipulations he would await the opinion of the governor and *ordonnateur* before giving a final decision.[20]

In the meantime on March 16, 1732, reinforcements for the New Orleans community arrived from France. [21] It is quite probable that Father de Beaubois recruited the sisters, as they arrived on the ship which carried him back to Louisiana.[22] The new recruits were Sister St. Pierre (Françoise Marguerite Bernard de St. Martin) and Sister St. André (Jeanne Melotte), professed religious of the Community of Caen,[23] and Sister St. François Xavier[24] (Charlotte Herbert), professed of Bayeux.[25] The Bishop of Bayeux in granting the three sisters permission to go to Louisiana praised their enthusiasm for missionary work and noted the great need for additional religious in the colony. He directed them to "retire" to the convent in New Orleans and practice their Rules and Constitutions as they would have in their French convents of Bayeux and Caen.[26]

The Governor and the *ordonnateur* reported that the conduct of these three religious "very regular" and that of the six already in the colony "very exemplary".[27] They also were expecting three more to arrive on the next vessel.[28] If the community increased to twelve, Périer and Salmon recommended that the payment made to each of the twelve sisters should be reduced to 500 livres a year "because they take some boarders whose payments will give some help." At that time the nuns had four or five boarders who paid 300 livres each.[29] The officials reported that they did not believe that discontinuing the pension for the orphans was justified and requested a fund for them in the future.

> It is work of charity and eventually they will become
> good mothers of families; whereas, if they should abandon
> them to their evil fate they would be so many libertines
> and in that case it would be necessary to establish a house
> of correction of which there is no need now.[30]

In the same report M. de Salmon sent a statement of the amount needed to complete the convent. He estimated that it would cost 39,168 livres 16 sols.[31] He reported that he had already let some contracts for roofing, as the timbers already set up would rot if it was not done soon. In the meantime, completion of the building was urgent. The religious, their boarders, and the orphans were living in two wretched houses "so closely lodged that they could scarcely turn around."[32] To delay finishing the convent would only increase the expense of the King, as the rent for the Kolly house was 1200 livres. The King would be obliged to continue this until the convent was ready for occupancy.[33]

In December, 1731, Salmon had written that once the Ursulines were in their new convent they would "have sufficient [space] for their parlor, dining room, kitchen and store-room with half the ground floor." They could break down some partitions in the other half of the ground floor to make wards for the sick. In addition to half of the first floor the religious would have "the entire second and third stories to make their sleeping quarters, those of the boarders, and of the thirty orphans."[34] When the sisters heard that such a proposal had been made, they were quite distressed. Even if the building was large enough, which it was not, the proposed arrangement would not be suitable. They enlisted the support of Father de Beaubois, and he succeeded in making Salmon see the anomaly of such a division of the first floor of the convent.[35] The *ordonnateur* was then faced with the difficult task of convincing

Count de Maurepas that the suggested plan was impracticable. He explained that he had been mistaken in thinking that the sisters would have sufficient room if half the lower floor were taken for the sick. They would need more living area as the community increased and as additional parents sent their daughters to the boarding school.[36] As the garrison in New Orleans increased, the number of sick would also be augmented.

Count de Maurepas, no doubt seeing in the proposed plan of division a measure of economy, wanted Salmon to execute it. He argued:

> It is not to be feared that the Ursulines can be crowded by this arrangement. Their number has been fixed at six and His Majesty has ordered for their support a sum of 3600 livres which he does not wish to increase. If they are in greater number, that is their affair, but they will be replaced only as they stand in need and only to the number of six.[37]

Far from the scene and unfamiliar with actual conditions, the minister and the king were dependent on their colonial representatives for information. In this instance Mother St. Augustin may have also written to Count de Maurepas to protest using part of the new convent for hospital wards, for a brief note from Maurepas to her exists in convent records for this period.[38] As a resident of Louisiana, Salmon understood the difficulties that not only the Ursulines but also the rest of the colonists faced. He always tried to make the home government appreciate the harsh living conditions. In this instance he must have succeeded, as no part of the completed convent was appropriated for hospital purposes.

Maurepas approved the contracts which Salmon had let to finish the monastery of the Ursulines as the "works were absolutely indispensable", but he cautioned the *ordonnateur* not to approve contracts in the future unless he had "received orders to that effect."[39] The work progressed at a dilatory pace. Exactly six years to a day after the Ursulines had come to New Orleans, the *ordonnateur* could only say:

> They are working every day to put the house of the [Ursuline] Religious in a condition to lodge them.

Their house would be roofed a long time ago if the tile furnaces had not succeeded badly. The contractor has lost more than half of the tiles. He hopes that it will be entirely covered at the end of this month, August, 1733. They are working now on the interior and on the stair and I hope that they will occupy it, at the latest, at the end of the year. I am very impatient that it may happen so that the sick may be better cared for. They are convinced that these Religious, who are very zealous, will do better than an overseer.[40]

The religious did obtain funds from the crown to support the orphans. The governor and the *ordonnateur* had explained to the king the probable fate of these girls if they were not housed with the nuns. The king consented to pay for the maintenance of thirty girls, giving 150 livres annually for each one. He was willing to incur this expense "as in giving to these orphans the means of becoming good mothers of families we will prevent the disorders into which their miseries would drag them."[41] But the governor and the *ordonnateur* "will take care not to leave them at the convent too long without getting them married off. They will be vigilant in providing education for the orphans, and they will make certain that the expense is advantageous to the orphans and the colony in general."[42]

After the Natchez massacre there had been more than thirty orphans at the convent, and the Company of the Indies paid for all of them. For the first half of 1731, the Company provided for forty-nine. A statement was presented to the king for an equal number with this explanation:

The [Ursuline] Religious have presented to us that in 1731 they had 49 orphans whom they fed and clothed and for whom the Company paid them 150 livres for each, and that they received, beginning with July 1, only 1037 livres 10 sols, whereas 3675 livres were due them.... They petition His Majesty to be kind enough to grant them the balance totaling 2637 livres 10 sols.... We owe them the justice of saying that they are not at all selfish. They have very much work with the orphans whom they educate well. They would not be able to do the work if they were only six as fixed by their salary. There are now nine of them. They live on almost nothing.[43]

In spite of this petition on behalf of the sisters, the king was adamant. He would pay for thirty and no more.

His Majesty is willing for you to continue to have paid to the religious the board and room of 30 orphans until a new order.

He forbids you to exceed the number of 30. He orders you even to diminish it, when there will be an opportunity to do so. According to the list which you sent of the orphans who are there at present, some will soon be old enough to be married.[44] You must be careful to provide for them so that the state will be relieved of this expense.

Concerning the representations that these Religious have made that they have received only 1037 livres 10 sols for the pensions of the orphans whom they have fed and clothed during the last six months of 1731, His Majesty, indeed wished to consider it, but not, however, for the 2637 livres 10 sols which they claim is due them, deducting the 1037 livres 10 sols which they have received, but only for the sum of 1212 livres 10 sols that he has ordered M. Salmon to have paid to them. That is all, indeed, that they can claim, since by all justice there would be due them for the 6 months only 2250 livres making half the sum of 4500 livres destined for this purpose.[45]

The King's word was final. The Ursulines would have to find some other means to pay the debts incurred in caring for the children.

The retrocession presented the nuns with another financial problem. The Company of the Indies had paid the annual rent of 1200 livres for the Kolly house, but no payment was made on the rent after July 31, 1931. Salmon called this to the attention of the minister of the colonies in his letter of March 30, 1732.[46] When no action was taken,

Madame Kolly[47] brought suit against the religious to obtain payment.[48] The sisters were not in a financial position to pay the accumulated rent,[49] nor was it their obligation. Governor Bienville, who had replaced Périer in March, 1733, and Salmon reported the suit against the Ursulines and appealed to the king in the nuns' behalf.[50] The minister of the colonies replied that he would like to have this rent paid for the sisters, but the king refused. Salmon persisted in his plea, reminding Maurepas that the Company agreed to provide a lodging for the religious until their convent was constructed. He pointed out their precarious living conditions.

> They are far from able to pay this rent which is now three years in arrears. They hope that in consideration of the two bad years through which they have just passed and during which they were obliged to buy grain and provisions at such high prices that the allowance of 150 livres for each orphan was not nearly sufficient to feed and clothe these children, that your lordship will have compassion and be willing to grant them a gratuity of 1800 livres. That is about half what is due Madame Kolly with whom they will settle for the balance.[51]

In August of 1734 Salmon dropped his suppliant tone, and pointed out plain facts to the minister of the colonies and indirectly to the king. After he had reviewed the facts as previously reported Salmon noted that Madame Kolly's attorney claimed that the religious owed 4500 livres for three years' rent on a house that was leased by the Company of the Indies not the religious. The Company, having paid rent through July 1, 1731, held that the rent was now the crown's responsibility. Salmon continued that along with the rights to the colony the king was also responsible for its debts. He did suggest a compromise of reducing the debt to half which would amount to 2250 livres. He concluded: "These Religious are so much the less able to pay this rent as they have just borrowed nearly 3000 livres to pay for household goods...for themselves and for the 30 orphans."[52]

By reducing the rent of the provisional convent to half, or 750 livres annually for the preceding three years, no injustice was done to

Madame Kolly. The 1500 livres annual rent was exorbitant as was shown when the entire property, "lots of ground, together with a house, kitchen, and other buildings thereon," was sold a year later for 1200 livres, 300 livres less than the annual rent.[53] The king at last yielded and granted the Ursulines a "gratuity of 1800 livres to pay the rent which they owe for the house which they have occupied up to the present."[54] It should be noted that although the king made the grant, he did it as a favor; Salmon had rather adroitly shown that it was a matter of justice.

As the king firmly refused to pay the salaries of more than six sisters regardless of the number in residence, or to provide for more than thirty orphans, the community was forced to find some means of reducing their living expenses. They decided to purchase another plantation and hoped to raise on it part of the provisions needed for the community, boarders and orphans. And so they purchased in January of 1733 a piece of land of ten *arpents* front on the river by the ordinary depth from Michel Vien and his wife Marie Françoise Le Verd.[55] (An *arpent* was equal to about 192 feet.) This property, located "on the other side of the Mississippi," was opposite Pointe St. Antoine.[56] The purchase price of 1000 livres was payable in three installments during the course of the year 1733. Father de Beaubois bought this property in his name for the Ursulines "as I have been obliged to do on account of the circumstances of the time and the complicated situation in which they find themselves and thus the Jesuits can not and ought not to have any claim on this land."[57] Although Father de Beaubois was under interdict for ecclesiastical reasons, he still showed himself a loyal friend and devoted assistant to the Ursulines.

Financial and ecclesiastical difficulties, the hardships of colonial life, and the vast amount of work exacted a heavy toll on the fragile health of Mother St. Augustin. She had become quite ill on the long voyage and did not ever completely regain her health in Louisiana. Sister St. Stanislaus wrote on April 24, 1728: "Our dear Mother Superior is always ill."[58] But one of the greatest trials for Mother St. Augustine was the deaths of three of the original missionaries. Sister St. François Xavier Mahieu, who had the heart of a true missionary, was the first member of the community to die. She originally asked to teach the Indians and Negresses, but as someone was already assigned to this work, she was given charge of instructing the day pupils. She was enthusiastic about her work, but was not destined to labor long. She died in less than a year on July 6, 1728.[59]

Three years later Sister St. Jean l'Evangéliste Judde, the Assistant Superior died. Her work was to instruct the Indians and slaves, "of which she acquitted herself with a truly apostolic zeal," until her last illness in July, 1731. Her superior recorded that "she possessed all the virtues that one could desire in a good and perfect religious." She gave the signal for rising each morning and was always the first to arrive at community exercises. She was always quick to share her own rations, for the poverty among the community was at times acute.[60] Shortly before her death she declared that she had never deliberately caused pain to any one.[61] Mother St. Jean l'Evangéliste's final illness lasted six weeks, during which she suffered from violent pains in her head and became totally blind. She died on the eve of the feast of the Assumption of Our Lady, August 14, 1731.[62]

Sister Ste. Thérèse Salaun, the youngest of the professed sisters who came in 1727, was the next to meet death. She had filled various duties in the house, and in spite of her delicate health her mother superior "always found her ready for anything." Sister Ste. Thérèse was ill for several months. Although the physicians tried one remedy after another, they seemed only to aggravate her illness. In her last hours she was assisted by Father Vitry S.J., who gave her the last sacraments. This is especially noteworthy as the Jesuits were under interdict at the time. Father Raphaël temporarily lifted the ban for the consolation of the dying sister. So peaceful was her death on September 5, 1733, that no one could tell just when she breathed her last. "Almost all the city assisted at her burial," wrote Mother St. Augustin. "It will be easy to appreciate the greatness of our loss, especially for the community just commencing and so small in number, since we are thereby reduced to eight, of whom several are in ill health."[63]

Two months later Mother St. Augustin went to join her spiritual daughters who had preceded her in death. She endured the trials and difficulties with an equanimity that was a source of admiration to those who knew her. Although endowed with rare talents and a keen intellect, she always sought advice from competent persons before making an important decision. On the feast of St. Ursula, October 21, 1733, she became very ill. Although she suffered from a high temperature all night, she was up the next day. But her condition became more critical, and she was confined to bed where she suffered for more than two weeks.

> The eighteenth day of her illness...she asked to receive the Sacrament of Extreme Unction which was administered by Reverend Father de Beaubois whom Reverend Father Raphaël...had permitted to assist her although he was under interdict... This interdict was not one of the least crosses of our holy Mother. She received the Last Sacraments with lively faith and a little while afterwards gave back her beautiful soul to God.[64]

The religious mourned the loss of Mother St. Augustin, not only as a cherished superior and loved mother, but also as a valiant woman who had courageously fended for them during six trying years. In his book, *The French Jesuits in Lower Louisiana*, Jean Delanglez S.J. sketched this Ursuline Superior against the background of contemporary troubles in Louisiana.

> This great woman was endowed with both physical and moral courage. Her straight-forward talk stands in sharp contrast with the fulsome, vulgar praise of the Company of the Indies so prominent in the correspondence of these years. When the rights of her Order were being threatened, she told Raguet a few plain truths that swept the Abbé off his feet. He had not been used to people so outspoken as Mother Tranchepain, and he quickly realized that it was a waste of time trying to browbeat her when the privileges of her Order were at stake. In the difficulties of Father de Beaubois with officials in Louisiana and in France, she did not hesitate one moment to take the defense of the Jesuit, who she thought was unjustly treated, although by doing so she was placing herself in danger of being subjected to the same vexations.[65]

Roger Baudier wrote in his work, *The Catholic Church in Louisiana*:

It was due to her valiant spirit, her indomitable courage and her sterling virtues, besides her unusual abilities as superior, that the Ursuline foundation at New Orleans, the first convent in the United States, was made possible and was maintained in the colony, despite the most vexing, trying and exasperating conditions that prevailed during the first decade.[66]

Six days after the death of Mother St. Augustin the community assembled to elect a new superior, according to the ceremonial of the Rule of Paris. Two Capuchins, Father Raphaël and Father Philippe presided. Mother St. André Melotte, who had come to Louisiana the previous year, was chosen superior. Mother Ste. Marie Yuiquel was made assistant superior, and Mother St. Pierre Bernard, who had accompanied Mother St. André to New Orleans, was chosen as treasurer.[67] Mother St. André would lead the Ursulines to the long-awaited convent eight months after Mother St. Augustin's death.

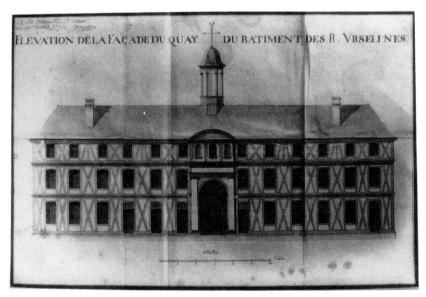

Ignace François Broutin's plan for first convent 1733. Courtesy Ursuline Archives & Museum.

The Ursuline Convent, seven years in the making, was finished and ready for occupancy in July, 1734. A solemn ceremony was planned to celebrate the change of residence on Saturday, July 17. A member of the community left this engaging description of the events surrounding the transfer from the Kolly House:[68]

> During the three days previous to the transfer to the new convent the weather seemed very unfavorable to this ceremony. Because of the continual rain which made the streets (*chemins*) impassable, we were uncertain until two o'clock in the afternoon what to do. Then the sky cleared and we carried out the plans in spite of the mud so discouraging especially ...for a group of some twenty young girls dressed as Angels. One young girl representing St. Ursula was clothed in a robe of cloth of silver with a long train of the same material. Her hair was dressed with bands of pearls and diamonds and a small veil ...the whole forming a superb crown. She held in her hand a heart pierced with an arrow. All was wrought with marvelous skill. Eleven young girls dressed in white and holding palms in their hands represented the eleven thousand virgins and accompanied St. Ursula. The little girls were angels.
>
> At five o'clock in the evening we rang our two bells as a signal. Immediately, according to the order of M. de Bienville, the Governor of Louisiana, the troops, both Swiss and French, began to march and drew up in order on both sides of our former house. The Reverend Jesuit and Capuchin Fathers five in number (three Jesuits and two Capuchins) namely, Reverend Fathers de Beaubois and Le Petit and Brother Parisel,[69] Reverend Father Philippe and Pierre, accompanied by quite a number of choir boys and chanters took their places in our chapel. Mm. Bienville, Governor, and Salmon, *Intendent,* honored us with their presence as did almost all the people of both the upper and the lower classes of the city.
>
> The Reverend Father Philippe, Capuchin Curé of the parish, incensed the Blessed Sacrament. They sang

some verses of the *Pange Lingua*, and Benediction having been given the procession began to march. We went out in order wearing our choir mantles, with veils lowered and each carrying a lighted candle of white wax. The Mothers Superior and Assistant were near the Blessed Sacrament which was carried under a rich canopy. The small community was composed of nine religious.... The troops, drawn up on both sides of the street, marched in perfect order, single file, leaving between them and us a distance of about four feet. The drums and fifes accompanied the songs and made agreeable harmony. The citizens led the procession. Our day pupils followed. Our thirty orphans, each with a candle in her hand, formed a third group. Then came the ladies of the congregation[70] each with a lighted candle. There were about forty of these ladies. The community and the clergy terminated the procession. The order was well kept in spite of the mud and the singing of the children. No one got out of order as the Jesuit Brother Parisel, wearing a surplice performed the office of master of ceremonies.

The procession entered the parish church where they had a reserved place for us in the sanctuary. The most Blessed Sacrament was placed on the altar and incensed. Then two soldiers wearing surplices and capes sang to music a motet to Ursula. This was followed by a beautiful sermon delivered by Reverend Father Le Petit of the Company of Jesus in which he showed that our establishment in this country was to the glory of God and the good of the colony. He praised our Institute very much on education of youth.

As we left the church it was noticed that the troops were lined up, kneeling, holding the muzzles of their guns against the ground and bowing to adore the Most Blessed Sacrament. This ceremony was very respectful and devout. I thought, however, there was reason to fear that their interior sentiments were not in conformity with it....

Some persons had charged themselves to sound

the bell of our new house; for these gentlemen had the kindness to give us one. As soon as they saw the procession approach, they rang it and did not cease until we had entered. The ceremony ended by benediction of the Blessed Sacrament, which we received in our inner chapel. From the moment we entered, the cloister was established.

As the next day was Sunday, we sang the Mass. The Blessed Sacrament was exposed and the *Te Deum* was chanted in thanksgiving. This had not been done the day before because it was late in the evening, and everyone was very much fatigued from the intense heat. Benediction of the Blessed Sacrament was given at five o'clock in the evening during which the Religious sang a beautiful motet with music, which was appreciated by all the persons who assisted at the ceremony.[71]

The Ursulines were delighted to be in their new monastery with cloister again established.[72] The convent, however, was too small and many amenities were lacking: there were no classrooms for the day pupils, no bakery, no laundry, nor a place to store provisions. To provide for some of the immediate needs, Father de Beaubois obtained from Governor Bienville and M. de Salmon the two main buildings that had formerly served as hospital wards. One building, which would be used by the day pupils, was moved across the street and attached to the convent. In this structure there was a small room for the portress as well as a parlor. The other building was dismantled, transferred into the enclosure, rebuilt, and rebricked. It would be used as a storehouse and laundry. Of course the sisters had to pay all the expenses, which amounted to more than 2200 livres.[73] This was an added burden as they had just recently borrowed money to purchase beds and other furnishings for the new convent. The furnishings from the Kolly House were in such wretched condition that they were not fit to move into the new building.[74]

The additional buildings addressed the need for more space in the convent, but a much more serious problem soon became evident. The "new" building was already deteriorating and demanded daily repairs. This was, to say the least, disheartening to the community that had waited for their permanent convent for seven years. Written records show

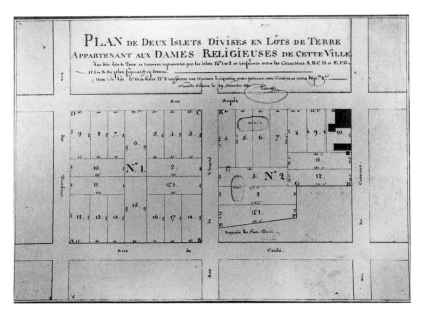

Plan for convent and hospital. Courtesy Ursuline Archives & Museum.

that the nuns suspected that the Company of the Indies had used convent appropriated funds on other projects, as at the time of the retrocession in 1731 only the framework of the building was finished. The Company left records that indicated an enormous sum had already been spent on the house. The crown appropriated 28,000 livres for the convent, but, noting previous expenditures on the convent, used 18,000 of that for the hospital ward, leaving only 10,000 for the completion of the convent which was inadequate. The nuns also soon realized that space for the nuns, boarders and orphans was at a premium. Records describe the rooms of the convent:

> There is on the lower floor only the chapel which is very small, two parlors, a room for the Superior, the dining room for the boarders, the kitchen, a small office, the refectory for the Religious, the recreation room for the Community and the room for the head nurse.[75] On the second floor are the dormitory and fifteen small bed rooms, with two rooms for the infirmary. There is no...sacristy, linen room, roberie, or pharmacy. The boarders and the

orphans occupy all the upper floor.... Our house in truth remained very imperfect and that has occasioned for us some great expenditures.[76]

Even though the new convent was far from satisfactory, it was a great improvement over the Kolly House. An increased number of boarders made it possible to organize their school in conformity with the *Réglements*,[77] the pedagogical scheme of the Ursulines of Paris. This program embraced a boarding school and a day school for girls, with the general management of the two following similar lines. The teaching technique was identical in both schools, and pupils were divided into classes according to age and ability. At the head of the boarding school was a Mistress General who devoted her entire time to supervision.[78] She maintained the balance between teachers and pupils and between teachers and parents. Several times a year the Mistress General visited the classes, examined the pupils, decided upon promotions and distributed awards. Her role would perhaps be put in the category of the 20th century school principal.

Under the Mistress General were two Class Mistresses for each division, responsible for order and discipline. They rotated their assignments every other week, acting on alternate weeks as an assistant to the person in charge that week. They attended to the spiritual education of the boarders and to their growth in Christian virtue. They gave catechism instructions and prepared the girls for reception of the sacraments.[79] The Class Mistresses were responsible for the health care of the girls and were forbidden to punish the pupils for their faults by depriving them of food, exposing them to cold, or exacting any other harsh measures.[80] No one, not even the Mistress General, was to punish a girl over twelve or thirteen without deferring to the Mother Superior.[81] In the spirit of Angela Merici, the teachers were urged to strive "to display a conduct full of sweetness and charity, of prudence, discretion and motherly foresight, full of goodness, and not too urgent or punctilious."[82] Collaborating with the two Class Mistresses were the special teachers for reading, writing, manual training,[83] spelling, and arithmetic. Many of the methods used continue to be employed. For example, framing problems in terms of the pupil's experience stimulated interest in arithmetic.[84] Part of each religion class[85] the nuns devoted to a review of the preceding lesson,

DU REGNE DE LOUIS QUINZE.
ROI DE FRANCE ET DE NAVARRE.
LA Pre PIERRE DE CE MONASTERE A ETE
POSÉE PAR TRES HAUTE ET TRES ILLUSTRE
DAME CATHERINE LE CHIBELIER EPOUSE DE
MESSIRE ETIENNE DE PERIER CHEVALIER
DE L'ORDRE MILITAIRE DE ST LOUIS CAPT.
DE FREGATES DE S.M. TRES CHRETIENNE
COMMANDANT GENERAL DE LA PROVINCE ET
COLONIE DE LA LOUISIANE.
L'AN DE GRACE MDCCXXX.

Cornerstone, Ursuline Convent. Courtesy Ursuline Archives & Museum.
Photo by Sister Jacqueline Toppino, O.S.U.

LES DAMES RELIGIEUSES URSULINES QUI LES
PREMIERES ONT HABITE CE MONASTERE
SONT.
SŒUR M. TRENCHEPAIN DE ST. AUGUSTIN, Supre.
SŒUR MARG. JUDE DE ST. JEAN L'EVANGELISTE.
SŒUR RENEE YVIQUEL DE STE. MARIE..
SŒUR MARIE LE BOULANGER ANGELIQUE.
SŒUR MARGUERITE DE STE. THERESE .
SŒUR CECILE CAVELIER DE ST. JOSEPH.
SŒUR M. MADELEINE HACHARD DE ST. STANISLAS.

PIERRE BARON INGENIEUR DU ROI. I.L. CALOT, CHAMBEL
LAN. GRATON. V.G. LE MAISTRE ET ANDRE DE
BATZ. ARCHITECTES. MDCCXXX.

Conerstone, Ursuline Convent. Courtesy Ursuline Archives & Museum.
Photo by Sister Jacqueline Toppino, O.S.U.

but couched in different terms so the pupils would understand rather than memorize the matter.

The organization of the day school[86] was similar to that of the boarding school with one additional feature. Each class was divided into groups of ten, presided over by a pupil-teacher called the *dixainière*. These pupil-teachers were girls distinguished by their intelligence, moral character, and school spirit. They assisted in hearing the catechism lesson, drilled the pupils, distributed and collected school books, and reported all misdemeanors whether committed at school or en route. The class day was shorter in the day school,[87] and less time was devoted to reading, writing, arithmetic, and sewing, in order to give adequate time for religious instruction. The dominant tones in both schools were order and thoroughness. No lesson was dropped until it was mastered. Promotion depended not upon a period of time spent in a class, but upon diligence and progress. Sister M. Monica concluded after a careful study of the *Règlements*:

> In the *Règlements* are to be found almost all the elements which are considered so valuable in present day teaching-methods; and besides these there is the proper securing of Attention and Interest, the right evaluation of Environment and of Individual Instruction; Memory, Imagination, Emotion, each has its place; and the special devotedness of the teachers to the character and personality of their pupils brings their teaching methods up to the first rank of enlightened systems of education.[88]

The educational methods that the Ursulines brought to New Orleans had been well-tested. They needed to adapt these methods to the particular conditions of the colony, but the fundamental principles were secure. One feature added in the New Orleans community was the education of orphans. The training given to these girls differed in that it was practical and emphasized manual skills, but religious instruction remained a key element in their education. As Father Le Petit S.J. reminded the nuns:

> They will remember that the orphans need to be taught manual labor and housekeeping rather than writing or even reading. They will not neglect in any way to

prepare them to earn their living. They need not, however, refuse to teach them the former things when they show ability to profit from them.[89]

From the writings of Mother St. Augustin and Sister St. Stanislaus we know that the first teachers of the oldest school for girls in the Mississippi Valley had religious fervor, physical courage, mental alertness, executive ability, and a sense of humor. They were women of keen observation and common sense. Their letters describe the food and how to cook it, the trees, the flowers, the mosquitoes, and the customs of the inhabitants, comparing and contrasting with a discernment that any teacher might well emulate. Their training was comprehensive, resourceful, and effective. Preparation for the teaching of Christian doctrine required the most study. This was so linked with the religious life of the teachers that the essence of their best teaching was the product of their individual lives, "action springing from contemplation." Having established their educational program, the Ursulines' transfer to the new monastery made it possible for them not only to expand their educational program but also to begin the principal work for which they had come to Louisiana: caring for the sick in the military hospital.

CHAPTER 6

The Military Hospital

The hospital building adjoining the convent was not yet completed when the Ursulines moved into their new home, but for once the officials hastened the work. M. de Salmon reported on August 12, 1734, that the principal room of the hospital had just been finished with flagstones and that the sick would be moved there as soon as the floor was dry, "at the latest at the end of the month."[1] Moved into the new hospital August 25,[2] the sick were for a short time left under the supervision of the treasurer and the hospital attendant. Sister St. Xavier Hebért, appointed to the office of head nurse, wanted to see how these gentlemen took care of their patients "not in order to do what they did, but better if possible." This arrangement lasted only a few days, as sympathy for the suffering patients encouraged Sister St. Xavier to assume her new responsibilities as soon as possible. She took complete charge on September l, and managed so well that the sick soldiers, who had previously come to the hospital only as a last resort, were now happy to be admitted. They began to seek admission without waiting until their illnesses became critical.[3]

Both before and after the retrocession of the colony to the Crown, Salmon had made every effort to improve conditions in the hospital. The parsimony of the king generally foiled his efforts, however, whenever there was a question of money. The king assigned only 5000 livres for the hospital, while[4] Salmon repeatedly insisted that the sum was inadequate.[5] During the four months from July to October, 1731, food alone had cost over 4869 livres.[6] Salmon further pointed out that the Company of the Indies had expended 15000 livres annually for this purpose.[7]

In March of 1732 the *ordonnateur* suggested to Maurepas that a contract be made with the Ursulines when they took charge of the hospital. He pointed out that the hospital desperately needed repairs,[8] as well as additional beds—only 29 existed, but there was a need for at least 40. The five thousand livres allotted by the king for drugs, food, linen and medicaments was clearly insufficient. Salmon proposed that the king offer to pay the Ursulines 200 livres per bed, which would amount to 8000 livres for 40 beds as well as the ration for each soldier's stay in the hospital. In return the sisters would agree to accept the poor of the colony at the rate of 200 livres per bed but without ration. All furnishings would be initially provided, but the sisters would be responsible for replacements. He concluded by saying, "I have conferred with Father de Beaubois about it and he has assured me that the Religious will do in that regard whatever your highness desires."[9]

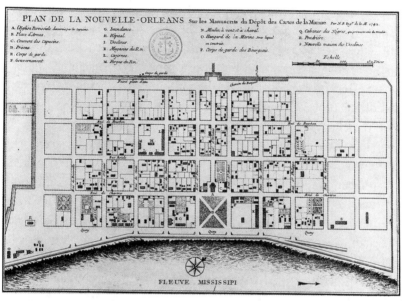

1742 Map of New Orleans. Courtesy Historic New Orleans Collection, 1974.25.18.99.

When the statement of expenses was forwarded in August of the same year, the officials in Louisiana again urged that a contract be made with the Ursulines. They argued that the government would save a great deal. The sisters would not derive any profit from it, if they gave the sisters only 8000 livres as Salmon had proposed. But the hospital would have to be furnished with beds, linen, and the necessary equipment.[10] Maurepas finally agreed to make an annual contract with the religious at the rate of 200 livres for each bed plus the ration of the soldier during his stay in the hospital. He added:

> If this expense does not exceed the sum of 5000
> livres allowed for remedies, food, linen, and medicaments

for the sick, His Majesty will approve it. In that case, you must be very careful that the sick are well treated. I ought to tell you, besides, that the ration of the soldier to be furnished to the Religious during his stay at the hospital ought to consist only in bread, two sols worth in all.[11]

Salmon had asked for forty beds, but the king refused to increase the number. "The number of twenty-nine would seem to be sufficient for the troops and you will have to do the best you can with that,"[12] was the answer.

Under the circumstances Salmon must have been quite perplexed. Food alone cost 8000 livres in 1732, and this sum did not include the expense for 2919 days' care of poor citizens received at the hospital.[13] The expense for 1733 had been somewhat less, owing to a decrease in poor patients. Because a hurricane had blown down one of the hospital buildings the previous August, Salmon had told many poor citizens that there was no room for them at the hospital. In any case it was the king's intention to treat only troops of the garrison.[14] The *ordonnateur* added conscientiously: "It is true, nevertheless, that misery has made itself felt still more keenly than last year, and I have been obliged to give them some rations in their homes."[15] Salmon, seeing the wretchedness of impoverished residents, pitied them and wanted to relieve them in their distress, but he could do little. By 1734, even though poor civilians were excluded from the hospital, the number of sick still exceeded twenty-nine. On August 12, of that year the admit rolls showed forty French soldiers, seven or eight Swiss, and others being brought in every day.[16]

The furnishings of the hospital were in deplorable condition. Soon after his arrival Salmon had drawn up an inventory of existing equipment and a list of needed articles which he forwarded to France.[17] Nearly three years later, the necessary articles had not yet arrived. Less than three weeks before the sisters were to take charge of the sick, the *ordonnateur* again reminded the minister of the destitute state of the hospital.

I have already written to your highness that the hospital is devoid of furnishings and utensils. The bedsteads are rotten, or are full of vermin. It would not be at all suitable to use them in the new ward. However, I have ordered those that are usable to be scalded, and I have had 25 new bedsteads made. The ticks are rotten. There are only 6 pairs of sheets. They are in rags. The mosquito bars (*tours de lits*)[18] are not in any better condition. I hope that your highness will give orders to send, by the vessel of the King, the necessary things that I have requested.[19]

In spite of the meager equipment, Sister St. Xavier did all she could to alleviate misery once she was installed as head nurse. The inspectors soon noted a marked change for the better, finding that under the sister's management there was little to regulate, but much to praise.[20] The forty to fifty sick soldiers cared for by Sister St. Xavier expressed gratitude for the care and attention given to them. She even provided special "sweets" which had never been available to patients previously.[21] In a joint letter of August 31, 1735, Governor Bienville and Salmon both testified to their satisfaction.

Since our hospital is served by the Religious, and we have lodged the soldiers there as comfortably as possible, we have noticed that the sick do not stay long, because they are well cared for.[22]

The sisters were grateful to God for the apparent success that attended their work of Christian charity. But while performing the corporal works of mercy, the nuns, as true daughters of St. Angela, also worked for the welfare of their patients' souls, which were often in a more pitiable state than their bodies.

The spirit of our holy Institute is spread by the solid good which our dear Sister does for their souls while caring for their bodies. More than thirty have died during the 14 months that she has been employed there. Only a few of this number have not made an edifying end. Many whose libertine lives gave just cause to fear have entered with surprising facility into the sentiments of piety and religion which have been suggested to them and have formulated sentiments beautiful enough to cause us admiration.[23]

When the Ursulines took charge of the hospital, Salmon proposed that they sign a contract to provide food for the sick. The sisters asked to study the situation first in order to determine the approximate cost of each patient's ration. They also asked to see the statement of what the treasurer had expended for food over a period of time.[24] In April, 1735, a final agreement had not been reached.[25] It is not certain whether or not a written contract was ever drawn up while Salmon was *ordonnateur*. M. Le Normant said there was none when he became *ordonnateur* in 1744.[26]

Seeing how proficient the nuns were in caring for the sick, Bienville

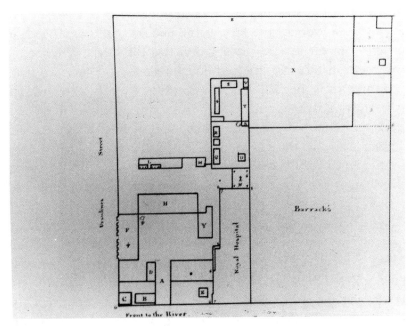

Plan of the hospital and the Ursuline Convent property from an iventory of public builidings made by Nicolas Foucault, 1766. Courtesy Ursulines Archives & Museum.

and Salmon proposed that they also assume the duties of the apothecary. The incumbent of the office in 1735 was inefficient and negligent, and Salmon canceled his contract.[27] He assigned the work to Dr. Prat, the physician at the Royal Hospital, who promised to do the work gratis.

Dr. Prat offered to teach the sisters to mix the drugs and to prepare the medicines.[28] There was also a Jesuit brother who had some experience in the preparation of medicines whom Salmon considered a possible instructor.[29] The sisters gave their best efforts to this work, but they realized that they lacked the training and the womanpower to meet this new challenge in addition to all of their other obligations. They appealed to the Ursuline Convents of France for volunteers, asking especially for a sister trained as a pharmacist. French sisters did agree to come to Louisiana. However, when the sisters were ready to embark, the ship's officers refused for unknown reasons to take them on board.[30]

Both Dr. Prat and Salmon petitioned that the pharmacist and the other sisters be given passage.[31] Salmon wrote to Maurepas in 1739, stressing the immediate need for more sisters. He spoke of the efforts the sisters gave to the hospital which was frequently filled to capacity, with patients being laid in the aisles at times. He praised the sisters virtue and dedication in the face of the endless work, and cited Sister St. Xavier's competence. He made it clear that the sisters were not asking for any additional funds, just additional personnel. He noted that for the past three years they had received no subsidy for the three additional nuns that had joined the original six.[32] Entreaty, urgency, insistence produced identical results. Nearly two and a half years elapsed before the arrival of reinforcements for the educator/nurses. Finally on February 12, 1742, the overburdened Ursulines joyfully welcomed Sister St. Louis de Gonzague Louchard, Sister Ste. Madeleine Bigeaud de Belair, and her younger sister, Sister Ste. Thérèse Bigeaud de Belair.[33]

One of the most intriguing things about the recruitment of additional sisters from France is the reaction of the French ecclesiastical authorities. Any sister wishing to leave for the missions had to have a "permission" from her bishop. One wonders whether these permissions were an exercise of power over the nuns or a genuine expression of concern for their welfare. Sister St. Louis de Gonzague[34] was a professed member of the Ursuline Community of Lisieux, and for several years had frequently petitioned the Bishop of Lisieux for permission to go to Louisiana. Her persistence was rewarded with a consent from the bishop in 1741.[35] Letters and records of her companions in the order give descriptions of her as a model of every virtue: humble, obedient, charitable, and compassionate, ever ready to give assistance to all who needed her help or sympathy.[36]

Sister Ste. Madeleine of the Ursulines of Landerneau made her vows at eighteen and expressed her desire to go to the Louisiana mission. Bishop of Laon, John Louis de Bourdonnaye, insisted on her giving mature consideration to her missionary vocation. He also wanted to be certain that the religious life as lived by the Louisiana community was regular and fervent. Only after he had been assured "that the community established at New Orleans devotes itself with fervor to the instruction of the young girls of the different nations that are there, and to the care of the sick in the hospital...and that the cloister and other religious observances are kept there with edification,"[37] did the bishop give permission for Sister Ste. Madeleine to transfer to New Orleans. For fifty years she lived and worked in New Orleans, dying in 1792 at the age of ninety-five.[38] Presuming that her early years in New Orleans were times of extremely hard physical and mental efforts, it is significant to note her achievements in later life. She became deaf and totally blind in her last years but continued to assist the poor of New Orleans, by soliciting help from friends.[39] She also persisted in encouraging spiritual renewal, writing three times to M. Ursin Bouligny, a colonel in the Regiment of Louisiana, urging him to make his First Communion and to remain ever faithful to his religious duties.[40] The four charming letters of Sister Ste. Madeleine make us regret that we know so little about this nun who remained so alert until the age of ninety-five.

At a young age Elizabeth Bigeaud de Belair showed unusual intellectual and spiritual gifts, and her parents gave special care to her training. When she was seventeen she joined her sister at Landerneau, where Sister Ste. Madeleine had been a religious for more than twenty years. Although Elizabeth had no intention of becoming an Ursuline, as a boarder she had studied the religious life and considered her own vocation. After two years Sister Madeleine had suggested to Elizabeth that she accompany her to New Orleans, even though Elizabeth had shown no desire to become a member of the order. Elizabeth accepted the proposal with "joy",[41] and she brought with her impressive letters of recommendation.[42] Elizabeth and Sister Ste. Madeleine left the Convent of Landerneau on April 4, 1741,[43] and traveled to Vannes to spend two days with their mother. Although the sacrifice of her dear Elizabeth was a severe trial to Madame de Belair, she gave them her blessing and the two sisters set out for La Rochelle to await the sailing of a vessel to Louisiana.

In accordance with the permission given by Bishop Henri Dubreuil de Pontbriand,[44] Elizabeth received the religious habit in the convent of the *Dames Hospitalières* on September 8, 1741,[45] and the name Sister du Sacré Coeur.[46]

While the two sisters were waiting at La Rochelle, Sister Ste. Madeleine became so ill that her departure was deemed impossible. Sister du Sacré Coeur and Sister St. Louis de Gonzague, who was also at La Rochelle, had reluctantly agreed to sail without her when Ste. Madeleine was unexpectedly restored to good health and able to embark with them.[47] It is easy to imagine the happiness of the overworked, sorely tried little community on the arrival of the three religious from France. Was either Sister Ste. Madeleine or Sister St. Louis de Gonzaque the pharmacist they had requested?[48] Sister Ste. Madeleine may have been, but historians consider Sister St. Xavier Hébert the first woman pharmacist in the United States. Sister Ste. Madeleine ended by being the last Ursuline to have charge of the Royal Hospital.[49]

There were still numerous deficiencies at the hospital. A pharmacy, a room for the chaplain, and another for the attending physician were urgently needed.[50] But as with the convent, it would be nearly seven years during which various plans would be considered before the work was completed. In the summer of 1737 Royal engineer Ignace-François Broutin drew a plan of a hospital wing consisting of four rooms—a pharmacy, a laboratory, a room for the surgeon, and another for the chaplain.[51] But "continual rains" in the summer, "bad weather" in winter, and other work on the barracks[52] hampered construction of the proposed building. Very likely it was not completed until 1742. By that time Broutin seems to have changed his plan, and, instead of the one wing originally projected, two were built. These twenty-by-forty feet additions provided facilities for a laboratory, kitchen, and additional room for the sick. With the exception of the convent, these buildings were all standing at the time of the transfer of Louisiana to Spain and were included in the inventory of public buildings made by Nicholas Foucault in 1766.[53]

Meanwhile Salmon, who knew only too well the procrastination that invariably impeded construction in Louisiana, asked the Ursulines to give over their recreation room near the choir[54] for a pharmacy until one could be built. The religious objected, and in a meeting of March 27, 1736, decided to offer to build a room adjoining the hospital at their own expense. Father Le Petit persuaded the *ordonnateur* to accept the proposal, and the room was built. The annalist succinctly recorded, "The house has been accepted, and built at our expense, and they no longer want it."[55] Did they ever use it? She does not tell us. When the drugs and medicines arrived in May, 1736, they were stored "in the room of the convent nearest the hospital."[56] Salmon had at times made demands that the religious could not grant, but they must have realized that he was acting only under the pressure of circumstances rather than with ill-will. As long as Salmon held the office of *ordonnateur*, the nuns had a friend on whom they could rely. It was far different when Sebastian Le Normant succeeded him in 1744. During his tenure they would become the victims of his spite and injustice.

As soon as he was in office, Le Normant began to question the nuns' administration of the Royal Hospital. At the time the sisters were receiving ten sols per day for each sick soldier or worker and fifteen sols for each Negro treated at the hospital.[57] Le Normant thought that these rates would have been reasonable had the sisters not also been supplied with a ration for each patient of flour, wine, brandy, sugar, soap, candles, oil, wood to burn, and "all that they asked for the daily use of the hospital, although they made other use of it."[58] This implies that Le Normant was charging the Ursulines with misappropriation of supplies. He cited as an example that they had received 1495 pots[59] of wine during 1744, the year before his arrival. Then he made a vindictive accusation:

> It is certain that the sick have not consumed the tenth part of it. They [Ursulines] have sold the rest, and they have likewise trafficked with a good part of the other supplies. Nevertheless, all these goods were bought in the colony on the account of the King at exorbitant prices, so that there has resulted not only a great abuse but also a considerable increase of expense.[60]

As though this were not sufficient, Le Normant accused the religious of having employed the Negroes assigned for the service of the hospital for their own benefit.[61] He also charged them with having profited from the rations given to the boys and apprentices[62] at the hospital. Le Normant estimated that it cost the French government more than 3 livres 10 sols a day for each patient, and he intended to abolish any abuses in expenditures. A few months later he reported, "I have attained my end."[63] His principal instrument was the contract of December 31, 1744.[64]

The first article of the contract specified that soldiers, marine officers, sailors, and workers in the service of the king, Negroes of the king, and crews of the king's vessels were to be admitted to the hospital on the orders of the *ordonnateur*. For each sergeant, corporal, cadet, drummer, or soldier of the troops garrisoned in Louisiana there would be paid 15 sols per day and a ration of bread.[65] The rate for each marine officer, sailor, worker, or seaman was 20 sols.[66] The same rate applied to the service of the poor inhabitants,[67] but only 14 sols per day were to be paid for each sick Negro or Negress admitted.[68] In turn the sisters were to provide food for the sick. The patients were to be given a sufficient quantity of broth made with fresh meat of good quality, the same quality of bread as was supplied to the troops, wine according to the physician's orders, and other necessary provisions.[69] The religious were responsible for the maintenance and replacement of all furnishings and utensils of the hospital. An inventory was to be made and was to be kept ready for examination at any time by the inspector of the hospital.[70] The religious were to furnish the lights and the wood for the stoves of the hospital wards, the kitchen, and the pharmacy.[71] For this purpose the king would give them 1500 livres a year.[72]

When Le Normant came to New Orleans there were seventeen Negroes and Negresses in the service of the hospital, including children, all of whom were fed and clothed at the king's expense. [73] Under the new contract Le Normant reduced the servants to Louison the cook, her 5 year old son, her 2 1/2 year old daughter, an unborn child, another Negress named Jeanneton, and two Negroes, all to be fed and clothed at the expense of the religious.[74] Baptiste, a Negro who was already employed at the pharmacy, would remain, and at his death the king would replace him.[75] Instead of seventeen servants there would be five, for M. Le Normant could hardly have expected the three children, one unborn, to do much work. With regard to provisions the contract indicated that every year on the arrival of the king's ships, the sisters were to receive ten barrels of wine, four quarts[76] of brandy, and the supplies that they had ordered from France, provided the total weight did not exceed six tons. On the delivery of the goods, the nuns were to pay the rate declared by the invoice from France plus forty per cent profit.[77]

Le Normant had attained his end to the great detriment of the Ursulines. What a story their correspondence of the next few years might have told! Unfortunately only brief *résumés* of some of their letters have been preserved in the correspondence of Abbé de l'Isle Dieu, who had become the new vicar-general in France for the Louisiana diocese.[78] These give a few scattered indications of the burden placed on the sisters by the contract of 1744 and of the treatment that M. Le Normant meted out to them.

> These good Religious have not ceased to write from March 7, 1745 to November 13 last [1745], by every means they could send their letters to me.[79]
>
> Judging from their letters, M. Le Normant, *Commissaire Ordonnateur* of this colony, treats them very badly and annoys them very much with regard to the Administration of the hospital, in which he accused them of having used malpractice. It may be very easy to justify them, judging from the means which they propose to throw light on their conduct that is, by examining the registers of their administration. They ask only to produce and to expose these to the examination and criticism of those whom he will wish to name as commissioners.[80]

It seems clear from this that Le Normant had failed to examine the books of the hospital to ascertain just what supplies had been received and how they had been used. It seems his charges were entirely without justification, as they were not based on fact.

In 1733 Bishop de Mornay had resigned as Bishop of Quebec rather than leave France for Canada. Monseigneur Dosquet then replaced him as Bishop of Quebec. The new bishop did not have an auxiliary, but needed someone to oversee ecclesiastical affairs in Louisiana. He appointed Abbé de l'Isle Dieu, a noted priest in France, to oversee Louisiana and Acadia. The Abbé was a very conscientious person, and from his office in France gave a great deal of time under difficult circumstances to advising those in Louisiana. During the controversy over the finances of the hospital, he made it clear that others were not complaining about the sisters.

> By all the letters that I receive from this colony these good Religious would seem to render there very great services, as much for the care of the sick of the hospital as for the education of the orphans, and the instruction of the children of the colony...as well as to the Negresses, whom they instruct separately, although these good and holy Religious are only twelve...during the fourteen years that I have had charge of the spiritual affairs of this colony there has come to me only praise of them, and the Capuchins have been the only ones who have troubled them under pretext of conflict of jurisdiction with the Jesuits. This no longer exists, since I put a stop to it.[81]

The vicar-general wanted to be just and not to accuse Le Normant wrongfully.

> God forbid that I should want to imply that M. Le Normant acts from ill-humor or antipathy, but it seems to me very strange that M. De Vaudreuil,[82] whom these good religious praise very much, daily helps them. M. de Salmon, who did as much for them, has never discovered on their part any bad administration and [there was the decisive argument] M. Le Normant accused them, even to declare them convicted of having ruined the hospital. It is for you, Sir, to verify the complaints that he makes of them and to judge if they are innocent, as I believe.[83]

Le Normant even went so far as to threaten to have the Ursuline Convent of New Orleans suppressed. To assure their position, the religious petitioned for letters patent from the king.[84] Such ill will on the part of the *ordonnateur* could not be passed over lightly by Abbé de l'Isle Dieu, and he spoke again of Le Normant's motives. "I do not want to judge M. Le Normant, but I suspect from the different letters that I have received that he is prejudiced against these good Religious."[85] A year later the situation had not improved. Again Abbé de l'Isle Dieu protested that good, holy women who performed great service to the colony were being harassed. He suggested that Governor Vaudreuil would agree with his comments.[86]

The matter dragged on for eight years. By that time the burden imposed on the religious was entirely out of proportion to the recompense received. When the contract was imposed in December, 1744, there were thirty patients at the hospital. By 1752 the number had risen to one hundred twenty.[87] The Ursulines explained this to M. Michel, Commissary of the Navy and Acting Intendant, when he succeeded Le Normant. Michel replied that he could do nothing to change the contract which they had made with M. Le Normant except with the consent and on the orders of the court.[88] This reply was quite reasonable, but it did not remedy the financial strain into which the religious had been plunged by the great increase in the number of sick.

On inquiring into the finances of the hospital, M. Michel was surprised to find that the Ursulines made a distinction between the revenue of the hospital and their own.[89] He was reverting to an old idea that had been prevalent before the Ursulines took charge of the hospital: That the revenue for the hospital, the salary of the sisters and the payments for the orphans should all go into a common fund.[90] This would have been not only an impractical method of handling the finances, but also a very unjust one. The mere pittance which the sisters received from the French government would not provide for their own needs, much less for support of the hospital, and the allowance for the orphans was not even sufficient to feed and clothe them.[91]

From France Abbé de l'Isle Dieu continued to champion the cause of the sisters and to stress in his communications to officials in France the poverty, inconveniences, disrespect and indignities they were subjected to. He carefully showed that it was next to impossible for the religious to reap any profits from monies they received. The nuns' compensation for the orphans was based on 30 orphans, whereas there were always more orphans residing at the convent than that. As for their salaries, the amount remained stagnant at 3600 livres regardless of the number of sisters residing at the convent. The Abbé noted that they could use at least 20 to 24 nuns given their many duties, but it would be impossible to support that number without an increase in compensation. The hospital fees brought no revenue to the convent, as all monies were put back into accounts for use at the hospital only. Finally the prelate noted that the religious who came from France brought no dowries, as they were originally professed in French convents. In fact, the New Orleans Ursulines had paid travel costs for religious from France amounting overall to 6110 livres. In addition the nuns had not been paid sums owed to them during the years 1743-1745.[92] The Abbé found it hard to believe that officials could ignore the poverty of the sisters.

> How do they expect this poor little community
> to enrich itself? Is it not rather astonishing that they are
> able to subsist and to fulfill all the charges for which
> they are obligated.... Is it not by their own economy and
> by their own industry that they have been able to support
> themselves without being a charge either to the hospital
> which they serve or to the State which has confided it
> to them?[93]

As if monetary problems were not trying enough, dissension among the physician of the hospital and the surgeons resulted in incivilities to the nuns. Outrageous discourtesies were not only humiliating, but detrimental to the service of the patients. The sisters were hampered in creating an atmosphere that would encourage patients to accept and cooperate with their treatment. When the sisters complained of their rude treatment they were usually ignored, and in some instances suffered further ill will.[94] The surgeons not only treated the nuns very badly, but threatened to remove them from the pharmacy and the hospital and replace them with Grey Sisters. One surgeon started a rumor that the Court had already given the orders for twelve Grey Sisters to come to Louisiana.[95]

The surgeons' lack of consideration for the nuns resulted in similar treatment of them by the patients. The contract of 1744 bound the sisters to maintain and replace the furniture and utensils of the hospital,[96] but the surgeons convinced the patients, especially the soldiers, that they were making a considerable profit on their agreement for services. Patients felt free to pillage and steal as much as they could of the furniture, goods, and utensils of the hospital, especially toward the end of their convalescence, when they were physically able to carry away their booty. They stole shirts, linens, wearing apparel and even the dishes. When they could not steal the dishes, they threw them on the floor and broke them.[97] This wanton destruction and theft entailed great expense for the Ursulines. Every year they were obliged to have La Rochelle send large numbers of replacement dishes and other supplies to substitute for those destroyed or stolen.[98]

The obligation of supplying the patients with palatable food was not always easy to fulfill. The sisters were paid 14 to 20 sols a day for each patient, depending on the rank or status of the individual. At times this small sum was totally inadequate to cover the cost of the food. As noted earlier, they were obliged to provide a "sufficient quantity of broth made with fresh meat of good quality."[99] The price of fresh meat (*viande de boucherie*) was not unreasonable, but it was so scarce that poultry frequently had to be substituted. Poultry was very dear, since chickens were worth 30 to 35 sols, a turkey 7 livres 10 sols and up to 10 livres each. Other products were also expensive—eggs according to the season were 18 to 25, even 32 sols 6 deniers a dozen, milk 2 sols 6 deniers a pot, wine up to 400 livres a barrel, and flour 200 livres a hundred.[100] Abbé de l'Isle Dieu commented:

> From this short summary it is easy to see that the price that they give to the Religious is not at all proportionate to the expense that the consumption of each sick person occasions them, and the more patients they have the more they lose.[101]

The Minister of the Colonies did not act immediately on the information that Abbé de l'Isle Dieu gave him. He asked the Governor and the *ordonnateur* in Louisiana for a clarification of the facts, "for it is just and it is my intention to give them the assistance which they really need to serve the hospital with the necessary facility."[102]

By the time this request reached New Orleans, Louis Billouart de Kerlérec had replaced the Marquis de Vaudreuil as Governor in February, 1752, and M. Dauberville had become *ordonnateur* in December of the same year.[103] These new officials did not consider the contract of 1744 burdensome to the nuns. The sisters had complained that the slaves furnished to the hospital by the contract were too few since the number of sick had quadrupled. Kerlérec and Dauberville maintained that these

Louis Billouart de Kerlérec, Governor of LA 1753-1763. Courtesy Historic New Orleans Collection, 1991.34.9.

slaves were allowed to the Ursulines only to help them in the service of the hospital, and that they were obliged to furnish as many more as they needed.[104] There was no such condition in the contract.

The Governor and the *ordonnateur* argued that it was not expedient to increase the rate per patient, as "that would be too strong a precedent for the future." They hoped that with the measures they were going to take, fresh meat would be more abundant in the future.[105] Yet Kerlérec described a week later, when petitioning that a room be built at the hospital for the officers, a somewhat different picture.[106]

It is, Sir, an indispensable necessity to build a room at the hospital of the King... for the officers whom we have seen perish of misery at home in case of sickness, deprived of all help. This is easy to believe if you will reflect on the small salary of the subalterns in a country where at the same time that everything is very dear, they do not find three-fourths of the time in winter and almost never in summer a morsel of beef to make broth.[107]

The contrast of attitude and reasoning in these two letters is remarkable. One may ask why the high price of provisions should work a hardship with the officers, but not with the nuns. Did Kerlérec intend to provide additional meat for the officers as well as for the Ursulines? Or was he using the description only to further the cause of an additional room? Even though they looked unfavorably on an increase in hospital rates, the Governor and the *ordonnateur* admitted that the sisters had discharged their duties faithfully even at a financial loss.

> ...it is certain that these Religious have had very much work to which they have devoted themselves with great zeal and it has not been without difficulty that they have provided for the maintenance of the sick. We think that if you are pleased to grant them a gratuity of seven to eight hundred livres for each of the years 1751, 1752, 1753 they will be amply compensated for the expense that they have had to make and for the wrong that they say they have suffered by not having received on time the furniture and utensils that had been promised them by Article 3.[108]

Not long after the financial recommendations were made Dauberville reported that the consumption of medications at the hospital was too high, and that there must be considerable abuse which could never be abolished as long as the sisters had charge of the pharmacy.[109] Did Dauberville investigate before making the charges? It is evident that he did not. He wrote, "I have reason to suspect[110] the false consumption" of the remedies in the hospital of the king.

> ...but in spite of all my care it will never be possible for me to prevent it, unless you are pleased to be good

enough to send me an apothecary to be charged only with the business of the pharmacy and of the composition of the medicine. As long as the Lady Religious will have some survey or inspection in this matter I can not hope, whatever care I take, to cut short the abuses which have been introduced.[111]

Despite supplications from the colonies, the home government was too preoccupied with other business to give consideration to a distant military hospital. In the summer of 1755, Abbé de l'Isle Dieu was still reporting to the Minister that the sisters were suffering from the same injustices. But during the next few years the Seven Years War in Europe overshadowed all other concerns, and correspondence on this subject either ceased or has been lost. In the end the officials must have been satisfied with the work of the Ursulines, since they continued to engage their services.

In July, 1762, Nicholas Foucault,[112] then the *ordonnateur*, chose to transfer some of the sick from the Royal Hospital to the *Hotel de Mars*.[113] He requested that the Ursulines go there to nurse the sick, bringing some of the Negroes from their plantation to serve this second hospital. The superior assembled the community and presented the request of the *ordonnateur* to them. After considering the reasons that M. Foucault gave, the community decided unanimously to limit themselves to the Royal Hospital "the sooner to hand over the whole to the King." The Ursulines had decided to discontinue hospital work as soon as possible and restrict themselves to the work of Christian education. While these developments were taking place, another change had been made in the living quarters of the religious. The first Ursuline Convent in New Orleans had been abandoned for a second, a fact that historians lost sight of for more than a century.

CHAPTER 7

ℭonvent ℭhanges and ℌrrivals from ℱrance

As early as 1734 the nuns knew that their "new monastery" was deteriorating. Mother St. André wrote that year that the house demanded repairs daily and could not last long.[1] Indeed eleven years after the nuns moved, the building was "decaying in every part."[2] It had been built of columbage construction, a heavy wood framework filled with brick in medieval fashion, with a foundation set on wooden sills. The skeleton structure had stood so long unroofed and exposed to rain during the protracted period of construction, that the beams and sills were beginning to rot even before the convent was completed. During the summer of 1745 colonial officials were obliged to have the building propped

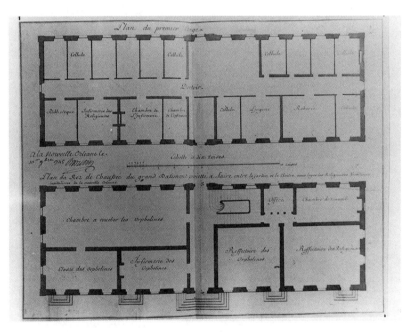

Plans of the first and second floors of the second Ursuline Convent. Signed by Ignace François Broutin, November 10, 1745. Courtesy Samuel Wilson, Jr., F.A.I.A.

133

up to prevent its falling and crushing those within.[3] This was a temporary expedient—until the Court would issue orders for the construction of a new convent.

Ignace Broutin, king's engineer, drew an elaborate plan for a new building and submitted it to officials in France.[4] Broutin's plan called for a main building with an entrance lodge on the site of the old convent with a chapel opening into the hospital, and a kitchen and laundry that would enclose a court in front of the main building.[5] The entrance was on the river side.

The cost of the new building was estimated at more than 77,000 livres. That seemed unattainable but necessary, as there was no other building that could serve the nuns' needs. It was also important to construct a solid building to avoid the costly repairs which had plagued the first convent. As finances would not allow execution of the entire plan, Governor Vaudreuil and M. Le Normant suggested in 1746 that only a main building be constructed at an estimated 49,600 livres.[6] The following spring a rather reluctant permission to begin work came from the minister. Noting the drain on the treasury due to the expenses of war, the authorization was for a building that would serve to lodge the religious.[7]

Two years later the convent was not yet begun. Finally on March 11, 1748, Maurepas renewed the permission to build the convent,[8] and work got under way. In the fall of 1748 Governor Vaudreuil, Claude Joseph Villars Dubreuil, the contractor for the second convent, and M. Dauberville reported on the progress:

> In conformity with your letter of March 18, we are working constantly on the building necessary to lodge the Religious. Indeed that which they occupy is no longer in a state to serve, and we doubt if it can hold against the violence of the gales which prevail in this country. For this new building we shall conform to what has been prescribed by your lordship.[9]

Work on the convent continued through the summer of 1749,[10] with competition from other projects. When Michel de la Rouvilliére arrived in New Orleans that summer as *ordonnateur*, he found some

Pierre de Rigaud de Vaudreuil (Marquis de Vaudreuil), Governor of LA, 1743-1753. Courtesy Historic New Orleans Collection, 1991.34.8.

of the government buildings in very bad condition and was anxious to hasten work on the convent so that some of the laborers could be employed on the king's buildings. At the same time he was determined that the buildings under construction should be solid. He praised engineer Broutin as a man with like intentions. Michel was chagrined to find that the iron gratings[11] for the windows of the convent had been forgotten. These items would entail considerable expense, as there were many openings in the building, which were "indispensable because of the hot climate."[12] The work was still far from complete in the fall, when Michel wrote: "I have had to draw the sum of 60 thousand livres on account of the building of the Religious, which is already above the casements of the second story (*premier étage*) and which will require at least this outlay before its completion."[13]

How much of the material of the first convent was utilized in the second is not known.   The main stair, which seems identical in plan[14] to the one in the original building, may have been reused. Some of the doors and windows may also have been salvaged.

The second convent was even smaller than the first.[15]   There were two full stories and an attic instead of three stories, no provision for a chapel, and no accommodations for the boarders. Where was the chapel? Was it at the corner of the cloister yard at Ursulines and Decatur Streets? A plan drawn by Gilberto Guillemard in 1793 shows a building in that place which he designated as the "ancient church."[16]   When Father Baudouin S.J. made the canonical examination before the profession of Mary Turpin in 1752, he took the novice "to the church" for the interrogation.[17]   It is hardly probable that he took this cloistered novice through the streets to the parish church which was some blocks away. It is more likely that the little church at the corner of Ursulines and Decatur Streets had been built or moved there some time between 1745 and 1752.[18]

The boarders may have been accommodated in a separate building. Father Le Petit, upon a visit of 1737, had recommended that "When the boarders will be in the new building, it will be necessary to have there a bedroom for the mistress, who will be able to watch over the conduct of the children."[19] An inventory of the buildings on the Ursulines' grounds in 1766 included an old brick structure of two stories which had formerly been used as a residence and school for the boarders.[20] It is doubtful that the rooms marked for the orphans' use on Broutin's plan of November 10, 1745 were actually used for that purpose.   The second floor space may also have been divided in a different manner and utilized for other purposes, as the original plan was evidently reduced. Either from the beginning or at a later date, the attic was partitioned into small rooms for the nuns' sleeping quarters. The primitive unfinished walls of cypress wood could still be seen until the building was restored during the mid-twentieth century.

It is impossible to say exactly at what date the Ursulines moved into their second convent, but it was probably in 1752 or 1753.   It was not until the statement of expenses for 1753 that the final payment of 29,984 livres 8 sols 7 deniers[21] was made.   Abbé de l'Isle Dieu stated in April, 1752 that the convent had been rebuilt, but that the Ursulines

Chartres St. Convent through the gatehouse. Courtesy LA Collection, Howard-Tilton Memorial Library, Tulane Univ., New Orleans, LA

had not yet moved into it nor reestablished cloister.[22] Since mail was a long time in transit, the sisters were probably settled in their new home some weeks before the Abbé learned of it. As the new building was within the old enclosure, the move was made without any of the fanfare that had accompanied the transfer from the Kolly house to this location.

It is remarkable that the facts about this building should have been so completely forgotten, and the second convent confused with the earlier structure.[23] There is no mention of a second building in any of the documents reserved in the convent archives. There are only a few scattered facts, which taken together would indicate that the first convent had given place to the second. Yet the documents in the National Archives of Paris, transcripts or photostats of which are in the Library of Congress, prove unequivocally that the old Ursuline convent now standing on Chartres Street was designed by Broutin in 1745. The Ursulines were to live for three quarters of a century in the second convent which was made of brick. This building is believed to be the oldest existing structure in the Mississippi Valley. Its venerable walls have survived, and the old stair, though deeply grooved with wear, is still as solid as the first day those pioneer Ursulines set foot on it. How many young girls passed through the portals of this ancient building can never be determined, as the records have long since disappeared. But each succeeding year girls trained according to Ursuline traditions went out into all classes of society to pass on to the next generation the enduring Christian principles learned from their Ursuline teachers.

As the work of the Ursulines expanded, an ever greater number of sisters was needed. This need was supplied by French communities, which for more than twenty-five years supplied reinforcements. The Company of the Indies had stipulated in the first contract that girls born in Louisiana were not to be admitted as religious without the permission of the Council.[24] They were anxious to provide educated young women as wives for the colonists, and even Father de Beaubois did not favor local women becoming nuns. According to Sister St. Stanislaus,

> All[25] the pupils would like to be religious but this is not to the liking of Reverend Father de Beaubois, our very worthy Superior. He considers it more expedient that they should become Christian mothers, in order to establish religion in this country by their good example.[26]

Before the arrival of the Ursulines, the girls of New Orleans were usually married at a very early age, normally between twelve and fourteen. Many had not even made their First Communion, but after the Ursulines came none were married unless they had first received instruction at the convent.[27] These future wives and mothers were thus assured before their marriage of some knowledge of Catholic doctrine and of their duties as Christians. By training these young girls, the Ursulines were doing the work for which the Company of St. Ursula had been founded.

If the work was to continue the religious needed to reinforce their ranks, as sickness, old age and death thinned their numbers. Relying on France for new volunteers was a precarious method of enlarging their ranks. No Ursuline Convent in France had any direct responsibility for the New Orleans community, whose original group were from six different monasteries. Each Ursuline Convent in France was independent of every other, with only the spirit of St. Angela binding them together.

Original front of Chartres St. Convent, now used as rear entrance. Courtesy LA Collection, Howard-Tilton Memorial Library, Tulane Univ., New Orleans, LA.

The original Company of St. Ursula had a Mother General. Because of the exigencies of the times, those instrumental in the expansion of the order did not keep this administrative feature, which would have assisted the New Orleans nuns. The wars of the eighteenth century also increased the difficulty of obtaining new recruits. In 1747 Governor Vaudreuil appealed to the Bishop of Quebec to send sisters from the Ursuline Monastery, "because of the difficulty and even the impossibility of having any come from France, on account of the war."[28] There were then eleven members in the New Orleans community, although they needed "at least thirty to fill the offices and charges of the house, and to put them in a position to discharge the services that they rendered to the colony."[29] More than a year later, November 7, 1748 the Bishop of Quebec wrote to the minister of the colonies for permission to comply with the request of Governor Vaudreuil.

Although the Quebec proposal did not materialize, the Ursulines received the first American born woman to enter a convent in the present United States[30]in New Orleans the following year. She was Mary Turpin,[31] a child of France and the New World. Her father Louis Turpin was keeper of the king's warehouses in Illinois. Dorothée, her mother, was an Indian and the widow of a Frenchman.[32] Dorothée's name signifies "gift of God," and she was that to her husband and daughter. An unusually pious woman, she instructed her young daughter Mary in the Catholic faith, aided by the Jesuit missionaries. After Dorothée's death Mary decided to give herself to God and began a spiritual program under the guidance of Jesuits. For several years she pursued a life of prayer, frequent reception of the Sacraments, fasting, and mortification. Although she had never seen a nun, she expressed a desire to join a religious order. Probably through the Jesuits she heard of the Ursulines in New Orleans, and asked her father's consent to join them. Her father was reluctant to give his consent, and her friends and associates, wanting her to stay in Illinois, predicted that she would be a servant to the religious. Mary, however, was determined to pursue her vocation. In the end she convinced her father to let her go to New Orleans.

Mr. Turpin asked that Mary learn about religious life before making her decision, and so after arriving in New Orleans she entered the boarding school. When after a year of study her decision remained firm, her father gave his permission for her to begin her novitiate on July 2, 1749. Five months later on December 7, Mary received the religious habit and the name Sister St. Martha. Father Baudouin S.J. had come for the canonical examination before her profession. Because the colonists had prejudicial feelings about Indians and their stability, he examined her closely. The priest's rather stilted testimony of approval is as follows:

We, Superior of the Ursuline Religious of New Orleans, Vicar General of Msgr. the Bishop of Quebec, to be convinced of the vocation of Mary Turpin called Sister St. Martha, a coadjutrix novice, have brought her out of the monastery and conducted her to the church, where after having asked her the necessary questions to which she replied in a manner satisfactory to us on the good quality of her vocation, we have consented that they proceed to have her make her profession, and we have brought her back to the conventual door and returned her into the hands of her Superior.[33]

Mary enthusiastically approached her assignments as a coadjutrix sister. She was skillful, neat, and exact. Her health failed within a few years, and despite being given tender nursing, she died November 20, 1761. The Ursulines had been happy to receive a native born woman into

Chartres St. Convent. Courtesy Ursuline Archives & Museum.

their ranks, but Mary Turpin remained the only one for some years.

The decade of the 1750's was more favorable to the Ursulines in adding desperately needed sisters. In early 1750 the nuns appealed once more to the French Ursulines, who once again responded affirmatively. Two religious from the community of Nevers arrived at La Rochelle in July of that year, waiting until September for passage to Louisiana.[34] During that time Abbé de l'Isle Dieu requested passage from Maurepas for "a young lady 26 years old, of very good will, excellent health, and with all the talents suitable to serve religion well."[35] Marie Madeleine Le Verme,[36] he wrote, was waiting at Nevers and could arrive in La Rochelle if sailing was delayed until September. Once Maurepas granted passage Mlle. Le Verme went to La Rochelle. On September 17, 1750,[37] the Abbé gave her "the holy habit of religion and the white veil for uniformity of dress and to avoid singularity on the ship." Mlle Le Verme then took the name of Sister St. François Régis.[38] Since the nuns had still not left in October, the Abbé asked for passage for Mlle Du Terrault of La Rochelle, a young woman in her early twenties "with good health, a strong constitution, and all the qualities requisite for a good religious."[39] The Abbé, pleading the cause of the New Orleans Ursulines, wrote to the minister for permission. In the letter he noted the duties the Ursulines had undertaken—caring for and instructing the orphans, day students, negresses, and boarders, and administering the military hospital.[40] Unless they enlarged their community, they would find it hard to continue in an efficient manner. He said: "This poor little community is reduced to 11 or 12 subjects, for the most part infirm and bent under the weight of years and work, and in spite of that, charged with rendering very great service to the colony."[41]

Whether the permission was refused or not given in time, Mlle Du Terrault did not sail. Only Sister St. Jacques Landelle, Sister St. Joseph de la Motte and the novice Sister St. François Régis, arrived in New Orleans on January 31, 1751.[42] Sister St. Joseph left Nevers in ill health, did not improve in New Orleans, and returned to France October 8, 1752 to her great disappointment and that of the New Orleans community.[43] Sister St. François Régis was professed in New Orleans on September 18, 1752.[44] Another novice who was native born was received but dismissed for ill health in December.[45] Despite the need for additional nuns, the Ursulines were very strict in their requirements, just as Mother St. Augustin had been in 1727 when she sent two of the original group back to France. The community would dismiss a postulant or novice whose health or conduct did not measure up to the demanding requirements of their Rule.

From France Abbé de l'Isle Dieu and Father Messaiger S.J., procurator for the Jesuit mission in Louisiana, continued to seek volunteers for Louisiana.[46] The Abbé expected to have three from Brest[47] on the ship which brought Governor Kerlérec and his wife to the colony in 1753, but only Sister St. Etienne des Champs of Bayeux, a twenty-eight year old coadjutrix sister, came.[48] She lived and worked in New Orleans for forty-five years "for the glory of God and the good of souls".[49] The two sisters who failed to come probably did not receive the consent of their bishop in time,[50] and the Abbé wrote in October, 1753 that they would soon leave Morlaix to go to La Rochelle. He was also expecting a third, "probably a secular," to whom he intended to give the veil before she left France; she did not sail with the others.[51] Finding communities who would allow volunteers to leave, as well as financing the journey were continuing problems for him.

As the Court is not accustomed to give help for these passages it is necessary to be content with two or three Sisters for this year, the more so as there is no religious who does not cost more than 600 livres from the day of her departure from her community until she reaches that of New Orleans. We can look for other subjects for next year.... The religious who are given to us leave their dowry in the communities where they have made profession and the seculars whom we receive do not have any, which, in spite of the custom to the contrary, would demand some indulgence and some favor on the part of the Court.[52]

It was a jubilant day when the Community of New Orleans welcomed the two promised missionaries in the spring of 1754. Sister Ste. Reine, Catherine Morice de l'Etang, and Sister Ste. Marie des Anges, Françoise Duplessis de Quemenor,[53] were both professed sisters of the community of Morlaix, which had been formed from the Bordeaux Congregation.[54] Upon their arrival they accepted the rules and customs of the New Orleans community and made the fourth vow on April 28.[55]

The following year four additional sisters arrived: Sister Ste. Thérèse de Jesus (Marie de Beaumont) and Sister St. Gabriel (Jeanne de Cormoray), both professed of Ancenis, Sister Ste. Anne (Rose Vincent de Limelec), professed of Pontivy, and a novice, Sister St. Ignace[56] (Marguerite Perrine du Liepure).[57] This novice was professed August 21, 1757 and spent forty-eight years in New Orleans before going to Havana in 1803.[58] There was also Martha Delatre, the orphan daughter of a physician of Mobile, who had lived several years at the orphanage where she learned to read, write, sew, and do housework. At the age of sixteen she entered the novitiate as a coadjutrix sister and was professed on March 25, 1759.[59] She was known in religion as Sister St. Antoine and was the last young woman to join the New Orleans community during the French regime. During her long life she saw the colony pass from France to Spain, return to France, and become part of the United States.

Staircase, Chartres St. Convent. Courtesy LA Collection, Howard-Tilton Memorial Library, Tulane Univ., New Orleans LA.

In spite of new arrivals, the loss of older nuns offset the addition of new members. One of those was Sister St. Stanislaus Hachard, who died on August 9, 1760, after thirty-three years of intense ardor for the work of Christian education in New Orleans. Sister St. Stanislaus had not complained of being ill and had spent the previous day in her normal routine. The next morning when she did not appear at Mass, one of the sisters discovered that she had died in her sleep. Her death was a great loss to the community, as she was exceptionally gifted and capable and had performed her duties with enthusiasm and charity toward all. She had lovingly been given the title of "Living Rule of the House".[60] Her letters to her father are a timeless memorial to her spirit and have commanded such interest as to be published four times.

Church historian Roger Baudier has written a fitting tribute to these heroic pioneer Ursulines of the French Colonial Period:

One of the consistently brightest spots in the religious panorama of Louisiana during the French colonial period was unquestionably the Ursuline Community, whose members did so much in the way of real Catholic work, translating their Faith and their Catholic principles into devoted and self-sacrificing labors that were a source of inspiration and edification at all times. The work of the Ursulines in imparting a Catholic education to the young women of Louisiana positively served as the foundations of the Catholic Faith in New Orleans and in many parts of the state. The Ursuline Convent was the nursery of Catholic families of Louisiana. Their pupils, well-trained in the Faith, went out into the life of Louisiana of that day as apostles of the Faith in Louisiana and helped to preserve it for the generations of today. The self-sacrifices, sufferings, trials, labors and devotion of these nuns during the colonial period has never been truly appraised and appreciated—perhaps never will, until on the day of the Great Assizes.[61]

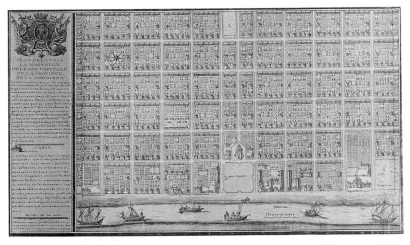

Thierry Map of New Orleans, 1755. Courtesy Historic New Orleans Collection, 1939.8.

From their difficult voyage and arrival in New Orleans in 1727 the Ursulines had faced what often seemed unsurmountable problems. The Company of the Indies and the Crown had failed to provide them with adequate housing and compensation for their work. Political and religious strife in the colony had directly affected them, and the instructions from abroad often failed to take the political as well as physical conditions of the colony into consideration.

The Ursuline communities of France continued to befriend the missionaries, and in Abbé de L'Isle Dieu the nuns found a considerate and supportive advisor. There are gaps of information in the story of the Ursulines during the French Colonial period, but the letters that have survived document an heroic struggle. Dedication to their objectives meant constant overwork, which caused the nuns to suffer to the point of exhaustion. The energy and labors of these first religious bore fruit in later years, especially during the Spanish Colonial period.

CHAPTER 8

The Advent of Spanish Control

The Seven Years' War which lasted in Europe from 1756 to 1763 was one of the largest conflicts between European nations in the continent's history. Almost all of the countries of Europe were involved on one side or another. In America the conflict was known as the French and Indian War, which actually broke out before the war in Europe. Despite its name, the war in America was primarily between the British and the French for control of territory. Spain was France's ally, and by the 1760's it was clear that they had lost the war, both in Europe and in America. Fighting did not take place in Louisiana, but diminished trade and isolation from France adversely affected the Colonial economy, while pleas for financial support went ignored. Finally Louis XV by the secret Treaty of Fontainebleau on November 3, 1762, transferred the portion of Louisiana west of the Mississippi River and the "Island of Orleans" to Charles III of Spain. By the Treaty of Paris, February 10, 1763, Canada and all the French possessions east of the Mississippi River, except the Island of Orleans, were ceded to Great Britain. France gave western Louisiana and New Orleans to Spain not only to repay her for the loss of the Floridas, but also because Louis XV and his minister, the Duc de Choiseul, did not want all of France's colonial empire in America falling into the hands of the British. In addition, France was completely discouraged by the difficulties and expenses consequent on governing a distant colony that for half a century had yielded little or no revenue.

Although Charles III accepted the gift of his cousin Louis XV, he did not immediately assume control. The year 1765 arrived, and Spain still had not taken possession of the territory. French officials continued to govern New Orleans during this period, and the residents continued to live as if they were still under French control. Governor Kerlérec, recalled in February, 1763, was replaced by another Frenchman, Jean Jacques Blaise d'Abbadie, who was made Director-General of the part of Louisiana not included in the cession to Great Britain. Nicholas Chauvin de Lafrénière arrived in New Orleans with him to serve as Procurator-

General of the Superior Council of Louisiana. Meanwhile political events in France continued to influence the Louisiana territory and New Orleans in particular.

In Europe the Jesuits were under fierce attack. In Portugal, prime minister Sebastião José de Carvalho e Mello, Marquês do Ponbal, had released anti-Jesuit propaganda in four languages during the late 1750's, the first time a government had attacked the Jesuit Order. Between 1759 and 1761 all Jesuits in Portugal and its overseas territories were arrested and deported to the Vatican states in Italy. In France the longstanding anti-Jesuit faction included political enemies who resented the Jesuits' privileged position at Court, as well as those who differed with them theologically. A single incident had enormous consequences for all of the French Jesuits. Father Lavalette, superior of the Jesuits on the island of Martinique, had used commercial credit in order to provide for some of the needs of his mission. When he was unable to pay his creditors for a debt in the neighborhood of two and a half million francs, the Jesuits refused to pay the debt, whereupon the affair was appealed to the *Parlement*. The *Parlement* ruled against the Jesuits in the Lavalette case, and on August 6, 1762, it recommended the expulsion of the Jesuits from France on the grounds that the order was "endangering the Christian faith, disturbing the peace of the Church, and in general building up far less than it destroys."[1] In Spain on April 2, 1767, troops descended on all houses, colleges, residences, and churches belonging to the Jesuits throughout the country. About 6000 Jesuits were packed into Spanish ships and transported to the Papal States in Italy, with many perishing aboard ship. These events in Europe swirling around the Jesuits would have a direct impact on Louisiana.

Shortly after his arrival in New Orleans M. de Lafrénière, notified the Jesuit superior that he had orders from France to take action against the Jesuits in Louisiana. Lafrénière then instituted proceedings against them before the Superior Council.[2] A Superior Council decree of July 9, 1763, tracking the decree of *Parlement*, declared that the Jesuits were hostile to royal authority, to the rights of Bishops, and to public peace and safety. To these charges the Superior Council added others, including allegations that the Jesuits of Louisiana were not taking care of their missions, were seeking only the improvement of their plantations, and were usurping the office of vicar-general.

It is unlikely that the Council really believed the charges. The majority had seen the missionaries regularly and were personally aware of their work. Nevertheless the Council, composed entirely of lay men, declared the vows of the Jesuits null and void. It ordered all their property, except personal books and clothes, to be seized and sold. It then delivered the vestments and plate of the chapel at New Orleans to the Capuchins, and razed all Jesuit chapels in Louisiana and Illinois to the ground. This left the colonists in many districts without a priest or place of worship. Every Jesuit was ordered to leave on the first ship sailing for France, and on arriving there to report at once to the Duke de Choiseul for pensions supplied by the sale of property. The majority of the Jesuits[3] embarked for France during the first months of 1764.[4]

The expulsion of the Jesuits was a severe blow to the Ursulines. A Jesuit had brought them to Louisiana, and a Jesuit had always been their superior, except during the short period when the Society was interdicted. A Jesuit had been chaplain at the Royal Hospital since 1737[5] and had done much to make the Ursulines' work there tolerable. Father Carotte S.J. was both chaplain of the Royal Hospital and spiritual director and chaplain of the Ursulines at the time of the expulsion.[6] The feelings of the nuns at the departure of their counselors and best friends may be better imagined than described. A new government was bringing uncertainty, and the departure of the Jesuits stood to deprive the religious of support and guidance. But with trust in God and strong determination, they could and did adjust to the changed circumstances. Election of a new superior was necessary and Father Dagobert and Father Prosper, Capuchins, were nominated April 11, 1764. After Devotion of the Forty Hours, customary before an election, Father Dagobert was unanimously chosen as superior.[7] The Capuchins of the 1760's had attained, through no effort on their part, the post which their predecessors had coveted.

Although the news of the cession of Louisiana to Spain leaked into the colony, French officials did not make a transfer until after M. d'Abbadie received the king's letter dated April 21, 1764. Louis XV's expressed sentiments in no way betrayed how little he really cared for his subjects in Louisiana:

I hope for the prosperity and tranquility of the
inhabitants of the colony of Louisiana and I promise myself

in consequence of the friendship and affection of his Catholic Majesty that he will be so good as to give orders to his Governor and to all other officials employed in his service in the said colony and city of New Orleans that the ecclesiastics and the religious...continue their duties and enjoy their rights, privileges, and exemptions that have been conferred on them by the titles of their establishments...that the inhabitants may be kept and maintained in their possessions: that they may be confirmed in the possession of their property according to the concessions which have been made to them by the Governors and the *Ordonnateurs* of the Colony, and that the said concessions may be accounted and reputed confirmed by his Catholic Majesty, although they had not yet been by me.[8]

Antonio de Ulloa, Governor of Loisiana 1766-1768. Courtesy Historic New Orleans Collection, 1991.34.12.

In his instructions to d'Abbadie more than a year earlier Louis XV left the religious communities established in Louisiana "free to live under the English or the Spanish rule."[9] The colonists did not wish to be handed over to the King of Spain. They were far from France and were attached to their sovereign. They wished to remain Frenchmen and sent Jean Milhet to intercede with Louis XV in their behalf. In Paris Milhet met Bienville, who regretted the dismemberment of Louisiana and grieved to see the last remnant of it transferred to Spain. In vain Bienville went with Milhet to see the Duke de Choiseul, who told them that the Treaty of Fontainebleau could not be annulled.[10]

By January of 1765 Spain had still not taken possession of the colony, and there was great unrest and dissension among the colonists over the prospect of Spanish rule. M. d'Abbadie died on February 4, 1765, and Captain Charles Philippe Aubry, commanding officer of the garrison, succeeded him. King Charles III appointed a scientist, Don Antonio de Ulloa, as governor in May 1765, but he did not formally take possession of Louisiana in the name of the Spanish King until January 20, 1767. Governor Ulloa was a scholar and cultivated person, but his threatening manner and inflexible personality made him unpopular. He made the Balize his headquarters and issued orders through Captain Aubry in New Orleans.

The Spanish governor's absence and apparent arrogance offended the former French subjects. The Superior Council in particular was irritated by the governor's absence. Ulloa issued commercial restrictions forbidding trade with the French West Indies, and this caused further resentment and discontent. A rebellious attitude continued to grow within the colony, and the Superior Council and governor were at odds on almost every issue. Finally on October 27, 1768, a mob took control of the city, and townspeople drew up a petition to expel the Governor for presentation to the Superior Council. Nicolas Chauvin de Lafrénière urged the Council at a meeting October 28 to order Governor Ulloa to leave. Despite some opposition, the measure was adopted.[11] Captain Aubry, who favored the Spanish governor, protested against the measure, but advised Ulloa to retire with his wife to a French ship in the river. Much to the governor's consternation the cable holding the ship was released or cut on the morning of November 1, so the governor and his wife chose to sail to the Balize. He did not return to New Orleans and subsequently sailed back to Spain.

As soon as Abbé de l'Isle Dieu[12] learned of the course of events in Louisiana, he counseled submission to the Spanish authority. The Abbé warned the colonists that if they did not yield willingly, their new masters would resort to force of arms "which would leave on one side the seed of discontent and insubordination and on the other a lack of confidence that it would be difficult to restore later."[13] This advice came too late.

Ulloa's departure and his bitter complaints against the colonists coupled with the revolt of 1768 against Spanish rule entailed tragic consequences. Charles III dispatched General Alexander O'Reilly,[14] an Irish Roman Catholic, to Louisiana with orders to crush the rebellion and reestablish Spanish control in the colony. O'Reilly arrived at the Balize on July 23, 1769, with twenty-two ships as well as cavalry, artillery, and infantry amounting to about two thousand men. He detailed Francisco Bouligny to notify Captain Aubry that he had come to take possession of the colony in the name of the King of Spain.[15] The leaders of the insurrection hastened to placate the new governor, and Lafrénière was among the first to go down-river to meet the new governor. O'Reilly received all graciously, but made no promises. The general and his imposing array of forces entered New Orleans with great ceremony, and it is curious that the event is noted by only a simple entry in the register of the Cathedral.

> The tenth[16] of the month of August in the year 1769, at twelve o'clock sharp, the entry of General Orrely [O'Reilly] and taking possession of Louisiana by that General in the name of Spain.[17]

After hearing from the Abbé de l'Isle Dieu, the religious of New Orleans dutifully participated in the fanfare surrounding the arrival of the General and the disembarkation of his troops. After the troops marched in parade formation in the elaborately decorated square, the Capuchin Fathers met General O'Reilly at the doors of the parish church and escorted him to the sanctuary. Those assembled sang the "Te Deum" and recited other prayers prescribed for joyful events. The Ursuline annals record that "Their small bell added its very modest voice to that of the parish church to acclaim their new lord."[18] Given their French origins it must have been disconcerting to the religious to see the white flag of France descend, but in support of peaceful negotiations they "prayed in their poor chapel, and begged the God of armies to appease the just anger of the newcomers, and to turn all to His greater glory."[19]

Shortly after the arrival of General O'Reilly, Captain Aubry reported on the activities of individuals involved in the recent revolt, and the chief insurgents were arrested while they were attending a reception at the governor's house.[20] The accused persons belonged to the most influential families of the city. Their wives had been educated by the Ursulines and their children were enrolled at the convent.[21] Five of the leaders[22] were condemned to death, and their sentences were carried out in the yard of the barracks which adjoined the courtyard of the Ursulines.

Don Allessandro O'Reilly, Captain General and Governor of Louisiana, 1769-1770. Courtesy Historic New Orleans Collection, 1991.34.14.

What a moment of anguish for the religious! .... They could hear all that took place. They heard the Spanish army form itself in the square. At three o'clock in the afternoon, the discharges of the executioners shook the windows of the Ursuline chapel where the relatives of the victims had taken refuge.[23]

Having accomplished his *tour de force*, O'Reilly turned his attention to the establishment of a Spanish form of government as King Charles III had ordered. Louisiana became a dependency of Cuba, and that caused some dissatisfaction in the colony. O'Reilly substituted the *Cabildo*, which had been the traditional form of municipal government in Spain and in the Spanish colonies in the New World, for the Superior Council as the governing body. He also smoothed the transition by leaving many of the principal offices of Church and State with Frenchmen in charge. The Bishop of Santiago de Cuba was designated as the spiritual director of ecclesiastical affairs. Reverend Doctor Don Santiago José de Echevarria Felguezua was named "Bishop of the Catholic Church in the City of Santiago, of Jamaica, and of the Provinces of Jamaica, and of the Provinces of Florida and Louisiana."[24]

The transfer of Louisiana to Spain must have created apprehension among the Ursulines, whom the Company of the Indies and the French monarchy had supported in their missionary work for over forty years. A principal concern was whether they could expect future recruits from France. No sisters had come from France since before the Seven Years' War, and the ranks of the New Orleans community were shrinking. Abbé de l'Isle Dieu had six religious whom he could have sent in the spring of 1769, but the unsettled conditions in both France and Louisiana prevented their departure.[25] There were no Ursuline communities in Spain, and the New Orleans group considered France their only source for replacements.[26]

Despite their uncertainties about the future, the nuns continued with their educational and nursing responsibilities. Indeed the hospital duties would continue for only a few more years. In 1762 the community had refused the request of Nicolas Chauvin Foucault, the Intendant, to take charge of a second hospital ward "the sooner to return the whole to the King."[27] Three years later, a report by Abbé de l'Isle Dieu on

July 5, 1765, indicated that he expected a change in the hospital's administration. He said, "In the event that the Court of Spain should judge proper to withdraw it [sic] from the hospital the community [Ursulines] could keep the pharmacy for the preparation of the remedies and medicines..." In the same report he referred to the necessity of arranging a method of payment for the other services the nuns were providing saying, "...but it would be a question of determining what the Court of Spain would judge proper to give them for the different employments to facilitate the means and ability to renew themselves with subjects..."[28]

Whether the Court of Spain or the religious themselves took the initiative in the withdrawal of the sisters from the Royal Hospital cannot be determined with certainty. Over fifty years after the fact, F.X. Martin, one of the first historians of Louisiana, wrote:

> The attendance of the Ursuline Nuns in the hospital, according to a bull they had obtained from the pope, was dispensed with; the service of these ladies had become merely nominal, being confined to the daily attendance of two nuns, during the visit of the king's physician. Having noted his prescription, they withdrew, contenting themselves with sending from the dispensary, which was kept in the convent, the medicines he had ordered.[29]

No record of a papal document dispensing the Ursulines from hospital duty has been found, and it may be that Martin misconstrued as factual the Abbé's suggestion that the Ursulines be retained to prepare medicines. A letter to the King of Spain from Mother Thérèse St. Xavier Farjon in 1800 states: "In 1770, Count O'Reilly took from the Ursulines the care of the hospital."[30] Twenty-five years later New Orleans Bishop Luis Peñalver y Cardenas wrote to the Spanish minister José Antonio Caballero: "When Count O'Reilly took possession of this province for our sovereign in 1770, he took from the religious the care of the hospital."[31] Three years later Governor Salcedo supplied a few more details.

> During the French domination the Ursuline Religious were here, as in other parts of France, in charge of the Military Hospital, but Count O'Reilly very wisely dis-

charged them of this obligation. His Majesty approved this step in view of the greater propriety, and of the benefit that the Institute would derive by having all the religious exclusively devoted to the teaching of both boarders and day students.[32]

The single brief note found in the convent archives suggests that the religious may have asked to be relieved of the hospital.

The first of the year 1770 we have given up the care of the hospital on account of the small number of religious who remain to us and the difficulty that there is to have any sent from France. Since the taking of possession by the Spanish of the country, ceded by the King of France, and the prohibition of commerce, there is very much difficulty and little hope of obtaining subjects to aid us. We hope that God who has commenced this mission will not abandon it, since it is so useful to this colony for the instruction of youth, to which we now limit ourselves, praying Our Lord that He deign to give it ever more and more His holy blessing.[33]

After 1770 the religious devoted their energy and resources exclusively to the instruction of girls and young women in the colony, regardless of their class. After receiving instruction from the nuns, young women were regularly sent to the St. Louis parish church to be baptized. Records show that many were slaves.[34]

The change from French to Spanish governance also affected the Ursulines' property. In 1764 Louis XV had instructed M. d'Abaddie to make an inventory of the king's property so that after the Spanish Commissioner had been put in "possession of the structures and Civil buildings," an evaluation could be made and the French king reimbursed by the Spanish monarch.[35] The inventory was completed on April 2, 1766, and included the buildings of the religious, some of which were in very bad condition.

There is the ground of the convent of the Ursuline

Ladies, religious nurses, containing fifty *toises* frontage on the river by one hundred twenty in depth on which are the principal building of the religious, two stories of brick, their parlor, the kitchen of brick, with its pits, a building serving for a chapel both for the religious and for the hospital, a small building serving as a free school for the day pupils, and a building of two stories in brick but uninhabitable on account of age, formerly used for the lodging and school of the boarders, another old building used as a dining room both for the boarders and for the orphans, another old building serving as a laundry, another used for a bake-house, and the latrines, a pigeon house, some cabins for the negroes, a garden and a cabin within for the gardener.[36]

This was only a general inventory and did not include an appraisal of the buildings. Another inventory with estimates was made the following year, but the buildings of the Ursulines still were not evaluated.[37] Governor Ulloa delayed signing the inventories, and they were still unsigned when he left Louisiana for Cuba in 1768. When Governor O'Reilly took charge, he insisted that the work be done over and that a reduction be made in the appraisals.[38] While this inventory was being prepared, M. Bobé, *ordonnateur*, asked to have the "buildings of the King, convent, etc. on the ground of the Ursuline Religious" evaluated. O'Reilly granted his request but indicated that the property had been used for charitable purposes and could continue to be used in that manner.[39] M. Bobé was not satisfied and wrote to the Duc de Praslin, Minister of the Marine:

I have suspended this work [of evaluating the buildings of the Ursulines] until the reception of your orders, taking the liberty to state that the King alone has supported the expense of their erection, repair, and maintenance, and that it is doubtful if the Religious will remain here, since there are no members of their Order in Spain.[40]

A month later Bobé again urged the evaluation of the Ursulines' buildings.[41]

What was his motivation? Governor O'Reilly apparently felt that the convent belonged to the sisters, and he did not want the Spanish government to have to pay for it.

Governor O'Reilly gave Bobé and his associates permission to evaluate the property, but made it clear that the members of the religious community were its owners and the buildings were of no use to the king. Bobé then set the value of the buildings at over 132,894 livres. His final report noted that Governor O'Reilly refused to include the convent as property of the king, since the religious were "useful to the colony for the education of youth."[42] O'Reilly explained his decision to the Spanish government:

> It is a pious work founded and given to the said Nuns, by His Most Christian Majesty in the year 1727 and experience has shown how very little income it has produced and how much good can be expected from it. Thus it seems to me that no payment for this building should be made, but that the evaluation should be made, and that I should explain to your excellency how I understand the matter.[43]

Although Governor O'Reilly was friendly to the Ursulines, even to visiting them in their cloister occasionally,[44] he did not adequately assess their necessities. While he did assist them in obtaining a salary from the Spanish government, his recommendations were for only one hundred twenty pesos a year for the same six religious as had been contracted 40 years earlier. He asked that thirty pesos a year be paid for each orphan housed at the convent, however, only twelve orphans would be financed under his plan versus the thirty previously supported by the French.[45] Why he limited the number of orphans to be cared for is not known. One would hope from the petitions Governor O'Reilly sent to Spain on behalf of the Ursulines that he appreciated their efforts in educating young women and girls in both the Christian faith, as well as in language and mathematical skills. But O'Reilly was faced with the enormous task upon his arrival in Louisiana of balancing church and state needs. He commissioned a survey of the essentials needed by the church in the colony, but unfortunately did not implement the recommendations. Governor

O'Reilly returned to Spain in October, 1770, and left the administration of the colony to Luis de Unzaga y Amezaga, colonel of the regiment of Havana, Cuba.

The change in government from France to Spain had no effect on the Capuchins in New Orleans. Father Dagobert, the superior, resided at the St. Louis parish church, assisted by Father Prosper, chaplain of the Ursulines, and Father Ferdinand, chaplain of the hospital.[46] There were four other French Capuchins in the colony,[47] but the seven men were taxed to provide church ministry throughout Louisiana. Abbé de l'Isle Dieu had expressed his anxieties regarding the spiritual life of residents of the colony in his letter of July 5, 1765.

That which afflicts me above all is the almost total deprivation of spiritual help in which this poor unhappy colony finds itself. I see there only four[48] Capuchins of whom two are infirm and too old to fulfill the duties of their ministry. It is unfortunate that as long as Spain is not pleased with the colonists it will not hasten to procure for them French missionaries, and it will not be possible nor permitted to send them until she [Spain] asks it.[49]

Shortly after taking office Governor Unzaga forwarded a report on ecclesiastical affairs to officials in Cuba. This report, together with the information previously received from Father Dagobert and General O'Reilly, evidently convinced Bishop Echevarria and the Spanish officials that additional priests were essential if the spiritual needs of the colonists were to be met. The bishop accordingly arranged for several Spanish Capuchins to enter the Louisiana Mission. The first group, four friars and their superior, Father Cirillo de Barcelona, arrived at New Orleans[50] July 19, 1772. Father Cirillo presented his credentials to Governor Unzaga and took up residence with the French Capuchins. There was some apprehension as to whether the French and Spanish friars would be compatible. Father Cirillo was an austere man with a vigorous personality and a flair for reform. He believed in strict adherence to Church law and the Capuchin rule.

Conditions in Louisiana shocked and scandalized Father Cirillo.

But although much had been neglected in the colony, his lack of missionary experience influenced his reaction to the situation. Father Cirillo was demanding and measured others by his own strict standards, a standard to which the French Capuchins did not conform. After the long separation from their home monastery and with no supervision from superiors, they had considerably relaxed their rule. Less than three weeks after his arrival Father Cirillo penned Bishop Echevarria an indictment of the religious and of the moral conditions as they appeared to him. His criticisms were directed at the French Capuchins rather than at the colonists in general.

> The people of this province are in general religiously disposed, and seem anxious for the salvation of their souls. They observe a profound silence during the divine worship.... With regard to the women, they are more honest than in Spain, and live more in accordance with the precepts of the Church. There are some small things in the morals and in the religious observances of these people, which might be better, but time will remedy these trifling evils.[51]

Having momentarily disposed of "these trifling evils," he went on to denounce the French priests, whom he considered unworthy of the title of Capuchins. He then turned his attention to the Ursulines:

> I cannot give you any information on these ladies if it is not that they live as they have always done, without being cloistered, and as if they were not religious at all. They have for confessor Father Prosper, seventy-two years of age, strong, robust, and capable of directing them. As for the violations of the rules and discipline, I will say nothing.[52]

Father Cirillo had been in New Orleans less than three weeks when he described the Ursulines. Since he was not fluent in the French language, one wonders from whom he acquired his information in such short time. Why did he describe the nuns as not cloistered? The Ursulines had observed cloister from the very beginning of their work in the city.

Did he make the charge because the nuns had formerly worked in the hospital? Or because they were obliged to cross the court yard in front of the monastery to go to the church? Governor Unzaga in a letter to the Bishop of Havana a month earlier had spoken of the Ursuline superior as being cloistered.[53] What applied to the superior undoubtedly applied to the other members of the community.

Far from reprimanding the nuns, Bishop Echevarria showed only compassion for them in orders issued three months later. He instructed those concerned with the welfare of the sisters to do all they could to alleviate their distress.

> Attend to the spiritual and temporal welfare of those poor Ursuline Religious, truly worthy of our esteem. Their institute causes us to look upon them as coadjutors of our ministry. The meager resources of their convent make us pity them. Their strict observance edifies us, and everything obliges us to commend them to our vicars, that they devote themselves to their relief, and do not cease thinking of ways of furnishing it to them, while for our part we carry out the ideas we have formed in their favor. Take care that they always have a vicar capable of directing them with ability, and do not omit appointing them each four months extraordinary confessors as is provided, advising us before hand of the persons in order that they may have our approbation.[54]

About a year later Bishop Echevarria wrote to Mother St. Jacques Landelle:

> Reverend Mother, you may be assured that the hopes you manifest of finding in me the counsels of a tender and compassionate father will not be in vain. The regularity of your community in keeping the observance and the small resources that you have to supply your needs have given birth in my heart to a true and sincere affection which causes me to act as favorably toward you as my means permit.. .. I appoint him [Father Cirillo] vicar of the convent in place of Father Prosper. His sound judgment,

his learning, and his piety render him suitable to direct a <u>community as regular as yours</u>.[55]

These letters are significant, for they indicate that the bishop viewed the Ursuline community as conforming with the regulations of the Church and their order.

In his instructions of November 12, 1772, Bishop Echevarria indicated that he was considering some plan for the Ursulines of New Orleans. His proposal once made was startling. The bishop it seemed wished to transfer the Ursulines from Louisiana to Cuba. Some twenty years before, authorities in Cuba had asked that an Ursuline be sent from New Orleans to create a new foundation in Havana. At that time Abbé de l'Isle Dieu did not favor the proposal and wrote to the Bishop of Quebec, saying he did not endorse the suggestion, but would at least investigate it.[56] When the earlier proposal was made the Ursulines had too few members for the work they were already doing, and they were trying to obtain additional religious from France.[57] The project was abandoned. Bishop Echevarria did not revive the former plan, as he wished to transfer the entire community from New Orleans to Havana. He made the proposal in a letter to Marques de Grimaldi on July 31, 1773. Grimaldi favored the project and thought that it deserved the king's approval. He advised the bishop to send a petition to Charles III of Spain through the minister of the Indies.[58]

Echevarria wrote directly to the king. The letter is interesting in that it refutes Father Cirillo's charges and reveals the bishop's conception of conditions in New Orleans—conditions of which he had no first hand knowledge. The bishop began by stating that his aim, now that Louisiana was part of his diocese, was to have religion "flourish" in the colony as it did in all the countries under the king's rule. He then spoke of his concern for the Ursulines, who deserved to be looked upon with the "same tenderness as a father looks upon his unfortunate children." He called their poverty to the king's attention and noted that it cost the royal treasury 120 piastras a year in support for the nuns (20 piastras each) and the orphans (30 each). Continuing, he described numerous difficulties related to the nuns—their former convent needed to be rebuilt and would be expensive, the orphans had been reduced to twelve instead of thirty, they used priests as their directors and the priests were needed elsewhere, and they had few recruits to swell their ranks.

The bishop then suggested to the king that all of the Ursulines in New Orleans be transferred to Havana, where he had a college which could be used to educate girls, along with funds to support the nuns. He indicated that the upper class citizens would send their daughters to be educated if there were capable mistresses to teach and care for the young women. Echevarria offered to provide a dwelling for the nuns and revenues to cover expenses. He noted, "...there they lack everything and at Havana they would have all things in abundance." He concluded that, "there remains nothing to be desired by this city or by my zeal except letters patent for a public school for young women where they could learn to become perfect wives, economical mothers, submissive daughters, and Christian examples."[59]

Negotiations relative to the transfer moved along at a dilatory pace. It was three years before the bishop's letter was finally taken up on April 23, 1777, by the Spanish monarch with his council, only to be delayed further by a request for additional information.[60] When the Cabildo of Justice and Administration met in ordinary session in New Orleans, August 22, 1777, it was presented with a sealed envelop addressed by the king to them. The contents included "a representation that the Bishop of Cuba made to His Majesty concerning the removal of the Ursuline Nuns of this City to Havana, Cuba, and a letter from His Majesty referring to said removal." The communication was read, and the officials agreed to file it and give an answer at a later date.[61] Two months later on October 11, 1777, the letters were again read and filed,[62] but Cabildo records do not reveal any subsequent action.

One may conjecture that the officials of Louisiana were unwilling to sacrifice their only school for girls in the interest of Havana. Bernardo de Galvez had succeeded Unzaga as governor of Louisiana on January 28, 1777. The wife of Governor Galvez was Félicité de St. Maxent d'Estrehan, a former pupil of the Ursulines. It is likely that she used her influence with her husband to prevent the transfer of the nuns. Like loyal Ursuline alumnae everywhere, she would not have wished to deprive the girls of Louisiana of education. It is doubtful that the Ursulines themselves desired the transfer, despite the glowing picture painted by the bishop. Hardship and privations had not affected their work in New Orleans. In addition the Ursulines were French, and they would have been extremely handicapped in their teaching by the Spanish language spoken in Havana.

Long before the letters of the bishop and the king reached the Council, many of the economic conditions cited by the bishop had been remedied. When the bishop noted that the convent was reduced to a "wretched cabin", it would appear that he was exaggerating. Was he talking about the 1734 building which was left standing after the second convent was built? Among the buildings the Ursulines listed in an inventory of 1766 was a two-story brick building, uninhabitable due to age, which had formerly been used as a school and lodging for the boarders.[63] The convent proper at the time of the letter was in bad condition, but not beyond repair. In 1773 the walls between the rooms of the convent were cracked open from "top to bottom". After examining the entire building contractors decided that the walls were not strong enough to support the tile roof, and that it should be replaced by a roof of shingles.[64] This was a satisfactory solution, as when the question arose twenty years later as to why the tile roof had been removed, no mention was made of the condition of the walls.[65]

The bishop's plan to transfer the Ursulines to Cuba was never implemented, and it would be twenty five years before the Ursulines would benefit from the Bishop of Cuba's generosity. He continued to show interest in the New Orleans community, and a practical expression of his appreciation for their work was his effort to secure additional religious for their community.

CHAPTER 9

The French-Spanish Blend

Under Spanish governance the Ursulines looked for additional sources to swell the ranks of their New Orleans community. It is quite probable that they appealed to Bishop Echevarria for suggestions of persons interested in the religious life, for in the summer of 1778 he sent three young women from Cuba that he thought had vocations to the religious life. They were well received at the convent and gave promise of becoming members of the community, a prospect that pleased the bishop. He wrote, "I have experienced very great pleasure and sincere satisfaction on learning that the three young ladies[1] whom I have sent to you have conformed so well to your desires...." Apparently, since the proposal to have the Ursulines transfer to Havana had been dropped, the bishop was eager to have the New Orleans convent well staffed. He indicated that if more religious were needed, the superior should contact him through the Governor and the vicar-general, and "I shall not have any difficulty to procure them for you."[2]

The Bishop was faithful to his promise, and during the next few years several of the young women who entered the novitiate were of Spanish lineage. The first two Spanish recruits to be professed arrived in New Orleans from Havana in August, 1778, for a four month residence in the boarding school. On December 8, 1778,[3] they entered the novitiate. Father Cirillo gave Sister St. Monica Ramos who was thirty years old and Sister St. Rita de Castillo who was nineteen their religious habits on January 25, 1779,[4] and with the authorization of Bishop Echevarria both made their profession two years later.[5] Of the twelve religious professed between the years 1781 and 1785, nine were Spanish and came from Cuba at the suggestion of Bishop Echevarria.

The Rule of Paris provided that young religious ordinarily remained in the novitiate for three years after their profession to complete their training. In 1745, the chapter decided that this point of the Rule, which had been dispensed with in the early years, should be observed again in the New Orleans community.[6] The community chapter agreed on January 31, 1782 to dispense Sister St. Monica and Sister St. Rita from this regulation as a special favor for them alone, since they were the first professed Ursulines of Spain. Immediately after profession they were given the right of active and passive vote. The chapter minutes make it clear that this exception was done with the permission of the vicar-general, Father Cirillo,[7] and was not to be a precedent for the future.

During the period the young women from Cuba were entering the community, some of the older French religious died. This gave rise to some concern that French traditions would die out in the community, and the spirit change unless religious imbued with old world monastic traditions could be secured.[8] Mother St. Jacques Landelle, who was serving her fifth triennial as Superior, expressed her fears to Father Aubert in 1785, when he was returning to France. Father Aubert therefore went to the flourishing monastery of Pont-St.-Esprit[9] in search of Ursuline volunteers for the Louisiana mission. This community generously consented that three of its members go to New Orleans.

As had happened in the past, difficulties and delays ensued during the waiting period. One of the volunteers, Sister Ste. Félicité, found a small statue of the Blessed Virgin in the attic of the monastery in the middle of some abandoned objects. It pained her to see the statue cast aside, and extricating it from the attic, she implored the Blessed Mother's assistance. "Good Mother, if you will quickly remove these obstacles, I shall carry this image of you to New Orleans where I promise to do all in my power to have you honored."[10] The next day good news awaited the missionaries. A Jesuit friend of the community had obtained permission from the King of Spain for the three sisters to depart for Louisiana.[11] Sister Ste. Félicité kept her promise, and the small statue of the Blessed Mother, fondly called "Sweetheart", has had a place of honor in the Ursuline convents of New Orleans for over two hundred years.

As was customary the Bishop of Uzès gave the sisters a "letter of obedience," a monastic instruction allowing a religious to relocate. But the letter for Sister St. Xavier and her companions is more than a letter of obedience; it was a summary of the preliminary activities connected with their departure and contained details that are especially relevant in view of later occurrences. The bishop began by commending the religious for volunteering to assist the New Orleans missionaries. He indicated that letters from Father Aubert, a former missionary in Louisiana, and

This small statue of the Blessed Mother, fondly called "Sweetheart" was brought from France and has had a place of honor in the Ursuline Convents for over two hundred years. Photo by Sister Jacqueline Toppino, O.S.U.

other letters which Reverend Mother Barral, the superior of Pont-St.-Esprit, had received between 1783 and 1785 confirmed that the New Orleans community was performing a meritorious service. M. Delaire, the vice-consul of Spain at La Rochelle who was in charge of the business of the religious of New Orleans, had verified that he was to furnish the expenses of the journey, as well as any passports or permissions from the Courts of France or Spain.

In the lengthy "letter of obedience" the Bishop of Uzès gave the religious permission in flowing language, recognizing that delays had been quite extensive. He carefully recorded that a letter sent to M. le Comte de Florida Blanca, minister of Spain, to M. d'Arenda, ambassador of Spain at the Court of France, on November 25, 1784, gave permission for the nuns' passage from the court of Spain. The bishop specified that they were to live under the orders of the Bishop of Havana and the superiors of the convent. He reserved the right, subject to the approval of the kings of France and Spain to recall them if they were needed in France. Finally he appointed Father Joseph Gabriel Chambon de la Tour, superior of the Missions of Sisteron, as their confessor.[12]

Since all ecclesiastical and royal approvals had been given to the French sisters, they anticipated a warm welcome in New Orleans. But in fact the reception by the New Orleans community was quite different. Reverend Mother St. Jacques Landelle, who had originally pleaded for the assistance from France, was no longer Superior. Sister Antonia de St. Monica Ramos, one of the first two religious to come from Cuba,

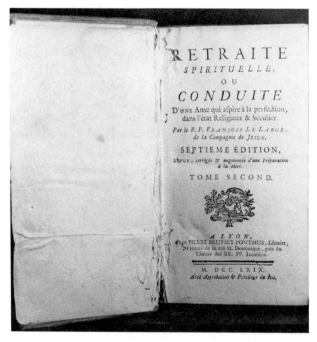

Retraite Spirituelle ou Conduite, 1763, book used by the Ursuline nuns.
Courtesy Ursuline Archives & Museum. Photo by Sr. Jacqueline Toppino O.S.U.

had been elected Superior in her place.[13] The arrival of the French sisters created a conflict within the community, and the annals do not make it clear whether it was related to Mother St. Monica or to the clergy. But one annalist writing years later suspected that the Spanish speaking sisters were not happy to have additional French religious join them.[14] The community assembled on February 12, 1786, the day after the arrival, and Mother St. Monica informed the three religious that they would take their rank after the last professed nun of the house. Bishop Cirillo, who had been named Auxiliary Bishop to the Bishop of Cuba, had given these orders.[15] In addition the French nuns would have neither active nor passive vote until four years from the date of their arrival. This amounted to punishing the religious for leaving their convent in France for work in New Orleans, but they submitted to the bishop's orders.[16]

Complications continued for the French sisters four months later when the community was again assembled to hear new orders from Bishop Echevarria. The French Ursulines were to remain at the convent as guests until the King of Spain gave orders regarding their status.[17] The bishop indicated that he would never have given his consent to the nuns' arrival without the king's permission. The Bishop of Uzès had clearly stated that permission had been granted by the King of Spain.[18] Bishop Cirillo should have been given the letter of obedience from Uzès, and Governor Miró wrote explicitly that the three religious had come "with the permission of His Majesty."[19] While all the various orders were circulating between bishops, courts, and local officials, the three religious must have felt oppressed and unwelcome. Bishop Echevarria also criticized Father Chambon de la Tour for bringing the French sisters, whose arrival had "caused discord."[20] The Spanish clergy obviously did not want any additional French influences in New Orleans.

When Mother St. Jacques learned that Bishop Echevarria disapproved of her soliciting the recruits from France without his permission, she wrote and asked for his pardon. He indicated that he would "forgive her in view of her age," but no more French subjects could be received to off-set the Spanish religious in the community. Alleging that the income of the community was inadequate, the bishop forbade Father Sedella to permit any young lady to receive the veil in the future, "no matter to what social class she might belong."[21] Possible rivalry between the French and the Spanish nuns must have worried the bishop, as there

*Bernardo de Galvez, Governor of Louisiana, 1777-1783. Courtesy
Historic New Orleans Collection, 1991.34.15.*

seems to be no other reason for him to have put such restrictions on
the order. The nuns considered the limitations drastic, and it was a special
source of grief to Mother St. Jacques. Her original intention in seeking
recruits from France had been to increase the size of the community,
while at the same time encourage strict observance of monastic tradition
through the influence of European nuns.

In addition to the ecclesiastical politics related to this matter,
colonial politics also became involved. The bishop rendered an account
of the events, and Charles III approved of the nuns remaining as guests
in New Orleans until he could have an investigation made.[22] A request
for facts was addressed to Estevan Miró, who had succeeded Count de
Galvez as Governor of Louisiana. Governor Miró expatiated on his reluctance
to furnish such a report, but added that he would do so lest he be

Esteban Miro, Commandant 1781-1785, and Governor of Louisiana, 1785-1791. Coutresy Historic New Orleans Collection, 1991.34.16.

censured for neglect of duty. He then proceeded to launch a denunciation of Mother St. Jacques, saying that she alone had instigated the recruitment, and neither government nor church authorities knew about it in advance. His letter indicates the strong rivalries between French and Spanish colonists.

> One idea alone dictated this: that the religious of French nationality should be greater than that of the Spanish in order to <u>outnumber</u> them in the elections. She [Mother St. Jacques] had no other excuse than a conversation with Count de Galvez in 1777 at the beginning of his government. In the course of this conversation he manifested to the above mentioned Superior how much he desired to have religious come from France.[23]

Miró continued in his report to say that Galvez had been fearful that there would not be enough nuns to teach the girls, and that he had been unaware that eleven nuns from Havana were available. It was Miró's opinion that the increase in French religious would delay the teaching of Spanish to the girls. Because the parents desired that the girls learn French, and because the majority of nuns were French, the Spanish language would be neglected. Miró then went on to criticize the nuns' confessor Father Chambon de la Tour for advising the French recruits to take status as guests of the community rather than agree to have the lowest rank and no vote as ordered by the auxiliary bishop. He conceded in ending the report that both bishops had given permission for the nuns to remain as guests, and that Father de la Tour had won the esteem of people in the city.

The people's high regard for Father Chambon de la Tour meant nothing to the king or hierarchy, and he was peremptorily ordered to leave the country.[24] The Spanish crown did reimburse him for the expenses he had incurred on the journey. He was allotted 3264 silver reales for his personal needs between February of 1786 and March of 1787 and was given 800 silver reales for the return trip. This was considered adequate, as he had lived at the pastor's house while in the city, and the Ursulines had contributed 100 pesos for the trip and a slave to assist him while in the city.[25] The generosity of the Ursulines to Father Chambon was expressive of their gratitude for his accompanying the French sisters.

How did Mother St. Xavier and her two companions occupy themselves while they remained as "guests" at the convent? Governor Miró in March, 1787, wrote that they were teaching students, and in spite of the nationalism that tinctured his outlook, he added a few words of praise. "Even though I have seen them only a few times they seem to me to be ladies of education and talent, and if it were not for the already mentioned inconvenience of increasing the number of French Religious, their coming would be appreciated."[26]

But Sisters St. Xavier, Félicité, and André were in New Orleans to stay. The king ordered that they should be received into the community without discrimination, take their rank in the community according to the date of their profession, and have both active and passive vote.[27] Mother St. Monica called the community together as soon as she received the order from the king, and the three sisters were formally received.

The three religious then completed their affiliation by making the fourth vow, the vow of instruction.[28] It was providential that King Charles III did not order Sister St. Xavier and her companions to return to France. Had the Ursulines of New Orleans been able to foresee the future in 1787, they would have marveled at the strength that these three women would give to their community in future years. How insignificant Mother St. Jacques would have considered the censures and humiliations it took to procure them.

During the mid-1780's financing for the needs of the community continued with the help of the Spanish government. Mother St. Jacques Landelle had appealed to the Spanish crown while she was superior for additional funds, requesting that the allotment of ten pesos a month be increased to twenty for six religious, and that the allotment of thirty pesos for each of twelve orphans be raised to sixty. She also requested repairs for the run-down church and construction of a brick wall to separate the monastery from the hospital. She asked that a priest be appointed to say Mass and to attend to the spiritual needs of the community.[29] The king referred her petition to colonial officials, but by the summer of 1785 Governor Galvez[30] had been appointed to the vice-royalty of Mexico. Since he still retained the captain generalship of Louisiana, he appealed to the king from Mexico to grant the requests because of the good that the Ursulines provided to the general public.[31] The king inquired of Governor Estevan Miró and Intendant Martin Navarro as to whether these requests were justified, and empowered them to act on them, "always being prudently economical in demands on the royal treasury."[32]

Miró and Navarro studied the petition carefully and decided because of the high cost of provisions to assign eighteen pesos a month to each of six religious and fifty pesos a year for each of twelve orphans living and educated at the convent. A priest had already been appointed as chaplain from among five priests assigned to the parish in 1784. Early in 1785 the officials approved the construction of a brick wall between the convent and the hospital, since the religious had frequently been annoyed by the troops.[33] The king[34] ordered the wall built, but the work was not begun until May 1789.[35] The delay came in the wake of the greatest disaster that had ever befallen New Orleans.

On Good Friday, March 21, 1788 the home of Don Vincente José Nuñez on Chartres Street caught fire from candles on a family

*Picture of Our Lady of Prompt Succor with scenes from the great
fire of New Orleans and the Battle of New Orleans below her feet.
Ursuline Archives & Museum. Photo by Sr. Jacqueline Toppino,
O.S.U.*

altar. Fanned by a strong south wind the flames spread rapidly, and
within a few hours 856 buildings were reduced to a charred rubble.
Among the areas and buildings affected were the business section, residences
of prominent citizens, the Capuchin presbyter, the Cabildo, the arsenal,
the public prison, and the historic St. Louis Church. An eye witness
described the actions of the Ursulines, who feared the worst.

> The Ursuline Religious, expecting momentarily the
> destruction of the monastery, had collected some precious
> objects and were assembled at the carriage gate, ready
> to abandon the cloister and to fly to the country.[36]

While they waited at the gate a strange phenomenon occurred. "Contrary to all natural laws and in spite of the wind," the witness said, "the flames receded."[37] The inhabitants then put forth every effort to save the row of buildings nearest the river and finally succeeded in extinguishing the fire.[38] Although the convent was spared, a rental property on Bourbon Street burned.[39] The loss would add to the nuns financial difficulties, as the house had rented for forty piastres a month.

At the request of Father Antonio de Sedella (Pére Antoine), a major gift was given to the Ursulines during this period by Don Andres Almonester y Rojas,[40] one of the great benefactors of the Catholic Church in Louisiana. Don Almonester in 1789 had a new brick church built for the convent,[41] facing Ursulines Street but attached to the main building.[42]

Don Almonester Y Roxas built a chapel for the Ursulines.
Courtesy Archdiocese of New Orleans.

The new church was much more convenient and eliminated the need for the nuns to cross a large courtyard when going to Mass or to choir. The nuns had suffered from cold and rainy weather in winter, as well as rain and hot weather in summer.[43] The church was completed and blessed on March 19, 1787,[44] and a tablet commemorating Don Almonester's generosity was placed in the facade fronting Ursulines Street.[45] The church was dedicated to the Blessed Mother under the title of Our Lady of Victory,[46] but Don Almonester requested that the church be called Our Lady of Consolation.[47] At a meeting of the community on August 23, 1787, all consented to make the change. In gratitude they would offer a general Communion for their benefactor annually on the feast of St. Andrew, and at his death they would recite the office of the dead with three nocturnes and have a High Mass celebrated.[48] Besides building the church, Don Almonester had financed extensive repairs to the convent and erected a three room brick building[49] to serve as classrooms for the boarders.[50]

To show appreciation for these favors, the Ursulines granted Don Almonester a seat in the sanctuary of their church, at the left of the Royal Vice-Patron.[51] To this seat were attached the privileges of the incense, the kiss of peace, and a candle, all to be carried out as for the governor general.[52] Don Almonester occupied this privileged place from March, 1787, until February, 1792, when Father Theodoro Henriquez,[53] auxiliary vicar-general, verbally ordered that it be taken from him.[54] This vexed Don Almonester and "caused much scandal."[55] Several months after his order Father Henriquez questioned Mother Marguerite de St. Ignace du Liepure as to why the honor had been extended to Don Almonester.[56] In a joint letter she and Mother St. Xavier Farjon explained that Don Almonester had expressed a desire for the honor, and since the municipal council did not attend, the religious did not find it inconvenient to grant his wish.[57]

Don Almonester was proud of his honor and would not relinquish it without protest. When the privileges had not been restored at the end of two years, he appealed directly to King Charles IV.[58] In his own good time the king inquired into the matter, again asking Mother St. Ignace why it was granted. She repeated the reasons she gave in 1792 and added that Don Almonester had sent a chair for the chapel which was still at the convent. The arrangement was only to show the gratitude of the community, and then she added "the right of patronage belongs to him who has built a church, even though it be erected from the very stones of the old one."[59] Father Henriquez was recalled to Havana in June, 1793, leaving the question of patronage to Father Patricio Walsh.[60] A royal order of August 14, 1794, directed Father Walsh to restore the seat with all its privileges to Don Almonester until some other order should be given, and to report to him the reasons for the deprivation of the seat.[61] Father Walsh restored the privileged seat to Don Almonester. The official record drawn up and signed before the notary Don Estevan de Quinones is of sufficient interest to be quoted almost in entirety.

I have just received a royal order, signed at San Ildefonse, the 14 August of the present year [1794] by his Majesty... addressed to Don Andres Almonester,...relative to a seat that he has in the church of the convent of the Ursulines. His Majesty orders that, Sunday the twenty-first of this month at the High Mass celebrated at eight-thirty at which the Baron de Carondelet, Governor General of

URSULINE CHAPEL BUILT IN 1787 BY DON
ANDRES ALMONESTER

Chapel built by Don Andres Almonester in 1787 for the Ursulines, side view. Courtesy Ursuline Archives & Museum.

this Province and Royal Vice-Patron will assist, the aforementioned Don Almonester be given possession of his seat. This seat should be placed on the Epistle side, outside the sanctuary. It should consist of a seat covered with a cushion but without a *prie-Dieu*. To this seat are attached all the privileges, the incense, the kiss of peace, and the candle, in the same way as it is observed for the governor general.[62] Don Almonester will be informed of it as well as the Reverend Mother Superior of the Convent in order that she may place there the seat in accordance with the prescribed terms. I shall send her a copy of this act that she may register it in the archives of the monastery and enforce it in so far as she is concerned.[63]

Father Walsh informed Charles IV that his order to restore Don Almonester's privileges had been executed so that he might "make it known to the Supreme Royal Council of the Indies."[64] In the meantime Father Walsh ferreted out all available documents relating to the controversy, to determine whether Don Almonester had legal right or if he deserved the privilege.[65] The search revealed only two items in the convent archives relating to the controversy, and Father Walsh concluded the matter in a formal and legalistic report. In it he noted that Don Almonester had assumed the seat without royal permission, which was against the law; therefore Father Henriquez deprived him of the seat. Once the king had granted the favor of his permission, Father Walsh could concede that the church was "a very appropriate place for the celebration of the divine office," and its benefactor "deserved to obtain the grace of patronage from His Majesty."[66] The final word was left to the Supreme Council of the Indies,[67] which remained silent, leaving the liberal benefactor of the Ursulines able to enjoy his honors without disturbance until his death in 1798.[68]

This episode is a typical example of eighteenth century Spanish concern with petty detail. Against the background of the momentous problems of the Spanish empire, the incident is insignificant, yet Charles IV treated it seriously. Competition for honorific privileges was part of the culture. When Nicolas Maria Vidal became lieutenant governor in 1793 for example, he appeared at the convent to apprise Reverend Mother

St. Ignace that it would be his privilege to receive the key of the tabernacle on Holy Thursday that year. Vidal noted that this had formerly been the right of the mayor, but that was before the colony had a lieutenant governor. Mother St. Ignace in turn sought the advice of Father Henriquez,[69] who referred the matter to Governor Carondelet.[70] The Governor's opinion was that Vidal should receive the key rather than Manuel Serrano, the mayor.[71]

A few days later it was the Baron de Carondelet himself who became piqued by what he deemed a reflection on his prerogatives as Royal Vice-Patron. Like his predecessor Carondelet was a stickler for convention and demanded observance of every formality relating to his dignity as governor, especially during public church services.[72] During the celebration of Mass in the Ursuline Church on April 11, 1793, Baron

Francisco Luis Hector de Carondelet, Governor of Louisiana 1791-1797. Courtesy Historic New Orleans Collection, 1991.34.18.

179

de Carondelet was given neither incense nor the kiss of peace, honors due him as Royal Vice-Patron. After Mass he reminded Father Henriquez that pastors were to observe the ceremonies stated in the laws of the Indies.[73] Father Henriquez, also present at the Mass, noted that he too had been left out of the honors. There followed a long notarial act passed before Quinones notifying Father Luis de Quintanilla, the Capuchin assistant pastor of the Church of St. Louis and chaplain of the Ursulines, that he had been negligent in the matter of honors due to the Royal Vice-Patron and also to Father Henriquez. In the future he was to conform to the regulations laid down in the laws of the Indies.[74] The absurdity of bickering over ceremonials while serious problems existed both in the colony and in the Church seems to have eluded the civil and church leaders.

After the fire of 1788 the colony was left without a parish church, and the *fabrica* without funds to build a new one. The colonists turned to the King of Spain for a new building, and in the meantime used a chapel of the Charity Hospital,[75] built by Don Almonester. The Ursuline Church of Our Lady of Consolation was also pressed into service temporarily. A parish church, although indispensable, might be years in coming, considering the red tape that invariably obstructed action by the Spanish government. Governor Miró and Bishop Cirillo were greatly relieved when Don Almonester again came to the rescue, offering to supply the funds to erect the church if the government would reimburse him. Work was begun in March, 1789. Two years later Governor Miró notified Bishop Cirillo[76] that he had received a royal *cedula* apprising him of the birth of the *Infanta* Maria Teresa. He asked that the event be commemorated by solemn ceremonies in the churches of the province from Wednesday, July 27, to Friday, July 29. These services were celebrated in the church of the Ursulines,[77] as the parish church was not completed until December, 1794.[78]

Parishioners awaiting a new church had found the Hospital of St. Charles totally inadequate. People had the option of being tightly packed inside in the heat or standing outside in heat, cold, or rain.[79] A residence was used as a church, but it burned in a second fire that swept through the city on December 8, 1794, destroying 212 houses within three hours.[80] After that fire the Blessed Sacrament was taken from the temporary church to that of the Ursulines, which Father Patricio

Walsh designated the parish church, informing Baron de Carondelet that his chair as Governor had been transferred there.[81]

When the second fire broke out the new St. Louis Church was finished except for the main altar. The artisans were encouraged to accelerate their work, and the dedication of the parochial church, which had been elevated to the status of a cathedral, took place two days before Christmas. On Christmas Eve, a procession reminiscent of the first Eucharistic procession in Louisiana sixty years before, filed down Chartres Street. The clergy, the governor, the city officials, and prominent citizens all assembled at the Ursuline Convent and in solemn procession escorted the Blessed Sacrament to the Cathedral. Father Joaquin de Portillo, rector of the Cathedral, sang the first High Mass in the new church. Benediction and the singing of the *Te Deum* closed the ceremonies, while outside artillery thundered a salute.[82]

During the late 1780's significant ecclesiastical changes affected New Orleans. In accordance with the King of Spain's wishes, the Holy See by a Decree of September 10, 1787, divided the diocese of Santiago de Cuba and created a new bishopric for St. Christopher of Havana, Louisiana, and the Floridas. José de Trespalacios, Bishop of Puerto Rico, was appointed first bishop of the new diocese, and Bishop Cirillo became his Auxiliary, continuing in charge of Louisiana and the Floridas.[83] The diocese would become the independent diocese of Louisiana and the Floridas on April 25, 1793. Bishop Cirillo asked the Ursulines to write a testimonial in his favor shortly before the division of the diocese.[84] Mother St. Monica complied and read the following to her assembled community a few days later.

I, Sister St. Monica Ramos, Superior of the Ursuline Convent of New Orleans, with all the choir religious of my community:

We certify with all the truth and sincerity of our hearts, that the most illustrious and Most Reverend Señor Don Fray Cirillo de Barcelona, Bishop of Tricaly and Auxiliary of the Island of Cuba, has served this community with the greatest exactitude and zeal, hearing confessions and administering to the sick the holy Sacraments and also salutary exhortations, without our ever having seen or heard anything repugnant to religious modesty so fitting a father and director of souls. On the contrary his good counsels have given us great edification, urging always peace and union among us who compose this mystic and religious body. He has never failed to celebrate the Holy Sacrifice of the Mass. Since our Most Illustrious Señor Doctor Don Santiago José Echevarria y Elguezua, our worthy prelate, is obliged to leave the chair of Cuba, we would be very happy if the said Most Illustrious Señor Don Fray Cirillo would succeed him in such a high employment and dignity preferring him to any other. And in case this our certification should be presented to the royal piety of our monarch (for whose life I pray to the God of Majesties) we wish it to serve as the most humble petition that some spouses of Jesus Christ and the most humble and faithful servants of our Catholic King can make. Given in New Orleans on August 23, 1787.[85]

The Religious signed Bishop Cirillo's testimonial,[86] which was addressed to the King of Spain rather than the Holy See, as the king controlled religious affairs in Spanish America according to a papal bull of Pope Julius III of July 28, 1508.[87] The king decided on the erection of new dioceses and their limits, provided for the maintenance of the bishop and the clergy, and made the episcopal nominations.[88] The choice of a bishop had long been made before the testimonial of the Ursulines reached Charles IV. It is significant only in that it seems extraordinary today for a bishop to have asked for such a testimonial from the religious. The elaborate praise of the testimonial reflects how dependent the Ursulines still were on the whims and financial support of the Court of Spain, local civil authorities, and the Catholic hierarchy. Knowing the great need which the Spanish officials and priests had for the esteem of their constituents, the religious made sure their testimonial reflected such.

CHAPTER 10

Challenges from the Clergy

When Angela Merici founded the Company of St. Ursula, she gave her daughters "the streets for their cloisters," but as we saw earlier the Ursulines became a religious order in 1612 with solemn vows and papal enclosure (cloistered). In New Orleans Mother St. Augustin Tranchepain and her companions observed the cloister so far as possible for religious engaged in hospital and educational activities in a mission country. Under French rule the ecclesiastical authorities did not question the fidelity of the Ursulines in this matter. Soon after the transfer to Spain's civil and ecclesiastical jurisdiction, however, Father Cirillo, a product of a strict Spanish monastery, found fault with the observance of cloister in New Orleans. On the other hand, Bishop Echevarria testified that he felt strict monastic discipline was observed in the Ursuline Convent of New Orleans, when recommending it to young women interested in the religious life.

Mother St. Monica Ramos was elected superior in 1785, when she was only four and one half years professed. She had acquired her knowledge of religious life in a Poor Clare monastery,[1] and after having observed cloister as practiced by a contemplative order, she apparently experienced difficulty in adjusting to the less rigid cloister of a community teaching in a mission country. She was particularly concerned about the way in which guests were accommodated on days of profession. Most convents had reception areas for guests, but the New Orleans parlor was not large enough. Guests were sometimes admitted to the recreation area or classrooms. Mother St. Monica took exception to this practice and put an end to it. She then wrote to the Bishop of Cuba on March 6, 1787, to tell him of her action and asked his approval for the earlier practice. It is a mystery as to why she wrote the letter, as she was asking approval for a return to a practice she had ended. In addition in 1786 Bishop Echevarria had ordered the community to receive no more novices, making the question of cloister at time of profession mute.

In answer to Mother St. Monica's letter, Bishop Echevarria refused to approve a return to the more liberal interpretation of cloister. He warned that permitting seculars in the cloister would be a violation of the decrees of the Council of Trent and papal bulls, which carried severe penalties. He urged her to "take the strictest measures" to avoid the abuses of the past, and in closing refused to allow her to return to the earlier practice.[2]

Until new religious were received there was no question of cloister violation. In addition, Bishop Cirillo in an account of his visitation to the convent in the fall of 1787 said that he had investigated "whether they observe the cloister inviolably in conformity with the Tridentine decrees and the pontifical bulls."[3] We assume that Bishop Cirillo felt they did, since he said nothing to the contrary. It does seem that rules and regulations were more important to the Spanish clergy than substantive issues relating to the lives of the religious.

One serious difficulty for the Ursulines was the demise of three of their fellow sisters, for this brought both sorrow and a reduction in their numbers. Sister St. Martha Lardas died November 22, 1786, when only twenty-eight years old.[4] Two years later death claimed Sister St. Ursula Lopez, a young Spanish sister who had been professed less than five years.[5] Within three weeks Mother St. Jacques Landelle, whose last years had been saddened by the prohibition of Bishop Echevarria, died at the age of seventy-two. Mother St. Jacques had come to New Orleans in early 1751 from the community of Nevers, France. She had filled various offices in the New Orleans community and had served as Superior during five triennials. She was especially gifted in caring for the sick during the period that the Ursulines were in charge of the Royal Hospital.[6] As each sister was laid to rest in the convent cemetery those remaining wondered how long the prohibition against additional members would last.[7]

Bishop Echevarria relinquished ecclesiastical jurisdiction over Louisiana without rescinding his prohibition, and four more years passed before Bishop José de Trespalacios, the new Bishop of Cuba, permitted the sisters to receive additional religious.[8] The permission was granted in June, 1791, and two young ladies received the habit that summer. Sister St. Ursula, Marie Regle Lopez, was a native of Havana and had spent seven months as a postulant learning French before entering the novitiate.[9] Sister St. François de Sales, Emilie Jourdan, had been educated at the boarding school and entered the novitiate at the age of sixteen.[10]

These two sisters made their profession August 20, 1793,[11] and were a very welcome addition to the community. Father Patricio Walsh, the bishop's delegate, officiated at the ceremony, assisted by Father Luis Quintanilla, chaplain of the convent, and Father Joachin de Portillo, pastor of St. Louis Church. During the next decade seven more young women were professed, giving the community continued growth.

While allowing the Ursulines to increase the members of the community, the clergy once again began to question the nature of the cloister which the community observed. On April 26, 1792, Bishop Trespalacios wrote to Mother St. Ignace Dupliepure, who had replaced Mother St. Monica as Superior in 1791, giving strict instructions to her in that regard. He ordered that no one, regardless of who she was

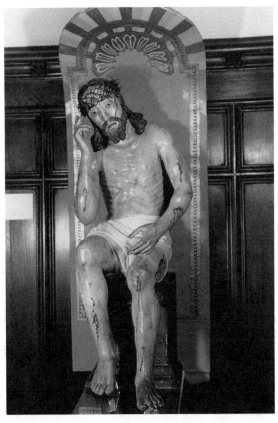

"Christ of Humility", statue from the Ursuline convent dating to Spanish period. Ursuline Archives & Museum. Photo by Sr. Jacqueline Toppino O.S.U.

could be admitted to the cloister either at the time of profession or for a visit. The wife of the governor and her companions were the only exceptions and could be present at professions by request. The bishop acknowledged the fact that the Ursulines kept their rule and observed the cloister, but warned them that he would be "obliged to use rigor, if I learned that they had disregarded this order."[12] Evidently the Ursulines had requested some relaxation in the cloister regulations. The bishop made it clear that he was granting no exceptions and that no changes should be made.

Father Theodore Henriquez, Auxiliary Vicar-General, was emphatic about enforcement of all church regulations. On May 4, 1793, he laid down precise policies for the admission and dismissal of boarding school pupils at the Ursulines' school. First of all he needed to be informed in writing (referred to as a memorial) of each admission and dismissal, so that he could give his approval. In addition he needed information on each student that wished to enter the school, because he would no longer allow students to enter the cloister without his "express permission."[13]

Mother St. Ignace lost no time in penning Father Henriquez a very candid reply in which she explained that the Church had approved the Ursulines' fourth vow of instruction, which was equally important to their other vows. Education of young persons, in fact, was one of the principal objectives of the order.

> This vow refers not only to the boarders and orphan girls living in the cloister, but also to the day pupils, commonly called externs, and to all other persons who may wish to be instructed in the principal mysteries of our holy Faith. The constitutions say that we can admit girls from the ages of 6 to 15, and that girls of more than 18 should be admitted only with the consent of the Superior and the council. We have faithfully observed this all along....[14]

Mother St. Ignace also objected to the "memorials" which would consume a great deal of the nuns' time—time they did not have with all of their other duties. She then acknowledged that the diocesan bishop was the first superior of the Ursulines, but the immediate superior was the priest elected by secret ballot of the community and approved by the bishop.

Mother St. Ignace asked Father Henriquez to postpone the enforcement of his order until a decision was made by the Bishop of Havana, to whom she was sending a copy of the order. Annoyed by Mother St. Ignace's candidness, Father Henriquez ordered her letter placed before her. He then commanded her to swear that she had written it or confirm the authorship of another. She was to tell the notary Quinones on what constitutions she based the facts stated in the letter and to place before the notary the Bishop's approval of the immediate superior (priest) chosen by secret vote of the community.[15]

Meanwhile Mother St. Ignace discussed with Governor Carondelet the inconvenience that Father Henriquez's order would impose on the religious.[16] Carondelet communicated with the Vicar-General who then became even more irritated. Henriquez said she had misunderstood the order he had given. He repeated his instructions and then warned her that, since she was now better informed, she was to obey the order in the future.[17] The response of Mother St. Ignace was respectful and devoid of subterfuge.

> We understood your order perfectly, both the letter and the spirit of its regulations. It was not lack of comprehension that prompted us to consult Baron de Carondelet, Governor and Intendant General, in our distress; but the many obstacles we foresee will be raised by the parents of the students in their fulfillment. The Rule of our Institute and the fourth vow that we make of teaching (and not of the cloistered life, although we observe it) have provided, since the foundation of the Ursuline Order, for the admission of girls up to the age mentioned in our constitutions into the cloister. In spite of these reasons we obey the decree and the commands of your Lordship, for we know that the vow of obedience includes the other vows. At the same time, it is clear that we shall practice the vow of teaching with a great deal of trouble and decrease of students for the parents will not agree to present memorials when sickness or other reasons force their daughters to go home for a certain length of time. In order to avoid all that trouble they will leave their daughters in ignorance of

the obligations of a Christian and they will live with the greatest liberty, without fear of God, in a country where there is no religion, as your Lordship has already experienced.[18]

Still not satisfied with this answer, a few days later Father Henriquez went to interview Mother St. Ignace, bringing the notary Quinones. She testified that the letter of May 4 had been written at her direction by Mother St. Monica Ramos. She then took the book of the constitutions and made extracts of the parts that referred to the admission of students, the election of a superior (priest), and the requirements for the profession of the religious. She was asked to show the decree of approbation and

Religious vestment used during the Spanish period. Ursuline Archives & Museum. Photo by Sr. Jacqueline Toppino. O.S.U.

confirmation of the superior, but she replied that no election had been made since that of Father Dagobert in 1765, as the community had conformed to the vicar-general.[19] After considering the information presented to him,[19] Father Henriquez reiterated his first instructions. If someone wished to enter the cloister of a monastery of nuns, the permission of the bishop or of the superior (priest) was necessary. This regulation must be followed regardless of the person's sex, age or condition, under pain of major excommunication, incurred *ipso facto*, as ordered by the Council of Trent. Written permission for entrance to the school must be obtained, but he agreed to modify the requirements for dismissal.[20]

Father Henriquez evidently believed that requiring parents to se[20] written permission from him for their daughters to attend the boarding school would increase enrollment. As evidence he pointed to Mr. Santiago Meder, an Englishman living at Des Allemands,[21] who had placed his three daughters at the convent, after having given his written consent.[22] Referring to Mother St. Ignace's objection that the memorials would require a great deal of work for the religious who were fully occupied in the service of God, he reproved her by invoking a "lesson" handed down by Benedict XIV in which he encouraged his subordinates to give all permissions in writing. Henriquez went on to say that if he could take the time to write the permissions, she should be able to take the time to ask him to do so. He concluded by saying, "We hope that following our example of punctuality, she will not excuse herself from the little fatigue that she might experience in cooperating in this temporal and external work of the education of young girls in obedience to her fourth vow."[23]

While Father Henriquez was holding himself up as a model for Mother St. Ignace and delivering his ultimatum on the question of the cloister, a letter bearing the decision of Bishop Trespalacios arrived in late June, 1793. Acknowledging receipt of her letter of May 22,[24] he emphasized that the religious must observe cloister while residing in the Spanish domain, regardless of whether it was required by their constitution. Boarders who were not obliged to observe cloister must nevertheless notify the superior of their arrivals and departures. Anticipating a change in the boundaries of the diocese he concluded: "I do not intend by this to bind in any way the administration of the Illustrious Bishop, Ordinary of your city, when he will take possession of his see. I know that you will obey him fully as the submission of your Reverence assures me, as well as all the religious who are under your government."[25] The boundaries of the diocese actually changed in April of 1793, and by the time these instructions were received the Ursulines were under a different administration.

Progressive development of the Catholic Church in the colony was severely hindered by directing church affairs from distant points through vicar-generals rather than a resident bishop. The remote-control management originated with the French and continued under Spanish governance. But during both periods the courts and civil governing authorities played a major role in deciding the direction of church affairs. Charles III appointed Bishop Cirillo de Barcelona as an auxiliary bishop, but he was not very effective in correcting religious abuses. In 1793 Charles IV convinced the pope to create the diocese of Louisiana and the Floridas which would have a resident bishop with full episcopal authority. The king then terminated Bishop Cirillo's administration and ordered him back to Spain. His letter to the bishop indicates the lengths the monarchy went to in dealing with colonial and church affairs.

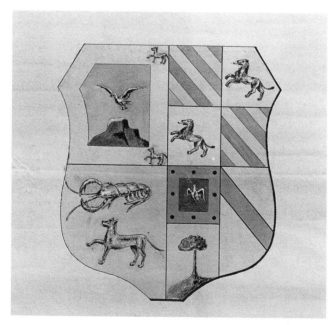

Coat of Arms of Bishop Luis Peñalver Y Cardenas, first Bishop of Louisiana and the Floridas, 1793-1801. Ursuline Archives & Museum. Photo by Sr. Jacqueline Toppino, O.S.U.

The deplorable state of religion and ecclesiastical discipline in the province of Louisiana, excited the compassion of my royal mind, and induced me to deliberate on the most efficacious means to remedy it: with this in mind I directed the Privy Council of the Indies,...to give me their opinion whether it would be proper to separate that province and Florida from his [the Bishop of Havana's] diocese, and to establish a bishop in them; and having done so...I saw fit to resolve that the necessary brief should be solicited therefore. His holiness having agreed thereto, and expedited the consistorial decree for the dismembering

Bishop Luis Peñalver Y Cardenas, first Bishop of Louisiana and the Floridas, 1793-1801.v Photo Courtesy Mary Therese Wolfe, O.S.U.

of said provinces, and a new erection of a bishopric in them, under date of April 25th of this year, and the corresponding step having been taken on the 26th of June following by my Privy Council.... I, the King.[26]

Bishop Cirillo had not been popular, and his efforts at reforming abuses and scandals had not endeared him to the citizenry. Roger Baudier wrote: "Certainly French extremists, atheists, skeptics, and the ridiculers of religion in the colony and those whose morals were at low ebb, shed no tears at his departure."[27] The Ursulines seemed to have appreciated Bishop Cirillo, given their remarks on his behalf in their petition to the king in 1787, but it should be borne in mind that they sent the petition at Cirillo's request.[28] Bishop Cirillo did not return to Spain, but remained in Havana and died in October, 1799. In the bull of April 25, 1793, creating the diocese of Louisiana and the Floridas,[29] Pius VI acknowledged that it was not practical for the Bishop of Havana to attempt to oversee church matters in Florida and Louisiana. Luis Ignacio Maria de Peñalver y Cardenas was selected for the difficult task of directing the affairs of the new diocese.

Born in Havana of a noble and wealthy family on August 3, 1749,[30] Peñalver was only forty-four years old when he was appointed bishop. As a young man he had studied at the Jesuit College of St. Ignatius and had completed his studies at the University of Havana, receiving the degree of Doctor of Theology in 1771. After ordination he had been assigned to judicial and administrative positions in the diocese under the direction of the Bishop of Santiago de Cuba and had become familiar with the difficulties of the church in Florida and Louisiana. When the larger diocese was divided, he was the choice to head the new diocese. Although he received his appointment in December of 1793,[31] Peñalver did not arrive in the colony until midsummer of 1795. During the interim year and a half Father Patricio Walsh directed the religious affairs of the colony as vicar-general.

The early 1790's were particularly trying times for both civil and religious leaders in Louisiana, as repercussions from the French Revolution were felt throughout the province. The French-speaking colonists were eager to read and absorb the revolutionary literature that was arriving from abroad, much of it extremely anti-clerical or at best disrespectful of Roman Catholicism. In addition to the literature, refugees from the French Revolution coming to Louisiana brought first hand accounts of a church all but uprooted by the new governing forces. The Spanish government could not countenance support for the French Revolution in Louisiana, and Governor Carondelet banned the singing of revolutionary songs and threatened to discipline those who showed sympathy to the French Republic.

Among the refugees of the French Revolution were three Poor Clare nuns, who lived with the Ursulines for nearly two years. They arrived in Baltimore in 1792[32] and went on to Illinois a year later[33], landing in New Madrid, Missouri. Governor Carondelet learned that all three religious were former members of the nobility, but were in destitute circumstances in Missouri. With the permission of Father Walsh[34] he provided passage to New Orleans, where the Ursulines received them.[35] The superior of the Poor Clares, Mother Marie Geneviève de la Marche, was descended from the house of Bourbon l'Arche. She had entered the Monastery of St. Clare at Tours, was professed in 1766, and had been elected superior in 1785. Mother Marie Marguerite Céleste le Blond de la Rochefoucault had been professed in 1784 and was the youngest of the group. Mother Marie Françoise Chevalier was about the same age as the Superior, as she had been professed at Amiens in 1762.[36]

The Poor Clares arrived with about 500 pesos left from money they had received for travel from French friends and relatives, including the Prince of Bourbon Conti. Since the Ursulines were also poor, Carondelet applied for a gratuity for the Poor Clares from the royal treasury. He asked that each nun be given eighteen pesos a month, the same amount paid to the Ursulines by the king,[37] who granted the subsidy.[38] Mother Marie Geneviève and her sisters remained with the Ursulines until October, 1796,[39] when they left for London. Their plans changed during the journey, and they stopped in Maryland, where they opened an academy in Georgetown. Mother Marie Geneviève died there four years later, and the others returned to Europe.[40]

Bishop Peñalver reached New Orleans in July, 1795, at the height of the political unrest and agitation provoked by the French Revolution. During the first three months after his arrival the bishop studied the problems of the new diocese and then reported to the home government. Although he experienced no difficulty in taking over church buildings, books, and other assets, reestablishing religious practices and reforming morals was another task. He reported that the residents seemed to have no regard for the Catholic faith. Out of the 11,000 members of the parish, only three or four hundred managed to receive Communion once a year, while many Catholics died without benefit of the last sacraments. He was appalled by the fact that many of the men, both married and unmarried, had concubines, and he was especially distressed to find that fathers procured mistresses for their sons in an effort to delay early marriage. In addition, he reported, slaves were not permitted to marry. On the other hand, Peñalver commended the Ursulines for their success in educating young women. "This is the nursery of those future mothers who will inculcate in their children the principles which they here imbibe. The education they receive in this institution is the reason why they are less vicious than the other sex."[41]

Despite his complimentary remarks about the Ursulines in his report, Bishop Peñalver also found them "decidedly French". He criticized the nuns for refusing to accept "Spanish women who wished to become nuns, so long as these applicants should remain ignorant of the French idiom." He also related that the religious had "shed many tears because they were obliged to read their spiritual exercises in Spanish books." The bishop's criticism seems unfounded, but was probably related to the fact that the report was going to the Spanish crown. The Ursuline community was made up entirely of French women until 1779, when the first Spanish women were received in the novitiate. The change in governance of Louisiana from France to Spain made little difference in the customs, language,[42] or culture of the populace or the Ursulines. Nine Spanish women came into the community between 1779 and 1786, and, after Bishop Trespalacios lifted his ban on reception of subjects, Maria Regla Lopez of Havana entered the novitiate. The latter "was admitted as a postulant for seven months so that she could learn French, the language native to that place."[43]

The Ursulines' requirements for entrance into the community were part of a time-honored tradition in religious communities that new members adapt to the established customs, whether it be speaking a particular language or wearing their skirts in a monastic style. Except for Mother St. Monica, the superiors, novice mistresses, and other officers of the community had been chosen from among the French sisters. Those responsible

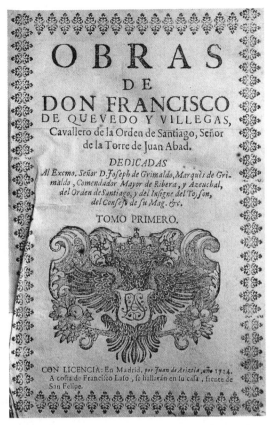

*Book dating from the Spanish period. Ursuline Archives
& Museum. Photo by Sr. Jacqueline Toppino O.S.U.*

for training the novices in the spiritual life and in teaching spoke French, and in some instances did not know Spanish. The rules and constitutions, the directory for the novices, the *règlements*, and all the books of the order that the novices were expected to study were in French. How could they learn from these works if they could not read them? It was for this reason that Spanish-speaking girls applying to the novitiate had to learn French. Did the bishop investigate the fact that the study of the various French works was designed to develop the spiritual life of the novices? Bishop Peñalver's criticism was poorly founded and perhaps formed after too short a time in the colony.

The religious had not neglected to study Spanish in any case. Bishop Echevarria had directed that Spanish be taught to the novices, and his successor insisted on it.[44] When Bishop Trespalacios ordered

Father Henriquez to notify the Ursulines that they must observe this injunction, he had the notary Quinones take the message to the convent and receive an answer from the superior. Mother St. Ignace testified before the notary that Bishop Echevarria's instructions had been filed in the archives, that she was familiar with them, and that they had always been observed.[45] Some days later, Trespalacios, while writing to Mother St. Ignace about the reception of novices, insisted "that all those who enter begin immediately to study the Spanish language, without however forbidding the French language which is useful for teaching."[46]

Bishop Trespalacios's determination to pressure the nuns into using Spanish emerged again in a petty but irritating regulation that became effective in July, 1791. From that time on, ordered the bishop, all official books of the house, all financial accounts, all records of receptions and professions, death notices, chapter meetings, and "all other events" were to be recorded in Spanish.[47] An annalist of later years, reviewing the period, wrote: "From 1791 to 1803 the annals were kept in Spanish, but there was not anything that merited to be written."[48] With a stroke of the pen she passed over a dozen years of interest to posterity that were perhaps too painful to record.

Another feature of the new bishop's report to the king was a commentary on the education of boys. Peñalver was concerned that many boys spent no more than two years in school.[49] Catholic education for boys and young men had been sadly neglected in Louisiana, he wrote, and the children often left school when they were only eight to ten years old. Frequently they returned to homes on distant plantations where they had no further religious training, and "where they daily witnessed the corrupt morals of their parents."[50]

Because of the educational circumstances of young men, the Ursulines felt an especially grave responsibility for the intellectual and moral formation of the young women in their schools. The girls needed to be prepared for the reality of life in the colony and be ready as adults to bring a Christian influence into the lives of their associates. The Ursulines felt an obligation to the Church to form future wives and mothers who had totally Catholic minds, and they fulfilled their duty admirably. Historian Roger Baudier concluded: "No one will deny that the faith in those days and in the succeeding several decades was preserved to a great measure by the good Creole mothers and other women who had been educated

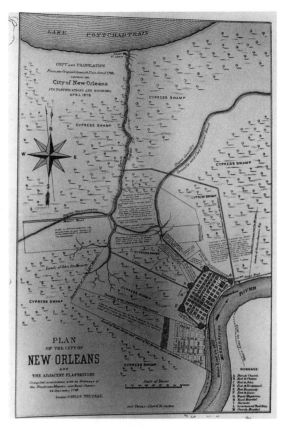

Map of New Orleans and environs, 1798 by Carlos Trudeau. Courtesy LA Collection, Howard-Tilton Memorial Library, Tulane Univ., New Orleans, LA. Photo by Sr. Jacqueline Toppino, O.S.U.

by the Ursuline nuns."[51]

A lack of adequate facilities continued to handicap the educational program, especially the boarding school and the school for the orphans.[52] A hurricane near the end of the century had destroyed an uncompleted building which they had planned to use for housing the children, and they were extremely crowded.[53] Another building was desperately needed, but no funds were available to build.[54] In a letter to Governor Miró, Mother St. Xavier described the congested living conditions.

> More than 70 orphans are lodged under the roof,
> in the story above the religious, or in the part below the
> community, so that the sick who are on the floor between

are very much inconvenienced by the noise above their heads as well as that from the first floor. The orphans themselves suffer very much from their restricted quarters, especially since their number is so greatly increased. This fact has already obliged me in several instances to refuse children who clamored for admission. The result of this is most unfortunate. If they do not receive an education at an opportune time, they soon lose the good desires that they had to acquire one. Advancing in age, they are ashamed and grow up in complete ignorance of the moral law and of religious principles. We cannot admit any more religious, who are indispensable to help with the teaching both of the boarders and of the day pupils, since we ourselves are obliged to lodge two together in a small room.[55]

The Ursulines applied to the king for a subsidy, asking that the money be taken from the surplus of a fund that had been established by Count de Galvez for the education of twelve orphans.[56] After five years of fruitless correspondence, and after Louisiana had passed from the jurisdiction of Spain, the king gave orders for the fund to be handed over to the royal treasury.[57] The religious and the girls remained in their very cramped quarters.

Until he was appointed President of the Royal Audiencia of Quito, Baron de Carondelet loyally supported Bishop Peñalver in his efforts to change the moral and spiritual decadence of Louisiana. Don Manuel Gayoso de Lemos succeeded Carondelet in August, 1797. Shortly after taking office he issued a set of instructions relative to grants of land. Two clauses treated of religious matters and were intended to check the spread of agnosticism and Protestantism.[58] But in spite of the cooperation between bishop and governor the spirit of indifference—even of scorn— for religion continued to grow.

The close of the eighteenth century witnessed additional political and ecclesiastical changes. In July 1799, Governor Gayoso died of a malignant fever and was succeeded by Don Sebastian de la Puerta y O'Farril, Marques de Casa Calvo, as governor pro tem of Louisiana. Juan Manuel de Salcedo, whom Charles Gayarré later described as "an infirm old man in his dotage,"[59] was appointed governor in October,

1799, but did not arrive in New Orleans until June, 1801. Salcedo was scarcely settled in office when Rome designated Bishop Peñalver as Archbishop of Guatemala. The loss of Bishop Peñalver would prove to be a severe blow to Catholicism in the colony. Under his administration the clergy had been given guidance and regulation, and there had been an improvement in the enforcement of church laws. But evangelization and moral reform had made little progress, owing perhaps to the people's disregard for religion[60] and perhaps to the punctilious, superficial nature of Spanish Catholicism. Louisiana needed a spiritual leader at this time, and political change would soon make the need even greater.

CHAPTER 11

ℛeturn to ℱrench ℛule and ℛepercussions

By 1800 political events in Europe had changed dramatically, as had the governmental structure of the United States of America. Napoleon Bonaparte was Emperor of France, and France was at war with Great Britain. The democratic government of the United States, grounded in a new constitution, was struggling but successful. Napoleon, regretting the loss of American territory in earlier years, sought to regain a foothold in North America through a secret treaty with Charles IV of Spain. Concluded on October 1, 1800, the treaty provided that the territory of Louisiana west of the Mississippi and New Orleans would be retroceded to France. Because of the French/English conflict and concerns that the English might attack Louisiana the treaty was concealed. Although the

A view of New Orleans from the Marigny Plantation, 1802. Courtesy Historic New Orleans Collection, 1958.42.

essential features were soon known in governmental circles, changes in the governing structure of Louisiana did not occur until 1803. In the meantime, life in New Orleans was not immediately affected.

The direction of Roman Catholic religious affairs in New Orleans became somewhat confusing after the departure of Bishop Peñalver in 1801. Father Thomas Hassett, who had been Bishop Peñalver's vicar-general, and Father Patricio Walsh, who claimed that the bishop had appointed him vicar-general prior to his departure, declared equal status in directing church affairs.[1] From Guatemala former Bishop Peñalver wrote to New Orleans with the message that Father Hassett and another priest, Father Francisco Perez Guerrero, were to direct affairs. They in turn wrote to the bishop of Havana for further information. In the meantime the Holy See in Rome had appointed Father Francisco Porro y Peinada, a Franciscan of the Monastery of the Holy Apostles at Rome, bishop of Louisiana and the Floridas. Before his departure, however, the Vatican learned of the cession of Louisiana to France from Spain and decided not to send Bishop-elect Porro to his diocese, although he had already been consecrated.[2] Rome evidently did not want to fill the vacant seat until the cession of Louisiana to France was publicly acknowledged.

In 1803 Louisiana became part of the United States. Rome still deferred the naming of a Roman Catholic leader, and the Catholics of Louisiana ended up the victims of ecclesiastical neglect for fourteen years. Roger Baudier deplored the depressing moral conditions of the Louisiana colony as

> ...the dark years of the diocese....What little Faith had been established was all but uprooted.... Indifference and even irreligion were rampant....As the Voltarian spirit and French Revolutionary ideas had free play,...casting blight upon religion.... And in the midst of this dismal situation, in the whole breadth and length of the vast diocese, there was one, solitary Catholic institution of learning, the Ursuline Convent![3]

Rumors of the cession of Louisiana to France had given rise to grave concerns about the future of the Ursulines. The prospect of living under the French government that had so recently persecuted priests and religious in France was so offensive to the nuns that Mother St. Monica[4] and several others began to take measures to secure their transfer to the domain of Charles IV of Spain.[5] On October 24, 1802, Mother St. Monica wrote to the king asserting that she, eight other Spanish sisters, and some French religious desired to live and die under the authority of "His Catholic Majesty". She asked that he permit them to go to Havana or to the capital of Mexico,[6] also requesting travel expenses and a gratuity for the sisters until they were able to provide for themselves.[7] Mother St. Monica sent the letter to the Marquis de Someruelos, the Captain General in Havana, asking him to forward it to the king.[8] Someruelos turned to the MarQues de Casa Calvo, who had returned to Havana after Salcedo became governor, for more information on the situation. Casa Calvo, a seasoned administrator, seemed optimistic about the Ursulines' future under a French administration. He felt that there would probably be no changes made to the status of the convent, as France was still predominately Catholic. In addition since the orphans were citizens of the Republic their expenses would be paid by the government, as would those of the nuns and priests. If for some reason the French government did not approve of the convent, then they should wait for a decision from the King of Spain.[9]

Some of the Ursulines, meanwhile, were urging that the community sell their property and leave New Orleans as soon as possible. Others thought it better to quietly await the development of events.[10] They consulted Father Hassett on the possible disposal of the property. Hasset knew that part of the community was opposed to the sale, but felt it just that those who were "going to live in another place should have their dowries."[11] The religious then authorized him to offer their properties for sale. Father Hasset made efforts to sell some slaves and houses in the city, but "by the protection of the Blessed Virgin there were always obstacles that prevented the sale."[12] Father Hassett then assembled the community to determine their wishes on whether to stay or depart. Thirteen choir and three coadjutrix sisters chose to go to Havana, while nine choir religious and two coadjutrix sisters indicated that if the French Republic would permit them to live as religious, they would be willing to remain.[13]

Before any action was taken, two visitors from Paris arrived warning that the arrival of Pierre Clement Laussat, Colonial Prefect, could mean seizure of the nuns' property and expulsion. They advised the religious to sub-contract or secretly sell some property so that they would have means to support themselves. The convent records reflect that this caused enough anxiety among the nuns to alter community records in case they were examined.[14] When the Ursulines learned that Colonial Prefect Laussat was at the Balize, their anxiety increased. Governor Salcedo sent a committee to meet the Prefect and escort him up the river. One of the members asked him what would become of the Ursulines. He replied, "It will remain as it is with all its possessions."[15] A messenger was secretly dispatched to bring this hopeful news to the community, but since the information was not official they continued to feel insecure.

1803 Map of the city dedicated to Pierre Clément de Laussat. French administrator in New Orleans at the time of the Louisiana Purchase. Map drawn by Antoine Joseph Vinache. Courtesy Historic New Orleans Collection. 1987.65 i-iii.

On Saturday, March 26, 1803, at four o'clock in the afternoon, Laussat arrived in New Orleans and went to the governor's house amid the firing of the cannons of the forts. Governor Salcedo received the Prefect, surrounded by his staff, the officers of the garrison and other troops, and by ecclesiastical and civil authorities. Laussat then went to the home of Bernard Marigny, not far from the convent, where he was to reside. On the following days he received visits from various committees and prominent citizens and affirmed the intention of the French government to maintain the prosperity of the colony.[16] When questioned about the destiny of the Ursulines, he responded that the religious could be at peace, for they would continue as they were with all their property. Laussat even sent the governor and the commandant to reassure them,[17] but the news still elicited various reactions in the monastery. Those who desired to leave were puzzled and distrustful, while the others "passed from excessive pain to joy inexpressible." Their fellow citizens also rejoiced with the religious.

> All the city had shared our affliction when we feared to be expelled. Now that the probability of destruction was past, there was universal joy. On the levee, in the streets, everywhere, was heard, "Our religious will remain with us."[18]

Lausset himself commented in his personal journal on the community's reception of the news that the Ursulines could stay. He noted that although religious worship, its ministers and their monasteries in France had suffered during the revolutionary years, in New Orleans the Catholic religion had been preserved by the Ursulines through their education of girls. The citizens of New Orleans, he wrote, had been very happy with the news that the Ursulines would remain in their city.[19] Just two days later he called on the Ursulines and the following greeting was recorded in convent records:

> My ladies, the need that the colony has of you, the good that you do here, the esteem of the public which you enjoy and which is justly due you have come to the knowledge of the French government which has decreed

that you will be preserved with all property. You may be certain that I shall protect you in all that depends on me. You shall be the coadjutrices of the government for the conservation of good morals, and the government will sustain you.[20]

In spite of these promises, Mother St. Monica Ramos and several others indicated that they intended to leave for Havana. Laussat did all he could to persuade them to remain. He assured them that General Victor would bring the order that the community was to be preserved, and he would have it recorded in the public papers. But it was to no avail, as he could not shake their resolution. Mother St. Ignace Du Liepure spoke so vigorously against French authority that the others feared the Prefect would take some action against her. Laussat had overlooked her words because she was more than seventy years old. When the others declared that if they left they did so of their own free will and with the permission of their superior, he no longer opposed their determination to leave.[21]

For some reason Mother St. Monica's letter to the king seems not to have been sent immediately, and the religious waited long and anxiously for an answer.[22] Governor Salcedo inquired about the king's decision on the Ursulines' fate, and a royal order of January 18, was finally communicated to the Governor by the Captain General on March 12. The document noted that the king would continue his aid to the Ursulines as long as they resided in his domain. If the French government wanted the nuns to stay in Louisiana, it would have to subsidize them from the French treasury.[23]

The decision of the king in their favor confirmed Mother St. Monica and her followers in their determination to live under the Spanish monarch,[24] and she asked Father Hassett for his assistance. Later in March Mother St. Monica and fifteen religious sent a formal petition to Salcedo and Casa Calvo, asking them to arrange for transfer to Havana at the first opportunity, to provide the necessities for the voyage, and to assign a priest as a companion for the journey.[25] The same day officials began to make preparations and asked Father Hassett to expedite those relating to the religious. The king's corvette *Diligencia* and the packet boat *St. Francis Borgia* were preparing to sail, and financial arrangements were made. Salcedo and Casa Calvo assured Father Hasset in May of 1803 that the royal treasury would assume the expenses of the journey, but a decision on payments to the departing nuns would be made later.[26]

Father Hassett responded to their letter, saying that he could only approve of the desire of the sixteen religious to live under the protection of the King of Spain. At the same time, he was convinced that no matter how good their intention, they would "always be defective in their execution since they were not guided and directed towards the desired end by discretion and prudence," no matter how good and praiseworthy that end might be.[27] Hassett wrote that the Ursulines had been devoted to their work of education, and the people of the city needed their continued presence. He said that he found no reason to allow them to leave the cloister, since they had no house or building assigned to them in Cuba. He acknowledged that the king had promised to provide for them, but only if the French Republic was unwilling to support them. Since the French had indicated that the community would be allowed to remain, he felt the Spanish monarch would want the sixteen to stay in New Orleans. He ended the letter by agreeing to abide by the decision of Salcedo and Casa Calvo.

Governor Salcedo and the Marquis de Casa Calvo apparently sympathized with Mother St. Monica and her companions, but differed with the vicar-general in the interpretation of the royal order. They felt that the king wished to admit all the religious who wished to come into his dominion and guaranteed to support the nuns, with no conditions attached. It was their opinion that in allowing the religious to leave they were fulfilling the king's wishes.[28] Salcedo and Casa Calvo added that if the religious were so appreciated in New Orleans "for their work of education and beautiful qualities," they would be "equally loved and appreciated in Havana," where they would be recognized for their merit and useful services. They rebuked Father Hassett by reminding him that the king's order did "not admit of explanations that delay their exact fulfillment."[29]

Father Hassett issued the Ursulines' permission[30] without further delay and agreed to make the arrangements for departure. He wrote to Salcedo and Casa Calvo that he had no intention of delaying the royal decision, but submitted his observations from a sense of duty. It was up to them to make the final decisions, since they knew the king's intentions and were "especially charged with seeing that his orders were properly obeyed."[31]

Although it was considered proper that "a priest, outstanding in holiness of life, should accompany the religious on their voyage and take care of their spiritual needs,"[32] there were already too few priests in the city to send one away. For that reason Father Hassett appointed Father Enriquez Boutin, pastor of Natchez and an "exemplary priest" who happened to be in the city at the time, to accompany them.[33] The vicar-general granted him faculties to celebrate Mass and to administer the sacraments to the passengers, soldiers and others on the vessel. He begged "His Excellency the Bishop of Havana to welcome him with all charity and love."[34] When the appointment was confirmed[35], Father Hassett sent word to Mother St. Monica that Father Boutin would sail on the *St. Francis Borgia*, and that he would celebrate daily Mass if the weather and other circumstances were favorable.[36] Those sailing on the *Diligencia* would have the services of the chaplain of that boat.[37]

The date for sailing was originally set for Friday, May 27,[38] but was postponed until Sunday, the feast of Pentecost. When the moment for departure came, it was with mixed feelings that the community assembled in the chapel for the last time to recite the prayers for travelers. Besides Mother St. Monica Ramos, superior, and Mother St. Ignace du Liepure, assistant and oldest member of the community, eight other Spanish religious were leaving: Sister St. Rita de Castillo, Sister St. Michel Mirabal, Sister St. Rafaël Mirabal, Sister St. Ursula Lopez, Sister St. Augustine Collazo, Sister St. Louis Vasquez, Sister St. Claire Yera, and Sister St. Rose Sanchez. Two French nuns, Sister St. Rosalie Bourque and Sister St. Stanislaus Langline were also leaving as were three Creole sisters: Sisters Ste. Solange, Sister St. Avoye Dusuau and Sister St. Marthe Chemite. Sister St. Angela Garder, who was Scotch, completed the group.[39] At ten o'clock at night, community annals record, "they left by the church door accompanied by Father Hassett, Governor Salcedo, and the Marquis de Casa Calvo, a military escort, and a great number of the most distinguished citizens."[40] From on board the vessel Mother St. Monica sent a message of gratitude and farewell.

My very dear Mothers,
In spite of my lack of facility to express myself

in French, I wish nevertheless, to do justice to your honorable manner of acting toward me and also toward the Sisters who wished to accompany me, by giving you the enclosed receipt, praying you to accept it as a tribute of our grateful hearts.

Be also pleased, my good and dear Mothers and Sisters, to accept the assurance that, without the events permitted by Divine Providence, we would never consent to separate ourselves from you, and that, notwithstanding the distance that separates us, we shall always remain united in heart and mind.[41]

The receipt spoken of shows the generosity of the small group left behind.

We the undersigned, certify that Mothers Ste. Félicité Alzas, St. Xavier Farjon, and Ste. Marie Olivier have indeed wished to give us all our personal linen and also a part of that in common such as sheets, table-cloths, napkins, etc.[42] Furthermore, they have had the generosity to send us on board a barrel of lard and another of oil, four sacks of rice and of coffee, some cases of white wine and of soap, some baskets of marchpane and other sweets. The good Mothers have also sent us some pieces of cloth, with the sum of $400 which we have not at all wished to accept before our departure knowing that they were not in a position to make such gifts as these.[43]

The inventory of supplies given to the departing nuns may have been written for a reason other than thanking the sisters. Shortly after having arrived in New Orleans, Laussat had heard that the religious were planning to take vestments and sacred vessels with them. He protested that this was in contravention of the agreement made between France and Spain.[44] Although the accusation against the nuns was not true,[45] it could have arisen out of a precautionary measure the nuns had taken before the French officials were scheduled to arrive. At the time Mother St. Monica, "with the consent of the councilors, had sent away by a small Negro named Auguste a chest full of ornaments for the church."[46]

Précis Elémentaire et Méthodique de la Nouvelle Géographie De La France, 1791, text used by the Ursulines. Ursuline Archives & Museum. Photo by Sr. Jacqueline Toppino, O.S.U.

They were hoping to prevent the confiscation of these objects and their use for unholy purposes. They had remembered only too well what had happened to Church property in France during the Revolution and had feared the same could happen in New Orleans.

Barbara Rita Labato, Catherine Bayona, Antonia Gonzales, and a free man of color, Santiago traveled with the professed Ursulines on the voyage.[47] Barbara Labato had entered the novitiate and received the habit and name of Sister Ste. Gertrude on December 15, 1785. Although she was very gifted, her poor health prevented her from following the regular life of the community and fulfilling the ordinary duties of a religious. After a year's trial, the nuns had asked her to withdraw from the novitiate. She loved the community, however, and pleaded to live as a perpetual boarder. She retained her place in the dormitory and in the refectory and assisted the nuns as her health allowed.[48] Catherine Bayona was one of the orphans cared for at the convent. Antonia Gonzales had also been placed among the orphans because of her mother's death.[49] Her father, who was employed at the Hospital, had consented that Antonia go to Havana and surrendered to Mother St. Monica all his rights over his daughter.[50]

The trip from New Orleans to Havana took twenty-five days, more than two weeks of which were consumed between New Orleans and the Balize, or mouth of the Mississippi. A week after they set out across the Gulf, they entered the harbor of Havana and disembarked on the afternoon of June 23.[51] As their coming was unexpected, there was no house prepared for them. Bishop Juan José Diaz de Espada y Landa and Captain General Someruelos decided that the nuns should be sent to three convents in Havana—six to the Carmelite monastery of St. Clare, six to that of St. Thérèsa, and four to the Dominican Convent of St. Catherine.[52] They remained separated in these convents for several months. Since the nuns could not open a school, their only source of income was the eighteen pesos a month for each of the six,[53] which was totally inadequate for supporting sixteen. Mother St. Monica brought the problem to the Captain General's attention and suggested that the religious be given twenty-seven pesos a month, as had been done in the case of the religious transferred from Santo Domingo.[54] Someruelos granted the desired gratuities,[55] and the king gave his approval for their continuation.[56]

While the Ursulines were separated, Mother St. Monica searched for a convent and eventually received the use of a building called St. John Nepomucene, which had formerly served as a house of correction for women. Amid great solemnity and accompanied by officials and prominent persons, they transferred to their new home on April 4, 1804. Ten days later Bishop Juan José de Espada assembled the community and appointed Mother St. Monica superior with Mother St. Rita as assistant.[57]

The professed religious, assisted by the four postulants, began their work of Christian education, instructing both boarders and day students. Until the convent was designated a monastery, however, the postulants could not receive the habit and make their vows. The nuns were encouraged by the king's appointment of Father José Miguel de Moy as their chaplain.[58] But the religious were to remain for many years without a designated monastery. Mother St. Ignace died April 24, 1811, and because the Ursulines did not yet have a burial place, she was interred in the sepulcher of the Carmelites.[59] A short time after her death, Havana officials received a royal decree, dated April 21, 1811 directing them to cede absolute ownership of the house of St.

John Nepomucene to the Ursulines so that they could establish it as their monastery. To enlarge the building and help defray the expenses of the house, the officials were also ordered to pay the sisters 8000 pesos

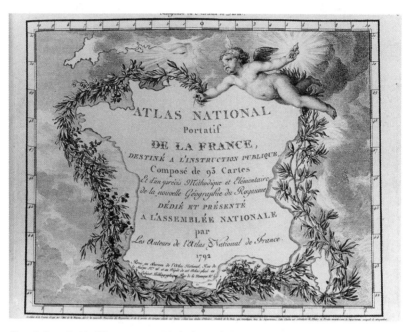

Frontispiece, Précis Elémentaire et Méthodique de la Nouvelle Géographie De La France, 1791. Ursuline Archives & Museum. Photo by Sr. Jacqueline Toppino, O.S.U.

each year for ten years.[60] For some reason, however, nothing was done until June 20, 1815, when the Supreme Council ordered the bishop to carry out the orders given four years earlier to establish the monastery.

Bishop Juan José de Espada established the Ursuline monastery of Havana by canonical decree on November 10, 1815,[61] restricting the number of religious to thirty-five. The Rules and Constitutions of the Congregation of Paris, with the modifications demanded by the climate and the laws of Spain, were to be observed. Bishop Espada named Mother St. Monica Ramos as superior for a first term of three years, and a few days later the community elected other officers. The postulants could receive the habit, and beginning with the first two from St. John Nepomucene in 1804[62] and repeating the ceremony every few days from December 23, 1815, to January 13, 1816, all were received. When Mother St. Monica reported to Bishop Espada that all the postulants had been received, she asked for dispensation from the novitiate and the four year temporary vows, since some of the women had been postulants for eleven years. During that time they had been under the direction of the novice mistress, had kept regular observances, and had instructed the girls of the academy. Since fourteen[63] of those who had come from New Orleans were still living, Bishop Espada granted the favor of dispensation from the novitiate to six who had received the habit, but obliged the others to make the two years of novitiate required by the constitution.[64] After more than twelve years of waiting, the Ursuline Community of Havana was canonically established with expectations of long and fruitful years of service to God under Spanish political jurisdiction.

The Ursulines were not the only ones who left Louisiana, either through fear of the French government or through a desire to spend their remaining years under the Spanish flag. As Spanish officials withdrew from the area, so did the clergy of Spanish origin.[65] Father Hassett, who had been designated to send reports relating to which clergy would remain in the province,[66] employed the notary Broutin to record each priest's intention as to his future allegiance. He sent circular letters to rural pastors to the same effect.[67] Father Hassett, who had so strenuously opposed the departure of the Ursulines, surprises us with his personal declaration:

> I...Canon of St. Louis Cathedral of New Orleans...Vicar-general...say that I want to live and die in the domains of our Catholic Monarch. When this province is handed over to the French Republic, I shall be ready to go to any place which His Majesty will assign me as soon as I finish the business with which I am charged.[68]

Father Walsh had also declared his intention to withdraw, adding that he had already sent his petition directly to the king. Father Antonio de Sedella (Père Antoine) also signified his intention of leaving, but rather than abandon souls, whose care he had taken for twenty years, he would wait until the French government provided priests. Father Quintanar, who also had a close relationship with the Ursulines, joined the others in placing his allegiance with Spain in a declaration overflowing with praise for Spanish governance:

I...Father Felix de Quintanar, Capuchin Monk, temporary pastor...of the Cathedral... chaplain of the Ursuline Monastery, declare that knowing the nobility of the Spanish blood, whose generosity flows through all Spanish people, being Spanish myself and counting myself among them, I say that having been born under the domination of my Catholic Monarch, the King my Lord, and having always been governed by his royal commands and laws which I have always respected and obeyed and will always respect and obey, I would make an ineffaceable black stain on the honor of my King and my nation if I were to leave the laws of my country and of my King to embrace those of a foreign place. I was born under my country's laws and I want to die under them.[69]

Considering the sentiments of the clergy, it is small wonder that Mother St. Monica and her companions were determined to abandon New Orleans. When the sixteenth Ursuline crossed the threshold of the chapel before departing for Havana, anxiety must have gripped the hearts of the eleven who remained in New Orleans. Even if the French government did not interfere with them, how could eleven do the work of twenty-seven? Would they be able to observe all of the Rule? If the Spanish priests left, would they have a chaplain? How could they support the orphans without the financial aid formerly given by the government?[70] These and many questions must have passed through the minds of the sisters who remained in New Orleans.

Who were these eleven Ursulines who dared to face an uncertain future in New Orleans? Three pillars of strength, Mothers St. Xavier Farjon, Ste. Félicité Alzas, and St. André Madier, who had been received coldly when they arrived from France in 1786, deserve first mention. Mother Ste. Marie Olivier de Vezin, Sister St. François de Sales Jourdan, Sister Ste. Scholastique Broutin, Sister St. Charles Carrière, Sister Ste. Madeleine Rilleux, and Mother Ste. Thérèse Mouy, [71] all Creoles, made up the choir religious. There were also two coadjutrix religious, Sister St. Antoine Delatre, a Creole, and Sister Marie Joseph Braud, an immigrant from Acadia. With tenacity and courage the women initiated the adjustments needed to continue both their religious life and their educational efforts among the boarders, orphans, day pupils, colored women, and children. Mother St. Xavier was elected superior, Mother Ste. Marie, assistant, and Mother Ste. Félicité, treasurer. Not having enough sisters to "say the Divine Office alone, they trained the orphans to sing and chant it so that the Office was said every day and all was done as usual".[72] During the summer of 1803 Félicité Nicolas joined the religious as a postulant and received the habit in November with the name Sister St. Jean l'Evangéliste. The community was shocked when she was stricken with a serious illness shortly before her profession and died within a

Napoleon Bonaparte discusses sale of Louisiana to United States with Talleyrand and Marbois. Courtesy Historic New Orleans Collection, 1974.25.10.64.

few days.[73]

While these events were taking place in the lives of the Ursulines and the clergy of New Orleans, United States envoys in France were making arrangements that would affect the future of the whole province of Louisiana. By the summer of 1803 rumors had reached Louisiana that the province had been sold to the United States. Laussat refused to believe the rumors and described the effect that the news produced in New Orleans as wild joy on the part of the Anglo-Americans, satisfaction on the part of the Spanish, and dismay on the part of the French. He wrote that he thought the rumors had been put forth by partisans of

President Jefferson, who were anxious to see their party remain in power.[74]

Signing of Louisiana Purchase. Courtesy Historic New Orleans Collection, 1974.25.10.65.

Laussat was mistaken. France had indeed sold Louisiana to the United States. The treaty of cession was dated at Paris on April 30, 1803, before the transfer from Spain to France had taken place. The Spain to France transfer was celebrated in New Orleans on November 30, 1803, amid solemn ceremonies and the boom of artillery rounds. Within weeks Laussat greeted the American commissioners, General James Wilkinson and William C.C. Claiborne, appointed by President Thomas Jefferson to receive Louisiana from the Colonial Prefect. The transfer to the United States took place with even more elaborate ceremonies on December 20, 1803. The emotions and sentiments of Louisiana residents, whose governance had been tossed from Spain to France to the United States in one year were mixed and confused. Difficult periods of adjustment awaited all.

As for the Ursulines, they would continue to be a major source of stability for the New Orleans community, especially through their care for the women and children. They had generously served the community since 1727 and had gained the respect of both elected officials and residents of the city. New challenges faced them in working under a new government, but their educational training and good management would serve them in good stead in the years ahead.

CHAPTER 12

$$\mathscr{A}djustments \quad \mathscr{U}nder \quad the$$
$$\mathscr{S}tars \quad and \quad \mathscr{S}tripes$$

John Carroll of Baltimore was the only Roman Catholic bishop in the United States at the time of the Louisiana Purchase. Father Thomas Hassett presumed that Louisiana would fall under Bishop Carroll's jurisdiction, and from New Orleans he sent an account of the ecclesiastical state of the province to the prelate on December 23, 1803.[1] There were twenty-one parishes in the territory, including New Orleans, he reported, but some were without priests. Of the twenty-six priests who were serving New Orleans or outlying parishes at the time Louisiana was retroceded to France, only four had agreed to stay in the territory. Whether or not any others would elect to remain under the United States was a mystery. The service of God and the many needs of Louisiana should have been cogent motives to induce the priests to both stay and increase their efforts. But *amor patriae* and the King's bounty, offered to all those who remained faithful to Spain, had been alluring inducements to seek refuge under the Spanish flag. Father Patricio Walsh was one of those entitled to a reward from the king. He had petitioned Charles IV for permission to leave Louisiana, but later decided not to abandon his post. As for Father Hassett, he was in poor health and wanted to retire to a more favorable climate, but he died on April 23, 1804. He was buried the following day in the sanctuary of St. Louis Cathedral behind the main altar[2].

As soon as the news of Louisiana's sale to the United States was made public, speculation and rumors arose concerning the fate of the Ursulines. The Paris newspaper *l'Univers* declared that "it was publicly announced in New Orleans that the American government would not permit the Ursulines to receive novices, and at the death of the last survivor, the convent would become the property of the State."[3] But whatever rumors may have been afloat, the United States government never made any such declaration. Since Louisiana was without a designated bishop and the vicar-general's intention was to leave, Mother St. Xavier

Thomas Jefferson, third President of the United States.
Ursuline Archives & Museum. Photo by Sr. Jacqueline Toppino,
O.S.U.

Farjon wrote to Bishop Carroll,[4] expressing her concerns for the future of the Ursuline community. He in turn wrote to James Madison, then Secretary of State, enclosing a copy of Mother St. Xavier's letter, and asked him to submit the letter to President Jefferson if he "deemed it worthy of it." The bishop verified that the "assiduity and disinterested devotion of the writer and her companions to the painful office of instruction, especially in a country, where it has been hitherto so much neglected," seemed "to require not only common protection, but special encouragement." He stressed the need to maintain and to promote an establishment that had supported both a free school and a boarding school for girls with frugality and self-denial for nearly one hundred years.[5]

In the meantime the Ursulines had made a friend among the American officials in New Orleans. Just a week after the official transfer

*William Charles Cole Claiborne, Governor 1803-1812 of the Territory
of Louisiana. Courtesy Historic New Orleans Collection, 1981.206.*

of Louisiana to the United States, Governor William C. C. Claiborne
visited the Ursuline community. The following day he wrote to Secretary
of State James Madison to inform him of the visit and of the deep
impression the nuns had made, saying in part:

> There is an Abbess[6] and eleven Nuns, the sole
> object of whose temporal care is the Education of Female
> youth;—they at present accommodate seventy three boarders
> and a hundred day Scholars, each of whom contribute
> to the Support of the House, in proportion to the means
> and conditions of their respective parents, and many receive
> their tuition gratis.[7]

The revenue the Governor referred to came from the fees for board and tuition for the pupils of the boarding school, which was normally $130 a year. To make it possible for less wealthy families to send their daughters to the convent school, some were admitted at half price. The only distinction made between the two groups was the "less delicate food" given those who paid only half. Besides the boarding school there was also a free day school for all who wished to attend it, "both rich and poor."[8] A second excerpt from Governor Claiborne's letter indicates his respect for the religious and presages an enduring friendship between him and the Ursulines.

> In the name of the President of the United States I undertook to give the Nuns a Solemn assurance, that they would be protected in their persons, their property, and the Religion of their Choice; and they in return expressed the highest confidence in the Government.[9]

Governor Claiborne's letter notwithstanding, the nuns waited several months for some reassurance from U.S. governmental officials regarding their status. Finally, the Ursulines addressed a letter directly to President Jefferson asking him to support a Congressional act guaranteeing their property and rights.[10] Their petition, they wrote, was not prompted "either by personal interest, or by ambitious designs." Since they employed their income in the exercise of charity and the education of youth, they had to know if they could rely with certainty upon the possession of the property which enabled them to fulfill their obligations. The nuns appealed to President Jefferson's sympathy for the poor and unfortunate. They pointed out that the orphans they cared for had no other means of existing, and that the Ursulines' training would help them to lead happy useful lives.[11]

Governor Claiborne visited the convent again April 8, 1803.[12] As he had done after his first visit, he again wrote to Secretary Madison in praise of the nuns. He found the Ursulines "most amiable" and reported that they carried on the work of education "with care and judgment." He considered "the Venerable Ladies as very useful Members of Society," and felt "very solicitous for their happiness and welfare."[13]

As the weeks went by Mother St. Xavier and the community

General James Wilkinson, named co-commissioner of the Territory of Louisiana along with W.C.C. Claiborne at the time of the Louisiana Purchase. Courtesy Historic New Orleans Collection, 1992.3.

daily expected an answer from Bishop Carroll, but none came. It must have been a day for celebration when the Ursulines received a respectful reply from President Jefferson himself:

> I have received, holy sisters, the letter you have written me wherein you express anxiety for the property vested in your institutions by the former governments of Louisiana. The principles of the constitution and government of the United States are a sure guarantee to you that it will be preserved to you sacred and inviolate, and that your institution will be permitted to govern itself according to its own voluntary rules, without interference

from the civil authority. Whatever diversity of shade may appear in the religious opinions of our fellow citizens, the charitable objects of your institution cannot be indifferent to any; and its furtherance of the wholesome purposes of society, by training up its younger members in the way they should go, cannot fail to ensure it the patronage of the government it is under. Be assured it will meet all the protection which my office can give it.

I salute you, holy sisters, with friendship and respect.[14]

Father Walsh was beset with his own difficulties. After the deaths of Fathers Hassett and Guerrero, Walsh was the only religious authority

Letter from President Thomas Jefferson to the Ursuline Religious. Original in Ursuline Museum. Courtesy Ursuline Archives & Museum. Photo by Sr. Jacqueline Toppino, O.S.U.

in the diocese. However weak his claim may have been,[16] he assumed the responsibility of directing the diocesan affairs. His administration soon ran into problems concerning disagreements between Father Antoine de Sedella (Père Antoine) and his assistants at the Cathedral. When matters worsened, Père Antoine resigned on March 5, 1805, and, accepting his resignation, Father Walsh promptly declared himself pastor of the Cathedral. If Père Antoine had kept silent and departed, affairs might have taken a different turn. Instead he enlisted the support of the Marquis de Casa Calvo, who attempted to dictate religious orders to Father Walsh. Gossip about the religious disagreements circulated throughout the city, and *Le Moniteur* invited all the Catholics of New Orleans to assemble in the Cathedral to elect a pastor and assistants. Father Walsh appealed to the city officials, warning that such a gathering had no authority to appoint a pastor. In fact, he pointed out, if a priest accepted such an election all his acts, as well as his power to administer the sacraments would be null and void.[17]

This warning did not prevent Catholics from assembling and nominating Père Antoine as pastor by acclamation. Père Antoine first declined, and then accepted the nomination of the assembled crowd. In the registers of the Cathedral he penned the following entry:

> On the 14th day of March, 1805, was named pastor of this Church of St. Louis of this city of New Orleans the Reverend Father Fray Antonio de Sedella and this was done on the petition and nomination of the majority of the people of this city, which is noted here to serve as information to posterity.[18]

Father Walsh responded to the proceedings on March 17, 1805 by issuing a pastoral,[19] which said that church functions could not be executed unless authorized by higher church authorities, according to the decrees of the Council of Trent. By assuming the pastorate without such authorization, those involved were not acting as ministers of the Church, but merely as crowd pleasers. Marriages performed and absolutions given by them, he said, were null and void, as were any other sacraments administered by them. Father Walsh then interdicted the Cathedral, thereby withdrawing the right to perform the sacraments, and designated the chapel of the Ursulines as the parish church, making it the only church where the sacraments could be administered and where Masses could be celebrated. He gave specific instructions that there would be three Masses each Sunday, with a sermon at the nine-thirty High Mass. Catechetical instruction would take place at 3:00 p.m. on Sundays, followed by Vespers.[20] Father Walsh assigned Father Jean-Baptiste Olivier, Chaplain of the Ursulines, and Fathers Pierre François de l'Espinasse, Jean Kouane, and Charles Lusson[21] to act as his assistants. They alone were authorized to exercise the duties of the priesthood in the city.

The designation of the chapel of Our Lady of Consolation as the parish church put the public on notice that the Ursulines were somehow allied with the vicar-general. His enemies accordingly became their enemies, and the nuns came in for their share of criticism. During a performance at the theater in New Orleans, the Ursulines were "held up to the public as an object of derision," and "the last act was marked with peculiar indecency and disrespect."[22] Learning that the theater management intended to repeat the performance, Mother St. Xavier asked Governor Claiborne to prevent future performances. Claiborne felt the policing of the theater a local matter and asked Mayor James Pitot to use his "influence and authority to protect" the Ursulines "from injury or insult."[23] The Mayor was instrumental in halting the next performance.[24]

During the meeting which proclaimed Père Antoine pastor of the Cathedral, those assembled chose a committee of laymen as a board of wardens to administer funds and revenues. They were known as Marguilliers, and when Father Walsh interdicted the Cathedral, they joined Père Antoine in opposing him. They declared that at the Ursulines' chapel Father Walsh maintained a schismatic "parish where they baptize, administer and marry the faithful of the legitimate parish."[25] Father Walsh was accused of having deceived the Ursulines and of having taken "advantage of their weakness, their frailty, and the inexperience of a cloistered sect to foment great and detrimental disorders."[26] Conditions were still unsettled when Father Walsh died August 22, 1806. The next day he was interred in the chapel of the Ursuline Convent near the altar, and many of the faithful came to show their high respect for him.[27]

Father Walsh's death left the diocese without leadership. Pope Pius VII had issued a rescript on September 1, 1805, placing the diocese of Louisiana under the spiritual supervision of the Bishop of Baltimore until a local bishop was appointed.[28] When Bishop Carroll learned of the death of Father Walsh and the religious turmoil in the territory, he appointed the Ursulines' chaplain, Father Jean Olivier, as vicar-general for the Diocese of Louisiana. On December 29, 1806, he was given "jurisdiction over all ecclesiastics, secular or religious, and over all members of the laity, with all necessary faculties."[29] Père Antoine refused to submit to the orders of Bishop Carroll and expressed his refusal in a letter of February 25, 1807. In the meantime, Father Olivier had formally announced to the Catholics of New Orleans that the chapel of the Ursulines would continue as the parish church, the only one in which any priest could administer the sacraments.[30]

As the controversy continued, the Marguilliers badgered Father Olivier and sent their demands to Bishop Carroll through correspondence and messengers. On April 5, 1808, Rome authorized Bishop Carroll to appoint an Administrator Apostolic for Louisiana, but unfortunately he delayed making the appointment. The bishop had hoped to name someone highly capable as administrator, but none of his priests wanted to accept the responsibility.[31] Finally in 1810 Bishop Carroll named Father Louis Sibourd, a French secular priest, as vicar-general of Louisiana, a less prestigious position than Apostolic Administrator. Sibourd arrived on December 29, 1810, and reaffirmed the Ursuline chapel as the official parish church. When Father Sibourd diplomatically encouraged Catholics to attend services in the chapel of Our Lady of Consolation, his entreaties met with a disheartening response—one man came to perform his Easter duty. Gradually Father Sibourd's sermons and instructions at the Ursuline chapel had their effect. There were twelve in the First Communion class on the first Sunday after Easter in 1811.[32] However, since the wardens of the cathedral continued to be inflexible, Bishop Carroll decided that Father Sibourd was not the person to manage the situation.

In an attempt to rectify the problems in Louisiana, recently elevated Archbishop Carroll[33] appointed Father Louis William DuBourg as Apostolic Administrator of the Diocese of Louisiana and the Floridas[34] on August 18, 1812. Dubourg was born at Cap Français, St. Domingue, on February 14, 1766, and educated in France. He entered the Company of St. Sulpice as a young man, but fled to Spain during the Revolution. He emigrated to the United States in 1794 and was ordained in 1796. He had been serving as president of St. Mary's College in Baltimore at the time of his appointment to the Louisiana post.

When Father DuBourg arrived in New Orleans, he established his pastorate at the Ursuline chapel and did not attempt to oust dissenting priests at the Cathedral. Père Antoine recognized him as the duly authorized church authority, but despite Père Antoine's recognition, Father DuBourg was received with great skepticism by the Marguilliers. They were irritated that Archbishop Carroll had once more selected someone other than Père Antoine for the leadership position. In the meantime, DuBourg suspended Père Antoine and interdicted the cathedral. Père Antoine withdrew, but his supporters brought him to the Ursuline convent, demanding that Father DuBourg reinstate him. Father DuBourg did not yield to the Marguilliers, nor did he take a public position against them. Rather than deal with the impasse, DuBourg fled the controversy. He departed from the convent and immediately left by boat for the upriver parishes. Father DuBourg was then absent from the city for several months, not returning until late in 1814. After his departure he wrote to Archbishop Carroll and attempted to justify his abrupt leave taking, but in the letter he failed to acknowledge the impact his departure would have on the troubled Catholic community in New Orleans.[35]

The religious turmoil in New Orleans, never a fertile field for vocations, made conditions worse for attracting novices. One young lady, however, Félicité Nicolas, entered the novitiate in August, 1803. The religious looked upon her as a gift from God intended to console and assist them for the loss of the sixteen who had gone to Havana.[36] Félicité was, however, the lone novice, and the nuns could not carry on their work without assistance. On April 2, 1804 Mother St. Xavier Farjon assembled the community to consider what measures they should take to obtain religious from France. They agreed to ask the Archbishop of Bordeaux to try to secure some nuns for New Orleans from his diocese or elsewhere, and they agreed to pay all the expenses for the journey.[37]

Some weeks later Father Jean-Baptiste Olivier wrote to the Archbishop of Bordeaux on behalf of the Ursulines, stressing both their great need for more nuns and the benefits derived from their apostolate in Louisiana. He praised their work saying that "the faith is preserved in this country only by the blessings that God showers on their labors."[38] A week later the religious themselves appealed, asking for three or four religious between the ages of thirty-six and forty-five, capable of sustaining the work of

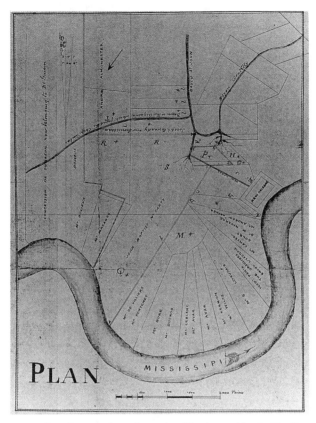

1805 Plan of New Orleans shows plot of land owned by the Ursulines for future use, on the right side of the picture before curve in river. Courtesy Historic New Orleans Collection, 1974.25.18.109.

the institute. If younger religious wished to volunteer, their age would not be a barrier. If there were some religious nearing fifty, viral in mind and body, as well as courageous and zealous, they would be received with open arms. All volunteers would be incorporated into the community and permitted to take their rank of profession. The house, although "not rich", was "in a position to furnish the religious with all they would need in health and in illness, without having to solicit help from seculars." Their chaplain and spiritual director was Father Olivier, a Frenchman and former curé in the Diocese of Nantes.[39] Following this appeal one professed religious came from Redon, France in 1806, but she remained only three years in the community.[40]

The withdrawal of two young sisters further depleted the ranks of the nuns. Because of ill health Sister St. François de Sales Jourdan asked permission to return to her home in 1809. She lived with her parents in retirement, renewing her permission every year until her death in 1818. During her last illness, Sister St. François de Sales asked to be brought back to the convent to die, but she was too ill to be moved. After her death she was dressed in the religious habit and buried in the convent cemetery.[41] The departure of Sister Ste. Madeleine Rilleux was the cause of real grief to the community. By her indiscreet manner of life, she drew down criticism and insults upon the nuns who had educated and trained her in the religious life.[42] The defection of one of their own was a very bitter trial for this already harassed community.

An even greater blow struck the community when Mother St. Xavier Farjon died on March 3, 1810. She had been one of the mainstays of the community since her arrival in 1786. As treasurer for a number of years she had greatly improved the financial condition of the community through her business acumen, even while devoting part of her time to teaching. She was especially enthusiastic about instructing slaves, whose confidence and admiration she merited. But it was in the office of superior, which she exercised for twelve years, that her prudence, charity, and equanimity showed to the fullest. Always kind and complaisant in her governance, she was also firm in maintaining exact regularity.[43] Her death left a vacancy that was difficult to fill.

Help was to come from another source. The three religious who had come to New Orleans from Pont-St-Esprit continued to correspond with some of the members of their former community, particularly with Sister St. Michel Gensoul, a cousin of Sister St. André Madier. Sister Michel had scarcely made her vows, when the French Revolution forced her to leave Pont-St-Esprit and seek refuge with relatives. After the Revolution she and two other ladies who had kept the spirit of St. Angela went to Montpellier and opened a boarding school for girls. While engaged in this work she received several letters from her cousin, Sister St. André, begging her to come to New Orleans and to bring with her some young, capable women with firm vocations to aid the New Orleans community in educating girls. Sister St. Michel asked permission of Bishop Fournier to go to New Orleans, but the bishop refused because he felt that the educational work that she was doing in France was more important. He said that only the pope could give her authorization. Sister St. Michel wrote to Pope Pius VII,[44] although political events made access to him difficult. Her letter recounted the information she had received from her cousin about the Ursulines of New Orleans. She related that the nuns were held in high regard and protected by both the civil and church authorities. She also mentioned that they were cloistered, which was evidently very important to the pope, and in great need of additional assistance. She concluded her request on a personal note:

> As for myself...I desire to unite myself to this elite band....In spite of my fifty years, I have, thanks be to God, the health, and the courage to undertake...this long

Small pope's statue of Our Lady of Prompt Succor. Sister Michel Gensoul had this statue commissioned under the title of Our Lady of Prompt Succor in thanksgiving for the pope's giving her permission to come to Louisiana in 1810. She brought the statue from France, and it stands in 1993 above the main altar in the Ursuline Chapel. Ursuline Archives & Museum.

and perilous journey....I am motivated only by the desire to reenter the religious state.[45]

Although Sister St. Michel wrote this letter to the pope in December of 1808, it was not sent until March 19, 1809. She had promised the Blessed Mother that she would propagate devotion to her under the title of Our Lady of Prompt Succor if a prompt and favorable reply to her letter was received.[46] While Sister St. Michel was trying to obtain permission for her group to come to New Orleans, Mother St. Xavier was having difficulty transmitting the money for their passage. She sent $900 to Mr. Philatus Havens, their agent in New York, with the request that he forward the money to Mr. Peter Walsh, agent general of the United States at Montpellier, to be delivered to Sister St. Michel. Mr. Havens replied that he could not send the money without the approval of the government, and in addition the embargo was an obstacle to their sailing.[47]

Mother St. Xavier then turned to Governor Claiborne, asking him to request that President Jefferson authorize Mr. Walsh to procure passage for Sister St. Michel and her companions. Since money could not be sent to France for the passage, the Ursulines in New Orleans would pay "their passage immediately after arrival at New York, New Orleans, or any other port."[48] At Mother St. Xavier's request Governor Claiborne forwarded to Secretary of State Madison a letter for Mr. Peter Walsh. In the event that the embargo should be continued, Claiborne asked that Mr. Havens be permitted to transmit a small sum of money to Mr. Walsh by some vessel that the government might dispatch to France, and that the same vessel on its return voyage "receive as passengers the ladies desiring to emigrate to New Orleans." He added, "The exemplary conduct of the Nuns of this City, has secured to them a great share of my esteem, and their temporal cares, devoted as they are, to the education of female youth, are of great public utility."[49]

Sister St. Michel received the "prompt" and favorable reply that she had prayed to the Blessed Mother to obtain. On May 7, 1809, she received a letter, dated April 28, 1809, from Cardinal di Pietro, who wrote in the name of Pius VII. The Pope was pleased that Sister St. Michel retained the Ursuline spirit and wished to devote her remaining years to the Christian education of youth in the United States. The cardinal said that the pope was aware of the positive effect on religious education the Ursuline monastery had produced in the "New World", and he gave his approval to the French nuns to join them in their work. The letter designated Sister St. Michel as the leader of the group, and concluded that the pope was

> ...convinced that your companionship, your knowledge, and the experience of your mature age will be of great help to them, not only during so difficult a voyage, but also in their future residence, to maintain and augment the fervor which has already been infused into them by your example, and to strengthen them in their pious and holy resolutions...[50]

Sister St. Michel relayed the contents of the letter to Bishop Fournier, and despite some obstacles she hoped to depart during early September of 1809. She had a large statue of Mary holding the Child Jesus made, which Bishop Fournier blessed under the title, Our Lady of Prompt Succor. Delays continued and it was not until the spring of 1810 that the group of religious could leave France.

Of the twelve young women who at first elected to accompany Sister St. Michel, only seven embarked with her at La Rochelle on Holy Saturday, April 21, 1810. On the vigil of Pentecost, June 10,[51] they arrived at Philadelphia, and after a short rest journeyed to Baltimore to meet with Archbishop Carroll. Because of danger of yellow fever he would not permit them to travel south until November 21.[52] Father Sibourd, who was going to New Orleans to assume the position of vicar-general, accompanied them, with New Year's eve bringing them to their journey's end. It was a day of joy and happiness for the small, overworked community of religious in New Orleans. Sister St. Michel again put on the religious habit and renewed her vows on the anniversary of her profession, January 25, 1811. That same day the seven young women who had accompanied her entered the novitiate.[53] Unfortunately three of the novices died during the first year of yellow fever and a fourth withdrew.[54]

The arrival of Sister St. Michel and her companions nevertheless renewed the spirit of the New Orleans community. She immediately became head of the boarding school, to which she devoted herself with untiring vigor. Under her direction the method of teaching was very much improved, and the work of education took on new life. The number of students increased considerably and necessitated some changes in the daily life of the nuns.

CHAPTER 13

Help and Hospitality

When individuals agree to share their lives with one another, it is necessary that some standards be set so that all can live peacefully. This was the primary reason that the New Orleans Ursuline community had observed the Rule of the Congregation of Paris since 1727. After the departure of the sixteen nuns to Havana, the remaining Ursulines considered altering their rules to align with the rules of the Presentation of Our Lady at Pont-St-Esprit monastery.[1] The changes that were proposed related to clothing, food, practices of penance, silence, the hour of rising, and the discontinuation of the discrimination between coadjutrix and choir religious.[2] But these requests, simple as they were, had to be processed through channels to Archbishop Carroll for his approval. In their petition for approval the nuns noted that while St. Angela had exhorted her daughters to comply with the rule, she had also made it clear that circumstances would at times necessitate changes.[3] Archbishop Carroll made only a vague reply to the Ursulines, and it was not until Bishop DuBourg was appointed Apostolic Administrator that action was taken. DuBourg, taking into consideration the difference between the climate and circumstances of New Orleans and those of the places for which the rules and constitutions were originally adopted, approved all the modifications that the community had proposed. The changes, formally approved on January 16, 1813,[4] made teaching duties somewhat easier.

After Mother St. Michel reorganized the boarding school, the number of students increased, necessitating additional space. The nuns then decided to try to obtain the Military Hospital from the U.S. government either "by purchase or otherwise".[5] Governor Claiborne contacted Secretary of the Treasury Albert Gallatin, noting that it might not be expedient to dispose of the hospital then, but he recommended that the "Government...make a donation to the ladies of the building...or concede to them the right of first purchase," when the time came to relinquish it.[6] Secretary Gallatin suggested petitioning Congress. Governor Claiborne drafted a petition for the Ursulines[7] and sent it to the Speaker of the House, Henry Clay, with the comment:

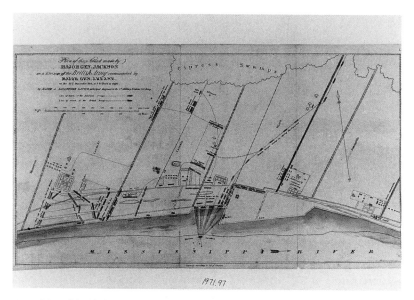

1815 Map of the Chalmette Battlefield. Courtesy Historic New Orleans Collection, 1971.97.

The Ursulines of this City are held in high estimation. Their deportment is exemplary correct, and their temporal care being wholly devoted to the education of Female youth, they have a just Claim to the Patronage of the Government.[8]

In the meantime, a number of physicians of New Orleans submitted a petition to Congress urging that the hospital be moved to a new location. The physicians said in the petition that the Ursulines and their students were subject to disagreeable odors of a "pestilential and epidemic nature," because of the proximity of the convent to the hospital. Three novices had actually died of yellow fever in 1811, but that had nothing to do with the location of the convent. The physicians argued though that moving the hospital to a new location would make it easier to prevent sickness, as the religious would no longer "be exposed to the vapors which are spread in the vicinity of the military hospital."[9]

The proposal to give the Ursulines the Military Hospital was filed and read in the U.S. House of Representatives and referred to a

Americans defend the City from the British, War of 1812. Courtesy Historic New Orleans Collections, 1959.160.4.

select committee chaired by Mr. J. Dawson.[10] Mr. Dawson was a strong proponent of the measure, and within a short time[11] he informed the Ursulines that a bill had passed authorizing the Secretary of War to exchange the plot of ground on which the hospital stood for one owned by the Ursulines. The bill stipulated that the land to be acquired by the government should be "conveniently situated for a Military Hospital and of equal value with the lots" on which the old hospital stood, including the value of the hospital.[12] For some reason the exchange was not made, perhaps because of preoccupation with the war with England.

During the last weeks of 1814 New Orleans was threatened by an attack from the British. Father DuBourg, having returned to the city, issued a letter to all the clergy directing that public services be held in all Catholic churches to ask God's protection.[13] When it became evident that the enemy would attack the city from below, General Andrew Jackson planned to stage his resistance at Chalmette. While the battle raged between the untrained American troops and the British veterans under Pakenham, many women and girls of New Orleans gathered in the chapel of Our Lady of Consolation. Pakenham's promise of "booty and beauty" could have only one meaning to the nuns and women of the city. In terror they spent the night of January 7, 1815, praying to Our Lady of Prompt Succor for victory for the Americans.[14] Mother Ste. Marie Olivier de Vezin, the superior of the Ursulines, made a vow in the name of the community to have a Mass of thanksgiving sung every year if the Americans were victorious. The morning of January 8 Father DuBourg offered Mass in the convent chapel for the success of General Jackson and his troops. The Mass was not finished when a courier entered the chapel crying "Victory is ours!" Immediately after Mass the *Te Deum* was sung, and every year on the anniversary of the battle a Mass of thanksgiving is offered in the chapel of the Ursulines of New Orleans.[15]

After the battle many of the sick and wounded soldiers were cared for at the convent. The school for the day pupils[16] was transformed into a hospital of more than fifty beds, and for the next three months the Ursulines became nurses again, caring for both American and British soldiers.[17] Mother Mary Teresa Wolfe recounted:

The tender care of these skillful and charitable nurses was so highly appreciated by their patients, that

Andrew Jackson and his troops are victorious over their British foes. Courtesy Historic New Orleans Collection, 1958.83.

British veterans were seen to weep like children when obliged to leave with their officers; while the Kentuckians and Tennesseeans no less grateful than brave, were for many years accustomed to send large baskets filled with bacon, fruit etc., as tokens of gratitude to their Ursuline Mothers, and especially to Sr. Ste. Angèle Johnston, whose devotedness to the sick and wounded entitled her to particular mention.[18]

Sister Ste. Angèle, although only a novice, helped to nurse the soldiers, as the other sisters could not speak English. When she was absent, communication between patients and nurses was labored. The ailing men would say to one another, "Wait until the little sister, the white-veiled one comes. She will understand you and give you whatever you want."[19]

Andrew Jackson's victory has always appealed to the people of New Orleans as bordering on the supernatural. General Jackson, though not a particularly pious person, regarded the victory as a "signal interposition of heaven" that required an external manifestation of gratitude. He asked Father DuBourg to order "a service of public thanksgiving to be performed in the Cathedral in token...of the great assistance we have received from the ruler of all Events, and of our humble sense of it."[20] In response Father DuBourg celebrated a solemn Mass of Thanksgiving at the Cathedral on January 23, 1815, with enthusiastic public participation. Before Mass, Father DuBourg received General Jackson at the door of the Cathedral and commended him for his suggestion of public thanks to God for the victory. The Ursulines also shared in the celebration when General Jackson and his staff came to the convent to thank the nuns for their prayers. Fittingly they were received by Mother Ste. Marie Olivier de Vezin, the first American-born superior of the Ursulines in New Orleans. The convent archives relate that "The Religious in their turn were happy to offer him their felicitations and to be able to contribute to the expense of a banquet which was given in honor of the illustrious General."[21]

The prominent part taken by Father DuBourg in the ceremonies honoring General Jackson contributed to his prestige as the administrator of the diocese and to a wider recognition of his authority. However, he still felt it necessary to go to Rome to lay his problems before the Sacred Congregation of the Propaganda. DuBourg appointed Father Louis

Rt. Rev. Louis William DuBourg, Bishop of Louisiana 1815-1825. This painting of him was sent to the Ursulines after the bishop returned to France. Ursuline Archives & Museum. Photo by Sr. Jacqueline Toppino, O.S.U.

Sibourd to manage the diocese during his absence, but as soon as he departed Père Antoine and his supporters challenged Father Sibourd's authority. When Archbishop Carroll was notified of this turn of events, he wrote Governor Claiborne, telling him that Father Sibourd was the ranking church official in New Orleans. The Governor, however, could do nothing, as internal church matters were not within his jurisdiction. Meanwhile the Marguilliers continued to refuse to recognize Father Sibourd, supporting only Père Antoine.

Again the Ursulines became anxious about the religious situation in New Orleans, and after DuBourg's departure considered relocating to another mission. Before making a decision they sought advice from

Pére Antoine de Sedella, Capuchin Priest who was a major influence on Roman Catholic affairs. Courtesy Historic New Orleans Collection, 1982.43.

Pope Pius VII, and, in a letter of May 2, 1815, they gave him details of the problems they faced. Reminding the pope that their monastery was the only institution in the country where women could be educated, they related their difficulties, emphasizing their need for spiritual direction. They praised Father Olivier's dedication but noted that, due to his advanced age, they feared to lose him.[22] They gave equal praise to Father DuBourg, saying, however, that his departure for Rome had thrown them into a state of uncertainty. They recounted the many burdens DuBourg had endured, and spoke of his "gentleness and kindness", as well as his accessibility. The religious expressed their opinion that the bishop's labors had not been in vain, especially because of his spiritual guidance and support for the education of young women. Finally, the nuns said that they would be forced to abandon their mission unless they were provided spiritual assistance and additional sisters. They asked for the pope's permission to reestablish themselves in France if conditions did not improve.[23]

Pope Pius VII responded to the Ursulines in October, 1815, and informed them that Father DuBourg had been consecrated as bishop of the diocese and would soon return. The Pope suggested that the Ursulines give up their idea of returning to France, as their work in New Orleans was much more useful. "Therefore, we exhort you to redouble your zeal for the Christian education of young persons of your sex, and for the eternal salvation of your neighbor,"[24] wrote the Pope.

Reassured by Bishop DuBourg's consecration as bishop of Louisiana and the Floridas, the nuns now abandoned the idea of leaving New Orleans. Still the diocese was without funds and had no more than eighteen priests to minister to thousands of Catholics over a large geographical territory. Already in Europe DuBourg had set out on an extensive tour preaching, seeking monetary contributions, and recruiting priests and seminarians as volunteers for service in America. Roger Baudier noted:

> The response of Catholic Europe to Bishop DuBourg should never be forgotten, because it was the zeal and charity of these people that made possible his reorganization of the Church in the Mississippi valley. This coupled with the self-sacrificing volunteers who dedicated themselves to the firm establishment of the Faith in Louisiana was the keystone of Bishop DuBourg's plan for the future of his diocese.[25]

During his visits to various cities in France, Bishop DuBourg also sought postulants for the Ursulines. Several volunteers entered the Ursuline Convent of Bordeaux, where they were tested to determine their spiritual and physical strength for the mission. Of these, nine women sailed from France and arrived in New Orleans on January 8, 1817. Unfortunately, Sister Ste. Thérèse Rey, professed of Sommières, died before the close of the year.[26] Sister Marthe Fortière, a Hospitalière, remained for only a few years with the Ursulines. In 1823 she left to assist Mlle Aliquot, who had established a school for Negro girls on St. Claude Street.[27]

A third volunteer from France, Sister Ste. Séraphine Ray, was

Mother St. Seraphin Ray, O.S.U. 1794-1881, professed 66 years.
Ursuline Archives & Museum. Photo by Sr. Jacqueline Toppino,
O.S.U.

to spend more than sixty years in New Orleans, serving thirty-three years as superior, fifteen years as assistant superior, and nearly half a century as novice mistress.[28] Thérèse Ray was born in 1795 during the French Revolution. To avoid arousing suspicion at the time of her baptism, her parents had placed her in a basket and carried the baby to a barn where she was baptized. At eighteen she had entered the convent of St. Charles at Pradines, where she received the religious habit from Cardinal Fesch, uncle of Napoleon Bonaparte. She was professed on Christmas Day, 1815, taking the name Ste. Séraphine. When Bishop DuBourg visited the convent the following year he was very impressed with her and encouraged her to join the Louisiana Ursulines. Sister Ste. Séraphine was a woman of broad views, fervent charity, and limitless energy. She generously taught the boarders, trained the young Negresses, governed the community and instructed the novices.[29]

In spite of his successes in recruiting clergy for Louisiana Bishop DuBourg was long delayed in returning to America. He had proposed to the Pope a division of the diocese and the creation of a see in Upper Louisiana, perhaps because while abroad he received news of the activities of Pére Antoine and the Marguilliers. Among other things, they had attempted to obtain a charter from the U.S. Congress depriving the bishop of his cathedral.[30] For this reason DuBourg petitioned Rome to permit him to reside in St. Louis and establish a seminary and other educational institutions in that part of the diocese.[31] Rome was informed that when Pére Antoine received copies of Dubourg's act of consecration and the Brief of the Sovereign Pontiff, he declared he had nothing to do with the pope or any bishops of his making. The papers were not registered in the archives of the Cathedral. Bishop DuBourg wrote that it would be "fatal to religion to attempt to land in New Orleans."[32] He also acknowledged his own lack of fortitude in dealing with the situation. In the meantime he contacted Bishop Flaget of Bardstown, Kentucky, asking him to sound out the people of Upper Louisiana regarding establishing the seat of the diocese in St. Louis. Would they contribute to its financial support?

Continually concerned about his reception in the new diocese of Louisiana and the Floridas, Bishop DuBourg lingered in Europe soliciting funds and volunteers for the mission. Not until June 2, 1817, did DuBourg and his party sail from Bordeaux, arriving at Annapolis, Maryland, on September 4. He then journeyed to Bardstown, Kentucky, where Bishop Flaget and priests and seminarians recruited in Europe awaited him. Together the group traveled westward and entered St. Louis on January 5, 1818. A large crowd had assembled to meet the group. Amid enthusiasm and rejoicing rather than rebellion and antagonism, the new bishop was installed in a cathedral he later described as a "poor old barn falling into ruins."[33] Once installed DuBourg began his plan to make St. Louis the center of spiritual life of the diocese. He opened a seminary, St. Mary's of the Barrens, which later became Kenrick Seminary. The seminary would provide training for many priests in years to come and was a major influence in the development of American Catholicism.[34]

While Bishop DuBourg had been successful in obtaining nine Ursulines for Louisiana, additional teachers were needed to foster Catholic

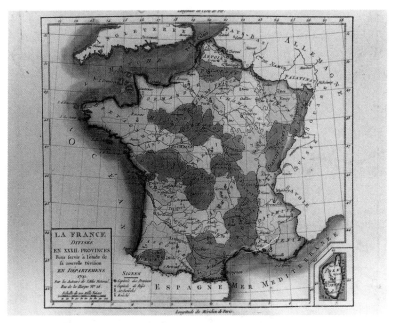

Map showing the provinces of France at the end of the 18th century, used for instructing students. Ursuline Archives & Museum. Photo by Sr. Jacqueline Toppino, O.S.U.

education in the diocese. The bishop therefore turned to a new congregation, the Society of the Sacred Heart, founded in Paris on November 21, 1800, by Madeleine Sophie Barat. Rose Philippine Duchesne was an early member of the order. She had been a member of the Order of the Visitation at Grenoble, but the convent had been closed during the Revolution. Mother Duchesne had wished to devote herself to foreign missions, and it was she who actually greeted Bishop DuBourg when he called upon the Religious of the Sacred Heart in January of 1817 to ask Mother Barat to provide sisters for his large diocese. At first she promised to have sisters ready to go quickly, but then later decided that it was not opportune for this young order to launch a new enterprise so soon. When she informed the bishop of her decision, he was not pleased. Mother Duchesne was extremely disappointed, and it was she who finally convinced Mother Barat to agree to send a few nuns to America the following spring.

The bishop was very pleased with Mother Barat's reversal of opinion and left instructions for the Sacred Heart nuns to go to St. Louis via New Orleans. The Ursulines, he explained, would give them hospitality when they reached America. On Holy Thursday, March 19, 1818, Mother Duchesne and four companions sailed from Pauillac, south of Bordeaux, aboard the *Rebecca*. After a voyage of two months, laden with almost as many perils and discomforts as that of the Ursulines a century earlier, the Religious of the Sacred Heart reached New Orleans. They traveled the last fifteen miles by carriage, one of the weary group recording this description in her journal:

> Monsieur Martial had sent a letter to the Ursuline Religious announcing our arrival. Two priests who were at the convent when the letter was opened did not wait to hear it through, but immediately went off to engage the carriages, which came for us with a cordial invitation

Philippine Duchesne R.S.C.J., 1769-1852, missionary of the Religious of the Sacred Heart to the United States.

from the Ursulines to hasten the pleasure they anticipated in welcoming us. It was about two-thirty in the morning when we reached New Orleans, so we went first to the priests' residence to await the dawn. As the angelus was ringing, we reached the Ursuline Convent. The religious received us with a charity of which every moment since has given new proofs.[35]

The charity of the Ursulines was an ever recurring theme in the letters these missionaries sent to France, and in the years to come was one of Mother Duchesne's strongest motives for thanks to God.[36] To the newcomers the good accomplished by the Ursulines was a source of hope and encouragement, for at that time "there were three hundred children profiting by the education and instruction given by the Daughters of St. Angela."[37] Since there was no message from the bishop awaiting the sisters, Mother Duchesne and her companions were happy to spend some time with the Ursulines. Mother Duchesne wrote of their stay with the Ursulines:

> While we wait we are fortunate in the good example and perfect charity of the Ursulines, who care for us like tender Mothers. Far from finding us a burden, as we really are, they speak only of their sorrow that we are not to remain in New Orleans.... Sunday I assisted at the instruction given here to three hundred persons of all colors and countenances. I noted especially some old Negresses who would much like us to stay here with their Mothers in Christ. That same day forty creoles, Negroes, mulattoes, etc., received their First Communion in the chapel of this house. When would <u>we</u> ever see so large a ceremony?
>
> This convent, as old as the city, was founded at the expense of Louis XV. The first nuns almost died of want, living as they did more in the marshes than on dry land, but now the house is well established. These religious are almost alone in upholding religion in this city. We cannot tell you what they have been to us.[38]

As the days passed and no word came from Bishop DuBourg, Mother Duchesne was somewhat disquieted. Only the cordiality of the Ursulines alleviated her anxiety. "The Bishop's silence has been far from consoling," she wrote. She then continued:

> No one could be more hospitable than the good nuns who would want us to stay on with them if they did not fear our getting ill. They have made us buy many things and have insisted on paying for them. The Superior told me today that we must use this house for storage and that our nuns coming from Europe must always stop here, choosing for the voyage a season in which a long stay in New Orleans would be desirable. They have also offered to do commissions for us after we are settled in St. Louis....
>
> The kind Ursulines are most solicitous about our journey. If it depended on them, our expenses would be small. I should not be surprised if they offer to give us more help. I am really anxious, not being able to count on the 10,000 francs which you sent for us to Bishop DuBourg....This sum may already be spent, and then there will be debts if we buy, or build.
>
> These good nuns, whose charity overwhelms us are expecting three religious and some priests who are to sail in September. Will you please send by them a beautiful embroidered flounce for an alb? I should be most grateful, as they have none in this house. They will have lavished upon us one hundred times its value, and that with a delicacy that I cannot express.[39]

Fear that a protracted stay in New Orleans might be detrimental to the health of the religious was another concern of Mother Duchesne. Adjusting to the debilitating heat was very trying, and mosquitoes plagued the newcomers. Mother Duchesne wrote that she looked like a leper. The Ursulines even offered their guests tobacco to burn in their rooms to drive away the insects that gave them no rest day or night.[40] Mother Duchesne became seriously ill with scurvy caused by the lack of fresh fruit and vegetables on the long voyage. Although at one point she feared death, she later noted that the skill and kindness of the sisters restored her. Mother Michel had noticed that Mother Duchesne took nothing but unsweetened coffee for breakfast. She encouraged Mother Duchesne to take a daily cup of coffee so sweet that it was almost like syrup and insisted that in America a substantial breakfast was not a luxury, but a necessity.[41] When Mother Duchesne grew better she wrote to Mother Barat:

> I cannot tell you of the touching kindness of the Superior of this house in this trial; it is quite inexpressible. We are the continual objects of kind attentions from her and the nuns. After having cared for me during my distressing illness, she now wants to help to defray the expenses of our journey, calling the 500 francs which she offers to give us a "widow's mite," which I scruple to accept. I have spoken frankly of the expected 10,000 francs without concealing my fear that it may already be disposed of. She shares our anxiety and she made me write to the bishop and approved what I had written. Moreover, she asked me to say nothing to her nuns of the possible 10,000 francs, lest hearing this might diminish their sympathy. You see, they make every decision in Chapter. We shall never be the losers in dealing with these religious, so I beg you to pay for the flounce for the alb ordered for them from Lyons... They want to keep us here, at least in the city, and promise us every success, assuring us of their help with an unselfishness that is admirable. However, while they wish to help our work, they see as we do that it is more for the glory of God that we go on to St. Louis in the Illinois country.[42]

One should not infer from Mother Duchesne's letter that she thought the Ursulines were wealthy. They wished only to share their modest means with those whom they knew would soon be suffering severe poverty and privation. Her description of the premises indicates the austerity of the Ursulines' lives.

Everything in this convent is in the greatest simplicity. The chapel is a large room with walls bare, as are those of the choir; the parlor is furnished with wooden benches and the pupils have many inconveniences....One sees here saints who have taught for thirty years and who have won many souls.[43]

June passed and the early days of July brought no word from Bishop DuBourg. Having prayed for counsel as to what to do, Mother Duchesne finally decided to go on to St. Louis when a boat became available. At departure time the Sacred Heart group wished to leave some material token of thanks behind, "but the nuns of St. Angela refused to accept anything, saying in their delicate charity that their visitors had been of invaluable service in the classes among the poor children, and they pressed upon them a generous gift for their mission."[44] Mother St. Michel expressed the sentiments of all when she wrote to Mother Barat:

The lively interest which your dear nuns aroused in us was the cause of our esteem for them and of the sincere friendship which will last all through our lives. We were naturally drawn to one another, as our two Orders differ only in name. They tend to the same end, and should form but one because of the religious affection we bear each other.

I think, dear Madame, that your daughters gave you too flattering an account of our hospitality offered them last year. Our Community will always rejoice to have had them as guests. The days that they spent here passed all too quickly for us, left us undying memories of the virtues of your religious. We hope to profit by their example of zeal for our Master and of devotedness to the salvation of souls, virtues which make them rise superior to the difficulties which encompass them. Their glorious enterprise, the spread of the Kingdom of Christ, brings with it much fatigue and anxiety but their trust in the Sacred Heart will sustain them.[45]

This statue of the Sacred Heart of Jesus was originally in the Dauphine Street Courtyard. Ursuline Archives & Museum. Photo by Sr. Jacqueline Toppino, O.S.U.

Mother Duchesne had been surprised to find that devotion to the Sacred Heart was already practiced by the Ursulines and their pupils.[46] She had hoped to be the first apostle of this devotion in the United States. In a letter to Mother Barat she wrote:

> Alas! We shall not have the glory of being the first to bring to the United States the devotion to the Sacred Heart. I have found here a picture of this Divine Heart, painted at Rome, and also a book of devotions to the Sacred Heart, printed in New Orleans.[47]

A French secular priest, Father Bertrand Martial, had accompanied the Religious of the Sacred Heart to New Orleans. Father Martial remained in New Orleans when they left, fully expecting Bishop Dubourg to call him to Upper Louisiana to open a boys' school. Meanwhile he joined Father Sibourd at the Ursuline Convent while he waited. Father Martial was a capable person with a winning disposition and quickly gained the respect of the people. He was especially appealing to youth. As Mother Duchesne described it: "the mulatto, creole, Negro, and American boys flock after Father Martial, who has three classes in Catechism every day."[48] The Ursulines hoped that he could continue as their chaplain.

Contrary to his expectations, Father Martial received orders to stay in New Orleans. His influence was remarkable and his prudence and affability helped to prepare the way for a rapprochement on the part of Père Antoine and the Marguilliers. The young priest saw the necessity of Catholic education for boys and proceeded to make plans for a college. With Bishop Dubourg's approval the project was initiated near the close of 1819 and was a decided success. The school was located below the city limits on ground belonging to the Ursulines.[49] The nuns were disappointed that Bishop DuBourg did not return to the city, but the community continued to give their financial assistance and moral support to the enthusiastic priests who were struggling to put order into the confused religious situation in the Crescent City.

CHAPTER 14

Loss of Property and Privacy

Although the principal reason for the Ursuline Community's existence in New Orleans was the spiritual and educational development of the young women of the area, material problems relating to their property and the use of it were major issues at times. We noted earlier problems associated with the proximity of the Convent to the Military Hospital. Although a wall separated the hospital grounds from the convent premises, it seems that soldiers would scale the wall and enter the courts and gardens of the convent at any time.[1] Drunken soldiers at times even entered the convent itself.[2] The religious considered the situation dangerous to the girls of the boarding school and orphanage as well as to themselves. Although an act of Congress of April 23, 1812, empowered the Secretary of War to exchange the Military Hospital for a parcel of ground belonging to the Ursulines, a variety of causes prevented the exchange.[3] When the situation had not improved by the summer of 1815, Mother Ste. Marie Olivier enlisted the services of Gallien Preval, a member of the City Council, to appeal to Colonel Ross, the commanding naval officer. After Preval paid Colonel Ross a personal visit, Ross promised to give strict orders that the disagreeable antics should be stopped.[4] This was merely a temporary solution, however, and a definitive settlement was still needed.

Mother Ste. Marie wrote to General Andrew Jackson in the summer following the Battle of New Orleans asking for assistance in solving the hospital problem. Jackson then took up the matter with Secretary of War Dallas,[5] who appointed a committee to "cooperate promptly and effectually" in the completion of the business originally assigned to General Wilkinson.[6] The three commissioners appointed by Secretary Dallas met with a like number representing the Ursuline nuns,[7] but they could not reach an agreement. The evaluation of the hospital property was a major dispute between the two sets of representatives. The commissioners representing the government valued the property at ten thousand dollars, while the commissioners representing the nuns valued it at twenty thousand dollars.[8] Another complication was that the United States commissioners

Letter of Secretary A.G. Dallas to Ursuline Nuns. Ursuline Archives & Museum. Photo by Sr. Jacqueline Toppino O.S.U.

felt the land offered by the Ursulines was an unsuitable location for the hospital. Two pieces of land had been offered, one in the Faubourg Annunciation above New Orleans and the other a piece contiguous to the property on which the barracks were built. The nuns reasoned that if the Annunciation parcel was rejected, the second piece of property would not be, since it added to the value of property already owned by the United States.[9]

In 1816 Sister St. Michel appealed to President James Madison[10] for settlement of the property matter, but her effort was unsuccessful. She and Sister St. Marie then sent a lengthy account of the dispute to Archbishop Carroll.[11] The archbishop was seriously ill at the time, and the matter was turned over to Father Ambrose Maréchal.[12] He in turn contacted Secretary Dallas,[13] who had previously pigeon-holed every

254

James Madison, President of the United States, original preserved in Ursuline Museum. Ursuline Archives & Museum. Photo by Sr. Jacqueline Toppino, O.S.U.

other appeal. No record of any action has been found from the next four year period. One suspects that the time and effort spent on bureaucratic entanglements must have been very trying for the religious. The delays and inaction may have been owing to the post War of 1812 recovery.

But in the meantime the Ursulines faced another property problem involving part of the grounds within their enclosure. In order to understand the full background, we must step back into the previous century. In 1797 the Spanish government considered erecting an addition to the Military Hospital on property which had been used for years as part of the recreational ground of the boarders and orphans. Mother St. Xavier Farjon was asked to produce the titles to the property, but they could not be found either in the convent archives or in the office of the notary public.[14] At that time Bishop Peñalver pointed out that it

Letter of James Madison to Ursuline Nuns. Courtesy Ursuline Archives & Museum. Photo by Sr. Jacqueline Toppino, O.S.U.

was not surprising that the religious could not find their titles, as less than one-eighth of the property owners had verification of their titles to property. He had noted then that sales records only went back to 1750, and even if records had existed fires and storms had destroyed many of them. He had then said "It is customary here to accept the deed of the last person from whom the right is derived as adequate proof both of right of ownership and of possession."[15]

As noted earlier, when Governor Alexander O'Reilly refused to include the Ursuline Convent and grounds in the inventory of properties of the French government, the Spanish had tacitly recognized the Ursulines' title.[16] At the time the Spanish required no proof of ownership from the Mother Superior, changed no boundaries, and altered no rights of possession.[17] In 1793, Governor Carondelet expressly recognized the nuns' title to the ground behind the barracks, proposing to exchange a lot belonging to the king for a lot of the Ursulines adjoining the barracks. The nuns consented and considered this transaction proof of ownership.[18] By 1797, however, Spanish officials thought otherwise. Still they failed to reach any agreement prior to the retrocession of the colony to France,[19] and the question was still not settled at the time of the Louisiana Purchase. It was to arise again in 1818.

An act of Congress passed in 1818 authorized the President to lay off in lots and sell the ground on which "the navy, military hospital and barracks" stood.[20] The plan included several lots within the Ursulines' enclosure as portions of the property. A search for title papers was renewed, but none were found. Mr. H.M. Brackenridge of Baltimore, an agent of the Ursulines, then discussed the problem with William H. Crawford, Secretary of the Treasury, who was in charge of supervision of the sale. Mr. Crawford was firmly opposed not only to the Ursulines' claim to title but to any application for further delay of the sale.[21] Seeing that he could make no headway with Secretary Crawford, Mr. Brackenridge wrote to President James Monroe and a few days later met with him. They examined at length the points made in Brackenridge's letter, which said in part:

> In...conversation with the Secretary of the Treasury, I learned that the proclamations for the sale of the property claimed by the nuns of New Orleans, had actually been made out. The secretary seemed to be unfavorably inclined to the application for delay, chiefly on the ground that...it was their own neglect that they have to blame in not having had a decision on their claim before this...They say it formed originally a part of their property, and was taken by the Sovereign, to whom the American Government succeeded, for specific purposes and for none other.[22] Moreover it is not merely the portion occupied by the United States which is to be affected; the gardens of the convent which lie in the rear of the Barracks will be destroyed...independently of the dispute as to title, the mode of disposing of the property is one which deeply interests them. The hospital, now a part of the United

States Possessions, they state is theirs by still stronger claim than the Barracks.[23]

President Monroe's comments at the meeting with Brackenridge indicated that he was favorably inclined toward the Ursuline position. The president was reluctant though to interfere in what related "more immediately to the duties of the Secretary."[24] Having received no orders to delay, Secretary Crawford proceeded to set the date for the sale on the second Monday of January, 1821.[25] The Ursulines then formally protested the sale in the *Gazette* newspaper,[26] and the sale was postponed.[27] At this point the nuns decided to write directly to President Monroe, basing one of their claims on the exchange of lots made when Carondelet was governor of Louisiana. The letter pointed out that Carondelet had been charged with preserving the king's property. His recognition of their claim to the land at that time clearly validated their present claim to the same property.[28]

Having repeated the evidence previously submitted, they asked that all proceedings related to the sale be suspended until their representative, Bishop DuBourg, could be heard. The bishop felt further correspondence was futile and a personal visit from him was necessary because of the value of the property. In correspondence to Rome he wrote:

> Although several times the Nuns entered a reclamation in writing, their claim received no acknowledgement. I was advised, therefore, by the lawyers to come to the seat of the Federal government, and thought it my duty to do so, in order to discuss the matter *via voce* .... This piece of property, indeed, is so valuable that I deemed that no effort should be spared to have this wrong righted.[29]

Before the bishop's departure for Washington, he presided over a special meeting of the community chapter during which the nuns decided to purchase the Military Hospital, which they still maintained was on their property.[30] Negotiations were completed and United States patents were signed and issued on August 7, 1821.[31] The Ursulines were forced to buy the hospital, since they were confined to less than a single square

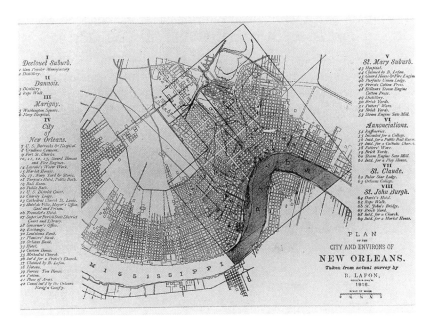

I
Declouet Suburb.
1 Gun Powder Manufactory
2 Distillery.
II
Dannois.
3 Distillery.
4 Rope Walk.
III
Marigny.
5 Washington Square.
6 Navy Hospital.
IV
City
of
New Orleans.
7 U. S. Barracks & Hospital.
8 Ursulines Convent.
9 Fort St. Charles.
10, 11, 12, 13, Guard Houses and Fire Engines.
14 Latrobe's Water Work.
15 Market Houses.
16, 17, Navy Yard & Stores.
18 Turpeau's Hotel, Public Bath.
19 Ball Room.
20 Public Bath.
21 U. S. District Court.
22 Clarris Lodge.
23 Cathedral Church St. Louis.
24 Hotel à la Ville, Mayor's Office.
Gaol and Prison.
26 Tremolet's Hotel.
27 Superior Parish State District Court and Library.
28 Governor's Office.
29 Exchange.
30 Louisiana Bank.
31 Planters' Bank.
32 Orleans Bank.
33 Hotel.
34 Custom House.
35 Methodist Church.
36 Intd for a Protest Church.
37 Claimed by B. Lafon.
38 Hotons.
39 Parish Tou House.
40 Prison.
41 Place of Arms.
42 Canal intd by the Orleans Navig'n Comp'y.

V
St. Mary Suburb.
43 Hospital.
44 Claimed by B. Lafon.
45 Guard House & Fire Engine.
46 Parfaite Union Lodge.
47 Ferrets Cotton Press.
48 Rilleux Steam Engine Cotton Press.
49 Distillery.
50 Brick Yards.
51 Potters' Ware.
52 Brick Yards.
53 Steam Engine Saw Mill.
VI
Annonciations.
54 Raffineries.
55 Inlended for a College.
56 Intd. for a Public Ball Room.
57 Intd. for a Catholic Church.
58 Potters' Ware.
59 Brick Yards.
60 Steam Engine Saw Mill.
61 Intd. for a Flag House.
VII
St. Claude.
62 Polar Star Lodge.
63 Orleans College.
VIII
St. John Burgh.
64 Davis's Hotel.
65 Rope Walk.
66 St. John's Bridge.
67 Brick Yard.
68 Intd. for a Church.
69 Intd. for a Market House.

PLAN
OF THE
CITY AND ENVIRONS OF
NEW ORLEANS.
Taken from actual survey by
B. LAFON.
1816.

MISSISSIPPI

The outlined area of this 1868 map shows the size of New Orleans in 1816. Courtesy Historic New Orleans Collection, 1950.57.35

block by the opening of the streets through their property.[32]

According to a 1728 plan drawn by French royal engineer Ignace François Broutin, the city of New Orleans was laid out in squares by streets running northeast and southwest. When the Ursulines moved from the Kolly house to their convent at the other end of town, not all the projected streets had been opened, although it is probable that Condé (today Chartres) Street was open as far as Arsenal (Ursulines) Street.[33] As the town grew, residents demanded that the streets obstructed by the convent property and government barracks be opened.[34] On May 19, 1819, New Orleans Mayor Augustin Macarty notified the Ursulines that on the fifteenth of the following June the streets would be opened "to reestablish communication as indicated on the primitive map of New Orleans." The delay would allow the religious time to enclose the grounds bordering these streets.[35] The nuns opposed this measure, as it would divide their grounds into three parts, confining their cloister to the square on which the convent stood. As an inducement to open Condé Street through the nuns garden, the City Council agreed on May 29, 1819, "to supply at its expense, the necessary planks and posts as well as the

259

labor to build a fence, with one or more gates on the side of said street."³⁶ This concession was not sufficient, however, to satisfy the nuns about abandoning the privacy that they had enjoyed for so many years.

Some months passed while the City Council initiated a search for early maps of New Orleans, and when two arrived from France the City Attorney exhibited them at the convent.³⁷ Since the Ursulines still resisted, the City Council passed a resolution on April 22, 1820, authorizing the City Attorney to bring action against them if they did not yield by May 1.³⁸ Faced with this alternative, the community agreed to the City Council's plan on condition that a board fence with the necessary gates as well as sidewalks be constructed at municipal expense.³⁹ By mid-October no action had been taken.⁴⁰ Apparently after the April resolution the sisters had intimated that the opening of the streets would force them to move to another location. This prompted the Council to appoint a committee that would make sure that if the Ursulines did move, the property would become public.⁴¹ The exact date on which the streets were opened is unknown,⁴² as convent records indicate only the year 1821, before the issue of ownership of the property was decided.

By November of 1822 the Ursulines had learned of the successful efforts of Bishop DuBourg in dealing with federal officials.⁴³ They received notice that the government had no intention of interfering "with any lands within their ancient enclosures."⁴⁴ President Monroe had consulted Attorney General William Wirt regarding the validity of the nuns' claims, and the Attorney General had rendered a favorable opinion:

> They [Ursulines] appear to have had a continued possession, of more than seventy years, of all the grounds embraced by their enclosure; which, I understand, embraces the whole of four squares bounded by Levee, Ursuline, Royal and Garrison Streets, except so much thereof, as is occupied by the Hospital, banks, quarters....
> To so much of these grounds, therefore, as is embraced by their enclosure, they have, I think, a title by possession which cannot justly be disturbed.⁴⁵

The opinion authorized agents of the United States to give the community legal title for all the property within their enclosure "not only by reason of concessions made by former governments, but more especially on account of the length of time of possession."[46] There was still to resolve the plot of ground behind the hospital between the convent and Hospital Street, still held by the federal government. Since the Ursulines owned a strip on the opposite side of the street behind the barracks, negotiations were soon under way for an exchange of these two properties.[47] By a single act of February 17, 1824,[48] the Ursuline nuns transferred to the United States all their title and claim to six lots situated in the square between "Condé, Hospital, Royale and Quartier (Barracks) Streets,"[49] and The United States relinquished all rights to six lots in the square between Levee, Ursulines, Condé, and Hospital Streets.[50] This same act confirmed the nuns' title to the residue of property within their enclosure. At long last the religious had undisputed possession of two entire squares extending back from the river.

While the nuns wrestled with problems related to property, opening of streets, and title settlements, regular community life and the classroom routine continued. In 1820, H.M. Brackenridge told President Monroe that the Ursuline Convent was "the school where the young ladies of all the best families" were educated; that it was "a most valuable institution;" and that all who were "acquainted with the ladies of Louisiana educated in this seminary" spoke "in its praise."[51] Yet very few of these young women were returning to join the ranks of their former teachers in perpetuating the work of Christian education. Other regions again would provide missionaries for the Louisiana area.

CHAPTER 15

Ursulines from Canada

By 1821 the fifteen Ursulines who made up the New Orleans community had realized that new members were not likely to come from the local area, as few had come in the past. Of the nine French religious who had come in 1817, only four were still members of the community. Only one American, Mary Bowling of Washington, D.C., had received the habit and the name Sister Francis de Sales on May 4, 1819.[1]

The fifteen[2] women fell into two age groups: those less than forty, and those over fifty, who were twice the number of the younger group. To fill the gap between the two age groups the community felt that they needed to recruit religious from an established community whose members were already trained in religious and spiritual matters. Mother St. Michel therefore wrote[3] to the Superior of the Canadian Ursuline Convent of Trois-Rivières asking for help, sending the letter in care of a Mr. Roland who was returning to Trois-Rivières from New Orleans. Either a copy of that letter or a duplicate letter was also included to be forwarded to the Quebec Convent.[4] In her letter Mother St. Michel, after relating the great need of the New Orleans community, requested that the Canadian sisters send two religious between the ages of 38 and 40 to New Orleans. She noted that even if they were older, but in good health, they would be welcomed. She did emphasize that the climate was harsh and the work very hard.[5] The New Orleans nuns offered to pay all the expenses[6] of the journey and to provide those who would come with all that they would need.

Bishop DuBourg, writing from St. Louis in July, 1821, eloquently pleaded the cause of Mother St. Michel and her sisters with Archbishop Plessis of Quebec. The age disparity among the nuns, rather than the small number available for the work they had undertaken, was the bishop's primary concern.

> A dozen young persons have joined within the last few years,[7] and the house, as regards members, seems no longer to give occasion for fear. But when I consider

Gaillard Cottage 1824 is typical of buildings in New Orleans at this period. Courtesy Historic New Orleans Collection, 00.38.

the age of the venerable pillars of this edifice, and that at the moment, perhaps near at hand, of their destruction, there remain but reeds to replace them...It is indispensable for the maintenance of the institution that there should come to it three or four religious already professed, of mature age, that is to say, about forty or forty-three years old, of proved judgment and virtue, who could fill the gap which separates the old from the young.[8]

Bishop DuBourg then asked Archbishop Plessis to support his request for assistance by contacting the two Canadian convents and encouraging the nuns to send mature members of their communities to New Orleans.

Mother St. Henri, superior of the Quebec convent, told Archbishop Plessis that her community had a sincere desire to assist the New Orleans community, but the sisters willing to leave did not have the qualities specified.[9] Indeed the archbishop rejected as not qualified two sisters from Trois-Rivières who volunteered.[10] However, the Canadian bishop must have given DuBourg some encouragement. In a letter written in early 1822 DuBourg spoke of "the hope of getting several subjects of distinguished merit."[11] Then, apparently fully confident that a group of nuns would be journeying southward, DuBourg in the same letter explained the plans he had made for the trip. Father Janvier, a priest of the Louisiana diocese who had been on leave of absence at Detroit, was preparing to leave for New Orleans. He intended to accompany three young women who wished to enter the New Orleans novitiate,[12] and he would meet the nuns from Quebec at Montreal. From there they would go to New York and travel to New Orleans by sea.

Before this letter reached Quebec the nuns of New Orleans were deeply grieved by the death of Mother St. Michel Gensoul on March 19, 1822. On that very day Bishop DuBourg wrote again to Archbishop

Chair used by each of the bishops and archbishops during services at the Ursuline chapels. Courtesy Ursuline Archives & Museum. Photo by Sr. Jacqueline Toppino, O.S.U.

Plessis:

As I write, her [Mother St. Michel's] remains are laid out in the choir of the convent, of which all are plunged in indescribable grief. Never was there greater cause for affliction than is theirs; for in Mother St. Michel they lose the firmest support of their house, and none of them can replace her as far as the talent and ability of her state are concerned. This death renders the situation of their institute extremely critical. It is now reduced to twelve choir nuns, of whom two are seventy years of age, one sixty-six, one or two very infirm, and the remainder too young for the higher offices. Your good nuns will therefore understand that they cannot make too much haste in coming to the aid of their Sisters, and that if instead of four they could send six subjects of mature age, and formed to the virtues and functions of their institute, they would much better fulfill the object they propose to themselves in this work of charity. All the conditions as to health and disposition that the solicitude of the late departed laid down are now set aside. We entrust ourselves absolutely, my lord, to your lordship's goodness and prudence.[13]

The two letters revived an interest in going to Louisiana, and several sisters offered to change communities. On May 3, Archbishop Plessis chose three: Sister St. Charles Borne, Sister St. Louis de Gonzague Bougie, and Sister St. Etienne Morin. They were all active members of the Quebec community, engaged either in teaching or in some other important responsibility. Sister St. Etienne, although only twenty-nine, had already been elected treasurer for a second term of three years.[14] Preparations for the trip were hastily made, as Father Janvier had been expected to come to Montreal in April. But the nuns received no word from him until June, and he did not arrive until July 16.[15] He had fallen from his horse while making a sick call and was unable to travel for some weeks. This delay may have started a rumor that reached Bishop DuBourg at St. Louis. Through a letter the bishop had been informed of a complicated change in plans on Father Janvier's part. DuBourg wrote to Plessis indicating that he had the highest regard for Janvier, and worried that the priest was changing his mind due to the climate and conditions in New Orleans.[16] Whether Janvier stayed in Detroit longer than necessary after his fall became inconsequential, as events in other areas would again delay plans.

In the summer of 1822 an epidemic of yellow fever had developed in New York, making it unwise for the religious to go there for departure. Bishop DuBourg suggested in a July 8th letter that they stay in Quebec until September or later. The delay gave the sisters sufficient time to

Depiction of the Sacred Heart of Jesus in painting originally brought from France by the early missionaires. Jesus is depicted as a burning heart. Photo by Sr. Jacqueline Toppino, O.S.U.

reflect on the step they were taking. Friends and relatives used very powerful arguments to persuade them to remain in Canada. The difficulties of the life, the severe heat, the customs and morals of the people, described as "devotees of liberty and pleasure," even the danger from pirates during the voyage were raised as reasons to remain in their own community. Still they remained firm in their resolve to go. Archbishop Plessis arranged for Father Thomas Maguire[17] to accompany the sisters to New York, and Father Janvier left in mid-September to arrange accommodations in New York and complete plans for the voyage.[18] Janvier seemed to have been concerned about finances, but not to the point of losing his sense of humor when he wrote:

> If the money that I have can bring us to the end of our journey without a penny over, I shall be satisfied; if it does not, I think that I dare to hope that the captain will not throw us into the sea, nor sell us to the Spanish. The religious of New Orleans have a good reputation, they say; we will draw a bill of exchange on their strongbox.[19]

Sisters St. Charles, St. Louis de Gonzague, and St. Etienne left the Quebec monastery at six o'clock on the evening of October 3, 1822. A crowd of friends and neighbors had gathered to wish them well and witness the unusual sight of the religious leaving cloister. Each sister entered a different carriage which then drove to the steamboat, followed by the crowd. At two in the morning they were under way, and by six that evening they were in Trois-Rivières. There Mother Ste. Hélène Lottinville joined them.[20] The missionaries reached Montreal on Saturday evening, October 7, and left the next morning with the three young ladies from Detroit, who had been recruited by Father Janvier. From New York Father Maguire wrote to Archbishop Plessis:

> ...our good Ladies arrived here yesterday, accompanied by Mr. Janvier who met them at Albany....Many miles of wearisome travel by carriage, especially from La Prairie to Lake Champlain; the continual noise of the machinery of the steamboats, the uncomfortable crowd

of passengers of every color and of almost every nation, all this added to the questioning of the curious, to a little seasickness, and to insomnia, fatigues them considerably; but good beds and rest have restored them and they are now in perfect health....I must add, nevertheless, that the religious from Trois-Rivières has suffered more than the others, probably because of the normal state of her health.

They are lodged here...with the Sisters of Charity who received them with all the cordiality and kindness that true charity inspires.... There is no danger of yellow fever in the quarter where we are.[21]

After a sojourn of ten days in New York, the party embarked on a packet ship[22] for New Orleans on October 21, the feast of their patroness St. Ursula. Within a few weeks a newspaper of November 12 related that pirates had taken the vessel on which the Ursulines had sailed and had held the passengers captive for twenty-four hours.[23] The Ursulines of Quebec must have been greatly disturbed over this news, which was misreported. Actually a shower of gun fire had driven off the corsairs, and no one had been harmed. Almost as bad, however, yellow fever was raging in New Orleans when the group arrived, and they had to remain outside the city at the home of Mrs. Jourdan. Sister St. Etienne wrote to her former superior in November and described their reception in Louisiana:

We are as much at home as if we had been here always. Madame Deslonde [mother of Mrs. Jourdan] told us yesterday that they were no more inconvenienced by us than if we had always been members of the family. We are near the college of Father Martial. The college is on the ground of the religious, where they intend to build a new convent. There is a chapel near the college that affords us the advantage of hearing Mass.[24]

Mother Superior St. Joseph Laclotte[25] and her sisters waited impatiently for the first white frost to clear the air so that they could greet their Canadian sisters. It was late in coming, but on December

5, 1822, the Ursulines joyfully welcomed their new members. Well coached children delivered complementary speeches, a solemn Mass of thanksgiving was sung, and the *Te Deum* chanted. Later there was a dinner for all the clergy of the city at the home of Father Sibourd, vicar-general and Ursuline superior.[26]

Coming from a large and prosperous community, the Canadians were struck by the poverty of the Ursulines of New Orleans. "Although we surely expected," they wrote, "to find a great contrast between our house here and our house at Quebec, there is a much greater one than we anticipated."[27] A member of the New Orleans community described the reaction of the Canadians to the conditions at the New Orleans convent:

> One of them wept hot tears on seeing the poverty of our house that she likened to the stable of Bethlehem, although we had spent several weeks preparing for their reception. The entire furnishings of the community room consisted, at that time, of two large benches, six little old chairs for the elder Mothers, and two armoirs, also old. The religious kept their work in one of these and the firewood in the other. The house was neither ceiled [sic] nor painted; and the door and windows were of rough wood.[28]

Because of the northern climate and available fabrics, the Canadian nuns' clothing was quite different. The New Orleans community had habits of a coarse material with single gimps and bandeaux, while the Canadians used double bandeaux and a finer material. They also wore black aprons. Still, a reasonable amount of good will achieved uniformity of dress. The agreed-upon product consisted of double gimps and black underskirt like the habit, as well as the habit over which there was no disagreement.[29] Clothing simply could not be allowed to be an impairment to the acculturation of the newcomers. The Ursulines were simply grateful for their presence:

> Divine Providence who watches over this house in a very special manner permitted us to find in these sisters religious according to the heart of God. They joined

to the virtues of their state an excellent spirit and great zeal for the glory of God.[30]

The religious were also very grateful to Archbishop Plessis for encouraging the sisters to come to New Orleans. The New Orleans community had been close to dissolution because of their shrinking ranks. Mother St. Joseph expressed the thoughts of all when she wrote to thank the archbishop:

Their arrival, by giving us renewed existence, has changed our sorrow into consolation and joy; we find in our dear Sisters...who were zealous enough to devote

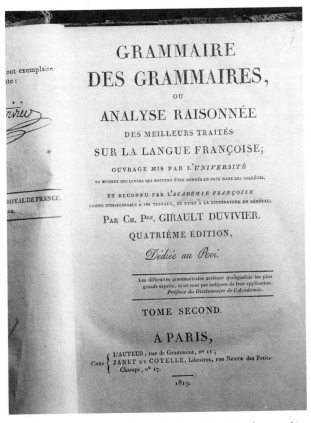

Grammaire des Grammaires, 1819. French book used in teaching students in early 19th century. Courtesy Ursuline Archives & Museum. Photo by Sr. Jacqueline Toppino, O.S.U.

themselves to this mission, qualities which surpass our expectations, and which could be looked for only in a community where such good order, regularity, and virtue exist, as in that whence they came.[31]

Assignments for the year were made promptly after the Canadians arrived. Sister St. Louis Bougie was made mistress of novices, and from the time of her appointment the novices began to spend more time in study.[32] Sister St. Charles Borne was entrusted with the boarders who were preparing to make their First Communion, and twenty-two young women received the sacrament the following spring.[33] This is all the convent records tell us of the first assignments of the newcomers, but Father Janvier implies in a letter to Mother St. Henri that they were given some of the more important duties in the house.[34] He indicated that this showed the great esteem in which the Canadians were held.

Sister St. Hélène, who was in poor health when she left Trois-Rivières, suffered very much in New Orleans. When doctors were unable to help her, it was decided that she should return to Canada. She left on April 16, 1824, to the regret of all.[35] Two of the young ladies from Detroit had already gone "on account of their health,"[36] and the third soon followed. The three remaining religious from Quebec labored in their adopted country with great generosity during their lives. Perhaps the greatest trial during their first months in New Orleans was the close confinement of the religious occasioned by the opening of the streets through the convent gardens and enclosure. The Canadians had seen the property which the Ursulines owned outside the city when they had stayed at Mrs. Jourdan's home. All of the community looked forward to the day when the nuns could exchange their cramped quarters on Chartres Street for the spacious grounds of this property.

CHAPTER 16

A Century Comes Full Circle

As New Orleans grew, the residential area of the city expanded to the open country that had once surrounded the Vieux Carré. The Ursulines foresaw that eventually the site on Chartres (Condé) Street might become undesirable for a cloistered community conducting a boarding school for girls. In the fall of 1818, they bought a tract of land[1] situated about two miles below New Orleans and on the same side of the river, at the site now occupied by the Industrial Canal. They purchased the estate of three *arpents* frontage on the Mississippi and eighty *arpents* depth from François Duplessis for $34,640.[2] On this property were two houses, one a quaint, oriental-looking building having one story and a belvedere; and the other a larger house with the potential for use as an academy.[3] In this building Father Bertrand Martial had evidently opened his school for boys in 1819, the one the Canadian sisters had observed. The nuns took no immediate steps toward erecting a new convent on the site, probably for financial reasons. In addition, before committing themselves in any way, the nuns wished to discuss the matter with Bishop DuBourg personally. Such an interview was impossible until the bishop returned to New Orleans.

In the winter of 1820, five years after his appointment to the See of New Orleans, Bishop DuBourg felt that at last it might be possible to visit the southern part of his diocese. Knowing the conditions and sentiments that still prevailed in the district, he set out with mixed emotions. On the way down the river he visited various parishes and received a friendly welcome on all sides. As he approached New Orleans, a large crowd of people headed by Father Sibourd, the vicar-general, and Père Antoine came to welcome their bishop about six miles from the city. It was a reception far different from what he had expected, given the years of religious tensions in New Orleans. Christmas Eve fell on a Sunday, and Bishop DuBourg presided at a High Mass celebrated at the cathedral by Père Antoine. This was the first time in nineteen years that a bishop had entered the cathedral in New Orleans. To the great joy of the Ursulines, Bishop DuBourg said the midnight Mass and the second Mass Christmas morning in their chapel. Then he celebrated pontifically in the cathedral.[4]

On New Year's Day, 1821, the Ursulines held a special chapter meeting at which Bishop DuBourg presided, and where the community decided to build another convent on the estate acquired three years earlier. Bishop DuBourg, however, returned to St. Louis that summer, and nothing was done to carry out the decision. He returned early in 1822, apparently to remain some time. On April 2, 1822, the Ursulines confided to him "the full and absolute direction" of the construction of the convent.[5] Even so, DuBourg did not feel it prudent for the nuns to leave the convent on Chartres Street until the question of the ownership of the property had been decided. He feared that since "they had been given the property by a former government for a special purpose, if they left it, the American government would claim it."[6]

In November, 1822 the complicated negotiations the Ursulines had gone through with United States officials regarding their ownership of the Chartres Street property and the documents of ownership they possessed were settled favorably for the religious. This gave them the assurance to go forward with their proposed new convent. On March 25, 1823 they signed a contract for $64,200 with Messrs. Claude Gurlie and Joseph Guillot, well known builders of New Orleans.[7] The contract specified the construction of a two story brick building one hundred eighty feet long and fifty feet wide "from out to out". The contractors obligated themselves "to construct, finish, complete and perfect the building totally in all the rules of art, without any interruption...and to have it remitted to the community, key in hand, in eighteen months...and even sooner if possible." In order to finish within the time specified, the contractors agreed not to undertake any other major enterprise while they were working on the convent. Construction was to begin May 1, 1823.

The specifications[8] were quite complete and detailed. The general plan of the new convent was somewhat similar to that of the Chartres Street convent. It had three stories, with wide galleries on the first and second stories and dormer windows on the third floor. The lower floor was divided into eight large rooms and four smaller ones. A hall extended the length of the building and another crosswise. On the second floor there were thirty[9] small rooms for the religious. The foundations were to be constructed solidly,[10] and the roof was to be guaranteed for two

View of Dauphine St. Convent from dirt road. Courtesy LA Collection, Howard-Tilton Memorial Library, Tulane Univ., New Orleans, LA.

years.[11] The specifications called for two coats of paint, grey and green, on all doors and windows, on all floors of the house and gallery, and on the columns, railing, banisters, jalousies and two stairways. All openings were to have small hooks both inside and out to stop the banging of doors and windows. Messrs. Gurlie and Guillot agreed to rent two slaves,[12] Charles and Honoré, from the Ursulines as workmen and to allow the religious to furnish any of the necessary materials at a deduction in the cost equal to the current market prices.

More than a year before signing the construction contract, the nuns had contracted with Edward Bradley, an Irish brickmaker, to furnish "six hundred thousand merchantable bricks on their plantation...at the price of two and a half dollars per thousand."[13] In the contract the nuns agreed to furnish Mr. Bradley and his workmen "with board, bedding and nine attendants; also all utensils, molds, wheel or wheels necessary for the making, wood for burning the bricks, and timber for erecting the sheds." Mr. Bradley consented to construct the sheds without extra charge and to furnish any quantity of odd shaped bricks at the same price as the plain ones. More than a hundred forty thousand bricks were ready when the contractors began construction in May, 1823.[14] Apparently the Ursulines were not satisfied with this, for about a month later they agreed to pay Bradley an indemnity of $125 to cancel the contract as soon as he had finished the kiln of bricks he was making.[15] The nuns then sold the bricks to the contractors for $10.00 a thousand, the current price.

Sketch of Dauphine St. Convent. Courtesy Ursuline Archives & Museum. Photo by Sr. Jacqueline, Toppino O.S.U.

At the outset the nuns had intended to construct only the convent proper rather than execute the entire plan.[16] But before the first building was finished, they decided to add a two story brick wing with a kitchen, bakery and workrooms at a cost of $17,972.[17] Its ground floor was divided into five rooms and a corridor, with a brick floor throughout. There were eight rooms on the second floor, which according to the original specifications could be reached only by an outside stair. Later a stair was built leading up from the kitchen.[18]

When the work was nearing completion, Mother St. Joseph Laclotte, Sister St. Louis and Sister St. Etienne went to see the new convent and plan how each area of the building would be used. Sister St. Joseph described the visit, as well as their reasons for leaving the cloister to view the new structure in a letter to her former superior, Mother St. Henri.

> The building is beautiful for this country and is situated in a place where the air is very salubrious, where we can walk and breathe with ease; but it is unfortunate that pecuniary circumstances do not permit us to have a church and a choir built at once. We will have a temporary one until times improve and until we can sell some land.[19]

She continued in the letter to explain that their leaving the cloister to visit the new convent had been necessary and was approved by the bishop. She wrote that certain construction problems could have been avoided if they had inspected the convent sooner.

During the weeks that followed this inspection, the Ursulines quietly prepared to leave the old monastery, hallowed by so many memories of the devoted religious who had preceded them. The mighty and the lowly, the rich and poor, the bond and the free, as well as countless young women had crossed its threshold. The majority of the religious had not set foot outside the cloister since the day its gate first closed behind them. When the move came it was not marked by the pageantry of the colonial transfer, nor did all move at the same time.

On July 26, 1824 the community sent the three Canadian sisters and a novice, Sister Ste. Claire Coskery, to prepare for the reception of the boarders, who came two weeks later with a few more sisters.[20] The Superior and several other religious remained in the city some weeks longer to continue the classes of the half-boarders (*demi-pensionnaires*), tuition pupils that spent the day at the convent, attended classes with the boarders, but returned home at night. But the new buildings were not completely ready, and for several weeks nuns and pupils occupied the two older houses on the land. It was obviously an unpleasant experience.

> It was a time of misery. They prepared the meals in the city and sent them out to us. Once the servant arrived about seven o'clock in the evening and showed us empty plates saying that the cart had upset.

Some were so frightened that they passed the nights without sleeping. Sister Ste. Marie, a novice, much amused by the whole affair, could not keep from bursting out laughing. The rats ran here and there; the dishes fell; the children cried.[21]

In spite of the dismal conditions, the nuns tried to follow the ordinary course of religious life as closely as possible. They said the office together, and on Sunday mornings a priest came to hear confessions and say Mass. Bishop DuBourg came occasionally and dined with the community, as there was no chaplain's house.

In September the convent was finally ready for occupancy, and the remainder of the community arrived. Regular community life could resume as before and assignments were given out. Each nun had a separate room, which was a blessing after the crowded conditions at the old convent. Until a chapel could be built a large room intended for the nuns' dining room was used for Mass. On Sundays a second Mass was said for the community and the people of the neighborhood in a small aged chapel a short distance to the east of the convent.[22] The chapel had been there for a long time and may have been the chapel of the old Capuchin plantation.[23] There the Ursuline pupils of the time made their First Communions.

Before their removal to the new convent the nuns thought that the larger of the two houses on the estate could be used for the boarders. Too late they realized that it did not provide adequate space, and so they had the attic of the convent wainscotted so that it could be used as a dormitory.[24] East of the convent and close to the levee, they built a one story brick residence for the chaplain [25] with plastered brick columns on three sides and a loggia of four large arches at the rear, "quite typical of the plantation *garçonnières* of the early nineteenth century."[26] On the opposite side of the convent they built a one story brick parlor to receive visitors.[27] These additional buildings, together with other developments and changes, raised the total cost of the project to $81,672 not including the $681.47 paid to Mr. Bradley for making some of the bricks.[28] By the middle of December, 1824, the nuns had cleared $27,126 of this debt, and paid the final installment on July 30, 1825.[29] They had already discharged the purchase price of the underlying plantation.

Chaplain's Residence, Dauphine St. Convent. Courtesy Ursuline Archives & Museum. Photo by Mother Marie de la St. Croix, O.S.U.

Where did this small community obtain such large sums of money? Convent records give few details, but most of the money was derived from the sale in 1811 of a plantation,[30] subdivided into the *Faubourg Religieuses* or Suburb Nuns. The buyer was M. St. Pé, who paid $76,000 for the land with all its slaves, buildings and other appurtenances.[31] M. St. Pé had given his note due March 1, 1812, for $6,000. The balance was to be paid in annual installments of $8,750, beginning January 11, 1813. Undoubtedly part of the money received from this sale was expended for the plantation purchased in 1818, and part may have been used to pay for the buildings. The nuns sold much of the property that they owned near the Chartres Street convent and elsewhere to raise the additional funds. On March 1, 1825, they sold twenty lots located in the two squares bounded by Ursulines, Chartres, Barracks and Royal at auction. The majority of these lots sold for between $1,000 and $1,500 each, although some sold for as little as $750. One corner lot with a house on it sold for $2,500. The total of the day's sales amounted to $24,190.[32]

Although the nuns were delighted with their spacious new convent and grounds, the Chartres Street convent held many memories for them.

Corridor of Dauphine St. Convent. Courtesy Ursuline Archives & Museum. Photo by Mother Marie de la St. Croix, O.S.U.

Rather than sell it and have no voice in its future use, they decided to give their convent to Bishop DuBourg and his successors as a residence.[33] They hoped that the gift would encourage the bishop to make New Orleans the seat of the diocese. The gift was contingent on certain conditions:

> 1. That on all Sundays and feasts an instruction, or catechism lesson be given to the Negresses of the district to replace that which we give on such days.
> 2. That we shall have two Masses on all Sundays and feast days when we shall be at our plantation.
> 3. That three Masses will be said at the death of each religious and four priests will assist at the obsequies.
> 4. That every year we shall be given a retreat of eight days, and a sermon on the feasts of the Order: the feast of our Father St. Augustine, of our Mother St. Angela, and of our Patroness St. Ursula.[34]

Bishop DuBourg was glad to accept the old convent with these stipulations.

The gift made it possible for the bishop to have not only a house of his own, but also a church "in which the first pastor of the diocese has not the shocking humiliation of depending on church wardens who regard themselves as absolute masters and altogether independent of the Bishop."[35]

The Ursulines had offered the convent to Bishop DuBourg before they actually moved to the new convent, and in the interim period he made plans for the use of the building. Father Martial had discontinued his school, and the bishop hoped to establish a college in the Chartres Street convent. He wrote to his brother in France in March, 1824, and noted that there was room for boarders, masters, and servants for a proposed college. The convent would also afford a private apartment with its own entrance for his use.[36] Once the nuns had moved out, however, the bishop found that repairs and remodeling of the convent would require a considerable outlay. The bishop felt though that the gift of the convent was too beneficial to be turned down. DuBourg had an apartment designed for his use which included a new entrance, a kitchen and a private stairway. The rest of the convent was rented to Father Portier for use as a college.[37]

In repairing the building the bishop contracted substantial debts. During the time he was administrator and later as a bishop he relied "in some degree upon the Ursuline Nuns of New Orleans for support."[38] The sisters were hard pressed to pay their own debts, but were reluctant to see the bishop financially embarrassed. They preserved few records of their generosity, but we do know that they paid $2600[39] for the kitchen that the bishop had built and for repair of the former parlors. The Society for the Propagation of the Faith contributed funds toward liquidating the balance of the debt.[40] Father Michael Portier opened his college in the building once it was repaired.[41] In 1826, he was appointed Titular Bishop of Oleno and Vicar-Apostolic of Alabama, and on November 5, 1826, he was consecrated as the first Bishop of Mobile. Father Portier resigned in June from the college, but remained there until the fall when he left for Mobile. A few months after his departure the other priests also departed, and the school closed, ending the work begun by Father Martial of educating Catholic boys in New Orleans.[42]

Bishop DuBourg's problems with New Orleans Catholics continued in the mid 1820's, and his acquisition and conversion of the convent to a residence was criticized. The Marguilliers, who were still very influential, spearheaded opposition to him, accusing him of clerical interference in the affairs of the city and violation of the civil rights of citizens. In newspapers and pamphlets they accused him of robbing[43] the Ursulines of their property and of lining his pockets with assets of the church. The Ursulines themselves came under fire for abandoning their school in the city and settling in the suburbs, where their critics said they were out of reach of civil authorities. They were further criticized for closing the free school. A free school had been offered by the Ursulines since their arrival in the city, with classes offered in mornings and afternoons. In earlier times the attendance had been quite large, but prior to the move to the new convent enrollment had dwindled to a small number. The parents may have been "humiliated by the name of free school."[44] Once settled in the new convent the Ursulines notified the public through an announcement in the spring of 1825 in the *Courrier de la Louisiane* that they intended to continue the free school.

The Ladies of St. Ursula inform the public that
on the 5th of April next, they will open in their New

Washroom, Dauphine St. Convent. Courtesy Ursuline Archives & Museum. Photo by Mother Marie de la St. Croix, O.S.U.

Monastery, the gratuitous external classes. They will teach Reading, Writing, Arithmetic, and Manual Work. The classes will open in summer at 8 o'clock and in winter at 9 o'clock a.m.[45]

The nuns also hoped to continue to care for the orphans in their new establishment, but politics in the city frustrated their wishes. Previously the city had supported twenty-four orphans whom the Ursulines cared for. The sisters fed, clothed, and cared for them in health and nursed them when sick. They also taught the orphans to read, write, sew, keep house, and to understand Christian doctrine. The city allotted each orphan only five dollars a month. After the move the City Council decided to withdraw the funding for the orphans. Convent records give only a brief account of the Council's reaction to their move:

> Towards the end of 1824 the house was very much calumniated and the authorities of the city determined to have the 24 orphans for whom the city paid $120 per month ($5 for each one) leave the convent. We had all those who were prepared make their First Communion on Christmas Day at Midnight Mass. Bishop DuBourg gave a beautiful instruction suitable to the feast and to the ceremony.[46]

The records of the City Council give a more detailed story and reflect that accusations were made, based on hearsay evidence. On October 9, 1824, Mr. Nicholas Girod, a former mayor of New Orleans, informed the Council that he had been told that the orphan girls whose board the corporation paid were not properly cared for at the convent. He asked that the girls be removed to the Poydras Asylum. Mr. Lebreton Davezac moved that an investigation be made before making the decision. A committee composed of Messrs. Girod, Davezac, and Wiltz was appointed to visit the convent and the Poydras Asylum to assess the conditions at each place.

When the committee arrived at the new convent, fourteen orphans were in school, as the others had not moved from the city yet. Several of the girls were barefoot, and the committee objected strongly to this.

Mother Superior explained that all the girls had shoes, but some preferred not to wear them in the warm fall weather. The committee contended that being barefoot was tantamount to being a slave and insisted that the girls be sent to put on shoes and stockings.

The methods of educating the orphans met with greater approval than did their apparel. The committee reported that there were two religious teaching the orphans, one in English and the other in French, and the subjects covered were reading, writing, and arithmetic. Evidently two of the orphans read for the committee, and they performed well. However, the committee was not satisfied with what they perceived as a different lifestyle for the orphans and the boarders. The report concluded that the orphans:

> ...serve the meals of the boarders, in a word they do almost all the work of servants... there exists between the orphans and the boarders a difference in dress, nourishment, education, occupation, necessary without a doubt, but which must certainly degrade these young unfortunate girls in humiliating them incessantly in their own eyes.[47]

At the Poydras Asylum the committee found fifty-six girls from five to fifteen years of age assembled in one class. They were taught reading, writing and arithmetic in English only, but almost all were wearing shoes and stockings! The committee found little fault with the lifestyle of the girls at the Poydras home.

> In this institution one sees equality reign which is the foremost of all benefits, and that which childhood appreciates above all. It is true that, destined to a frugal and laborious life, that their table is simple, as is their dress.... There is no domestic care, no household work from which they are exempt, but this work is alternately the task of all and each of them serves, and is in her turn served by her companions.[48]

The committee's report and the discussion that followed its presentation showed a clear bias for the Poydras Home. The convent girls did "almost all the work of servants," while the girls from the Poydras facility did "domestic cares and household work." The City Council was piqued because the Ursulines had moved to the country and had made no provision for a day school in the city.[49] Regardless of how the committee reported, the Council probably would have voted for the removal of the orphans from the convent. Although the Ursulines grieved to see the girls go to a non-sectarian institution, the girls were taken to the Poydras Asylum[50] on February 3, 1825.[51]

Nuns and front view of Dauphine St. Convent. Courtesy Ursuline Archives & Museum. Photo by Mother Marie de la St. Croix, O.S.U.

The boarding school continued to be very successful. There were seventy-two boarders at the time of the transfer to the new convent.[52] Unfortunately, the nuns in 1825 accepted a girl as a boarder whose reputation was questionable. When they became aware of the facts in the situation, the nuns dismissed her. Some parents then withdrew their daughters, posing a threat that enrollment might decrease. In fact it continued to increase and by January, 1828, the boarding school had eighty boarders and was larger than it had ever been.[53] Sister St. Charles related details of their daily life in the Academy in an 1825 letter to Mother St. Catherine and the members of her former Canadian community:

> In the boarding school here we teach Christian doctrine, sacred and profane history, mythology, geography, English, arithmetic, grammar, writing, embroidery, etc.[54] Instruction in such accomplishments as voice, piano, and drawing is not included in the ordinary tuition.[55]
>
> We had every reason to believe that our transfer which places us two miles from the city would displease the parents and that they would withdraw their children to place them in other boarding schools, so that they would not be deprived of seeing them as often as they desire. On the contrary, they are enchanted with our new monastery which seems to them to offer to their children very satisfactory advantages. The air is salubrious and the location is beautiful.
>
> We also have the consolation of teaching some children from the plantations. They were obliged to leave the city at the time of the epidemic. Their education would be retarded unless they employed tutors, and then religious instruction would be set aside.
>
> At present we have 56 girls. There are six mistresses who are on duty with them a week at a time. The outing on Thursday is most pleasant. The mistresses take their pupils to a small lake surrounded by weeping willows. In this rustic place, free from all restraint and work, they enjoy the innocent pleasures suited to their age.[56]

Besides the regular classroom instruction, the girls were also taught to sew and to do various kinds of house work. Each week four or more girls were appointed as helpers and assisted in sweeping the classrooms, setting the tables and serving at table.[57] Until 1824, the boarders went out once a month to spend the day with their parents, but the nuns thought this "frequent" going out interrupted their studies too much. To avoid the "frequent" interruptions the girls were given three days vacation every three months. Later they were permitted fifteen days vacation in the month of January and eight days in the month of June.[58]

As the boarding school grew a greater number of sisters was needed, and fortunately the community increased. Sister Marie de l'Incarnation Le Roy, an old friend of Mother St. Joseph Laclotte, came in 1825. She had wanted to come with Mother St. Joseph in 1810, but she was doing such excellent work at a large academy at Montpellier that her director encouraged her to stay. She was also the sole support of her mother. But when she was finally free to leave France, she came to New Orleans. Although she was much older than the other novices, the training period was a source of enrichment to her. Her prior experience as a teacher and administrator, as well as additional talents, made her a valuable teacher for the New Orleans girls.[59] Some local women also entered the novitiate, and Mother St. Louis, the novice mistress, wrote to Mother St. Henri in June of 1826 with elation:

Can you believe that in a country where one scarcely
sees one postulant in six years, six have entered the novitiate

Gallery of the first floor, Dauphine St. Convent. Courtesy Ursuline Archives & Museum. Photo by Mother Marie de la St. Croix, O.S.U.

Garden, Dauphine St. Convent. Courtesy Ursuline Archives & Museum. Photo by Mother Marie de la St. Croix, O.S.U.

since All Saints? ...I am quite satisfied with my novices. They are good and are striving to become virtuous.[60]

The success of the boarding school and the novitiate was a source of joy to Bishop DuBourg. The bishop often found temporary respite from his worries and troubles when he visited or said Mass for the Ursulines and their students.

For many years it had been obvious that DuBourg needed assistance in administering the vast diocese. Roman Catholic terminology defines the position of coadjutor as a bishop who is appointed to assist another bishop, often having the right of succession. In 1823 Father Joseph Rosati, a member of the Congregation of the Mission order, was appointed a coadjutor to the bishop of Louisiana. His appointment carried the proviso that he would be designated as bishop of one of two dioceses into which Louisiana was to be divided within the next three years. Bishop DuBourg was quite pleased with this appointment, as he considered Father Rosati "a man of prudence, zeal, eloquence, modesty, and strength of body."[61] Father Rosati was consecrated a bishop in Donaldsonville,

Louisiana on March 25, 1824, and shortly after that visited New Orleans. During his stay he said daily Mass at the Ursuline chapel, officiated at Holy Week services, and on the day of his departure preached a sermon.[62] On a second visit to New Orleans in the fall of 1825, Bishop Rosati went straight to the Convent to avoid exposure to yellow fever. He was lodged in the chaplain's house and remained at the convent for almost a month, saying Mass each day.[63]

But the appointment of a coadjutor could not solve DuBourg's problems. He had considered resigning on numerous occasions, and in February, 1826, wrote to the Prefect of Propaganda asking that his resignation be accepted. Without waiting for a reply he decided to go to Rome and make his request personally. Before leaving New Orleans the bishop wrote a touching farewell letter to the Ursulines, containing a paragraph for each sister, from Mother St. Joseph down to the youngest novice.[64] DuBourg left for St. Louis in April of 1826, but when conferring with Bishop Rosati in St. Louis he did not reveal his letter of resignation. After leaving the United States, he did not again return.

Rumors that Bishop Dubourg would not return surfaced shortly after his departure. Apprehensive about what this might mean to the community, Mother St. Joseph confided her fears to Mother St. Henri:

> Our holy and respected Bishop, who is another St. Francis de Sales by his wisdom, his virtue, his kindness and his goodness, has gone to Europe for the affairs of his diocese. Many people believe that he will not return again to this country, but I need to have confidence that he will not abandon us and that he will return again to the post where Providence places him, where, indeed, he finds a field very difficult to cultivate.... It would be a terrible blow for us if we should lose our good, worthy, and respected father. This thought is too sad to contemplate.[65]

It is interesting to note that historians view DuBourg as having been a poor administrator, but he obviously was a warm and understanding person in his individual dealings, as evidenced in descriptions of him in the Ursuline records. The rumors referred to by Mother St. Joseph were true, and Pope Leo XII approved DuBourg's resignation on July 3, 1826, the same day that the bishop arrived at Havre, France. After DuBourg was appointed Bishop of Montauban, France,[66] he sent a portrait to the Ursulines, which hung in the community room for many years. Clergy and laity had mixed emotions about the bishop's resignation, but it was generally acknowledged that he had experienced a multitude of problems in managing the large diocese.

Before leaving for Europe Bishop Dubourg had urged Bishop Rosati to visit the lower part of the diocese, and on May 22, 1826, the bishop arrived in New Orleans. He established his residence at the old Ursuline convent and began to confer with clergy. Père Antoine had been reconciled with Bishop DuBourg, but Bishop Rosati made sure that he established a working relationship with him. Rosati also called on the Ursulines and said Mass at their chapel, having established a friendly relationship with them on previous visits to the city. He later administered the sacrament of Confirmation to twelve girls, and assisted at Mass on the feast of St. Angela on June 11th, confirming four more young women. After his visit he wrote to Bishop David, Auxiliary of

Chapel for the religious, Dauphine St. Convent. Courtesy Ursuline Archives & Museum. Photo by Mother Marie de la St. Croix, O.S.U.

Bardstown: "The Ursuline Convent could not go better. They have twelve novices and 90 boarders."[67]

Bishop Rosati was not notified of Bishop DuBourg's resignation until November, 1826. Along with the notification came a brief from Pope Leo XII creating the Diocese of New Orleans, which included the entire state of Louisiana, whose Constitution had been approved by Congress in 1812. The remainder of the Louisiana Purchase territory was designated as the Diocese of St. Louis. Bishop Rosati was asked to administer both dioceses. Rosati was willing to serve St. Louis and the upper valley, but he dreaded being assigned the New Orleans area. He wrote to Pope Leo XII and to the superior of the Lazarists begging not to be appointed to lower Louisiana. He would find it "better to continue poor and eat cornbread in Missouri than to have all manner of comforts in Louisiana,"[68] he wrote.

Bishop Rosati returned to New Orleans in March 1827, to the joy of the Ursulines.[69] He stayed for some time in the chaplain's residence of the convent, and during that time made his episcopal visitation of the community.[70] An episcopal visitation was one in which the bishop,

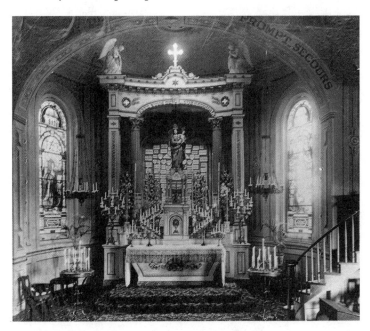

Our Lady of Prompt Succor Altar, Dauphine St. Convent. Courtesy Ursuline Archives & Museum. Photo by Mother Marie de la St. Croix, O.S.U.

as head of the diocese in which an Ursuline convent was located, examined the goals and undertakings of the community. Part of the "visitation" entailed personal interviews with each member of the community. During his visitation Bishop Rosati confirmed and ratified the dispensations from certain points of the Rule and Constitution Bishop DuBourg had given.[71] He defined the limits of the enclosure and gave directions for the building of certain cloister walls. He called for strict enforcement of the rule of cloister, even to the point of never being seen:

> The religious acting as portress will never open the carriage gate, but only the small gate which is near it; the Negro will enter by that one and will open and

Holy Water Font, Dauphine St. Convent. Courtesy Ursuline Archives & Museum. Photo by Sr. Jacqueline Toppino, O.S.U.

Cross from Dauphine St. Convent. Courtesy Ursuline Archives & Museum. Photo by Sr. Jacqueline Toppino, O.S.U.

close the other, so that the religious may never be seen from the road.[72]

The bishop approved the printing of a new edition of the Rules and Constitutions, as well as the revision of the book of customs and ceremonials.[73] He encouraged the sisters to decide on which customs to adopt for the New Orleans community and then to conform to them. The bishop recommended several improvements in the boarding school and stressed the strict observance of certain rules already in force.

> The boarding school demands all the attention
> of our pastoral solicitude and all the zeal of the community.
> We have noticed that it admits of several improvements

which will assure the progress of the children and lighten considerably the work of the religious.

1. The Mistress General will be in complete charge of the boarding school. She will superintend the children, and will also see that the Mistresses acquit themselves of their duties.

2. The Superior will appoint a religious who will have one or several assistants to correspond with the parents of the boarders.

3. There will be a Mistress of Study who will supervise the children while they are in the study room.[74] She will not teach in the classroom. It is important that this should always be the same person; she will be especially charged

Self photo by Mother Marie de la St. Croix, O.S.U. Courtesy Ursuline Archives & Museums.

with the good conduct of the children; however at other times they may continue to have the mistress of the week.

4. They will not form unnecessary classes. Therefore, all the children will be divided into several classes according to their ability. The first class will comprise those who are just beginning and who do not know how to spell. The second, third and fourth will include the children of the same ability in reading and grammar, and each class will have a mistress. During one half of the day they will occupy themselves with English and during the other half with French. They will hold the different classes in reading and grammar at the same time.

5. They will be inexorable in not sending the boarders to the parlor except on Thursdays and Sundays; and they will be supervised at all times by a religious. They will permit only the visits of the fathers and mothers, brothers and sisters, uncles and aunts; as to other persons, they will be admitted only when they bring a written permission from the father of the boarder. They will keep this letter and will inform the parents of it.

6. They will set a suitable time for the instructors of the accomplishments (music, painting, etc.); and they will request them to be exact in coming at the hour appointed. They will not send the children to them, if they come at another time, especially if the children would have to miss a part of another class.

7. They will supervise the boarders carefully even during the morning meditation.[75]

After the visitation Bishop Rosati affirmed that an excellent spirit permeated the community, the Rule was well observed, and all the religious displayed great enthusiasm for their educational endeavor. The bishop continued throughout his administration to show interest in the work of the Ursulines. "This good prelate is very devoted to our community", wrote Sister St. Etienne.[76] Sister St. Louis de Gonzague summed up the opinion of the community following the visitation.

Front yard and Mississippi River, view from Dauphine St. Convent. Courtesy Ursuline Arhcives & Museum. Photo by Mother Marie de la St. Croix, O.S.U.

> The community has been well pleased with his Lordship and I believe that he has been well pleased with us. I hope that the good God will deign, in His mercy, to give him to us as our pastor. He seems to be as much loved and respected as any bishop can be in this diocese.[77]

Bishop Rosati was appointed Bishop of St. Louis in 1827, but continued to be the administrator of the New Orleans diocese. He left New Orleans after the appointment, depriving the Ursulines of his presence at the one hundredth anniversary of their arrival in New Orleans. The centennial was celebrated on August 7, 1827, with Father August Jeanjean officiating.[78] Almost all of the clergy of the city assisted at the High Mass which was sung by the religious and accompanied by the music instructors on their instruments.[79]

> It was a day of joy in the Lord and of gratitude at the remembrance of the benefits by which it had pleased Divine Providence to preserve and renew this community

when it seemed that it could no longer exist after the departure of the sixteen religious for Havana in 1803.[80]

Sorrow for the death of Mother St. Joseph on December 10, 1827, followed the joyful centennial celebration a few months later. Only a few weeks before her death she had completed six years as superior. Mother St. Félicité Alzas, one of the three religious who had responded in 1786 to Mother St. Jacques Landelle's appeal for assistance succeeded her. Mother St. Félicité was not as well educated as Mother St. Joseph, but she had a mild, kindly temperament. Her generous nature endeared her to all, and she was given the affectionate title *La Bonne Mère.*[81]

With equal justice the Ursuline Convent could have been called *La Bonne Mère de la Louisiane.* For one hundred years the women of the Ursuline community had continued their educational work without interruption in a region almost devoid of Catholic educational institutions.[82] The Roman Catholic faith had been kept alive in the colony, now a part of the United States, through the instruction that the Ursulines had given young women. The mothers were the communicators of religious values, and those whom they educated had very strong values and knowledge. Until the arrival of Phillipine Duschene and her companion members of the Religious of the Sacred Heart, the Ursulines were the only Roman Catholic religious women teaching in the Louisiana territory.

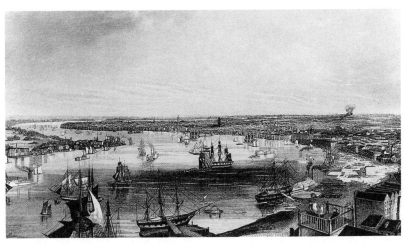

1852 painting shows the tremendous growth of the City by mid-ninteenth century. Courtesy historic New Orleans Collection, 1959.184.15.

A century of pioneering was complete. Though many years would elapse before Catholic education would become widespread in Louisiana, the Ursulines had prepared the way at the cost of innumerable sacrifices and heroic perseverance. In August of 1837, they could look back and rejoice that they had made great progress since the morning that Mother St. Augustin and her companions trudged down Chartres Street. They had made changes and adaptations demanded by the times but had essentially adhered to the traditions of St. Angela. Through love of God and their personal generosity and charity, the Ursulines had continued the work of their foundress in forming Christian wives and mothers who would educate their own Christian families and continue the restoration of Christianity envisioned by St. Angela.

Epilogue

In March, 1992, spring put its gorgeous touch on New Orleans. The trees all sprouted new leaves with lots of pollen to shake the noses of the inhabitants, the azaleas were glorious and petunias and inpatients were starting to peek out of the ground. The Ursulines who spent their years here during the period of this book (1727-1827) must have found this to be the most beautiful time of the year. They were assailed by heat, mosquitoes, rain, and storms and had no air conditioning, heat or Sewerage and Water Board pumps to assist them. So spring must have been very special in terms of giving them a reprieve from the elements of the weather. Spring of 1992 was very special to the Ursuline community of New Orleans for many reasons. In November of 1991 Sr. Damian Aycock, O.S.U., in recognition of the contributions of all religious to Catholic schools and for the pioneering role of the Ursuline Sisters in the United States' Catholic School Network, received the Elizabeth Seton Award from the National Catholic Educational Association. She was a guest at a ceremony in which the President of the United States gave his congratulations to the Ursulines throughout the country. Ursuline Academy High School was also honored in 1991 with the School of Excellence Award, which Sister Carolyn Marie Brockland O.S.U. and members of the Student Council received in Washington, D.C.

In 1992 Ursuline Academy cares for children from birth through high school. The young children of teachers are lovingly cared for until they are approaching three years of age. They can then enter the toddler program and progress from that to pre-kindergarten through high school if they are female. Boys are welcome until four years of age. The elementary school prepares girls for the college preparatory courses of the high school. An accelerated course of studies is offered for eighth grade students, which gives them an opportunity to pursue advanced studies in high school.

A survey conducted by Patty Stern Habans '64 in 1991 indicated some very interesting statistics. The list of living alumnae at that time totaled 4,000 persons, 1,210 of which replied to the survey. The oldest alumna was 95 years of age and the youngest responding was 20. There were 735 alumnae living in the greater New Orleans area. Of those alumnae, 109 of their daughters had graduated from Ursuline, and 34 had daughters attending the school. Membership in the Roman Catholic church was the predominant religion listed in the survey. Of those who responded 750 different occupations were listed. Homemaker, educator, physician, attorney were some of the most frequently listed ways in which the graduates of Ursuline in the twentieth century were fulfilling the mission of St. Angela to give Christian impact to society at large.

Appendix - Book Patrons

Jeanne M. Aber
Marcia McWaters Abide
Mr. and Mrs. Jack Abodie
Eunice Knop Accardo
Ronald W. Ackman
Charleen Wegmann Adam
Rose Mary Ainsworth
Clare Monjure Aiuvalasit
Roy R. Alberts
Martha Anciola Allen
Michelle Buisson Alley
Priscila F. Almendral
Janet Rivet Anderson
Yvonne Stelly Anderson, M.D.
Mr. & Mrs. Julio Andino
Mr. & Mrs. H. Keith Annison
Anonymous
The Anzelmo Family
Susan Ducasse Aparicio
Mrs. Blake Arata
Anne Spansel Arbo
Doris G. Arcement
Archdiocese of New Orleans
    Archives
Andrea Ann Arcuri
John L. Ardoin
Amy Armbruster
Linda Labanca Armbruster
Julie Mailhes Arms
Frederick & Dorothy Arndt
Arndt Family
Jack & Alanna Arnold

Ruth Ida Steger Artigues
Diana Aspiazu
Mrs. Normand D. Aucoin
Verna Boulet Aucoin
Fernand J. Aycock, Jr.
Sister Damian Aycock, O.S.U.
Sister Joan Marie Aycock, O.S.U.
Shirley Schaub Babcock
Margaret Medo Babin
Loretto Morvant Babst
Mary Ellen Badeaux
Debra A. Baehr
Mae Aycock Bakewell
Mrs. J. Luis Baños
Paddy Pittman Barattini
Doris Chase Baril
Mr. & Mrs. Robert A. Barnett
    (Lisa Zaccaria)
Jean Lala Barousse
Rose Merle Failla Barrett
Carolyn Casey Barrois
Mrs. Anna L. Barrois
John S. Bartlott, Jr.
Beverly Klundt Baudouin
Gertrude Marie Beauford
Sister André Becker, O.S.U.
Sister Gertrude Becker, O.S.U.
Sister Barbara Becnel, O.S.U.
Judith Crawford Beeler
Catherine Cassagne Benedict
June Blanchard Benedict
Henry R. & Amelia J. Bennett

Marilyn Ragusa Bennett
Earleen Fournet Bergeron
Pat Bergeron
Alice I. Bertheaud
Gladys G. Bessolo
Adele Marie & Peggy Flynn
    Bienvenu
Mrs. Elaine Graves Bilski
Dorothy M. Bising
Judy Radke Blakemore
Margaret Drown Blattmann
Mrs. Emanuel Blessey
Patricia Stewart Blouin
Joan Vath Blythe
Convent Boarder
Alan & Blanche Bobowski
Edwin & Marjorie Boehm
Miss Paula A. Boesch
Lindy Boggs
Nora C. Bolling
Maria Palermo Bologna
Joseph M. Bonin
Ashley & Laura Bonner
Jody Lynn Bonura
Margaret Booker
Mr. & Mrs. J. Patrick Booker
Mrs. Harry Hamilton Booker, Jr.
Theresa LaBarbera Boone
Margaret Bourg Booth
Kathryn P. & Alison L. Bordelon
Frances Wagnon Borrello
Jean Aucoin Bossier
Lisa Bothman
Rev. Claude Boudreaux, S.J.
Connie Connor Boudreaux
Rev. Msgr. Edw. L. Boudreaux
Mrs. Rosalie Kerber Boudreaux

Claire Weilbaecher Bourgeois
Gi Gi Paulette Bourgeois
Mr. & Mrs. George Michael Bour
    geois
Sister Glenda Bourgeois, O.S.U.
Patricia McCord Bourgeois
Dayle Lacour Bradford
Marilyn Boudreaux Brandt
Nathalie Forstall Brasher
Eloise Carey Braud
Mrs. Carol Hinrichs Braud
Mary M. Bray
Dr. & Mrs. Frederick W. Brazda
Donna Mayeux Breaux
Ned & Alice Breitenmoser
Lorraine F. Brennan
Mrs. Claire Lally Brennan
Dr. & Mrs. Del Britsch, Jr.
Sister Carolyn Marie Brockland,
    O.S.U.
Mrs. E. S. Brodtmann
Lisa Boudreaux Broekman
Linda Ormond Brooks
Irma Vial Brou
Fr. Douglas C. Brougher
Mrs. Virgie Broussard
Mrs. Celeste H. Brown
Suzanne Toca Browne
Marion Schexnayder Bruno
Jane Rodrigue Bryant
Elaine B. Buisson
Mr. & Mrs. Robert Bullick, Jennifer
    & Stephanie
Odessa Elston Burch
Edmund J. Burke, M.D.
Eileen Dalio Bush
Louise Byrd

Alberta Bostick Byrne
Madeline Warren Calhoun
Reverend Ronald L. Calkins
Sister Ruth Marie Call, O.S.U.
Mr. & Mrs. William Callaghan
Danielle Cambre
Marjorie A. Cambre
Grace E. Cameron
Melba Puig Campbell
Patricia Campbell
Julie Cangelosi
Suzanne Artigues Cangelosi
Mrs. F. F. Canik
Bettie Keller Caplis
Michele A. Cappel
Geralyn W. Caradona
Shirley J. Carbo
Marion Clade Carlton
Jane M. Gisevius-Carpenter
Betty P. Carrere
Marie Ramoneda Carriere
Miriam Ann Block Carroll
Donna L. Carter
Hazel M. Carter
Mrs. Jules A. Carville, Sr.
Dolores Herbert Casey
Mr. & Mrs. Taylor Casey
Mrs. Philip (Edna) Casolino
Leslie Castay
Jackie & Sam Catalanotto
Diane L. Centanni
Mr. & Mrs. Warren Anthony
    Cervini, III
Joyce Laborde Cessac
Frank & Mary Marks Cezus
Terry Dorvin Chamberlain
Mr. & Mrs. Connor John Chambers

Mr. & Mrs. Leo P. Cham-
    pagne, Sr.
Ana Maria Redmann Chandler
Anthony & Brenda W. Chappell
Mrs. Robert H. Charbonnet
Mr. & Mrs. Carlton I. Charles
Mrs. Marion T. Chedville
Janet Horil Cheralla
M. L. Christovich
Gasper A. Chwalek
Emery Clark
Dorothy Nebe Clasen
Allison Stern Clement
Dr. W. S. Coker
Mary Ann Helm Coker
Claire Brechtel Collier
Janet Marie Combes
Mrs. Iliff P. Conger (Loras Mary
    Walsh)
Evelyn Moragas Conino
Mr. & Mrs. C. R. Connally
Colleen M. Connolly
Mr.& Mrs. Armand J. Constantin,
    Jr.
Ed Cooper, M.D.
David Coote
Rosario "Chari" Coote
Mrs. Paul D. Cordes
Johanna Kunz Corniels
Asta Viguerie Cotonio
Mary Lillian Carey M. Courtney
Peggy Duvieilh Cozad
Gerry Klundt Crane
Pat O'Leary Crane
Gayle Graham Crawford
Anne Lousteau Creel
Russ & Claire Cresson

Adele Q. Cressy
Joyce Lafaye Crews
Mr. & Mrs. Boyd L. Crigger
Cheryl, Julie & Tim Cronan
Clayre & Linda Crook
Mildred D'Aubert Crouere
Pat Peltier Crum
Marcia L. Culley
JoAnn Ruttiger Curtis
Concetta M. D'Alessandro
Gloria Cahill D'Antoni
Mr. & Mrs. George A. d'Hemecourt, Jr.
James Dahman
Anna Marie Tripolino Daigle
Carol Mashburn Daigre
Mary Bergevin Dalton
Patricia F. Danflous
Mrs. Patricia Finney Daniels
Elcy Eble Daussat
Anne Harrison David
Nancy Weilbaecher Davis
Norma Carrillo Dean
Lisa Noe Deane
LaJuan Dickey DeBarbieris
Naomi Armshaw De Blanc
June C. deBoer
Ines V. DeGruy
Dorothy Deichmann
Mr. & Mrs. Scott E. Delacroix
Emily Ann DeLatte
Kimberly Ann DeLatte
Mr. & Mrs. Floyd E. delCorral
Mr. & Mrs. Edward J. Deleery
Joe and Mildred Deleery
Sister Jean Marie Deleery, O.S.U.
Mr. & Mrs. Mark Denegre & Family

Eugene (Gene) Denton
Marianne Summerville de Reyna
Lidwin & Greg de Silva
Mary Weilbaecher Desimone
Beverly deVerges DeSonier
Winston DeVille
Mary Jane Morgan Dewberry
Adele Allain Di Giovanna
Maureen Cicero Dicharry
Mr. & Mrs. Randy Dickmann
Mrs. Thompson M. Dietz (Anna Joyce)
Nancy & Carl Dolce
Dr. Constance C. Dolese
Gloria Beaullieu Doll
Dominican Sisters, Congregation of St. Mary
Mrs. Beverly C. Dominique
Bridget Donovan
Nancy R. Dreux
Dr. & Mrs. Edward J. Driscol
Bob & Julie Du Rocher
Lynn Garcia Dube
Charles G. Duffy III
Jeannette Dufilho
Rhea Horil Dufour
Dorothy Joan Barry Dulaney
Dolly Duplantier
Sally & Adrian Duplantier
Bertha Hanley DuPont
Bridget Molony Dupuy
Diana Durham
Kathleen Murphy Durio
Eldred Martinez Durocher
Mary Eble Eastin
Enid Faust Eckhardt
Col. & Mrs. Richard J. Ecuyer

Eloisa Maestri Edelmann
Mary Elisabeth Edwards
Veronica McCune Edwards
Karen Guerra Elizondo
Susan Haydel Elmendorf
Sondra Eglé Elvir
Mark & Sharon Erikson
Charlotte Grisaffi Eschman
Ann Haro Estingoy
Mrs. Peter Everett, III
Lisette Robbert Fabacher
Rita Rexer Fair
Doris Digby Faler
Pamela Castagna Falgoust
Andrée Lavie Fant
Janie Shay Farley
Helen E. Farris
Mary K. Caire Faust
Lindalee Horil Favaloro
Melissa D. Favaloro
Rosemary Baudier Favaloro
Mr. & Mrs. Charles J. Ferro
Rosemary Mano Ferro
Carlee Blamphin Feske
Jack C. & Ann Everard Fielder
Linda Marie Goll Finley
Betty Ricau Fischer
Rita Stock Fitzpatrick
Sister Michelle Fitzwilliam, O.S.U.
Winifred S. Flanagan
Peggy Fleming
Sherri Hughes Floyd
Mary L. Block Fonseca
Deidre R. Foreman
Mary E. Foscue, M.D.
Susan B. Fox
Sally Thomas Fradella

Patricia Kehoe France
Elinor Ernst Francis
Mrs. Esther Ravize Garcia Francisco
Margaret Monvoisin Fuller
Angela Fulton
Bernice Ory Fulton
Cathleen Rea Furlong
Mrs. Harold A. Fuselier, Jr.
Katherine Gallo
Mrs. Guido J. Gallo
Paulette Crouere Gamard
Miss Katherine R. Gambel
Anne Lacassagne Ganucheau
Rose De Abreu Garbarino
Johanna Maisano Garcia
Mrs. Shirley DeBlanc Garic
Marie Souchon Garrett
Betty B. Gatipon, Ph.D.
Mrs. Regina D. Gaudet
Rosemary W. Gaudry
Susan M. Gaudry
Jean Arnoult Gaul
Ellen Isabel Geheeb
Mr. & Mrs. Lawrence J. Genin
Helen Schell Gerig
Donna R., Charlotte R., & Rochelle
    R. Gerstner
Marcia Giglio
Julie Combes Gill
Tara Mc Auliffe Gilliland
Kathryn L. Gilmore
Mr. & Mrs. Michael Charles
    Ginart, Jr.
Anne Generes Githens
Joan G. Glynn
Dr. & Mrs. Gerald F. Goetz
Myron Gogarty

Stephanie & Stacey Gonzales
Betty Kehoe Gordon
Catherine Harang Gouaux
Lorena Guidry Gouaux
Mr. & Mrs. Henry E.
Gowland, Jr.
Eileen Dempsey Grace
Sister Miriam Teresa Graczak, O.S.U.
Dr. & Mrs. David Y. Graham
Mrs. Helen M. Graham
Eugene & Norma M. (Liedecke)
Green
Rosalind Michelle Green
Jennifer W. Greene
Shirley Kross Greiner
Inez P. Grieshaber
Janice Donaldson Grijns
Suzette LeBlanc Grogan
Mrs. Arthemise Tallon Gros
Katherine Sylvester Groves
Douglas Lanaux Grundmeyer
Elaine Toscano Grundmeyer
Sarah Elaine Grundmeyer
Mr. & Mrs. Ronald Guarino
Camille Edwards Guarisco
Ann M. Guenther
Dr. & Mrs. Stuart J. Guey, Jr.
Ogden & Kathleen Guillory
Blanche J. Guillot
Patricia Stern Habans
Marie Tripp Hanemann
Butsie & Jerry Hansen
Prof. Kirk O. Hanson
Mr. & Mrs. Warren Harang, Jr.
Charlotte Dussé Haro
Mary Lee Berner Harris
Laura Harrison

Patricia Mackel Harrison
Lyndall Keller Hart
Denise St. Martin Hartman
Jo A. Harun
Jerry & Karen Haskin
Dr. Gene C. Hassinger
Sister Mary Francis Hassinger,
O.S.U.
Marguerite R. Hathway
Sister Elizabeth Susan Hatzen-
buehler, O.S.U.
Mrs. Robert E. Hay
Patricia Walt Hays
Mrs. Bonnie Peyrefitte Hebeisen
Boyd & Barbara Helm
Mrs. Martha Elmer Hendricks
Chris Christopher Hermann
Mary Margaret Abbott Hevron
Elizabeth R. Hilsman
Brenda J. Hingle
Allison K. Hinyub
The Historic New Orleans Collec
tion
Kathleen Dowling Hite
Mr. & Mrs. Michael Hoban
Evelyn (Tiblier) Hoffman
Judy Kirn Hollier
Erin Maronge Holloway
Rhea Weilbaecher Holt
Margaret Gravois Holwill
Mr. & Mrs. Ferdinand J. Horil, Jr.
Wendy E. Horne
Mrs. James S. Hotard
Katherine M. Hough
Victoria C. Hu
Mrs. Alma C. Hughes
Mrs. Martin Hunley

Joy Lacour Hurley
Danny Hurtig Memorial Library
Dr. Eduard A. Imko
Mrs. E. J. Ireland
Veda T. Jackson
Carola Jacob
Mrs. Mildred Hatrel Jeansonne
Gayle Daniel Johnson
Marshall B. Jones
Mr. & Mrs. Robert E. Jones
Mr. & Mrs. C. Palmer Jones
Elaine Le Boeuf Jordan
Dr. & Mrs. Robert C. Judice
Sandra Davis Jung
Mary C. Kaehler
Peg Muldrey Kane
Mr. & Mrs. William S. Kaska
Ms. B. J. Kaska
Irene A. Kaster
Eugenie Luck Kearney
Katherine Stewart Keene
Barbara Kellam
Sister Madeline Kelly, O.S.U.
Rosalie Lemieux Kemk
Gerardine A. Kennedy
Mrs. Norman R. Kerth
Sister Susan Kienzler, O.S.U.
Rose Marie Crucia Kirkwood
Ken & Beverly Klundt
Charlotte Laguaite Knauer
Clarence Koehn
Mr. & Mrs. Michael J. Kondracki
Nancy Amato Konrad
Judith Byrnes Kountoupis
Mr. & Mrs.Frank J. Kozicki
Mrs. J.V. Leclere Krentel
Nancy Bode Kritikos

Lorraine Bahan Kroll
Judith A. Kron
Mrs. John L. Kron
Mary Ann Richarme Krupsky
Larry LaBarrere
Jennifer M. Labit
Dr. Mary B. LaCoste
Eugenie R. La Cour
Brigette Anne LaGarde
Kathleen Boyle LaGarde
Lauren Elizabeth LaGarde
Rachel R. Laiche
Elizabeth Lala
Marie Charvet Lala
Mary Lambert
Dr. & Mrs. Ralph E. Lambert
Ethel Langenstein Lanaux
Sister Doris Landers, O.S.U.
Michelle O. Landrieu
Verna Landrieu
Coleen Perilloux Landry
Dr. & Mrs. Alphonse D. Landry
Floyd P. Landry
Jeannette Louise Landry
Marcelle Barbazan Landry
Sister Pierre Landry, O.S.U.
Ruby Landry
Gloria Welker Larrieu
Faye Lousteau Lasseigne
Verlyn A. Latino
Laureene B. Leach
Doris E. LeBlanc, M.D.
Mary Lachin LeBlanc
Marion Schlosser LeBon
Dr. Marietta M. LeBreton
Marie Leckert
Elma Ireland LeDoux, M.D.

Julie L. Leger
Merriellin Lindeman Lehner
Antoinette Ruttiger Letinich
Carolyn Eble Levy
Robert & Elizabeth Lewis
Dana Marcile Licata
Maureen Cronan Lillich
Susan Bridges Linnstaedter
Patty Treuting Lipari
Esther Landry Lirette
Jacqueline Laurent Lister
Kara Foundas Litchfield
Angela Liuzza
Mrs. Salvador R. Lococo
Sarah, Jane, & Elizabeth Lodwick
Mrs. Wm. J. Long
Dariann Ballina Lopez
Janet Groetsch Lotherington
Louisiana Colonials - Founders
    Chapter
Rev. Msgr. J. Anthony Luminais
Shirley Peyrefitte Lund
Maureen Lundergan
Karen Parr Luthringshausen
Joy Chalona Lyons
Dr. & Mrs. Joseph N. Macaluso,
    Jr. Family
Mrs. Vic A. Maceo
Doris Rivet Macgowan
Marjorie Darney Macklin
Claire M. Madere
Jeanne Douglass Madere
Marshall Madere
Leslie Ainsworth Maggio
Lisa Plaisance Mahiger
Dorothy Vignol Majors
Msgr. Charles J. Mallet

Elaine N. Malloy
Lee Cangelosi Maloney
Mr. & Mrs. L.J. Malus, III
Mrs. Catherine Mandot
Sister Ann Mangelsdorf, O.S.U.
Bridgit R. Maniger
Diane Manning
Carol Kramer Mannino
M. Enid Byrne Markezich
Charles J. & Karen Marks
Christopher A. & Diane Marks
Dawn C. Marks
Gayton S. & Sandra Marks
Lucille Heaney Marks
Mr. & Mrs. T. R. Marley
Julie Ehret Martin
Mrs. Joseph A. Martin
Carolyn Champagne Martinez
Barbara N. Massony, M.D.
Mrs. Charles A. Matassa
Erin L. Matherne
Marcelle B. Maurin
Dione M. Mayeux
Sister Marie McCloskey, O.S.U.
Donna O. McNamara
Helen Cassidy McGrail
Jeanne Guillory McAllister
Judith S. McMullen
Mary Jane McKee
Margaret McNamara McAuliffe
Patricia Keiffer McAuliffe
Meghan Greer McCaffery
Paula Diodené-McCaskell
Charlotte L. McCrory
Mrs. Michael A. McDermott
Mary C. McDonnell
Kay McGartlin

Kathleen McGoey
Ann McHugh
Mrs. Sarah L. McHugh
Marjorie C. McKay
Mary Alice T. McKay
Judy Fife Mead
Michele Bernard Mehrabadi
Mrs. June Smith Ménard
Stanley J. Mendelson
Joan Gunning Merkle
Beulah Bertel Merritt
Jo Ann Anselmo Merse
Mary McCune Messonnier
Lois Manint Meyer
Sandy Meyer & Family
Linda Cousin Meyers
Ida Chirieleison Mialaret
Mida Castell Michell
Diane Hubbell Michelli
Charlotte Milazzo
Maria Levet Millet
Lisa A. Mills
The Mir Group
Pamela Haydel Mistretta
Dee Dee Englisbee Mitchell
Ethel S. Molony
Mrs. Lawrence A. Molony
Carol Levy Monahan
Mr. Paul A. Monju, Sr.
Rita Mae Montalbano
Jim & Mary Jean Moore
Joan Menard Moore
Margaret (Levet) Moore
Mrs. Walter G. Moore
Sandra Falk Moore
Barbara Lyné Moreira
Cheryl Gregoratti Morock

Janet Watson Moseley
Dorothy Mossholder
Adrienne Johnson Mouledoux
Gloria Lachin Mouledoux
Dorothy S. Mouton
Jo-Ann Fazzio Mueller
Kathleen E. Muldrey
Mrs. Joseph P. Mulhern
Ann G. Muller
Evelyn Jordan Mumme
Mary Alice Lennox Murdoch
Sister Angela Murphy, O.S.U.
Elaine Villars Murphy
Lynne Li Rocchi Murphy
Suzanne Crouere Neal
Carol Nelson
Mr. & Mrs. A. James Nelson, IV
Marilyn Krieger Neville
Lumina C. Newchurch
Margaret Ann Morgan Newman
Mary Stern Niven
Kathryn A. Nizer
Mary H. Noone
Geradine G. North
Mrs. Rosemonde J. Nugent
Marianne O'Hara
Dr. Marian & Bill O'Neil
Edward T. & Mary W. O'Shay
Wilma B. Ogattio
Elmere Ehrett Oldenburg
Dimitrij & Christiane Oleksij
Don & Mavis Olivier
Elizabeth M. Olivier
Henry R. Olivier, M.D.
Joan Bonvan Organ
Mr. & Mrs. E. J. Ourso
Elizabeth A. Owens

Mr. & Mrs. Nathel C. Pacini, Sr.
Angela C. Palmisano
Madeline Panipinto
Gayla, Caroline & Megan Paredes
Cordelia Partridge
Irma Geheeb Peltier
Lauralee Horil Perez
Magdalene P. Perino
Ruth M. Perkowski
Anna R. Persich
Mrs. Muriel McKay Pfister
Mary Jane Phillips
Solange Picot
Dr. & Mrs. Wayne Pierce
Mr. & Mrs. Wayne R. Pietri, Sr.
Robin Clark-Pigg
Carmen Breaux Pigott
Hilda W. Pilcher
Julie Schutten Pitot
Maureen McKay Poché
Mrs. Paul A. Poissenot, Sr.
Mary Fitzpatrick Pollard
Monastery of Poor Clares
Jeanette Ruli Pou
Danna L. Powell
Sister Mary Jacuqeline Pratt, O.S.U.
Sr. Mary Margaret Prenger, O.S.U.
Mr. & Mrs. John L. Prevost
Sister Consuelo Price, O.S.U.
Sylvia Probst
Alvin Regina Puderer
Kathleen Puglia
Mrs. Leslie Webster Quantaro
Leo & Druscilla Quebedeaux
Gayle Freidenberg Queyrouze
Kathi Moss Quinn
Amanda Rabalais

Amy Schremp Ramon
Margaret Denechaud Ramsey
Mr. & Mrs. Felix D. Rando
Millie Rappold
Elisabeth Ainsworth Rareshide
Mrs. John E. Ray (Joan Lennox)
Sandra Russo Ray
Sister Mary Ready, O.S.U.
Irlee Leclere Redmann
Gloria Hernandez Redmond
Patricia Gunning Reese
Religious of the Sacred Heart-New
    Orleans
Terry Failla Reymond
Linda Hingle Rhodes
Anne S. Ricci
Miriam Dwyer Rice
Janet Mary Riley
Harry & Debbie Rivero
Adele Rivet
Sister Teresita Rivet, O.S.U.
Phyllis De Blanc Robert
Rev. Thomas J. Rodi
Ruby Lanier Rodriguez
Joan Lisso Rogers
Cludette Sellers Romero
Marilyn Rook
Susan Y. Roos
Mr. & Mrs. Gary S. Roques
Olive A. Rosato
Mr. & Mrs. Allyn P. Roussel
Sister Magdalita Roussel, O.S.U.
Althea de Latour Ruello
Ellen Beach Ruiz
Jean Gardner Russo
Mrs. Pedro Sabi & Daughter
St. Matthew the Apostle School

Merla Leber Salathe
Winifred Wegmann Sampson
Sergio San Antonio
Norris M. Sartin
Mrs. Lucille Bourg Sauer (Leonard)
Paul & Jo Nel Savoy
Loislyn Blanchard Scardino
Joan Joanen Schade
John & Ann Scharfenberg
Ray Schelfhout
Wandah M. Scheuermann
Jackie Rice Schexnayder
Madge Warrick Schexnaydre
Zoe Callac Schluter
Kathleen Schmitt
Bernard R. Schmitz
Deborah Jefferson Schmitz
Carolyn Coogan Schof
Danielle A. Schott
Gerald & Priscilla Schroeder
Catherine O'Connell Schulze
Merle Albert Segura
Jeanie Mailhes Sellers
Mrs. Mary Sette
Laura Cangelosi Sewell
Mr. & Mrs. Michael F. Sewell
Marilyn Kingsmill Shaak
Jeanne Culivan Shackleford
Sheila Walt Shaler
Leslie Ménard Sharkey
Mrs. Linda Robinett Shea
Sister Julia Shea, S.P.
Barbara Ann Siefken
Carolyn Margaret Siefken
Gerald E. Siefken
Mary Ethel Booker Siefken
Janet Haydel Signorelli

Mr. & Mrs. Clive L. Sills
Mr. & Mrs. Jeffrey C. Sinclair
Elizabeth Riley Sintes
Martha Guedry Skelly
Lois M. Skinner
Wm. M. & Doris (Deleery) Slagle
Dr. & Mrs. William Slaughter, III
Carmen Suárez Smedley
Billie Childress Smith
Carol Zengel Smith
Carolyn R. Smith
Catharine Pittman Smith
Eleanor G. Smith
Mr. & Mrs. Hugh J. Smith, Jr.
Suzanne Brigtsen Smith
Thoy Jourdan Smith
Joanne M. Spedale
Elizabeth Fitzgerald Sporar
Adelaide Caneza Sprague
Renée Bravo Spratt
Lisette M. St. Mard
Shelby Macgowan St.Romain
Teresa G. Staub
Sue Maynard Steel
Alice Morvant Steiner
Melissa Ann Steudlein
Beverly d'Aquin Stevens
Julienne Territo Stewart
Irene Miranne Stokes
Marjorie R. Stone
Andrea Fay Stringos
Therese Thibodeaux Stuckey
Tracy C. Styron
Sister Lourdes Suarez, O.S.U.
Sarah Anne Spinks Suddreath
Trudeen Dempsey Swain
Mr. & Mrs. Timony F. Swoop

Betty Sue Talbot
Suzanne Schiro Talbot
Mrs. James P. Tallon
Walter A. Taney
Mary Ann Tantillo
Charlene & Joe Taranto
Mr. & Mrs. James E. Taylor, Jr.
Helen A. Tentler
Ellen B. Terrell
Hilda Landry Theriot
Katherine Tumminello Thiesse
Mrs. Enola C. Thomas
Beverly Richard Thomassie
Judie Gabler Tidwell
Mr. & Mrs. Jose Tijerina
Laura Favret Tobin
Sister Jacqueline Toppino, O.S.U.
Sylvia Landry Torregano
Laurelee Roger Toscano
Ann Hughes Towns
Mrs. Betty Breland Trachtman
Peggy B. Trainor
Thelma Mae Mouledoux Trapolin
Elizabeth S. Trayner
Mrs. James L. Treadway
    (Yvonne D.)
Debora Tremont
Salva D'Antoni Treuting
Adelaide Marston Trigg
Mr. & Mrs. Verne W. Tripp (Rita)
Theresa Trosclair
Blaine Rittiner Twibell
Irish Ursuline Community, Georgia
    Ursuline Academy of Dallas,
    Alumnae Assoc.
Ursuline Academy, Kirkwood, MO

Ursuline Academy Elementary, New
    Orleans
Ursuline Academy High School, New
    Orleans
Ursuline Central Province
Ursuline Community, Bedford Park,
    NY
Ursuline Community Villa Maria,
    Frontenac, MN
Ursuline Community, Wilmington,
    Delaware
Ursuline Convent of the Sacred
    Heart, Toledo, Ohio
Ursuline Convent, Springfield, Ill.
Ursuline Merici Heights Com-
    munity
Ursuline Sisters of Alton, Illinois
Ursuline Sisters of Decatur, Ill.
Ursuline Sisters of Galveston -
    Houston
Ursuline Sisters of Kirkwood, MO
Ursuline Sisters of Laredo, TX
Ursuline Sisters (Martha Way)
Ursuline Sisters of Mount Saint
    Joseph, KY
Ursuline Sisters of St. Joseph's,
    Malone, NY
Ursuline Sisters Northeastern
Province
Ursuline Western Province
U.S. Daughters of 1812, Chalmette
    Chapter
Nora Vabulas
Louis & Anita Valente & Family
Mrs. Mary Ann G. Valentino
Rose L. Vales
Mary Margaret McFaull Vallon

Carmela Matassa Van Hook
Betty Ann Roy Vaughan
Gayle Cousins Ventola
Gertrude Vera
Allys D. Vergara, Ph.D.
Mrs. Louis P. Verges
Charmaine Vernon
Mrs. Alfredo Vichot
Barbara Palm Vignes
Carolyn T. Villarrubia, M.D.
Audrey S. Vitter
Vizard Family
Margaret Roussel Vizzi
Audrey Mary Vogt
Bill & Diane Voigt
Marguerite M. Volz
Louise Allen Wagstaff
June Trosclair Waguespack
Mrs. Carol Gisevius Waguespack
Robert & Rowena Walsh
Mary Doyle Walther
Mr. & Mrs. Milton M. Walther
Marjorie Gelpi Walton
Mrs. Bernadette Warchol
Janice Rodrigue Watermax
Winifred M. Watson
Ann Elizabeth Webb
Elois L. Weber
Jacqueline Uber Weber
Deanne Derbes Webster
Mrs. Marguerite Teresa Wefel
Catherine Lyons Wegmann
Lillian Kerth Wegmann
Marion Nix Wegmann
Alma Soignier Weilbaecher
Dorothy M. Weilbaecher
Sister Loyola Weilbaecher, O.S.U.

Dr. & Mrs. Maurice O. Weilbaecher, Sr.
Dr. & Mrs. Robert G. Weilbaecher
Cynthia Johnson Weiss
Ann Alston Stirling Weller
Helen McCown Wettermark
Sandra Gelis Wich
Patricia J. Wilcox
Dr. & Mrs. Frederick A. Wild, Jr.
Kathryn Eberle Wildgen
Rosemary Regina Challoner Wilkinson
Bethanne Breisacher Williams
The Family of Conrad S. P. Williams, III
Donna Marie Williams
Rita Kehlor Williams
Mrs. Clotilde W. Willis
Alvis Ann Wilson
Jane L. Wingerter
Judge Lorain F. Wingerter
Warren & Elaine Wingerter
Sister Vera Marie Wingerter, O.S.U.
Barbara Breaux Winn
Sandra Tridico Wolf
Mr. & Mrs. Roland & Dorothy Wolter
John Woodford
Leonora Hassinger Woods
Helen M. Woolley
Alexine Ward Wyndelts
Lisa Baiamonte Yamin
Anne Marie Moore Youngblood
Merrill Richard Zeringue
Zara Lyn Zeringue
Marjorie C. Zibilich
Lilly May Mayer Zimmer

MEMORIALS

Camille E. Bartlott
Valentine Marie Fernandez Block
Mr. Harry Hamilton Booker, Jr.
Mr. & Mrs. Martin E. Deleery
Mrs. Edward F. Donohue
Nancy and James Donovan
Brooks Fain
Sister Columba Fitzwilliam, O.S.U.
Sr. Maureen Gaffney, O.S.U.
Sister Jane Frances Heaney, O.S.U.
Stella Glynn Kehlor
Sister Elizabeth Marie Landry,
    O.S.U.
Dr. Loy R. Olivier
Dr. Robert M. Olivier
Cora Bourgeois Richard
Mr. & Mrs. Earl A. Richard
Dr. Pedro Sabi
Mother Mary John Sevin, O.S.U.

Abbreviations

AAB.: Archives of the Archdiocese, Bordeaux, France.

AAQ.: Archives of the Archdiocese, Quebec, Canada.

    E.U.: *États-Unis*

    V.G.: *Vicaires Généraux*

AASL.: Archives of the Archdiocese, St. Louis, Missouri

AC,B.: Dispatches of the Ministers of the Marine and orders of the king to officials in Louisiana.

AC,C11A: *Archives des Colonies, Correspondance Générale, Canada.*

AC,C13A: *Archives des Colonies, Correspondance Générale, Louisiane.*

AC,D2d: Lists of missionaries in Louisiana. Report of December 1, 1744.

AC,Fl.: Pay warrants of missionaries in Louisiana.

ACNO: Archives of the City of New Orleans, Louisiana.

ACU., H.C.: Archives of the *Colegio de las Ursulinas,* Havana, Cuba.

AGI., P.C.: *Archivo General de Indias, Papeles procedentes de Cuba.*

AGI., S.D.: *Archivo General de Indias, Audiencia de Santo Domingo.*

AMUQ.: Archives of the *Monastère des Ursulines, Québec, Canada.*

AUC., N.O.: Archives of the Ursuline Convent, New Orleans, Louisiana.

CAA., N.D.: Catholic Archives of America, Notre Dame University, South Bend, Indiana.

CCB., N.O.: Conveyance Office Book, New Orleans, Louisiana.

HTML.: Howard Tilton Memorial Library, Tulane University, New Orleans, Louisiana.

L.C.: Library of Congress, Washington, D.C.

LSML.: Louisiana State Museum Library, New Orleans, Louisiana.

NANO.: Notarial Archives, New Orleans, Louisiana.

NAUS., S.D.: National Archives of the United States, Department of State, Washington, D.C.

NAUS., W.D.:   National Archives of the United States, Department of War, Washington, D.C.

SLO., B.R.:   State Land Office, Baton Rouge, Louisiana.

CHR.:   *Catholic Historical Review.*

ICHR.:   *Illinois Catholic Historical Review.*

LHQ.:   *Louisiana Historical Quarterly.*

MA.:   *Mid-America.*

MPA., Fr. D.:   *Mississippi Provincial Archives,* French Dominion.

MVHR.:   *Mississippi Valley Historical Review.*

RACHS.:   *Records* of the American Catholic Historical Society.

SLCHR.:   *St. Louis Catholic Historical Review.*

Chapter 1

1. [Mère Marie de Chantal Thibaut], *Sainte Angèle Mérici et l'Ordre des Ursulines par une Religieuse du même Ordre* (2 vols.; Paris: J. de Gigord, 1922), I, 6.

2. Sister M. Monica, *Angela Merici and Her Teaching Idea* (New York: Longmans, Green and Co., 1927), Appendix, Note A, 407-408, summarizes the facts as given in various biographies.

3. This is the most probable date, although historians give other dates ranging from 1470 to as late as 1516. Cf. Abbé V. Postel, *Histoire de Sainte Angèle Mérici et de tout l'ordre des Ursulines* (2 vols.; Paris: Librairie Poussielgue Frères, 1878), I, 4.

4. After the death of John Merici and his wife, biographers speak only of Angela and her elder sister.

5. Some historians relate that as Angela prayed she was enveloped by a heavenly light and she saw a luminous ladder, like that of Jacob, reaching to the heavens. A throng of maidens clothed in shining robes, each with a royal diadem, and escorted by a multitude of angels, descended. As Angela gazed at the glorious spectacle, she saw among them a dear friend of whom she recently had been bereft. "Angela", the well-known voice said, "know that God has shown you this vision to signify that before you die you are to found a company like these virgins." Then the shining procession reascended into heaven. Cf. Postel, *Histoire de Sainte Angèle Mérici*, I, 31-34. Many of the details seem to have been invented to embellish the account.

6. Of this event in Angela's life, Sister M. Monica, *Angela Merici and Her Teaching Idea*, 46, says: "Nothing in her whole experience played such a positive part in her life as this subtle, intangible episode, known as the Vision of Brudazzo. No matter whether or not one accepts or scoffs at what savants call the laws of mysticism, the measure of a man's professed intercourse with the world of the unseen is proven by its influence upon his living act. In the gradual unfolding of this woman's life is shown very curiously the power of suggestion exerted by this event of her girlhood. At the time it happened both inheritance and environment had shaped her to receive a new impetus, and there is no doubt at

all that from this inspiration arose her life-work, her new and very original teaching-idea."

7. Filipo Maria Salvatori, S.J., *Vita della S. Madre Angela Merici fondatrice della Compagnie di S. Orsola ossia della Instituto delle Orsoline* (Rome: Lazzaroni, 1806), 17, cited by Sister M. Monica, *Angela Merici and Her Teaching Idea*, 46, says: "it had been included in the revelation, either by some particular instruction, or by intimate mental illumination, that the company of whom she was destined to be the mother should be specially consecrated to the education and spiritual advantage of her neighbor."

8. They were Barbara Fontana, Simona Borni, Clara Gaffuri, Laura Peschiera, Caterina Dolci, Dominica Dolci, Maria Bartoletti, Pellegrina Casali, Chiara Martinengo, Dorosilla Zinelli, Paola Peschiera, Margherita Dell'Olma.

9. As there was no cloister, so there was no distinctive religious habit. Angela prescribed merely that her daughters dress in a simple and modest manner.

10. From the earliest Christian times, women consecrated their virginity to God while living in the midst of their families. There was even a ceremonial of public and official consecration. However, these virgins, whether consecrated singly or in groups, made no pretense of perpetuating themselves as an organization.

11. According to tradition, Angela had a dream, or vision, of St. Ursula, who exhorted her to begin the work envisioned at Desenzano. For this reason Angela called the institute which she established the Company of St. Ursula. In any account of St. Ursula it is difficult to distinguish legend from truth. However, certain facts seem to be incontestable. There was at Cologne at the end of the fourth or middle of the fifth century an illustrious martyr by the name of Ursula. She came from what is now Great Britain and was accompanied by numerous girls whom she had trained in virtue. Ursula and her companions were martyred as Christians by the barbarians. St. Ursula was held in high esteem by the people of the Middle Ages. The name of St. Ursula became synonymous with protectress of young girls and of those who instruct them, and even of students in general. The renowned universities of Paris, Vienna, and Coimbra in Portugal were placed under her patronage. The church of the Sorbonne in Paris was also dedicated to St. Ursula.

12. There is a French translation of the Primitive Rule of St. Angela in Mère Marie de St. Jean Martin, O.S.U., *L'Esprit de Ste. Angèle Mérici* (Rome, 1947), 643-647. The Primitive Rule comprised only twelve chapters. The last treated of the administrative organization of the Company but only in broad outlines. It states in part: "*Pour le gouvernement de cette Compagnie, il est établi qu'il faut élire quatre vierges des plus capables de la Compagnie, au moins quatre matrones veuves, prudentes et de vie honorable, et quatre hommes murs et de moeurs éprouvées. Que les Vierges soient comme les enseignantes et les guides dan la règle de la vie spirituelle; les matrones comme des mères, pleines de sollicitude pour le bien et l'utilité de leurs filles et de leurs soeurs spirituelles; et les quatre hommes, comme des agents et des pères pour les nécessités courantes de la Compagnie.*" The office of Superior General was definitely established, and before her death Angela indicated that she desired the Countess Lucrezia de Lodrone to succeed her.

13. That the elections might be fully authenticated a notary public assisted at the chapter and drew up the act. This document shows that there were fifty-nine voters present, including the Foundress, and that thirteen members were absent making a total of seventy-two.

14. The edition followed here is that drawn up in 1673 by P. Jean-Marie Cristoni, spiritual director of the Ursulines of Brescia at that time. Cristoni testified that this was the Rule as it came "from the mind and heart of Angela." The spirit, but not the exact content of Angela's Rule, was preserved. Chapter XII of the Primitive Rule was replaced by twelve chapters that treat in detail the administrative organization of the Company.

15. Chapter XXIII

16. Chapter XIX

17. Cardinal Guidiccioni even went so far as to advocate the suppression of all religious orders, except four, for he said, "All Orders become relaxed, and then do more harm to the Church than they did good in the beginning." Stewart Rose, *Ignatius Loyola and the Early Jesuits* (London: Burns & Oates, 1891), 264.

18. Angela's secretary, Gabriel Cozzano, recorded that while she was dictating the Rule to him she would exclaim, "Oh that it might please God to have the whole world come under the shadow of this rule." Sister M. Monica, *Angela Merici and Her Teaching Idea.* 180.

19. Testament of St. Angela, Eleventh Legacy.

20. Most Rev. Cesare Orsenigo, *Life of St. Charles Borromeo* (St. Louis: B. Herder Book Co., 1945), 63-64; passim.

21. Quoted by Postel, *Histoire de Sainte Angèle Mérici*, I, 322.

22. Orsenigo, *Life of St. Charles Borromeo*, 111.

23. "Le Problème Grégoire XIII" a manuscript in the possession of the author, prepared by Mother Marie Vianney Boschet, gives this date in preference to 1572 as is given by most historians.

24. *Geschichte der heiligen Angela Merici und des von ihr gestifteten Ordens der Ursulinen bearbeitet von einer Ursuline* (Innsbruck: Fel. Rauch, 1893), 224.

25. The Congregation of Brescia continued to exist, as Angela had left it, until the invasion of upper Italy by the French revolutionary armies under Napoleon in 1796. The conqueror suppressed the Company and confiscated its property.

26. Testament of St. Angela, Eleventh Legacy.

27. Postel, *Histoire de Sainte Angèle Mérici*, I, 239; [Thibaut], *Sainte Angèle Mérici et l'Ordre des Ursulines*, I, 296.

28. Françoise de Bermond played a more or less important role in the foundation of three congregations: Avignon, Bordeaux, and Paris. All three influenced the formation or continuation of the New Orleans foundation.

29. In the beginning only the simple vows of chastity, obedience, and stability were required of the sisters. The vow of poverty and observance of the cloister were not all obligatory. Cf. *Annales de l'Ordre de Ste. Ursule* (2 vols.; Clermont-Ferrand: Ferdinand Thibaud, 1857) I, 36.

30. Madame Acarie later became a Carmelite nun and was beatified under the name of Marie de l'Incarnation. She is not to be confused with Blessed Mary of the Incarnation, Marie Guyart-Martin, foundress of the Ursulines of Quebec.

31. [Thibaut], *Sainte Angèle Mérici et l'Ordre des Ursulines*, I, 347-348.

32. Father Coton, S.J., who was charged by the king with the religious instruction of the dauphin, the future Louis XIII, was so impressed with the work of Mother de Bermond that he borrowed her books and used her method in teaching his royal pupil.

33. When Madame de Sainte-Beuve announced her intention of applying to Rome for permission to erect the Paris foundation into a monastery of solemn vows, the Ursulines of Provence recalled Mother Françoise de Bermond.

34. The daily recitation of the Office of Our Lady was substituted for the Breviary, except on certain feast days.

35. Father Le Jeune arrived at Quebec July 5, 1732, with Emery de Caen who carried credentials empowering him to take possession of Canada again for France. Cf. Colby, *Founder of New France* (Toronto: Glasgow, Brook and Co., 1935), 129.

36. Reuben Gold Thwaites (ed.), *Jesuit Relations and Allied Documents* (72 vols.; Cleveland: The Burrows Brothers, 1897), V, 11. Hereinafter cited as *Jesuit Relations.*

37. Father Poncet was Claude Martin's professor at Orléans. Later he consecrated his labors to the Canadian missions.

38. *Mary of the Incarnation, Foundress of the Ursuline Monastery Quebec* by an Ursuline of Quebec (Quebec: L'Action Catholique, 1939), 28.

39. One night during the octave of Christmas 1634, Mother Mary dreamed that she and a young woman made a voyage to a vast unknown country where they were met by the Guardian robed in white. He directed them to a small church where she had a vision of Our Lady and the Child Jesus. Later, during 1635, while at prayer one day, she heard distinctly the words: "It was Canada I showed you. You must go there and build a house for Jesus and Mary." *Les Ursulines de Québec, depuis leur établissement jusqu'a à nos jours* (4 vols.; Quebec: C. Darveau, 1878, I, 4-6; *Jesuit Relations,* LVI, 247-251.

40. *Jesuit Relations,* VIII, 239.

41. Mother Mary of the Incarnation wrote of this first Ursuline Convent in the New World: "All we have for a house are two little rooms that serve as kitchen, dining room, living room, classroom, parlor, and chapel." *Lettres de la Vénérable Mère Marie de l'Incarnation, première supérieure des Ursulines de la Nouvelle-France* (Paris: Antoine Vuarin, 1684), 328.

42. As the community was composed of members from both the Bordeaux and Paris Congregation, they followed a rule which contained elements of both rules, e.g., the Ursulines of Tours took the fourth vow

of Paris, while the Paris Ursulines adopted the religious habit of Bordeaux. This rule of Quebec was followed until 1681, when Bishop Laval obliged them to adopt the constitutions of Paris.

43. Boarding school for Indian girls.

44. Charlotte Barré, a girl of nineteen, had come to Quebec with the Ursulines in 1639, while Catherine Lezeau was a Canadian.

45. *Les Ursulines des Trois-Rivières depuis leur établissement jusqu'a à nos jours* (2 vols.; Trois-Rivières: P.V. Ayotte, 1888) is the best account available of this foundation. Cf. *Edits, Ordonnances Royaux, Déclarations et Arrêts du Conseil d'Etat du Roi Concernant le Canada* (7 vols.; Quebec: E.R. Frechette, 1854), I, 288-296; AAQ., Reg. A, 595-601.

46. The Florida of the sixteenth century included the present Louisiana. It was the name long employed to designate the Spanish possessions and the land claimed by the Spanish north of the Gulf of Mexico and east of the Great Plains.

47. The King of Spain, not the Holy See, had established the diocese and appointed Father Suarez to the bishopric, but the approbation of Rome and the consecration of Father Suarez were expected to follow. This procedure was in accordance with the practice of the time. Cf. Francis Borgia Steck, O.F.M., "Interesting Incidents in the Catholic History of the Southwest," *Fortnightly Review*, XL (June, 1933), 121-122.

48. Edward Channing, *A History of the United States* (6 vols.; New York: Macmillan Co., 1909), I, 60.

49. This Company, which was sometimes called the Mississippi Company, was the famous speculative body connected with John Law's banking scheme. In 1719 it became the Company of the Indies, and two years later its privileges were revoked and the king appointed *commissaires* to conduct the affairs of the bankrupt company. They remained in charge until 1723 when the Company of the Indies was again reinstated, only to relinquish its charter in 1731. Thus from 1717 to 1731 the religious affairs of Louisiana were bound up with the activities of the Company, as it enjoyed the right of patronage in Louisiana as granted in the original charter. Cf. AC, C13A, 9:417-421; 12:224-258.

50. Le Baron Marc de Villiers, *Histoire de la Foundation de la Nouvelle Orléans (1717-1722)* (Paris: Imprimerie Nationale, 1917), 17-38, weighs the pros and cons for the various dates given for the foundation of New Orleans. This work is translated in LHQ, III (April, 1920),

158-251.

51. The district of the Capuchins extended west of the Mississippi from the Gulf of Mexico to the confluence of the Ohio and the Mississippi; that of the Carmelites was east of the Mississippi as far north as the Wabash; that of the Jesuits included the Illinois settlements and the country along the Missouri River. Cf. AC, C13A., 10:296-296v; ll:220-221.

52. AC, C13A., 10:296v; ll:221; B43:243-244. The Carmelites had incurred the displeasure of the Bishop of Quebec, his coadjutor, Monseigneur de Mornay, and the French Court. "They had gone to Rome without consulting the bishop, for a Bull of Prefecture and, as Bishop de Mornay stated, this was not recognized in France. In other words, the Carmelite Fathers should have gone first to Paris and not direct to the Holy See. The French Court, thoroughly Gallican, would not brook anyone seeking religious authority from Rome without first securing approval of the French ministry. Just how widespread Gallicanism had become in France can be ascertained from the fact that both Bishop St. Vallier and Bishop de Mornay opposed the Carmelites for this reason." Roger Baudier, *The Catholic Church in Louisiana.* (New Orleans, Louisiana: Library Association, Public Library Section, 1972), 52. Cf. also Jean Delanglez, S.J., *The French Jesuits in Lower Louisiana (1700-1763)* (Washington, D.C.: The Catholic University of America, 1935), 93-98.

53. AC,C13A, 10:297-297v; 11:22lv-222v.

54. Father de Beaubois was a dynamic, clever, realistic individual. Quick tempered, he could neither hide his antipathies nor refrain from speaking his mind about people. He was a man of broad vision, an excellent administrator, and considerate of his subordinates. His superiors considered him prudent and very capable of governing men. Cf. Camille de Rochemonteix, *Les Jesuites et la Nouvelle-France au XVIIIe siècle* (2 vols.; Paris: A. Picard et fils, 1906), I, 286; Delanglez, *The French Jesuits in Lower Louisiana*, 116-117; Claude L. Vogel, *The Capuchins in French Louisiana (1722-1766)* (Washington, D.C.: The Catholic University of America, 1928).

55. AC, B43:342-343; 363-363v; AC,C13b,l:n.f.

Chapter 2

1. Jean Delanglez, S.J., *The French Jesuits in Lower Louisiana (1700-1763)*, 114. The Sisters of Charity of St. Vincent de Paul, founded in 1633, have always been popularly known in France as "the Grey Sisters" from the color of their habit. They are not to be confused with the Grey Nuns, a community well known in Canada.

2. AC,C13A, 10:75

3. AC,C13A, 7:20. Translation given in *MPA., Fr. D.*, II, 294ff.

4. AC,C13A, 10:75

5. AC,C13A, 10:75v-76

6. AC,C13A, 10:61v

7. After studying the data at his disposal, Delanglez, *French Jesuits in Lower Louisiana*, 131, concluded: "As a hypothesis one might say that the choice was purely accidental." This hypothesis hardly stands in view of the direct statements made at the meeting of the Board of Directors of the Company, March 20, 1726, cited above and that of Abbé Raguet quoted below.

8. Abbé Raguet was appointed ecclesiastical director of the Company of the Indies, May 20, 1724. He acted as liaison officer, as it were, between the Company and the Church. He continued in office until the Company was dissolved in 1731.

9. Louis François de Mornay, Superior of the Capuchin Monastery of Meudon, was appointed coadjutor of Bishop St. Vallier by the French court in 1713. Bishop de Mornay was charged with the care of the Catholic Church in Louisiana, but he remained in France and governed that section of the diocese of Quebec from afar. Even when he was made Bishop of Quebec, he steadfastly refused to leave France and finally resigned in 1733. Cf. Auguste Gosselin, *L'Eglise du Canada depuis Monseigneur de Laval jusqu'a la Conquête* (3 vols.; Quebec: Laflamme & Proulx, 1911-1914), II, 2ff; *Bulletin des Recherches Historiques*, IV, 258-265; *CHR*, VI, n.s., 49ff; *MA*, I, n.s., 296ff.

10. AC,C13A, 10:54-54v.

11. AUC., N.O., Annals, I, 51.

12. *La Revue Canadienne* (October, 1881), 596.

13. Benjamin Sulte, *"Les Gouverneurs des Trois-Rivières,"* *Bulletin des Recherches Historiques,* II, 70.

14. Madeleine Hachard, *Relation du Voyage des Dames Religieuses Ursulines de Rouen à la Nouvelle-Orléans* (Paris: 1872), 4.

15. Ibid., 15

16. Abbé Raguet wrote to Bishop de Mornay, May 8, 1726: *"Sans eux* [the Jesuits] *je n'aurais pu parvenir à avoir ces Religieuses."* AC,C13A, 10:54v

17. AUC., N.O., *Noms de toutes les Religieuses Professes et Novices de Notre Monastère.* The community of New Orleans consisted of two groups, the choir religious who engaged in teaching, and the coadjutrix religious who performed the household duties. The superior and older choir religious ordinarily were called "Mother", the others "Sister".

18. AC,C13A, 10:57v

19. AUC., N.O., *"Lettres Circulaires",* I, 208; Mère St. Augustin de Tranchepain, *Relation du Voyage des premières Ursulines à la Nouvelle Orléans et de leur établissement en cette ville par la Rev. Mère St. Augustin de Tranchepain, Supérieure, avec les lettres circulaires de quelques unes des Soeurs, et de la dite Mère* (New York: Cramoisy Press, 1859), 56.

20. AUC., N.O., *Délibérations du Conseil,* I, i; *Journal depuis 1727 jusqu'en 1853,* 2.

21. AC,C13A, 10:28

22. AC,C13A, 10:28-28v; Hachard, *Relation,* 2.

23. AC,C13A, 10:76.

24. AC,B43:584-592. Several articles of this contract are quoted by Delanglez, *French Jesuits in Lower Louisiana,* 112-114.

25. In AC,C13A, 10:84-87v there is a first draft of the contract which differs but little from that signed September 13, 1726. The actual contract signed by the Ursulines and the officials of the Company of the Indies (AC,C13A, 10:88-99; AC,A23:76-79v) is printed in B.F. French, *Historical collections of Louisiana* (5 parts; New York: Wiley & Putnams, 1846-1876), Part III, 79-83. There is a certified copy of the same in AUC., N.O., as well as a contemporary copy made in *Délibérations du Conseil,* I, 2-8. A translation is given in [Wolfe], *Ursulines in New Orleans,* 167-173.

26. Articles I-III.

27. Article V.

28. Article II.

29. As long as the Superior of the Jesuits was also Superior of the Ursulines, the latter were assured that at least one member of the administrative board was devoted to their interests.

30. Article VII.

31. The *arpent* is an old French measure equivalent to slightly less than 193 linear feet. Cf. *MPA., Fr.D.,* II, 166.

32. Articles IX-XII.

33. Articles XIV-XXI.

34. All too frequently the food had been totally unfit for the patients. M. Villeneuve was even convicted of having furnished "plenty of roast dog" to the hospital. Cf. *LHQ.,* I (Jan. 8, 1917), 113, for abstract of sentence.

35. Article XXIV.

36. Article XXV.

37. Articles XXVI and XXVII.

38. The majority of the religious who had volunteered for Louisiana belonged to his jurisdiction.

39. Delanglez, *French Jesuits in Lower Louisiana,* 97, 132.

40. AC,C13A, 10:31.

41. "*Je suis persuadé que les religieuses y feront du bien . . .*" AC,C13A, 10:33v.

42. *Ibid.,* 10:34.

43. *Ibid.,* 10:31.

44. *Ibid.,* 10:54-54v.

45. *Ibid.,* 10:34.

46. *Ibid.,* 10:57.

47. *Les Constitutions des Religieuses de Saint Ursule de la Congrégation de Paris* (Paris: Gilles Blaizot, 1646), Part III, Ch. I, 3-8.

48. AC,C13A, 11:260v.

49. *Ibid.,* 12:228v.

50. *Ibid.*

51. This letter of Bishop St. Vallier seems to have disappeared, but this arrangement can be deduced from other sources. Cf. AC,C13A, 11:272v; 12:228v.

52. AC,C13A, 10:35v.

53. *Ibid.*, 10:231-231v.

54. *Ibid.*, 10:28-29.

55. Perhaps Cardinal Fleury was instrumental in bringing about this change on the part of the archbishop. When the latter had refused permission for Sister François Xavier Mahieu to join the Louisiana missionaries, Mother St. Augustin "was obliged to appeal to Cardinal de Fleury." Cf. AUC., N.O., *Lettres Circulaires*, I, 196.

56. AC,C13A, 10:319. The official statement giving a religious permission to transfer from one convent to another was referred to as a letter of obedience, or simply as an obedience.

57. Abbé Raquet, J. Morin. D'Artaguette, Diron, Castanier, Deshayes. P. Saintard signed for the Company.

58. *Soeur Catherine de Broscoly de St. Amand, première Supérieure des Ursulines de France; Soeur Marie Tranchepain de St. Augustin, Supérieure; Soeur Marie Anne Le Boullenger de Ste. Angélique, Dépositaire*, signed for the Ursulines.

59. AC,C13A, 10:100.

60. Ac,B43:639-640. Certified copy in AUC., N.O. There is a translation of this *brevet* in *Publications of the Louisiana Historical Society*, IV, 101, and in [Wolfe], *Ursulines in New Orleans*, 175-176.

61. AC,C13A, 10:67-68.

62. Hachard, *Relation*, 5 AUC., N.O., *Délibérations du Conseil*, I, i-l.

63. Hachard, *Relation*, 1-23, gives a detailed account of this journey from Rouen to Paris to Hennebont in her letter to her father, February 22. 1727.

64. *Ibid.*, 8-10.

65. *Ibid.*, 11-12.

66. *Ibid.*, 14-15.

67. A list of those assembled at the Hennebont convent is appended to this letter. There are some discrepancies in the spelling of the names as written by Mother St. Augustin and those signed by each individual on page i of the *Délibérations du Conseil*, I, AUC., N.O.

68. AC,C13A, 10:69-70. The coach fare from Paris to Rennes was 40 francs and the charge for a carriage from Rennes to Hennebont, a day's journey, was twenty francs per person. Cf. Hachard, *Relation*, 7, 13. Besides there was the expense of rooms and meals along the way.

Since The Company had contracted for six only, the allotment of 500 francs per person for the journey applied only to that number.

69. AUC., N.O., *Délibérations du Conseil,* I, l.

70. Hachard, *Relation,* 27.

71. In *Lettres Circulaires,* 228 (AUC., N.O.) her name is given as Mother Ste. Marie Eviguel de St. Goustant.

72. AUC., N.O., *Délibérations du Conseil,* I, 1. In addition to the three vows of Poverty, Chastity, and Obedience, the Ursulines of Paris made a fourth vow to devote themselves to the education of girls.

73. The principal source of biographical data is AUC., N.O., *Lettres Circulaires des Religieuses décédées,* I, 207-211.

74. Henry Renshaw, "The Louisiana Ursulines," *Publications of the Louisiana Historical Society,* II (December, 1901), 26-27.

75. AUC., N.O., *Lettres Circulaires,* I, 199.

76. *Ibid.,* 231 In the same place we read: *"Elle céda à la pré le droit de fondatrice."* This may imply that Father de Beaubois addressed himself first to Sister Ste. Angélique.

77. *Ibid.,* 203-204.

78. *Ibid.,* 228.

79. *Ibid.,* 195-196; Tranchepain, *Relation,* 39-45.

80. AUC., N.O., *Lettres Circulaires,* I, 196; Tranchepain, *Relation,* 42.

81. AUC., N.O., *Lettres Circulaires,* I, 211. In her community of Elboeuf, Sister St. Joseph had the name Sister Cécile des Anges.

82. Hachard, *Relation,* 26-27; 108-109.

83. AUC., N.O., *Lettres Circulaires,* I, 224.

84. Hachard, *Relation,* 25.

85. AUC., N.O., *Lettres Circulaires,* I, 2224.

86. AUC., N.O., *Actes de Prise d'Habit et de Professions,* I, l; Hachard, *Relation,* 17.

87. The Ursuline novices wore white veils which they exchanged for black on the day that they made their first vows.

88. Scarcely anything is known of Sisters St. Michel Marion and Ste. Marthe Dain who left New Orleans to return to France, November 25, 1727, or of the two postulants, Sisters Claude Massy and Anne de François, who were not admitted to profession.

1. Hachard, *Relation*. There is a translation of this in [Mother Thérèse Wolfe], *The Ursulines in New Orleans and Our Lady of Prompt Succor. A Record of Two Centuries, 1727-1925* (New York: P.J. Kennedy & Sons, 1925), 177-238.

2. There are two accounts of this voyage of the Ursulines to New Orleans. That of Mother St. Augustin Tranchepain, *Relations du voyage des Fondatrices du Monastère de la Nouvelle Orléans écrite aux Ursulines de France*, in AUC., N.O., *Journal depuis 1727 jusqu'en 1853, 7-24*, is in large part very similar to that of Madeleine Hachard cited above; but in several instances is less detailed. A slightly abbreviated edition of the Tranchepain Relation, with the obituary letters of Mother St. Augustin and the three religious who had preceded her in death, was published by Shea in the Cramoisy series (1859). A translation of this Relation is found in the *LHQ*, II, 1-23; another in *United States Catholic Historical Magazine*, I, 28-41.

3. Hachard, *Relation*, 22.

4. Mlle de la Chaise must have been lodged with the nuns, as there were only twelve religious, counting the two postulants. Sister St. Stanislaus refers to Mlle de la Chaise as always staying with them. Cf. *Relation*, 51 in which Mother St. Augustin wrote: "... *nous y trouvames un peu serrées, mais nous y étions seules, ce qui nous faisait beaucoup de plaisir.*" AUC., N.O., *Journal depuis 1727*, 7. But later, when pirates were sighted she wrote: "*Mademoiselle de la Chaise, qui a voulu être ses nôtres, pleurait amèrement . . .*" and added "*. . . triste liberté pour des Religieuses que d'être sur un vaisseau ou il est impossible d'avoir un moment à soi.*" *Ibid.*, 11.

5. Hachard, *Relation*, 50

6. *Ibid.* 54-55.

7. Another community, not the Ursulines, was to make this foundation. Letters patent were issued, November 16, 1731, for the establishment of a convent by the Religious of Notre Dame of Perigueux at Cap Français, Santo Domingo. They were to have a school for the education of girls. Cf. Paris, *Bib. Nat. Mss. fr. nouv. acq. 2551: 146-147*

8. "We [the Ursulines] were on the deck watching all this work; it was the desolation of desolation to see the poor passengers, who were trembling for their trunks and regretting their sugar, for even the sailors had their little barrels. Not one was exempted from it, not even the officers who had some also. All the sugar was thrown into the sea without discrimination." Hachard, *Relation*, 64.

9. Governor Périer and M. de la Chaise reported the company's loss as 62 barrels of brandy and four barrels of unrefined sugar. Cf. AC,C13A, 10:184.

10. The ordinary sailing time was three, or at most three and a half months. Cf. AC,C13A, 11:366.

11. At the mouth of the Mississippi River, the royal engineer, Adrien de Pauger, erected in 1721 a beacon, *une balise.* from which the outpost derived its name. Cf. Samuel Wilson, Jr., "Early Aids to Navigation at the Mouth of the Mississippi River," *United States Naval Institute Proceedings*, LXX (March, 1944), 279.

12. *Ibid.* Wilson says that the *Gironde* "could not cross the bar." However, the ship must have crossed later, perhaps after unloading part of its cargo, as Périer and de la Chaise reported: "This ship [the *Gironde*] remained at the Balize wind-bound until August 12 when it left and arrived here [New Orleans] the 22nd, where we had it ascend to have it repaired." AC,C13A, 10:184v.

13. "Our Reverend Fathers are taking with them a cabinet-maker, a locksmith and several other workmen. As for us, my dear father, be not scandalized at it, for it is the custom of the country, we are taking a negro to wait on us." Hachard, *Relation*, 73-74.

14. *Ibid.*, 73-74.

15. The picture, "The Landing of the Ursulines of New Orleans", is not historically correct. Only one-half of the Ursulines arrived August 6. Those in the sloop did not come until the next day. There were no Capuchins at the wharf to meet them. The cat may or may not have actually gotten as far as Louisiana. At any rate Madeleine Hachard had written from Lorient. "We are also taking a pretty little cat which wishes to be one of our community, supposing apparently that there are in Louisiana, as in France, some mice and rats." Hachard, *Relation*, 18.

16. Reuben Gold Thwaites (ed.) *Jesuit Relations and Allied Documents*

(72 vols.; Cleveland: The Burrows Brothers, 1897), LXVII, 273.

17. Fathers Soeul, Dumas, and Poisson, *Ibid.*, 278.

18. *Ibid.*, 277;279.

19. AC,C13A, 10:313

20. *Ibid.*

21. This house was directly across the street from Father de Beaubois' residence, the only one in the block bounded by Chartres, Bienville, Iberville, and Royal Streets. Cf. LSML., *Plan véritable à la Nouvelle Orléans, le 15 mai 1728, Broutin*; Delanglez, *French Jesuits in Lower Louisiana*, 101.

22. There are some notable exceptions. F.X. Martin, *The History of Louisiana from the Earliest Period* (2 vols.; New Orleans: Lyman and Beardslee, 1827-1829), I, 263, locates this building in the proper square but does not indicate its ownership. Roger Baudier, *The Catholic Church in Louisiana*, 104 says: ". . .the Company placed at their disposal the former house of Bienville then located in the square bounded by Bienville, Chartres, Decatur, and Iberville Streets." But page 134 and *passim* he refers to this residence as the Kolly house. Gravier in Hachard, *Relation*, 121, n. 6, says: "The provisional house destined for the Ursulines was that which Bienville had just left. It was situated at the southwest between the streets Bienville, Royal, Saint Louis and Chartres. Delanglez, *French Jesuits in Lower Louisiana*, 135 and *passim* refers to the provisional convent as the Kolly house.

23. M. de Kolly was the "principal party interested in the Ste. Reine Concession." LSML., Doc. No. 27/118, May, 1727.

24. LSML., *Louisiane - Recensements* (Bound volume of manuscripts), 204. The general census of the City of New Orleans(January, 1732), 282-302, lists the "Succession Kolly" as occupied by the Ursuline Religious.

25. AUC., N.O. *Journal depuis 1727*, 41.

26. Hachard, *Relation*, 78.

27. AC,C13A, 10:173; *MPA, Fr.D.*, II, 537.

28. AUC., N.O., *Délibérations du Conseil*, I, 252.

29. This plan, dated May 15, 1728, is in the LSML, New Orleans. There is a copy and various modifications of the original in the Library of Congress. It has also been printed in several works, among others, Stanley Clisby Arthur, *Old New Orleans* (New Orleans: Harmanson, 1937),

20.

30. No. 48. It is significant that on this plan No. 1, diagonally across Chartres St., is marked as "granted to Bienville". Perhaps the proximity of these two squares has led to confusion as Martin and Gravier (Cf. n. 22, supra) both locate the provisional convent in the correct square; but Gravier attributes the ownership to Bienville.

31. Further evidence appears in the documents relative to the rent of this house which will be cited in their proper place. Cf. also AC,C13A, 22:30v.

32. Bienville sold one house in New Orleans to Mr. Dutisne, captain and commander in Illinois, January 30, 1725. "Records of the Superior Council of Louisiana," *LHQ.*, II (October, 1919), 478. He had yet another house which, on his return to New Orleans in March, 1733, he peremptorily ordered Périer to vacate. Cf. AC,C13A, 10:197; ll:144. *MPA., Fr. D.,* II, 557-558; 601.

33. Glass was being used in the colony even at this early date. Cf. AC,C13A, 10:197; 11:144. *MPA., Fr. D.,* II, 557-558; 601.

34. Hachard, *Relation,* 91. The sketch of the "Provisional Convent, 1727-1734," in [Wolfe], *Ursulines in New Orleans,* opposite page 12, is evidently the artist's conception of this building. As far as the writer has been able to ascertain the original is a pen sketch in the manuscript volume of the history of the Ursulines in New Orleans written by Mother Thérèse Wolfe and was done for the Columbian Exposition in 1893 and preserved in the Ursuline Museum, New Orleans.

35. Hachard, *Relation,* 85.

36. AUC., N.O.*Délibérations du Conseil,* I, 252.

37. AC,C13A, 11:273v; Hachard, *Relation,* 79.

38. AC,C13A, 11:274.

39. AC,C13A, 10:359-359v.

40. Hachard, *Relation,* 79.

41. This was probably the first girls' boarding school within the present limits of the United States.

42. AC,C13A, 10:314v.

43. AC,C13A, 11:273v; Hachard, *Relation,* 85, 98.

44. AC,C13A, 11:274.

45. Hachard, *Relation,* 85.

46. AC,C13A, 11:274v.

47. AC,C13A, 11:256.

48. They expected to place the orphan boys at the hospital, when it would be built, until they were of an age to serve as apprentices. Cf. AC,C13A, 11:145.

49. AC,C13A, 11:120; ll:145; 13:265; AC,B55:626v. The Board of Directors of the Company of the Indies approved this grant in their meeting of June 3, 1729. Cf. AC,C13A, 11:348v-349; *MPA., Fr. D.,* III, 653.

50. AC,C13A, 11:384.

51. Hachard, *Relation,* 97-99.

52. Cf. AC,C13A, 10:75-77v; 11:232v; 260. This is also evident from the terms of the contract. Cf. AC,C13A, 10:88-98.

53. AC,C13A, 10:173.

54. AC,C13A, 10:276v.

55. Hachard, *Relation,* 84.

56. AC,C13A, 11:273.

57. Hachard, *Relation,* 84, 93.

58. *Ibid.,* 227.

59. AC,C13A, 11:321v; 328v; *MPA., Fr. D.,* II, 631.

60. This lead plate is preserved in the Ursuline Museum, New Orleans. The writer has not been able to determine when it was removed from the original building.

61. Sr. Marie Tranchepain de St. Augustin, *Supérieure;* Sr. Marie Judde de St. Jean l'Evangéliste, Sr. Renée Yuiquel de Ste. Marie; Sr. Marie Le Boullenger de Ste. Angélique; Sr. Marguerite de Ste. Thérèse; Sr. Cécile Cavelier de St. Joseph; Sr. M.M. Hachard de St. Stanislaus; Pierre Baron, *Ingénieur du Roi;* I.L. Calot; Chambellan; An. Graton; V.G. Le Maistre et André de Batz, *Architectes.* It is to be noted that the name of Broutin, who probably had more to do with the design of the building than any of the other engineers or architects, with the possible exception of André de Batz, was omitted from this plate. Cf. Samuel Wilson, Jr., "An Architectural History of the Royal Hospital and the Ursuline Convent of New Orleans," *LHQ,* XXIX (July, 1946), 573-577.

62. AC,C13A, 10:359v.

63. AC,C13A, 10:273-273v.

64. Abbé Raguet is referring here to a house of correction for

women of dissolute life. Cf. AC,C13A, 13:265v' AC,B55:626v.

65. AC,C13A, 11:232-232v.

66. AC,C13A, 11:280.

67. Pointe de St. Antoine was in the locality of the present day Chalmette. Cf. "Documents Concerning Bienville's Lands," *LHQ,* X (January-April, 1927), 8, 12, 16, and accompanying map. It is to be noted that Henry P. Dart, in his editorial note to these documents makes the error of locating Pointe St. Antoine directly opposite New Orleans. Cf. "Early Census Tables of Louisiana," *LHQ,* XIII (April, 1930), 205ff; "Records of the Superior Council," *LHQ.,* III (July, 1920), 428; see entry also for May 31, 1729. Herman de Bachelle Seebold, *Old Louisiana Plantation Homes and Family Trees* (2 vols.; New Orleans: Pelican Press, 1941), II, 2, erroneously locates this plantation above New Orleans.

68. AUC., N.O., Petition, September 20, 1727.

69. Hachard, *Relation,* 35-36. The Ursulines paid the current purchase price. Fourteen or fifteen Negroes belonging to the Company escaped the same day and in the same manner.

70. *Ibid.,* 36.

$\mathcal{C}hapter$ 4

1. AC,C13A, 11:272v; 12:228v.

2. AC,C13A, 11:256v.

3. AC,C13A, 10:359.

4. This controversy has been fully treated by Claude L. Vogel, *The Capuchins in French Louisiana (1722-1766)* (Washington, D.C.: The Catholic University of America, 1928), 119-193, and Jean Delanglez, S.J., *French Jesuits in Lower Louisiana,* 163ff.

5. Contract of the Jesuits with the Company of the Indies, Article 24. AC,C13A, 12:264.

6. AC,C13A, 10:192; *MPA., Fr. D.,* III, 553.

7. "Saint-Vallier's letter to Beaubois was sent to France, for the bishop did not know where the Jesuit was. Moreover, it was the ordinary route of the mail from Canada to Louisiana.... The letter arrived in

Paris in December when de Beaubois had just left Lorient. Being forwarded to Louisiana, it did not reach there until the following August, coming with the other mail on the ship that brought the Ursulines to the colony. Dated August 4, 1726, it reached its destination one year later." Delanglez, *French Jesuits in Lower Louisiana*, 172-173.

8. Father de Beaubois here defines a permission as an order. "I am writing says Bishop Saint Vallier...to agree with you that as vicar-general you may exercise all the functions you wish in Louisiana and New Orleans. It is not then a question of doubting whether or not your powers are sufficient, since I am explaining them in your favor. But since it is more a question of what is becoming than of what you have the right to do, I leave it to your prudence to decide what you will do." AC,C13A, 12:228v.

9. AC,C13A, 10:314-314V.

10. Mother St. Augustin also makes the mistake of calling this permission an order.

11. AC,C13A, 111:272v-273. Letter is dated January 5, 1728.

12. *Ibid.*, 273.

13. AC,C13A, 11:276-276v. Sister St Stanislaus in writing to her father about this retreat says that there were sometimes two hundred present for the conferences. This is undoubtedly an over-estimation as four years later the census of New Orleans showed only 169 women or girls of an age to marry and 74 Negresses. Cf. LSML., *Louisiane Recensements* (Bound volume of manuscripts), 302.

14. "*ne battre que d'une aille.*" AC,C13A, 11:275.

15. "Records of the Superior Council of Louisiana," (Feb. 15, March 13 and 20, 1728(*LHQ.*, IV (April, 1921), 243; 247-248.

16. This incident was related to Abbé Raguet by Mother St. Augustin, AC,C13A, 11:274-276v, and by Father Raphäel, AC,C13A, 11:264-269. Cf. Delanglez, *The French Jesuits in Lower Louisiana*, 189-190.

17. *Les Constitutions des Religieuses de Sainte Ursule de la congrégration de Paris* (Paris: Gilles Blaizot, 1646), Part III, Chap. I, 7.

18. AC,C13A, 11:276.

19. AC,C13A, 11:264v. It would be interesting to know who the "*personnes dignes de foi*" were that the Capuchin should set their word against that of the Ursuline Superior. Father Raphäel made frequent

use of this type of expression in his letters.

20. AC,C13A, 11:277-278.

21. AC,C13A, 11:256; Hachard, *Relation*, 95-96;Delanglez, *The French Jesuits in Lower Louisiana*, 186, *passim.* Roger Baudier, *Catholic Church in Louisiana*, 104, 107.

22. AC,C13A, 11:278-278v.

23. Father de Beaubois refers to the "rich establishment which they offer them at Cap St. Dominique." AC,C13A, 11:256v.

24. "*comme l'oiseau sur la branche.*" AC,C13A, 11:278v.

25. AC,C13A, 11:262v.

26. *Ibid.*

27. AC,C13A, 10:360. This was written one month before the departure of the two religious.

28. AC,C13A, 10:314v

29. AUC., N.O.*Délibérations du Conseil,* I, 5.

30. Hachard, *Relation*, 51.

31. He was punished in the sense that he recognized and sincerely regretted all the evil that resulted from his intended act of kindness.

32. AC,C13A, 10:315.

33. AC,C13A, 11:256v; 12:34; Vogel, *Capuchins in French Louisiana,* 79; Delanglez, *The French Jesuits in Lower Louisiana,* 182.

34. AC,C13A, 11:256v.

35. AC,C13A, 12:2v.

36. AC,C13A, 11:12; *MPA., Fr. D.*, III, 588. Underscoring in the original.

37. Périer is probably referring to the journal which de la Chaise kept and sent at intervals to Raguet. Cf. AC,C13A, 11:249; 12:5.

38. AC,C13A, 12:6v.

39. This variable style was characteristic of Abbé Raguet. ". . .any fair-minded person by comparing a few letters of Raguet comes to the conclusion that the Abbé could accomplish mental somersaults which argue for an excessively nimble mind." Delanglez, *The French Jesuits in Lower Louisiana*, 224.

40. AC,C13A, 11:232v; 11:279-281v.

41. AC,C13A, 11:279-279v.

42. AC,C13A, 11:280v-281.

43. *Ibid.*, 280-280v.

44. *Ibid.* 281-281v.

45. Delanglez, *The French Jesuits in Lower Louisiana,* 192-193.

46. AC,C13A, 11:239-239v.

47. The recall of Father de Beaubois is treated fully in Delanglez, *The French Jesuits in Lower Louisiana,* 203-248; Camille de Rochemonteix, S.J., *Les Jesuites et la Nouvelle-France au XVVIIIe Siècle* (2 vols.; Paris: A Picard et fils. 1906); Vogel, *Capuchins in French Louisiana,* 152-165.

48. AC,C13A, 11:239.

49. This delay is easily explained. The Jesuit appointed to succeed Father de Beaubois died before the order reached him. Another superior had to be appointed. This was Father Le Petit, a missionary stationed in the Choctaw country. Father Le Petit had not yet reached New Orleans when Father de Beaubois left.

50. AC,C13A, 12:280v-281

51. AC,C13A, 11:260.

52. AC,C13A, 11:253.

53. AC,C13A, 11:254.

54. AC,C13A, 11:260-260v.

55. AC,C13A, 11:5v.

56, AC,C13A, 11:256v-257v.

57. AC,C13A, 11:256v.

58. AB51:90; AC,C13A, 12:255.

59. AC,C13A, 12:255.

60. AC,C13A, 11:226-226V.

61. The development of these congregations is treated in Abbé V. Postel, *Histoire de Sainte Angèle Merici et de l'Ordre des Ursulines* (2 vols.; Paris: Poussielgue Frères, 1878); *Geschichte der Heiligen Angela Merici und des von ihr gestifteten Ordens der Ursulinen bearbeitet von einber Ursuline* (Innsbruck: Fel. Rauch, 1893); Mère Marie de Chantel Thibaut, *Sainte Angèle Mérici et l'Ordre des Ursulines* (2 vols.; Paris: J. de Gigord, 1922).

62. AUC., N.O., *Délibérations du Conseil,* I, l.

63. *Ibid.,* 9. The entry is dated June 20, 1728.

64. AC,C13A, 10:89, Art. I.

65. AC,C13A, 10:70.

66. Madeleine Hachard, Thérèse Massy, and Anne de St. François were received as novices on January 19, October 21, and November

1, 1727, respectively. AC,C13A, 10; Hachard, *Relation*, 17, 35.

67. AC,C13A, 10:314v.

68. AUC., N.O., *Lettres Circulaires*, I, 2.

69. AC,C13A, 12:255.

70. Regarding this matter Gov. Périer wrote: "The thing is so much the more terrible as it has been reported by a religious and a priest. If I were not as firm as I am in my religion, such blows would make me a renegade." AC,C13A, 11:239.

71. Further on Périer remarked: "I pity Father Raphäel in having three or four bad subjects. If they continue to send him men of this character, their mission will fall of itself. I have as much reason to complain of them as I have cause to praise the Jesuit Fathers." AC,C13A, 11:239v.

72. AC,C13A, 11:239-239v.

73. Delanglez, *The French Jesuits in Lower Louisiana*, 192.

74. *Les Jesuits et la Nouvellel-France au XVIIIe Siècle*, I, 313.

75. "No one, having put his hand to the plow and looking back, is fit for the kingdom of God." Had Mother St. Augustin wished to quote Scripture she might have riposted with "When they persecute you in one town, flee to another."

76. Recall that he had written on April 3, 1728: "As to Rev. Father de Beaubois . . . Be very certain that neither his successor, nor he himself if he remained, would exercise any authority over you, neither as superior nor as confessor." AC,C13A, 11:233.

77. AC,C13A, 11:244-245v.

78. AC,C13A, 11:232v.

79. AC,C13A, 11:259.

80. AC,C13A, 12:283-284v. All the professed sisters signed this letter.

81. "If Father de Beaubois had a spark of the vindictiveness some assert he had, what an opportunity for him to get even with the Company of the Indies, who had all to lose if the Sisters should leave . . . But the Jesuit was sufficiently high-minded to spurn such a pretty revenge, for he had seen the good that was being done by the Sisters; and the benefits conferred by them outweighed his own resentment." Delanglez, *The French Jesuits in Lower Louisiana*, 193.

82. Underscoring in the original.

83. AC,C13A, 11:241-241v.

84. AC,C13A, 11:249-249v.

85. Abbé Raguet had encouraged the keeping of a journal to be sent to him at regular intervals. When he gave this advice to Governor Périer, the governor replied: "As to the advice which you give me to keep a journal in imitation of M. de la Chaise, I know, as I know myself, that the keepers of Journals are liars, victims of their passions, sycophants . . . Even though I might be sufficiently virtuous to avoid these three vices, the Company would lose very much if I passed two-thirds of my time in writing. Here I ought to work more than to write. . . If the time that M. de la Chaise spent in keeping his journal had been employed in affairs of business or new administration, they would perhaps be entirely up to date. . . On the other hand a man makes a mistake today which he repairs tomorrow. I would forget the good; and I would have said the evil. It is a man that I destroy in your mind." AC,C13A, 12:5-5v.

86. AC,C13A, 11:249-249v.

87. AC,C13A, 11:226v.

88. Mgr. Henri Têtu, "Mgr. Duplessis de Mornay," *Bulletin des Recherches Historiques*, IV (Aug. 1898), 264.

89. AC,C13A, 11:171v; 11:203v; 12:214-223; 12:280; Rochemonteix, *Les Jesuites et la Nouvelle-France au XVIIIe Siècle*, 314. Vogel, *Capuchins in French Louisiana*, 167.

90. AC,C13A, 11:282v; 12:280v.

91. AC,C13A, 11:282V.

92. AC,C13A, 11:282-283. Al the religious were present at this interview.

93. Part III, Ch. I, 5.

94. Abbé Claude Berthelon was a regular chaplain on the vessels of the Company plying between France and Louisiana. He remained in New Orleans from March, 1727, to May, 1732.

95. AC,C13A, 11:282v. Delanglez, *The French Jesuits in Lower Louisiana*, 194-196, quotes in full the letter giving an account of this election.

96. The original act has disappeared, but an exact copy of it was made in the *Délibérations du Conseil*, I, 12-13. de la Chaise reported this election to Abbé Raguet as follows: "The death of the Bishop of Quebec has produced a good effect in this colony. Since it took away

from Father de Beaubois all his powers, it was necessary to proceed to the election of a new superior for the Ursuline Religious. Father Raphaël who wished only to maintain the right of his Bishop, appointed him in order not to cause any change . . . The ladies appear to desire to keep Father de Beaubois for their superior and Father Raphaël makes no difficulty about agreeing to it." AC,C13A, 11:171v.

97. AC,C13A, 11:203-204.

98. AC,C13A, 11:283v.

99. AC,C13A, 11:171v. At that time Mother St. Augustin asked Abbé Berthelon to act as their superior until the arrival of Father Le Petit, the successor of Father de Beaubois. Cf. AC,C13A, 12:281.

100. AC,C13A, 12:281. Father Raphaël's letter to Raguet giving an account of the interview, though somewhat prejudiced, shows that he was willing to give a liberal interpretation to these instructions. Cf. AC,C13A, 12:280-282. This letter is quoted by Delanglez, *The French Jesuits in Lower Louisiana*, 196-197.

101. AC,C13A, 12:281v.

102. It is worth noting that the major Jesuit superiors in France were opposed to the members of their order acting as superiors or confessors to the Ursulines. Father D'Avaugour made this clear in a letter of March 19, 1728: ". . . whatever Jesuit remains at New Orleans he will not be permitted to concern himself with the [Ursuline] Religious ("*qu'il ne se mêle. . . pas des Religieuses*"). Independently of what happened, Father de Beaubois would have been forbidden to be either their superior or their confessor. "It is better that these offices be in the hands of others than in ours." AC,C13A, 12:209-209v. It was "only due to the extraordinary circumstances that prevailed in New Orleans for thirty-three years that the Jesuits were allowed to continue in this office." Delanglez, *The French Jesuits in Lower Louisiana*, 199.

103. AC,C13A, 16:19.

104. AC,C13A, 18:107v.

105. This grave measure was taken by Bishop de Mornay because Father de Beaubois had returned to Louisiana as Jesuit superior of the mission.

106. AC,C13A, 16:19; AC,B59:576.

107. de la Chaise died in New Orleans in February, 1730 and was succeeded by MacMahon whom Salmon replaced in October, 1731.

Bienville returned March 3, 1733 to replace Périer as governor.

108. AC,C13A, 16:15.

109. In the Margry transcripts in the *LSML,* the letter of Bienville and Salmon, March 8, 1733, is abbreviated. This has resulted in a definite change of meaning in the statement made with regard to the Ursulines. "*Ces mêmes Religieuses, quoique prêtes àse soumettre aux orders de l'Evêque* . . . " Grace King, *Jean Baptiste Le Moyne, Sieur de Bienville* (New York: Dodd, Mead and Co., 1893) 291, incorporated essentially this erroneous transcript. Vogel, *Capuchins in French Louisiana,* 168, has taken if from King.

110. AC,C13A, 16:18.

111. *Ibid.*

112. AC,C13A, 16:18v; 17:197.

113. AC,C13A, 16:16. Father Hyacinthe was sent back to France in May, 1733. Cf. AC,C13A, 16:15-16. At New Orleans and in its vicinity there remained only Father Raphaël and two other Capuchins, one up the river at Les Allemands and the other at the Balize.

114. AC,C13A, 18:1107.

$\mathcal{C}hapter$ 5

1. AC,C13A, 12:27-45. This is Governor Périer's account of the event.

2. Roger Baudier, The Catholic Church in Louisiana, 122. J.J. O'Brien, *The Louisiana and Mississippi Martyrs* (New York: The Paulist Press, 1928); Delanglez, *The French Jesuits in Lower Louisiana,* 251-252.

3. Delanglez, *The French Jesuits in Lower Louisiana,* 63, 249.

4. AC,C13A, 12:426.

5. AC,C13A, 13:21, 13:122.

6. AC,C13A, 11:120, 11:145.

7. *Jesuit Relations,* LXVIII, 198-201; quoted in [Wolfe] *Ursulines in New Orleans,* 272.

8. AC,C13A, 16:87.

9. AC,C13A, 16:87v-88.

10. *Jesuit Relations,* 281.

11. AC,C13A, 13:104.

12. AC,A23:76v., marginal note.

13. AC,G1, 412:107. Among those present at the funeral services were Gov. Périer and two councillors, Bruslé and Dausseville.

14. AC,C13A, 13:104.

15. Cf. Delanglez, *The French Jesuits in Lower Louisiana,* 261, for an appreciation of the worth of Salmon.

16. AC,C13A, 13:266.

17. AC,C13A, 13:265v; AC,C55:626v.

18. AC,C13A, 13:265v.

19. AC,B55:627.20. *Ibid.*

21. AC,C13A, 14:7v.

22. AC,C13A, 20:297v.

23. AC,C13A, 14:7v

24. She was called Sister Ste. Marie at Bayeux. AC,C13A, 20:197v.

25. AUC., N.O., *Noms de toutes les religieuses professes et novices de notre monastère, et de toutes celles des autres monastères qui sont venues à son secours; Délibérations du Conseil,* I, 15.

26. AUC., N.O., Obéissance de Sr. Ste. Marie Hébert, Sr. St. Pierre Bernard, Sr. St. André Melote.

27. AC,C13A, 14:7v.

28. *Ibid.,* 8.

29. *Ibid.*

30. AC,C13A, 14:8-8v.

31. AC,C13A, 15:74.

32, *Ibid.,* 74v.

33. Elsewhere this rent is given as 1500 livres a year. Cf. AC,C13A, 19:71-72.

34. AC,C13A, 13:122; 15:74v.

35. AUC., N.O., *Délibérations du Conseil,* I, 257-58.

36. AC,C13A, 15:75.

37. AC,B57:795.

38. AC,B57:749.

39. AC,B57:794v-795.

40. AC,C13A, 17:197v.

41. AC,B57:836.

42. *Ibid.,* 836v.

43. AC,C13A, 16:88v-89.

44. To marry the orphans off as soon as possible was the constant theme of the instructions sent to the *ordonnateur*. As the writer has not found any of the lists of orphans, it cannot be said with certainty at what age the king and his minister considered them marriageable, but it was probably any time after the age of puberty.

45. AC,B59:575v-576.

46. AC,C13A, 15:74v.

47. Madame Kolly remained in France. After the death of her husband and son in the massacre of 1729, she claimed the plantation of Ste. Reine and the house in New Orleans. Cf. AC,B57:850-851.

48. AC,C13A, 16:88.

49. *Ibid.*, 88v.

50. AC,C13A, 16:88v-89.

51. AC, C13A, 18:112-112v.

52. AC,C13A, 19:71-72.

53. *LSML.*, Doc. No. 2453 (10469). This property was purchased with part of a legacy left by Jean Louis, a sailor, to establish a charity hospital. Bienville and Salmon explained the low purchase price as follows: "It has cost only 1200 livres because there were very many repairs to be made, which amount to 2500 livres. Cf. AC,C13A, 22:30v.

54. AC,B61:645v-646; AC,C13A, 19:71, marginal note.

55. AUC., N.O., Bill of sale, January 1733.

56. Although on the opposite side of the river this plantation was probably near that granted the Ursulines by the Company of the Indies in 1727 at Pointe St. Antoine. In February, 1728, a certain Vien (spelled Viel on map) held eight *arpents* of land opposite Pointe St. Antoine, Cf. "Documents Concerning Bienville's Lands," *LHQ,* X January, 1927, 16. This strip of land with an additional two *arpents* is probably the plantation purchased by the Ursulines.

57. This statement was added to the bill of sale, August 8, 1733, the date of the final payment, and signed by Father de Beaubois.

58. Hachard, *Relation,* 37. [Wolfe], *Ursulines in New Orleans,* 203.

59. AUC., N.O., *Lettres Circulaires,* I, 196-197; [Wolfe] *Ursulines in New Orleans,* 203.

60. AUC., N.O., *Lettres Circulaires,* I, 199.

61. *Ibid.*, 202.

62. *Ibid.*, 199-202; Tranchepain, *Relation*, 45-48; [Wolfe] *Ursulines in New Orleans*, 19-20.

63. AUC., N.O., *Lettres Circulaires*, I, 203-205; Tranchepain, *Relation*, 48-53; [Wolfe] *Ursulines in New Orleans*, 19-20. In the last account there is an error in the year of her death.

64. AUC., N.O., *Lettres Circulaires*, I, 211; Tranchepain, *Relation*, 59-60; Ursuline Annals, I, 198-199.

65. Delanglez, *The French Jesuits in Lower Louisiana*, 133-134.

66. Roger Baudier, *Catholic Church in Louisiana*, 125.

67. AUC., N.O., *Délibérations du Conseil*, I, 16; Ursuline Annals, I, 199.

68. The descriptions of this event given in [Wolfe] *Ursulines in New Orleans*, 22-24, and *Ursulines in Louisiana 1727-1824* (New Orleans: Hyman Smith, 1886), 16-17, are substantially the same. Both purport to be a translation of this contemporary account, but the translators have taken wide liberties which have completely altered the meaning in some instances.

69. Brother Parizel was one of the six Jesuits who accompanied Father de Beaubois to Louisiana in 1727. He remained at New Orleans. Cf. Delanglez, *The French Jesuits in Lower Louisiana*, 378-379.

70. *"les dames de la congrégation"*. These were probably members of the Sodality of the Blessed Virgin, as this expression was sometimes used to designate them. Cf. AUC., N.O., *Premier Registre de la Congrégation des Dames Enfants de Marie*, 285.

The Sodality of the Blessed Virgin was established May 28, 1730. The original act says: *"avec permission . . . du R. p. de Beaubois supérieur de ce Monastère."* *Ibid.*, 3. This is difficult to explain unless we assume that a period of probation preceded the formal reception and that this was begun or at least arranged for, before Father de Beaubois left New Orleans in April, 1729. The act is signed by Father Doutreleau "j. et g. vic. et. Sup." and by Sr. M. de St. Pierre, Supérieure. It is obvious that these signatures were added at a later date, since Father Doutreleau did not become vicar-general until after the death of Father Le Petit, October 13, 1739, and Mother St. Pierre was not elected superior until November 17, 1739.

71. AUC., N.O., *Délibérations du Conseil*, I, 253-255.

72. In March, 1732, Périer and Salmon had reported that the Ursulines observed the cloister as far as it was possible in a house which was not enclosed by walls. Cf. AC,C13A, 14:7v.

73. AUC., N.O., *Délibérations du Conseil,*I, 256.

74. AC,C13A, 19:72-72v.

75. The floor plan by Broutin, March 19, 1733, shows also a small room for the portress and a third parlor. AC,C13A, 17:306. There are copies of these plans in the Library of Congress. Since a room for the portress and a parlor were located in one of the old hospital buildings, some change may have been made in the plans after March, 1733.

76. AUC., N.O., *Délibérations du Conseil,* I, 257-258.

77. The *Règlements des Religieuses Ursulines de la Congrégation de Paris; divisés en trois livres* (Paris: Louis Josse, 1705) was first printed in 1652 "so as to be more easily communicated to the houses of the same Order who may wish to make use of it as a very important method in the Christian and secular education of the children in their institutes." The writer has followed the edition of the 1705, as a copy of that edition was preserved in AUC., N.O., for more than two centuries. There is an excellent commentary on *Règlements* of 1705 in Sister M. Monica, *Angela Merici and Her Teaching Idea* (Longmans Green and Co., 1927), 362-392.

78. *Règlements,* Pt. I, Chap. II. Undoubtedly when the teachers were very few and the boarders less numerous, the Mistress General also taught in the classroom.

79. Two very long chapters of the *Règlements,* Pt. I., Chaps. IV and V, give detailed directions for instructing the boarders "in things of piety" and preparing them for their first confession and Communion.

80. *Ibid.,* Pt. I, Chap. III, 26.

81. *Ibid.,* Chap II, 7.

82. *Ibid.,* Chap. III, 2.

83. In modern parlance, it was vocational training and consisted of plain sewing, embroidery, tapestry, painting, lacemaking, etc. *Ibid.,* Chap. VII.

84. *Ibid.,* Chap. VIII, 3.

85. In 1737, Father Le Petit, S.M., recommended that the nuns use the "same catechism for all the little girls, whether day pupils, boarders or orphans. It is fitting that it be taught at the parish church." AUC.,

N.O., *Délibérations du Conseil,* I, 27.

86. Part II of the *Règlements* is devoted to the day school.

87. The day pupils were in class ordinarily about four hours a day, an hour and a half in the morning and two hours and a half in the afternoon. Pt. II, Chap. I, 6.

88. Sister M. Monica, *Angela Merici and Her Teaching Idea,* 391.

89. AUC., N.O., *Délibérations du Conseil,* I, 27.

Chapter 6

1. AC,C13A, 19:72.

2. AUC., N.O., *Délibérations du Conseil,* I, 258.

3. *Ibid.*

4. AC,C13A, 15:76.

5. *Ibid.,* 121-121v; 15:76.

6. AC,C13A, 13:121.

7. *Ibid.*

8. In August, 1732, a wind storm blew down several buildings belonging to the king, among others one of the hospital buildings built only of wood and covered with shingles, 50 feet in length and 20 in width. "The furniture and 26 beds were crushed. Fortunately, the sick who had felt the first shaking of the building, which was built only of wood and very old, had withdrawn." AC,C13A, 17:29-29v.

9. AC,C13A, 15:75v-76.

10. AC,C13A, 17:293.

11. AC,B57:795v.

12. *Ibid..* 795.

13. AC,C13A, 19:27v; AC,B59:611v.

14. AC,C13A, 19:28-28v.

15. *Ibid.,* 28v.

16. AC,C13A, 19:73.

17. AC,C13A, 13:23-24v.

18. These *tours de lits* enclosed the entire bed as a protection against mosquitoes. In his letter of August 19, 1734, Salmon asked for

600 aunes de toile de hautbrin for this purpose. AC,C13A, 19:78.

19. AC,C13A, 19:73-73v.

20. Salmon said of Sister St. Xavier: "This Religious is charged with the care of the hospital and is an excellent subject. . . She takes excellent care of the sick." AC,C13A, 20:197v-198.

21. AUC., N.O.,*Délibérations du Conseil,* I, 258-259.

22. AC,C13A, 20:205-205v.

23. AUC., N.O., *Délibérations du Conseil,* I, 259.

24. AC,C13A, 20:221v.

25. *Ibid.*

26. AC,C13A, 29:116.

27. AC,C13A, 20:72-73; 21:65-65v; 21:257-257v.

28. AC,C13A, 20:73.

29. AC,C13A, 20:106.

30. AC,C13A, 23:112.

31. AC,C13A, 12:112v; 23:137-137v.

32. AC,C13A, 24:156-156v.

33. They were respectively, Catherine Paul Eulalie Louchard, Marguerite Antoinette Bigeaud de Belair, and her sister, Jerome Perrine Elizabeth, Cf. AUC., N.O., Letters of Obedience. In *Lettres Circulaires,* I, 234, Sister St. Louis de Gonzague's name is given as Catherine Eulalie de Lavardière.

34. She was known as Sister Ste. Marie in the community of Lisieux.

35. AUC., N.O., Letter of Obedience.

36. AUC., N.O., *Lettres Circulaires,* I, 234.

37. AUC., N.O., Letter of Obedience, March 20, 1741. Signed: J.L. Ev. de Léon.

38. AUC., N.O.*Lettres Circulaires,* I, 240.

39. *HTML.*, Bouligny-Baldwin Papers: No. 49a, Soeur M. Madelaine de Jésus to Madame Bouligny, Sept. 4, 1788.

40. *Ibid.,* No. 52, Jan. 3, 1792; No. 57, July 26, 1792; No. 58, July 27, 1792. M. Ursin Bouligny was a son of Don Francisco Bouligny, O'Reilly's aide-de-camp, and of Marie Louise de Senechal d'Auberville (Francisco's wife).

41. AUC., N.O., *Lettres Circulaires, I, 216; [Wolfe]* Ursulines in New Orleans, 28-30.

42. These documents are all preserved in AUC., N.O. They were written by Olivier Perz, confessor of the Ursulines of Landerneau; the Superioress of the same; Joseph Desboys de Lamallat, priest, Doctor of Theology, and Licenciate of Law; and the Bishop of Léon.

43. AUC., N.O., *Lettres Circulaires.* O. 233.

44. Bishop Pontbriand had personally interviewed her before permitting her to receive the habit. Cf. AUC., N.O., *Lettres Circulaires,* 217.

45. AUC., N.O., Testimonial letter of Frère Richard, Superior of the Augustinian Fathers of La Rochelle.

46. Her name was later changed to Sister Ste. Thérèse.

47. AUC., N.O.,*Lettres Circulaires,* I, 218; [Wolfe] *Ursulines in New Orleans,* 30.

48. Delanglez, *The French Jesuits in Lower Louisiana,* 293, n. 32 says: "She was in New Orleans in 1739," and cities AC,C13A, 25:182. The writer has not found anything in this document to substantiate this statement. Furthermore, according to the official list of members of the New Orleans Community, Sister Ste. Radegonde de St. Marc arrived February 14, 1736, and no one else came for six years.

49. AGI., S.D., 2585 (87-7-22):826. The convent records do not indicate that either one was employed at the hospital. Since the Ursulines had given up the hospital about nine years before the death of Sister St. Louis de Gonzague, and some twenty before that of Sister Ste. Madeleine, it is possible that their biographers simply failed to record their work at the hospital.

50. AC,C13A, 20:72v; 23:5v-6.

51. AC,C13A, 17:28. For the plan and a description of this structure. Cf. Samuel Wilson, Jr., "An Architectural History of the Royal Hospital and the Ursulines Convent of New Orleans", 600-602.

52. AC,C13A, 22:4-4v; 22:11v.

53. AC,C13A, 46:47; Wilson, "Architectural History", 601.

54. The floor plan of the convent shows this room directly across the hall from the inner chapel. Cf. AC,C13A, 17:306' Wilson, "Architectural History", 589.

55. AUC., N.O., *Délibérations du Conseil,* I, 19.

56. AC,C13A, 21:257.

57. AC,C13A, 29:116v.

58. AC,C13A, 29:116v.

59. The *pot* is a measure containing two French pints, equivalent to 3.29 English pints. Cf. *MPA., Fr. D.*, II, 318.

60. AC,C13A, 29:116v-117.

61. *Ibid.*, 117.

62. These boys and apprentices were probably orphans. It had been the plan to place the orphan boys at the hospital when it would be built. Cf. AC,C13A, 11:145.

63. AC,C13A, 29:117v.

64. AC,C13A, 28:342-345.

65. Article 13.

66. Article 14.

67. Article 15.

68. Article 16.

69. Article 2.

70. Articles 3 and 4.

71. Article 5.

72. Article 18.

73. AC,C13A, 29:117.

74. Article 10.

75. Article 11.

76. As a liquid measure the capacity of the *quart* was approximately 20.56 gallons. Cf. *MPA., Fr. D.*, 297.

77. Article 12.

78. Bishop Dosquet of Quebec, who succeeded (1763) Bishop de Mornay, appointed Abbé de l'Isle Dieu as his vicar-general in France to look after the affairs of his diocese in Louisiana. "The Abbé seems to have been a man of exceptional qualities and priestly zeal, prudence, tact, and intelligence, handling Church affairs to the entire satisfaction of Bishop Dosquet as well as his successors and the French Court." Roger Baudier, *Catholic Church in Louisiana*, 133.

79. The Ursulines also protested to the Bishop of Quebec. That prelate in turn referred the case to Maurepas, but that was as far as the bishop could go since he did not know all the details of the situation and the reasons which caused Le Normant to act as he did. He points out that the Ursuline establishment was useful to the colony, and "it was only just that these women who sacrifice themselves to go to the

colony" should not be annoyed. AC,C13A, 86 (Pt. 4):261v; AAQ., *Lettres*, II, 521-522.

80. AC,C11A, 86 (Pt. 4):272v-273.

81. *Ibid.*, 273-273v.

82. Marquis de Vaudreuil succeeded Bienville as governor in 1743.

83. AC,C11A, 86 (Pt. 4):273v-274.

84. AC,C11A, 86 (Pt. 4):275.

85. *Ibid.*, 277.

86. AC,C11A, 89:267.

87. AC,C13A, 36:330v; AC,C11A, 98:400v.

88. AC,C13A, 36:331.

89. *Ibid.*

90. AC,C13A, 16:89v-91.

91. *Ibid.*, 91.

92. In November, 1745, there were due them 5751 livres; 10 sols for 1743; 7964 livres for 1744; and 7964 livres for 1745. AC,C11A, 86 (Pt. 4):274v. CF. AC,B95:349-349v. For the years 1748-1752.

93. AC,C13A, 36:331v-332.

94. AC,C13A, 36:332v-333.

95. *Ibid.*, 333.

96. Part of the furniture and utensils provided for by Article 3 of the contract of 1744 had not arrived in 1752. Cf. AC,B95:337.

97. AC,C13A, 36:333v; AC,C11A, 98:400v.

98. AC,C13A, 36:333v, marginal note.

99. AC,C13A, 36:342-342v.

100. AC,Ci3A,36:333v-334.

101. *Ibid.*, 334.

102. AC,B93:337.

103. Kerlérec was appointed in February, 1752 and Dauberville in December of the same year.

104. AC,C13A, 37:42.

105. *Ibid.*, 42v.

106. The request, made April 23, 1753, was for a room of ten or twelve beds. AC,C13A, 37:48. In December nothing had been done. Dauberville wrote: "I can assure you, Sir, that this increase is as indispensable for the protection of the men as for the prompt cure of the sick who can not fail to suffer very much and often to communicate their sickness

by lying always two in a bed as they are obliged to do. The room which actually serves can hold at the most 30 beds if they are so close that there remains scarcely room to pass or to wait on the sick . . . A room for the officers . . . is very necessary. It is easy to understand that an officer whose entire resource is 30 to 40 livres a month is not in a position to have himself treated at the barracks . . . Since his salary would not suffice to have a domestic, it is necessary that he have recourse to the hospital in which, up to the present, he has found himself mixed with the soldiers which is very indecent. I am persuaded that this is contrary to your intentions. There are some who died there perhaps more from grief at seeing themselves so debased than from the seriousness of their illness. AC,C13A, 37:175v-176.

107. AC,C13A, 37:48-48v.

108. AC,C13A, 37:43-43v.

109. AC,C13A, 38:151v.

110. Underscoring that of the writer.

111. AC,C13A, 38:157v-158.

112. Dauberville was succeeded by Bobé-Decloseaux (1757), who was replaced by Rochemore (1758). Foucault was appointed January 18, 1762.

113. This was a hospital intended for the officers. (AC,C13A, 46:48v). It was located in the square adjoining the Ursulines on Barracks Street between Royal and Decatur. Cf. AUC., N.O., "*Cahier renfermant toutes les pièces relatives aux réclamations du fiscal pour le domaine royal du roi d'Epagne: entre autres pièces curieuses se trouvent trois plans de terrains et bâtisses des casernes de l'hôpital et du couvent en ville*", 116.

114. AUC., N.O.,*Délibérations du Conseil*, I, 49.

$\mathcal{C}hapter$ 7

1. AUC., N.O., *Délibérations du Conseil*, I, 256-257.

2. AC,C13A, 29:17.

3. *Ibid.*, 17-17v.

4. Samuel Wilson, Jr., "An Architectural History", 603-608, Plates 13-18.

5. AC,C13A, 29:17-18.

6. AC,C13A, 29:17v-18.

7. AC,B83:297-297v.

8. AC,B87:255v.

9. AC,C13A, 15(sic):16-16b. The volume number as given on the transcript in the Library of Congress is 15, but this is evidently an error as it is filed with those of volume 32 and is chronologically correct.

10. AC,C13A, 33:107v; 33:109v.

11. One who spent many weeks studying this building and making measured drawings of it says: "Of the iron grilles . . . only one remains today, that in the window at the foot of the main stair, a fine piece of wrought iron consisting of a cross member near the top, with another on the sill, embedded in the jambs of the window and pierced by six square-pointed vertical bars. If all the windows of the building were thus barred, the cost of these grilles must have been considerable. They may however have been only in the windows of the ground floor." Wilson, "An Architectural History", 609-610.

12. AC,C13A, 35:92-92v.

13. It is to be noted that this amount is more than ten thousand livres in excess of the estimate. The *premier étage* always referred to what we call the second story or floor.   AC,C13A, 34:218-218v.

14. Broutin's plans of March 19, 1733 (AC,C13A, 17:306) and November 10, 1745. *LHQ*, XXIX (July, 1946), 586-589; 605-609.

15. A comparison of the present day building with the plan shows that it was of greater length than was at first intended.

16. Copy in AUC., N.O., also one in HTML.

17. AUC., N.O., *Délibérations du Conseil*, I, 25.

18. M. de Kerlérec mentions discontinuing work on a chapel in a letter of Dec. 6, 1758. This chapel, however, seems to have been for the new hospital under construction. Cf. AC,C13A, 40:129v-130.

19. AUC., N.O., *Délibérations du Conseil*, I, 25.

20. AC,C13A, 46:48.

21. AC,C13A, 37:173v.

22. AAQ., V.G., III, 101.

23. The discovery that the present building is the second convent in the square is due to Mr. Samuel Wilson, Jr. who found the original

plans in the National Archives in Paris.

24. AC,C13A, 10:98v.

25. "All" is certainly an exaggeration.

26. Hachard, *Relation*, 99.

27. *Ibid.*, 98.

28. AC,C11A, 89:272.

29. *Ibid.*

30. Willliam A. Styles, "Pioneer American Nuns," *Ave Maria*, LV,n.s. (February 7, 1942), 167-170, gives an account of some American-born women who became nuns, but only Mary Turpin entered a convent in the present United States.

31. Biographical data has been taken from AUC., N.O., *Lettres Circulaires*, I, 255-256; Part of this account has been incorporated in [Wolfe] *Ursulines in New Orleans*, 39-41, but the author has introduced some substantial changes. Cf. also "The First American Nun," *ICHR.*, I (October, 1918), 173-175; Laurence J. Kenny, S.J., "The First American Nun in This Country," *ICHR.*, I (April, 1919), 495-499.

32. The record of their marriage is in Kaskaskia church register. "In the year of 1724, on the 11th of September, after the publication of the three banns between Louis Turpin, relict [widower] of Marie Coulon, and Dorothy Mechiperousta, relict [widow] of Charles Danis, I Nicholas Ignatius de Beaubois, religious priest of the Society of Jesus, Pastor of this parish, received their mutual consent of marriage in presence of the subscribed witnesses: Nic. Ig. De Beaubois, Louis Turpin. Her mark + Marie Metchiperousta, etc." Quoted by Kenny, "The First American Nun", 493.

33. AUC., N.O., *Actes de Prise d'Habit*, 4a.

34. AC,C11A, 96:217.

35. *Ibid.*, 217v.

36. This and Levermé are the spellings used in the convent records. In one letter Abbé de l'Isle Dieu spelled it l'Everme (AC,C11A, 96:217v) and in another Levermé (AC,C11A, 96:221).

37. AUC., N.O., *Noms de toutes les Religieuses.*

38. AC,C11A, 96:221-221v.

39. *Ibid.*, 221v.

40. Abbé de l'Isle Dieu also saw the good that could be expected if the men were given religious instruction. The same "would likewise

happen among the Negroes if they would give them two brothers of the school to instruct them, to cultivate their reason and to civilize their morals by the principles and teachings of religion as I have had the honor of representing and of asking the Court during twenty years. It is religion alone that can form not only Christians but also men and subjects for the states." AC,C11A, 96:222v.

41. AC,C11A, 96:222-222v.

42. AUC., N.O., *Noms de toutes les Religieuses*.

43. AUC., N.O., *Ursuline Annals*, I, 249. AC,C13A, 35:5v.49. AUC., N.O., *Noms de toutes les Religieuses*.

44. AUC., N.O., *Noms de toutes les Religieuses*.

45. *Ibid.*

46. AC,C11A, 99:205.

47. AC,C11A, 98:402v.

48. AUC., N.O., *Noms de toutes les Religieuses*.

49. *Ibid.*

50. Their letter of obedience (AUC., N.O.) is dated October 15, 1753 and is signed by Guy Evêque de Tréguier. In this letter the bishop does not distinguish between Canada, the center of ecclesiastical authority for the French colonies in America, and Louisiana. ". . . *nous avons permis et permettons de vous transporter dan la communauté de votre ordre établié au Canada*".

51. AC,C11A, 99:205; AUC., N.O., *Noms de toutes les Religieuses*.

52. AC,C11A, 99:205v.

53. AUC., N.O., *Ursuline Annals*, I, 255.

54. Morlaix was founded (1638) indirectly from Bordeaux through Laval (1618), Dinan (1621), and Tréguier (1625). Cf. *Sainte Angèle Mérici et l'Ordre des Ursulines*, II, 217.

55. AUC., N.O., *Ursuline Annals*, I, 256.

56. *Ibid.*

57. Sometimes written *Du Lièvre* or *Duliepure*.

58. AUC., N.O., *Noms de toutes les Religieuses*.

59. *Ibid.*; [Wolfe] *Ursulines in New Orleans*, 41: *Actes de Prise d'Habit*, 16. The record of her profession is signed by the three Jesuit Fathers Morand, Carette, and Maximilian Le Roy. This was the last ceremony at the convent at which a Jesuit assisted and signed the record until 1832.

60. AUC., N.O., *Lettres Circulaires,* I, 224; *Ursuline Annals,* I, 264-265; [Wolfe] *Ursulines in New Orleans,* 34-35.

61. Roger Baudier, *Catholic Church in Louisiana,* 176.

Chapter 8

1. Rochemonteix, Camille de, S.J., *Les Jésuites et la Nouvelle-France au XVIIIe* (2 vols.; Paris: A. Picard et fils, 1906), I, 396.

2. François Philibert Watrin, S.J., *"Bannissement des Jésuites de la Louisiane," Jesuit Relations* LXXX, 212-301, is the classic account of this event. Father Watrin had spent thirty years in Louisiana and at the time of the suppression was the superior of the Illinois Mission. Cf. also François Watrin, "Memoir on the Louisiana Missions," *Researches of the American Catholic Historical Society,* XVII (1900), 89-93; J.J. O'Brien, "Sketch of the Expulsion of the Society of Jesus from Colonial Louisiana," *Publications of the Louisiana Historical Society,* IX (1916), 9-24.

3. Four did not go to France. Father LeRoy went to Mexico, Father Carette to Santo Domingo, and Father Baudouin, who was a native of Canada and advanced in years, was permitted to remain in New Orleans. Father Meurin returned to the Illinois Mission. *Jesuit Relations,* LXX, 267-269, Cf. Delanglez, *The French Jesuits in Lower Louisiana,* 522, 526ff; Rochemonteix, *Les Jésuites et la Nouvelle France au XVIIIe siecle,* I, 404-405.

4. Father Bernard Viel, born in New Orleans, was among the Jesuits expelled from the colony. He was the only native Louisiana priest at the time, and the first to enter the priesthood. He died in France as an Oratorian.

5. *Jesuit Relations,* LXXX, 243.

6. Delanglez, *The French Jesuits in Lower Louisiana,* 527.

7. AUC., N.O., *Délibérations du Conseil,* I, 50.

8. AC,C13A, 44:56-57.

9. AC,C13A, 43:222v.

10. François Xavier Martin, *The History of Louisiana from the*

Earliest Period (2 vols.; New Orleans: Lyman and Beardslee, 1827-1829), I, 351.

11. Charles Gayarré, *History of Louisiana: The French Domination* (2 vols.; New Orleans: Redfield, 1854) II, 192-203;365-380.

12. After the death of Bishop Pontbriand in 1760 the Chapter of the Diocese of Quebec selected Abbé de l'Isle Dieu to act as vicar-general, and he continued his supervision over the Church in Louisiana.

13. AAQ., V.G., IV, 188.

14. An Irishman of ability in the Spanish service, he had served with distinction in Europe, had acted as governor of Havana rebuilding the fortifications dismantled during the British occupation, (1762-1763) and now was called to cope with the situation in Louisiana.

15. Details of this event are given in "*Carta de D. Alejandre O'Reilly à D. Julian de Arriaga dandole cuenta de su viaje à Nueva Orleans, 31 de Agosto de 1769,*" in Manuel Serrano y Sanz (ed.), *Documentos Historicos de la Florida y la Luisiana siglos XVI al XVII.* (Madrid: Libreria General de Victoriano Suarez, 1912), 304-312.

16. In the above letter (n.15) the date is given as August 17.

17. James S. Zacharie, "The Cathedral Archives," *Publications* of the Louisiana Historical Society, II (February, 1900), 13.

18. AUC., N.O., *Ursuline Annals,* II, 30-31.

19. *Ibid.,* 31.

20. AGI., S.D., (81-1-7), Nos. 9 and 10, October 27, 1769, give an account of this event, the official accusation, the sentence and its execution.

21. AUC., N.O., *Ursuline Annals,* II, 33.

22. Nicholas Chauvin de Lafrénière (the same who was foremost in the expulsion of the Jesuits), Jean-Baptiste Noyan, Pierre Caresse, Pierre Marquis, and Joseph Milhet were originally sentenced to be hanged, but as no hangman could be found, O'Reilly was forced to have them shot. Six others were condemned to imprisonment in Morro Castle in Havana.

23. AUC., N.O., *Ursuline Annals,* II, 34-35.

24. Roger Baudier, *Catholic Church in Louisiana,* 179.

25. AAQ., V.G., IV, 188. In this letter to the Bishop of Quebec the abbé expressed his deep concern for the Ursulines in New Orleans.

26. The first Ursuline foundation in Spain was made during the

French Revolution by four religious from Oloron. Their first residence was at Valencia whence they moved to Murviedro and finally to Molina de Aragon. This last and permanent establishment was made in 1812.

27. AUC., N.O., *Délibérations du Conseil*, I, 49.

28. AGI., S.D., 2585 (86-7-); 1355.

29. *History of Louisiana*, II, 21.

30. AGI., S.D., 2645 (87-2-26):406.

31. *Ibid.*, 416.

32. AGI., P.C., 155B, Pt. I, 99-104; 1572, packet C, No. 18, 1133-1138, Manuel de Salcedo to Senor Marques de Sommeruelos, September 12, 1803.

33. AUC., N.O., *Délibérations du Conseil*, I, 8.

34. Roger Baudier, *Catholic Church in Louisiana*, 183, citing St. Louis Cathedral Archives.

35. AC,C13A, 44(pt. 4):56.

36. AC,C13A, 46:48.

37. AC,C13A, 47:15.

38. AC,C13A, 50:21-22v; 50:69-69v,

39. AC,C13A, 49:161-161v.

40. *Ibid.*, 16lv. Cf. also AC,C13A, 50:21-22.

41. AC,C13A, 49:169.

42. AC,C13A, 50:70.

43. AGI., S.D., 2587 (86-7-22); 674-675.

44. AUC., N.O., *Ursuline Annals*, II, 38.

45. AGI., S.D., 2678 (87-4-4):73-88. A record of the payment of these allotments for the years 1770 to 1803 is found in AGI., P.C., 538B.

46. Roger Baudier, *Catholic Church in Louisiana*, 183.

47. *Ibid.*, 180.

48. As shown above there were really seven.

49. AAQ., V.G., IV, 188.

50. He was forty-two years old when he came to Louisiana. On his way to the colony he stopped in Cuba. There he made the acquaintance of Bishop Echevarria whose friend he became.

51. AGI., S.D., 2594, Cirillo to Echevarria, August 6, 1772. A translation of almost all this letter is given by Gayarré, *History of Louisiana, Spanish Domination*, 57-63.

52. Shea, *History of the Catholic Church in the United States*, II, 546, makes the following statement: "The coming of Father Cyril in the name of the Bishop of Santiago de Cuba, was hailed with delight by the Ursuline Nuns, who were thus brought into relation with a Superior to whom they could expose their wants and trials." If they hailed his coming "with delight" this "delight" must have waned quickly if he made his opinion of them unknown to the religious themselves. As we shall see later, the nuns did come, in after years, to have a very high opinion of Father Cirillo.

53. AGI., S.D., 2594 (87-1-4): 889-890.

54. AGI., S.D., 2594 (87-1-4): 698. Emphasis added.

55. AUC., N.O., October 1, 1773. Emphasis added.

56. AAQ., V.G., III, 101.

57. *Ibid.*

58. AGI., P.C. 1400: March 28, 1774.

59. AGI., P.C., 1400, Bishop of Cuba to the King of Spain, March 24, 1774; AGI., P.C., 180-1: Nos. 11 and 12. AUC., N.O., Contemporary French translation.

60. AGI., P.C., 180-1: No. 11 and 12.

61. ACNO., Records and *Délibérations* of the Cabildo, 267.

62. *Ibid.*, 269.

63. AC,C13A, 46:48.

64. AUC., N.O., *Délibérations du Conseil,* I, 73-74.

65. *Ibid.* As there was no record of the removal of the tile roof, Rev. Mother Xavier Farjon called a meeting, October 27, 1795, of all the nuns of the community "even the coadjutrix Sisters, although the latter never attend these meetings" and asked them why the tile roof had been removed. Mother St. Ignatius Duliepure and Sisters St. Antoine Delatre and Marie Joseph Braud were the only professed members of the community in 1773 who were still living in 1795. They gave an account of the condition of the house and of the removal of the tile roof, and their statements were recorded.

Chapter 9

1. This is the only time that the third one is ever mentioned in the convent archives. There is no record of how long she remained nor why she was not admitted to the novitiate.

2. AUC., N.O., Bishop of Cuba to Mother St. Régis, October 13, 1778.

3. AUC., N.O., *Actes de Prise d'Habit*, 33, 35.

4. *Ibid.*

5. *Ibid.*, 34, 36. Father Antoino de Sedella was present for the ceremony and signed the register for the first time.

6. AUC., N.O., *Délibérations du Conseil*, I, 60.

7. *Ibid.* This entry dated January 31, 1782, is signed by the officials of the community and Father Cirillo.

8. Some years earlier an effort had been made to obtain some Ursulines from France. February 3, 1783, Abbé de Villars, vicar-general, wrote from Paris to the Bishop of Quebec: "I wrote some years ago to the Superior of the Ursulines of New Orleans, on the subject of Ursulines from France that they had asked for at the time of the death of M. de l'Isle Dieu, 1779. If they are still in need, I think I could procure some young ladies of merit disposed to go to join them. I presume that the court of Spain would not oppose it." AAQ, V.G., VI, 30. This request was probably made as the result of a conversation with Count de Galvez who suggested to the Ursuline Superior that religious be obtained from France. Cf. AGI., S.D., 2552 (86-6-16) No. 199.

9. AUC., N.O., Letter of obedience given by the Bishop of Uzès, September 22, 1785.

10. AUC., N.O., *Ursuline Annals*, II, 106-107. Sister Ste. Félicité kept her promise and today this statue has a place of honor in the small chapel of the Ursuline Convent of New Orleans.

11. *Ibid.*, 107.

12. AUC., N.O., Henri Benedict Jules de Bethy, September 22, 1785.

13. Mother St. Monica Ramos was professed only four and a half years when she was elected superior, July 12, 1785.

14. AUC., N.O., *Journal depuis 1727 jusqu'en 1853*, 37-38.

15. At the request of the King of Spain, Bishop Echevarria asked the Holy See to appoint Father Cirillo de Barcelona as his Auxiliary to serve the Louisiana section of his diocese. July 18, 1782, the King officially notified Father Cirillo of his appointment as Auxiliary Bishop of the Bishop of Cuba. Pope Pius VI, however, did not issue the Bulls of appointment until June 6, 1784, and the consecration did not take place until March 6, 1785. Cf. Roger Baudier, *Catholic Church in Louisiana*, 200.

16. AGI., S.D., 2552 (86-6-16). No. 199, Miro to Sonora: AUC., N.O., *Journal depuis 1727 jusqu'en 1853*, 38.

17. CAA., N.D., Echevarria to Sedella, April 26, 1786; AUC., N.O., *Journal depuis 1727 jusqu'en 1853*, 38.

18. CAA., N.D., Senora to Cirillo, (No. 42), July 17, 1786; Senora to Echevarria, August 6, 1786.

19. AGI., S.D., 2552 (86-6-16), No. 199.

20. CAA., N.D. Echevarria to Sedella, April 26, 1786.

21. *Ibid.*

22. CAA., N.D., Sonora to Echevarria, August 6, 1786; Echevarria to Sedella, November 25, 1778.

23. AGI., S.D., 2552 (86-6-16), No. 199 Miró to Sonora, March 24, 1787.

24. CAA., N.D., Sonora to Cirillo, June 17, 1786; Cirillo to Sedella, May 17, 1786; AGI., P.C., 102, Miró to Chambon de la Tour, December 29, 1786.

25. AGI., S.D., 2544 (86-6-8), 323-326, Miró to Valdes, June 15, 1788.

26. AGI., S.D., 2552 (86-6-16) No. 199, Miró to Sonora, March 24, 1787.

27. CAA., N.D., Cirillo to Sedella, August 22, 1786.

28. AUC., N.O., *Journal depuis 1727 jusqu'en 1853*, 38.

29. AGI., S.D., 2544 (86-6-8): 138-140, Miró and Navarro to Valdez, February 20, 1788; *Ibid.*, 2576 (86-7-13), 336, Porlier to Valdez, September 11, 1787.

30. AGI., S.D., 2576 (86-7-13): 335-336, Porlier to Valdez, September 11, 1787.

31. AGI., S.D., 2551 (86-6-15) : 72-73, Condé de Galvez to Sonora, March 22, 1785.

32. AGI., S.D., 2576 (86-7-13): 336-338, Porlier to Valdez, September 11, 1787.

33. AGI., S.D., 2544 (86-6-8): 138-142, Miró and Navarro to Valdez, February 20, 1788, enclosing Miró and Navarro to Porlier, February 20, 1788.

34. King Charles III died December 14, 1788, and was succeeded by Charles IV. The news did not reach Louisiana until the early months of 1789. The day set for the usual ceremonies incident on the accession of a new sovereign was May 7.

35. AGI., S.D., 2645 (87-2-26); 405; AUC., N.O., *Le roi d'Espagne ordonne de bâtir la muraille de séparation. . . 1788.* This wall is marked on a plan drawn by Gilberto Guillemard, April 10, 1793. Copy in AUC., N.O., and in *HTML*. Reproduction of the plan in *Messenger of Our Lady of Prompt Succor*, January, 1940 and in *Catholic Action*, January 11, 1940.

In October, 1789, Mother St. Monica asked Governor Miró to have the wall extended across the front of the convent grounds near the levee. Miró refused, saying that he could have built only that portion specified in the royal order. He told her that he was sure that this would have been granted had it been asked in the original request made to the king. Cf. AGI., P.C., 15b, Mother St. Monica Ramos to Estevan Miró, October 14, 1789, and Miró to Mother St. Monica Ramos, October 15, 1789.

36. AGI., S.D., 2544, No. 5, Miró and Navarro to Valdez, April 1, 1788.

37. *Ibid.*

38. AGI., S.D., 2544:488; AUC., N.O., Private Archives, III, 102. The total loss was placed at 2,595,561 pesos. CF. AGI., S.D., 2544:503.

39. This house represented the dowries of three of the religious. In October, 1785, Bishop Cirillo had asked the community to give him the dowries of Sisters Ste. Claire, St. Raphaël, and St. Louis de Gonzague, a total of 4500 pesos, in exchange for this house. All the community consented. After receiving the money, the bishop made a gift of 500 pesos to the community. CF. AUC., N.O., *Maison Rue Bourbon vendue par Mgr. Cyrille de Barcelona. . . aux Dames Ursulines. . .6 octobre 1785.*

40. Don Andres Almonester y Rojas, descendant of a noble Andalusian family and royal standard bearer for the colony, was foremost among

the public-spirited men of that time. He made a great fortune in New Orleans, and at a cost of $50,000 built the St. Louis Cathedral. He also built a parish house, the Charity Hospital, the town hall and the cabildo, offered one of his houses for a school for boys and founded the leper hospital.

41. Father Antoine de Sedella obtained this favor for the Ursulines. Cf. AUC., N.O., *Délibérations du Conseil*, I, 67-68.

42. AUC., N.O., plan drawn by Gilberto Guillemard. Cf. n. 35 *supra*.

43. AGI., S.D., 87-4 (L.C., I, 22-28): 25, 30.

44. CAA., N.D., Charles IV through Taranco to Father Patricio Walsh, August 14, 1794.

45. *Norman's Guidebook of New Orleans* (New Orleans: 1845), 98; Roger Baudier, *Catholic Church in Louisiana*, 366.

46. Roger Baudier, *Catholic Church in Louisiana*, 365. The entry in AUC., N.O.,*Délibérations du Conseil*, I, 65, indicates merely that the chapel was dedicated to the Blessed Mother.

47. When he petitioned the king for the right to build the church, Almonester asked that it be dedicated to Our Lady of Consolation. Cf. AGI., S.D., 2531 (85-5-22), September 8, 1785.

48. AUC., N.O., *Délibérations du Conseil*, I, 65.

49. AGI., S.D., 2544:187. Bishop Peñalver y Cárdenas in a letter to the king, March 7, 1796 refers to the spacious classrooms constructed by Almonester. Cf. AGI., S.D., 87-4 (L.C., I, 22-28), 26. The writer has not been able to locate this building. It does not appear on Guillemard's plan of 1793 (Cf. n. 35 *supra*), which is a detailed plan showing the location of all the Ursuline buildings. The convent proper is designated "Convent, school-room, and lodging for the boarders and orphans." There is a building marked as the day school. It is possible that this building was the one financed by Almonester and at first used for the boarders, for in an account published in 1825, Almonester is credited with having built "*l'église, le choeur, et les écoles pour les externes.*" Cf. *Recueil des Lettres des Evêques et des Missionaires des Missions des Deux Mondes*, (Louvain: Valinthout et Vandenzande, 1825), 408.

50. They numbered 64 in 1796. Cf. AGI., S>D>, 87-4 (L.C., I, 22-28), 25, 30.

51. *Ibid.*, 31

52. AUC., N.O., Patricio Walsh before Quiñones, December 19, 1794.

53. Rev. Don Theodoro Thurso Henrique Henriquez, D.D., was appointed Auxiliary Vicar-General and Ecclesiastical Judge of the Province of Louisiana by Bishop Trespalacios of the Diocese of St. Christopher of Havana, in February, 1792.

54. AGI., S.D., 87-4 (L.C., I, 22-28), 25, 30; CAA., N.D., Charles IV to Patricio Walsh, August 14, 1794.

55. CAA., N.D., Charles IV to Patricio Walsh, August 14, 1794.

56. CAA., N.D., Theodoro Henriquez to Mother St. Ignace Duliepure, August 18, 1792.

57. CAA., N.D., Mother St. Ignace Duliepure and Mother St. Xavier Farjon to Theodoro Henriquez, August 18, 1792.

58. CAA., N.D., Charles IV to Patricio Walsh, August 14, 1794.

59. *Ibid.*

60. Father Patricio Walsh, an Irish priest from Spain, came to Louisiana in 1792 and served as chaplain of the hospital in New Orleans. When Louisiana was made an independent diocese in 1793, he was appointed administrator and served in that capacity until Bishop Peñalver arrived in 1795. Upon the departure of Bishop Peñalver for Guatemala in 1801, and after the death of Fathers Hassett and Guerrero, he claimed to be vicar-general and administrator under an appointment that had been made by Bishop Peñalver. He died August 22, 1806, and was buried under the chapel of the Ursulines. Roger Baudier, *Catholic Church in Louisiana*, 242.

61. CAA., N.D., Charles IV to Patricio Walsh, August 14, 1794; Taranco to Patricio Walsh, August 18, 1794.

62. The seat was to be so placed that Don Almonester would have his back to the people. AUC., N.O., Walsh to Almonester, December 13, 1794. (Copy)

63. AUC., N.O., Patricio Walsh before Quiñones, December 19, 1794.

64. CAA., N.D., Walsh to Taranco, January 14, 1795.

65. *Ibid.*; AUC., N.O., Walsh to Mother St. Xavier Farjon, January 3, 1795.

66. CAA., N.D., Walsh to Taranco, January 14, 1795.

67. AGI., S.D., 87-4, August 29, 1796.

68. He was interred in the present St. Louis Cathedral which he had erected. Indicating the place of his burial is a large marble slab on which are inscribed his coat of arms, his titles, his dignities, and the services rendered to church and state in Louisiana.

69. CAA., N.D., Mother St. Ignace Duliepure to Father Theodoro Henriquez, March 16, 1793.

70. CAA., N.D., Henriquez to Carondelet, March 18, 1793. Francisco Luis Hector, Baron de Carondelet, was appointed March, 1791, to succeed Estevan Miró who had asked to be relieved as governor of Louisiana. Carondelet assumed office December 30, 1791, as the sixth Spanish governor of Louisiana.

71. CAA., N.D., Henriquez to Mother St. Ignace Duliepure, March 19, 1793.

72. For Carondelet's insistence on the observance of honors due him in the St. Louis Cathedral see Roger Baudier, *Catholic Church in Louisiana*, 226, 244.

73. CAA., N.D., Carondelet to Henriquez, April 21, 1793.

74. CAA., N.D., Henriquez before Quiñones, April 22, 1793.

75. The original Charity Hospital of St. John established in the first house occupied by the Ursulines and later rebuilt on the same site was virtually destroyed by a severe storm in 1779. Don Almonester rebuilt the hospital, under the patronage of St. Charles, on a new location just at the edge of the city, now Rampart and Toulouse streets.

76. Without a church and without a home after the fire of 1788, Bishop Cirillo went to San Antonio, Florida where he remained from July 18, 1788, until June 12, 1789. He then returned to New Orleans. During his absence Father Antonio de Sedella acted as vicar-general.

77. ACNO., Records and Deliberations of the Cabildo, III, 132.

78. Don Almonester said that the groundless opposition he had encountered would have discouraged a man less interested in the public welfare. Cf. AGI., S.D., 2554:186.

79. ACNO., Records and Deliberations of the Cabildo, III, 220.

80. Gayarré, *History of Louisiana: Spanish Domination*, 355-356.

81. Roger Baudier, *Catholic Church in Louisiana*, 225, citing AGI., P.C., 102 (1794).

82. Roger Baudier, *Catholic Church in Louisiana*, 226, citing St. L.C.A.

83. Shea, *Catholic Church in the U.S.*, II, 557-558.

84. AUC., N.O., *Délibérations du Conseil,* I, 65.

85. AGI., S.D., 2590 (6-7-27): 348-349.

86. It bears the signatures of Mother St. Monica Ramos and the twelve other choir religious. The three French religious, Mothers St. Xavier Farjon, Ste. Felicité Alzas, and St. André Madier were among those who signed.

87. Ludwig Pastor, *The History of the Popes* (St. Louis: B. Herder Book Co., 1923), VI, 448.

88. John Gilmary Shea, *History of the Catholic Church in the U.S.*, II, 582-584.

Chapter 10

1. ACU., H.C. *El Libro de Defunciónes;* D. Pedro G. De Villaumbrosia, *Historia Chronológica y General de la Orden de Santa Ursula* (4 vols.; Zaragoza: José Bedera, 1866), IV, 271-272. Mother St. Monica did not receive the habit of the Poor Clares. She simply remained in their monastery in Havana "for some time" preparatory to entering the novitiate, but withdrew to go to New Orleans to join the Ursulines.

2. AUC., N.O., Bishop of Havana to Mother St. Monica Ramos, April 27, 1789.

3. AGI., S.D., 2590 (86-7-27): 316-330; same 437-456.

4. AUC., N.O., *Lettres Circulaires,* 237.

5. *Ibid.,* 239.

6. *Ibid.,* 240-241.

7. After the death of Mother St. Jacques the community consisted of nine religious, five French, three Creole, one Acadian, professed before 1781, while the community was still thoroughly French, and of eight Spanish, two Creole, one Scotch professed between 1781 and 1785.

8. AUC., N.O., Private Archives, III, June 17, 1791.

9. ACU., H.C., *El Libro de Defunciónes.*

10. AUC., N.O., *Lettres Circulaires,* 248.

11. AUC., N.O., *Noms de toutes les Religieuses Professes.*

12. AUC., N.O., Bishop of Havana to Revered Mother St. Ignace Duliepure, April 26, 1792.

13. CAA., N.D., Henriquez before Quiñones, May 4, 1793.

14. CAA., N.D., Mother St. Ignace Duliepure to Father Theodore Henriques, May 4, 1793.

15. CAA., N.D., Henriquez before Quioñones, May 6, 1793.

16. CAA., N.D., Henriquez to Mother St. Ignace Duliepure, May 10, 1793.

17. *Ibid.*

18. CAA., N.D., Mother St. Ignace Duliepure to Father Henriquez, May 10, 1793.

19. CAA., N.D., Quiñones, New Orleans, May 14, 1793.

20. CAA., N.D., Henriquez before Quiñones, June 3, 1793.

21. A settlement of Germans some 30 miles up the river from New Orleans.

22. CAA., N.D., Henriquez before quiñones, June 3, 1793.

23. *Ibid.*

24. The letter of Mother St. Ignace to Bishop Trespalacios, May 22, 1793, is no longer extant; but it is hardly probable that Mother St. Ignace wrote that the Ursulines were "not bound to the cloister by their constitutions", since Chapter IV laid down very strict regulations relative to the cloister. Probably she told Bishop Trespalacios, as she had Father Henriquez, that they took the vow of instruction and not the vow of cloister, although they observed it. ". . . *y quatro Voto que hacemos de ensenanza (y no de clausura aunque la guardamos)."* CAA., N.D., May 10, 1793.

25. AUC., N.O., Bishop of Havana to Mother St. Ignace Duliepure, June 11, 1793.

26. This letter signed at San Lorenzo, November 23, 1793, is quoted in full in John Gilmary Shea, *History of the Catholic Church in the U.S.,* II, 567-568.

27. Roger Baudier, *Catholic Church in Louisiana,* , 219.

28. AGI., S.D., 2590 (86-7-27): 348-349.

29. The diocese thus created was bounded on the north and east by that of Baltimore and on the south and west by those of Linares and Durango.

30. This is the date given by Roger Baudier, *Catholic Church*

in Louisiana, 223. Shea, *Catholic Church in the U.S.*, II, 571, gives April 3.

31. Shea, *Catholic Church in the U.S.*, II, 571.

32. *Ibid.*, 412. This account says that they were accompanied by a lay brother.

33. *Ibid.*

34. Father Walsh applied to the Bishop of Havana for approval of the permission given. CAA., N.D., Walsh to Trespalacios, January 5, 1795.

35. AGI., S.D., 2588 (86-7-25): 565-566.

36. *Ibid.*; AGI., S.D., 2579 (86-7-25): 612; AGI., P.C., 538B, gives Mother St. Luc as one of the companions of Mother Marie Geneviève instead of Mother Marie Françoise.

37. AGI., S.D., 2588 (86-7-25): 566-568.

38. AGI., S.D., 2579 (96-7-16): 613; AGI., P.C., 538B, Aranjuez, May 22, 1795.

39. AGI., S.D., 2579 (86-7-16): 612.

40. Shea, *Catholic Church in the U.S.*, II, 412; Henry De Courcy, *Catholic Church in the U.S.* (New York: Edward Dunigan & Bro., 1857), 79. Mother Marie Geneviève was buried in the cemetery of the Sulpicians of Baltimore.

41. AGI., S.D., 2673:1153-1159. A translation of this report is given in Gayarré, *History of Louisiana, The Spanish Domination*, 376-379. Shea, *Catholic Church in the U.S.*, II, 572-575, quotes from Gayarré, but makes a few changes in the wording.

42. In 1771 the Spanish government decided to establish schools in Louisiana to teach Christian Doctrine, elementary education and grammar. AGI., P.C., 174: No. 66. The Louisianians, who were addicted to the French language, evinced little interest in the Spanish schoolmasters. ". . .no pupil ever presented himself for the Latin class; a few came to be taught reading and writing only; these never exceeded thirty, and frequently dwindled down to six. . .As late as 1788. . .the effort to introduce the Spanish language in Louisiana had remained a practical failure. In New Orleans the courts were conducted in Spanish, but for the rest the people . . . clung to the French tongue, and insisted on sending their children to French schools. On this rock of Gallic stubbornness, therefore, the hopeful project of the Spanish monarch was

shipwrecked." David K. Djork "Documents Relating to the Establishment of Schools in Louisiana, 1771, *MVHR.*, (March, 1925), 561-562.

43. ACU., H.C., *El Libro de Defunciónes.*

44. CAA., N.D., Theodoro Henriquez to Mother St. Ignace Duliepure, February 7, 1792; Bishop of Havana to Mother St. Ignace Duliepure, June 11, 1793.

45. CAA., N.D., *Auto expedido á la Superiora de Monasterio de Ursulinas . .* , New Orleans, February 7, 1792.

46. AUC., N.O., Filipe, Bishop of Cuba, to Mother Ste. Marguerite Duliepure, April 26, 1792.

47. AUC., N.O., *Délibérations du Conseil,* I, 70.

48. AUC., N.O., *Journal depuis 1727 jusqu'en 1853,* 41.

49. CAA., N.D., General proceedings of the visit of the Diocese of Louisiana and in particular of New Orleans by Don Luis Peñalver y Cárdenas, 1795.

50. Shea, *Catholic Church in the U.S.,* II, 575; Gayarré, *History of Louisiana, The Spanish Domination,* 376.

51. Roger Baudier, *Catholic Church in Louisiana,* 219.

52. In 1800 Mother St. Xavier Farjon wrote that they always had from 50 to 60 boarders and more than 100 day pupils. AGI., S.D., 2645 (87-2-26), 407. Bishop Peñalver about the same time gave the number of boarders as 80. AGI., S.D., 2645 (67-2-26), 420. Perhaps the bishop included in this number the orphans who numbered at least 24, of whom 12 were supported by the king and 12 by the Foundation of Count de Galvez. AGI., P.C., 15b, Miró to Mother St. Monica Ramos, January 8, 1789.

53. CAA., N.D., The King to the Bishop of Louisiana, March 20, 1801; AGI., S.D., 2640 (87-2-21), 37.

54. AUC., N.O., Sister St. Xavier Farjon to Gayoso de Lemos, April, 1799, (Copy); AGI., S.D., 2640 (87-2-21): 37; CAA., N.D., The King to the Bishop of Louisiana, March 20, 1801.

55. AUC., N.O., April, 1799, (Copy).

56. AGI., S.D., 2552 (86-6-16), No. 210; 2576 (86-7-13): 248-250; 2672 (87-3-26): 53-55; 2640(87-2-21): 36-39; CAA., N.D., The King to the Bishop of Louisiana, March 20, 1801. Cf. also correspondence between Mother St. Monica Ramos and Governor Miró (1787-1790) in AGI., P.C., 14 and 15b.

57. AGI., S.D., 2533 (86-5-24): 213-215.

58. François Xavier Martin, *The History of Louisiana, from the Earliest Period* (2 vols.; New Orleans: Lyman and Beardslee, 1829), II, 154.

59. Gayarré, *History of Louisiana, The Spanish Domination*, 592, quoting dispatch of Laussat to his government.

60. Roger Baudier, *Catholic Church in Louisiana*, 246.

Chapter 11

1. Shea, *Catholic Church in the U.S.*, 580-581; Roger Baudier, *Catholic Church in Louisiana*, 249. After Bishop Peñalver had taken possession of his see of Guatemala, he notified the Canons of the Cathedral, Father Hassett and Father Francisco Perez Guerrero. They, uncertain of their authority, wrote to the Bishop of Havana for advice. He expressed the opinion that the direction of the diocese depended on the two canons.

2. He was sent instead to the see of Tarrazoma, Spain.

3. Roger Baudier, *Catholic Church in Louisiana*, 249.

4. Mother St. Monica had been elected Superior again, July 12, 1800, at the expiration of the second triennial of Mother St. Xavier Farjon.

5. CAA., N.D., Mother St. Monica Ramos to the Marques de Casa Calvo, May 19, 1803.

6. Some historians seem to have erroneously associated this request to go to Mexico with the conspiracy of Aaron Burr. Cf. Walter Flavius McCaleb, *The Aaron Burr Conspiracy* (New York: Wilson Erickson, Inc., 1936), 33; Carlos E. Castaneda, *The Mission Era: The End of the Spanish Regime, 1780-1810*, Vol. V. of *Our Catholic Heritage in Texas, 1519-1936* ed. by James P. Gibbons, C.S.V. (7 vols.; Austin: Von Boeckmann-Jones Co., 1942), 275. McCaleb and Castenada both cite Matthew L. Davis, *Memoirs of Aaron Burr* (2 vols.; New York Harper and Brothers, 1837), II, 382. Relative to Burr's activity in New Orleans, Davis wrote: "The Catholic bishop, resident at New Orleans, was also consulted, and prepared to promote the enterprise. He designated three priests, of the order of

Jesuits, as suitable agents, and they were accordingly employed . . . Madame Xavier Tarjeon [Farjon], superior of the convent of the Ursuline nuns at New Orleans, was in the secret. Some of the sisterhood were also employed in Mexico." Castaneda says that "some of the Sisters were to be employed in Mexico." Burr spent an hour at the Ursuline Convent in June or July, 1805 (Davis, *Memoirs*, II, 371), but it is utterly incomprehensible that Mother St. Xavier cooperated in any way with Burr in his harebrained scheme relative to Mexico. Burr told his daughter that the Bishop conducted him "to the cloister", but that was impossible as there was no bishop in New Orleans from the time Bishop Peñalver left in 1801 until five years after Bishop DuBourg was consecrated in 1815. Who were the three Jesuits? The Jesuits had been expelled from Louisiana in 1763 and the order suppressed in 1773. Although former Jesuit Father Viel returned to Louisiana in 1792, he had probably gone to France by the summer of 1805. Cf. Roger Baudier, *Catholic Church in Louisiana*, 229, 239, 251. There were no Ursulines in Mexico in 1805 and except for the instance cited above in 1802 there is no record that the Ursulines entertained any thought of going there until several decades later.

7. AGI., S.D., 2672 (87-3-26): 56' AUC., N.O.. The King of Spain to the Bishop of Havana, July 25, 1803; Thomas Hassett to Mother Monica Ramos, March 16, 1803. Father Hassett implies in this letter that he did not know that Mother St. Monica had written to the king until he received a communication from her dated March 10, 1803.

8. ACU., H.C., Someruelos to Mother St. Monica Ramos, November 19, 1802 (Copy).

9. AGI., P.C., 1572:91, Packet A, No. 10, Casa Calvo to Someruelos, November 8, 1802.

10. "*sans que l'union des coeurs ni la paix fussent altérées,*" AUC., N.O., *Délibérations du Conseil,* I, 85.

11. AUC., N.O., Thomas Hassett to Mother St. Monica Ramos, March 16, 1803.

12. AUC., N.O., *Relation de ce qui se passa dans notre Communauté à l'Epoque de la Rétrocession.*

13. *Ibid.*; Pedro G. de Villaumbrosia, *Historia Cronológica,* IV, 273.

14. AUC., N.O., *Délibérations du Conseil,* I, 85-86. Dismayed

by the impending evil and alarmed lest the Colonial Prefect examine the books, the nuns "jumbled the accounts". It is possible that they also destroyed other records and papers, thereby depriving the present day historian of vitally important information about the community and its schools.

15. *Ibid.*

16. Alcée Fortier, *A History of Louisiana* (4 vols.; New York: Manzi, Joyant & Co., 1904), II, 221-222.

17. AUC., N.O., *Délibérations du Conseil,* I, 86.

18. *Ibid.*

19. Quoted by Fortier, *History of Louisiana,* II, 233-234, citing Colonial Archives, Paris.

20. AUC., N.O., *Délibérations du Conseil,* I, 86.

21. Villaumbrosia, *Historia Cronológia,* IV, 273-274. The account given in the *Délibérations du Conseil,* I, 85-86, does not mention Mother St. Ignace as taking any part in the discussion, but that given by Villaumbrosia is wholly in keeping with her ardent, outspoken character. The author has based his account on information furnished him by a member of the Ursuline Community of Havana who lived with Mother St. Ignace during the last four years of her life. *Ibid.,* 283-290.

22. AGI., P.C., 1572, Packet C., Letter No. 4, Mother St. Monica Ramos et al. to Salcedo and Casa Calvo, May 19, 1803. The king apparently replied to Mother St. Monica's letter of October 24 by a letter to the Bishop of Havana dated July 25, 1803. In reality it confirmed what had already been done. AUC., N.O. (Copy).

23. AUC., N.O., Salcedo and Casa Calvo to Mother St. Monica Ramos, May 14, 1803, quoting from the royal order of January 18, 1803; CAA., N.D., copy of same; Thomas Hassett to Mother St. Monica Ramos, May 18, 1803 quoting same part of royal order.

24. CAA., N.D., Mother St. Monica Ramos to Thomas Hassett, May 16, 1803.

25. CAA., N.D., Mother St. Monica Ramos et al. to Salcedo and Casa Calvo, May 20, 1803, enclosed in Salcedo and Casa Calvo to Thomas Hassett, May 20, 1803. Same in AGI., P.C., 1572:908, Packet C, Letter 4.

26. CAA., N.D., Salcedo and Casa Calvo to Thomas Hassett, May 20, 1803. In his reply, May 21, 1803, Father Hassett repeats this

letter almost verbatim.

27. CAA., N.D., Thomas Hassett to Salcedo and Casa Calvo, May 21, 1803; AUC., N.O., copy of same.

28. CAA., N.D., Salcedo and Casa Calvo to Thomas Hassett, May 23, 1803.

29. *Ibid.*

30. CAA., N.D., Thomas Hassett before Broutin, May 26, 180331. CAA., N.DThomas Hassett to Salcedo and Casa Calvo, May 24, 1803.

32. CAA., N.D., Thomas Hassett before Broutin, May 26, 1803.

33. CAA., N.D., Thomas Hassett to Salcedo and Casa Calvo, May 26, 1803.

34. CAA., N.D., Thomas Hassett before Broutin, May 26, 1803. Father Broutin must have returned as soon as possible for he was appointed to Ascension Church at Lafourche, July 22, 1893. Cf. AGI., P.C., 6120.

35. CAA., N.D., Salcedo and Casa Calvo to Thomas Hassett, May 26, 1803.

36. CAA., N.D., Thomas Hassett to Mother St. Monica Ramos, May 27, 1803.

37. AGI., P.C., 1572, Packet C, Letter 4, (L.C. f. 910), Salcedo and Casa Calvo to Someruelos, May 31, 1803.

38. CAA., N.D., Salcedo and Casa Calvo to Mother St. Monica Ramos, May 23, 1803; Mother St. Monica Ramos to Thomas Hassett, May 23, 1803.

39. Some of these names are spelled in almost as many ways as there are documents in which they appear. Cf. AGI., P.C., 1572, Packet C, Letter 4 (L.C., 914-915); AGI., P.C., 593, Letter 212; AGI., S.D., 2599: 376-377; ACU, H.C. *El Libro de Fundación*, 1-1v; AUC., N.O., *Délibérations du Conseil*, I, 86; Villaumbrosia, *Historia Cronológica y General*, IV, 275-276.

40. AUC., N.O., *Relation de ce qui se passa dans notre Communaute à l'Epoque de la Rétrocession.*

41. *Ibid.* Translation in [Wolfe] *Ursulines in New Orleans*, 55.

42. They had humbly asked and received the permission of Father Hassett to take these things and also some books with them. CAA., N.D., Mother St. Monica Ramos to Thomas Hassett, May 26, 1803; Thomas Hassett to Mother St. Monica Ramos, May 26, 1803; ACU., H.C., Act signed by Mother St. Xavier Farjon, Felicité Alzas, and Marie

Olivier, May 25, 1803.

43. AUC., N.O., *Relation de ce qui se passa dans notre Communauté à l'Epoque de la Rétrocession.*

44. "*Je n'ai pas besoin de vous expliquer ce que vous savez comme moi, que toute propriété publique, soit royale, soit communale, est comprise dans la remise de possession de la Colonie d'entre nos mains, d'après les conventions qui tiennent nos Gouvernments respectifs, nour manquerons l'un et l'autre à notre devoir si nour tolérons qu'il en fut rien soustrait.*" AUC., N.O., Laussat to Salcedo, ll Germinal, an ll. (Copy). Cf. also Salcedo to Mother St. Monica Ramos, April 2, 1803; Thomas Hassett to Mother St. Monica Ramos, April 4, 1803. Same in CAA., N.D.

45. CAA., N.D., Thomas Hassett to Salcedo, April 4, 1803.

46. AUC., N.O., *Délibérations du Conseil, Ibid.,* 86.

47. The Spanish government paid the passage of these four seculars also. AGI., S.D., 2599:372-384, No. 212 with enclosures; 387-390, No. 213 with enclosures; AGI., P.C., 593, Letter 212: AGI., P.C., 1572:908-912, Packet C. Letter 4.

48. AUC., N.O., *Noms de toutes les Religieuses professes et Novices de Notre Monastère.*

49. AGI., S.D., 2599:387; AGI., P.C., 593, Letter 212, enclosure No. 2.

50. ACU., H.C., Act signed by Juan Gonzales at New Orleans, May 27, 1803, in the presence of Fernando Mancevo and Eusevio Regueira.

51. ACU., H.C., *El Libro de Fundación,* 1v

52. *Ibid.,*; ABI., S.D., 2599:220, No. 342; Villaumbrosia, *Historia Cronológica y General,* IV, 279.

53. AGI., P.C., 593, Letter 212; AGI., S.D., 2599:220-221, No. 342.

54. AGI., S.D., 2599:220-221, No. 342; 2599:223-225.

55. AGI., S.D., 2599: 223-225.

56. AGI., S.D., 2599:227. The sixteen religious continued to receive this pension during their lifetime. Sister Marie de Ste. Ursule, being the last to die, received this pension until 1851. Cf. Villaumbrosia, *Historia Cronológica y General,* IV, 279-280.

57. ACU., H.C., *El Libro de Defunciónes,* 2; Villaumbrosia, *Historia Cronológica y General,* IV, 279-281.

58. Villaumbrosia, *Historia Cronológica y General,* Iv, 281-284.

59. *Ibid.*, AUC., N.O., *El Libro de Defunciónes*, 5.

60. ACU., H.C., *El Libro de Fundacion*, 2v-3.

61. ACU., H.C., *Decreto del Iltmo Sr. Don Juan José Diaz de Espada y Landa*, November 10, 1815 (Copy).

62. One of the first four postulants died in 1806, and Bishop Espada appointed another one in 1808 as an instructor at the Colegio de San Francisco de Sales. CF. Villaumbrosia, *Historia Cronológica y General*, IV, 281-282.

63. Besides Mother St. Ignace Duliepure already mentioned, Sister St. Louis Vasquez also had died, January 9, 1815. ACU., H.C., *El Libro de Defunciónes*, 5v.

64. Villaumbrosia, *Historia Cronológica y General*, IV, 291.

65. Roger Baudier, *Catholic Church in Louisiana*, 252.

66. CAA., N.D., Salcedo and Casa Calvo to Thomas Hassett, May 26, 1803.

67. CAA., N.D., Thomas Hassett to Salcedo and Casa Calvo, June 4, 1803; Thomas Hassett before Broutin, June 6, 1803; Thomas Hassett to Patricio Mangan et al., June 10, 1803. In the last letter, a circular one, Father Hassett also asked for an inventory of the vases, vestments, sacristy linen, and the amount of funds on hand.

68. CAA., N.D., (1803), No. 157. Document referring to transfer of Louisiana and the Floridas to France and calling for a declaration of intention by Fathers of the territory.

69. *Ibid.*

70. The pension of the six religious was stopped the day the sixteen left for Cuba, and that of the orphans ceased the day the colony was handed over officially to France. Cf. AGI., S.D., 2599, No. 212, enclosure No. 2.

71. Mother St. Thérèse was the first pupil of the boarding school to be admitted to the novitiate. She had spent nine years at the convent and had for one of her teachers Sister St. Stanislaus Hachard. Cf. [Wolfe] *Ursulines in New Orleans*, 42-43. Mother St. Thérèse is sometimes omitted from the list. Perhaps she was already incapacitated for at the time of the death of Mother St. Xavier in 1810 she is referred to as the "old Mother St. Thérèse incapable of doing anything on account of her infirmities." AUC., N.O., Private Archives, III, 116.

72. *Ibid.*, 114-115.

73. *Ibid.*, 123.

74. AC,C13A, 52:150-150v.

Chapter 12

1. Thomas Hassett to Rt. Rev. John Carroll, December 23, 1803. This letter is quoted in full in Shea, *Catholic Church in the U.S.*, II, 582-584.

2. St. L.C.A., Reg. 5, No. 37.

3. *Annales de l'Ordre de Ste. Ursule* (2 vols.: Clermont-Ferrand: Ferdinand Thibaud, 1857), II, 666-667.

4. This letter seems to be no longer extant. Its general contents may be inferred from the letters of Bishop Carroll to James Madison, Jan. 14, 1804 (referred to as of Dec. 14, 1804 in following letter) and James Madison to Bishop Carroll, July 20, 1804, copies in AUC., N.O. Letter quoted in [Wolfe] *Ursulines in New Orleans*, 59.

5. AUC., N.O., J. Carroll to James Madison, January 14, 1804 (Copy).

6. Claiborne always referred to the superior as the abbess although this title has never been used in the Ursuline Order.

7. Dunbar Rowland (ed.), *Official Letter Books of W.C.C. Claiborne, 1801-1816* (7 vols.; Jackson, Miss: State Department of Archives and History, 1917), I, 315. Hereinafter cited as *Of. Let. Bks.*

8. AGI., P.C., 155B (L.C., Pt. I, 99-104), Salcedo to Someruelos, September 12, 1803; same in AGI., P.C., 1572 (L.C., Packet C, No. 18, 1133-1138).

9. *Of. Let. Bks.*, I, 315, Claiborne to Madison, December 27, 1803.

10. There are two letters addressed by the Ursulines to Thomas Jefferson that treat identical matter, but differ slightly in wording. One in NAUS., S.D., Misc. Letters: ALS, dated April 23, 1804 and endorsed as received June 8, 1804 is printed in Clarence Edwin Carter (Comp. and ed.), *The Territorial Papers of the United States*, Vol. IX, *The Territory of Orleans, 1803-1812* (Washington: U.S. Government Printing Office,

1940), 231-232. The other in L.C., Papers of Thomas Jefferson, 141:2447-2448, is dated June 13, 1804. The unsigned copy in AUC., N.O., printed in [Wolfe] *Ursulines in New Orleans*, 60-61 dated March 21, 1804, is undoubtedly a first draft. Jefferson's reply was most probably to that of April 23, Cf. note 15 *infra.*

11. The allusion here is not only to the orphan girls who were quickly drawn into a life of immorality when left unprotected, but also the hundreds of colored women and girls who had been taught by the pioneer Ursulines. This work was still being carried on, particularly by Mother Marie Olivier de Vezin, who devoted herself to this task for forty years.

12. *Of. Let. Bks.,* II, 85-89. Address delivered in his honor at the convent and Claiborne's reply.

13. *Ibid.,* II, 90, Claiborne to Madison, April 10, 1804.

14. AUC., N.O., Thomas Jefferson to Sr. Thérèse de St. Xavier Farjon, May 15, 1804. A facsimile of this letter appears opposite page 60 in [Wolfe] *Ursulines in New Orleans,.* The date, apparently added by a different hand, is very probably erroneous. On a polygraph copy in L.C., Papers of Thomas Jefferson, 142:24602 there is a contemporary notation "date omitted. It was 1804, July 13 or 14". Apparently Jefferson's letter was in reply to that of the Ursulines of April 23, received June 8. The notation regarding the date may have been added by Jefferson when he received the second and practically identical letter from the Ursulines on July 26. Cf. *Ibid.,* 141:24464, covering letter of Claiborne to Jefferson, June 15, 1804.

15. *Le Moniteur de la Louisiane,* Sept. 13, 1804. This only complicates the matter of the dates. The letter of the Ursulines to Jefferson is given as of June, 1804, while the reply is dated May 15, 1804.

16. For the dispute over jurisdiction Cf.. HTMO., Documents in Spanish and French Relating to Padre Antonio de Sedella and His Ecclesiastical Differences with Vicar-General Patrick Walsh of the St. Louis Cathedral in New Orleans, 1778-1807; Roger Baudier, *Catholic Church in Louisiana,* 250, *passim.*

17. Roger Baudier, *Catholic Church in Louisiana,* 256, citing Archives of the City of New Orleans, March 13, 1805.

18. *Ibid.,* 257, citing St. L.C.A.

19. AUC., N.O., *Lettre Pastorale,* March 27, 1805. Signed, Patrick

Walsh, Vicaire-Général.

20. *Ibid.*

21. Father Lusson originally sided with Père Antoine and after the death of Father Walsh he refused submission to Father Sibourd. This whole period is treated in some details in Roger Baudier, *Catholic Church in Louisiana*, 250-305; Shea, *Catholic Church in the U.S.*, II, 582-597.

22. *Of. Let. Bks.*, 84-86, Claiborne to James Pitot, June 8, 1805; Claiborne to the Lady Abbess of the Ursuline Nuns, June 8, 1805.

23. *Ibid.*

24. There was a similar performance presented about a year later and Claiborne again intervened in their behalf. Cf. *Of. Let. Bks.*, III, 344-45, W.C.C. Claiborne to the Lady Abbess of the Ursuline Convent, June 24, 1806; same to the Mayor of New Orleans, June 24, 1806.

25. HTML., Documents in Spanish and French Relating to Padre Antonio de Sedella. . . 1778-1807, 34.

26. *Ibid.*, 22.

27. Shea, *Catholic Church in the U.S.*, 590, citing Louis Kerr to Bishop Carroll, August 29, 1806.

28. On September 21, 1805, Propaganda wrote to Father Walsh telling him that his powers of vicar-general had ceased and that faculties for the governance of Louisiana had been conferred upon Bishop Carroll, to whom he would henceforth be subject. Father Walsh probably received this letter before his death. Cf. Peter Guilday, *The Life and Times of John Carroll* (2 vols.; New York: The Encyclopedia Press, 1922), II, 706.

29. HTML., Documents in Spanish and French Relating to Padre Antonio de Sedella . . .1778-1807, 8-9.

30. *Moniteur de la Louisiane*, February 28, 1807.

31. Cf. Guilday, *Life and Times of John Carroll*, II, 71032. Shea, *Catholic Church in the U.S.*, II, 641; Roger Baudier, *Catholic Church in Louisiana*, 263.

33. In 1808 Bishop Carroll became Archbishop, with suffragan sees at New York, Philadelphia, Boston, and Bardstown.

34. The letter of appointment will be found in *CHR.*, IV (April, 1924), 56.

35. Shea, *Catholic Church in the U.S.*, II, 671; Roger Baudier, *Catholic Church in Louisiana*, 265; Cf. BCA, Item 3E10.

36. AUC., N.O., *Actes de Prise d'Habit,* 89.

37. *Ibid.*

38. AUC., N.O., Certified copy of the original in AAB.

39. AUC., N.O., Certified copy of letter of Sister Thérèse de St. Xavier et al. to the Archbishop of Bordeaux, May 21, 1804. The original in AAB is countersigned by Father Patricio Walsh.

40. AUC., N.O., *Noms de toutes les Religieuses.*

41. *Ibid.*

42. *Ibid.*

43. AUC., N.O., *Lettres Circulaires,* 244-246.

44. AUC., N.O., Sister St. Michel to Pope Pius VII, December 15, 1808 (Copy).

45. *Ibid.*

46. [Wolfe] *Ursulines in New Orleans,* 68.

47. Sister St. Xavier Farjon To Governor Claiborne, October 30, 1808, in Carter *Territorial Papers of the U.S.,* IX, 804-805.

48. *Ibid.*

49. *Of. Let. Bks.,* IV, 245-246, Wm. C. C. Claiborne to James Madison, November 8, 1808.

50. AUC., N.O., Michele, Cardinal di Pietro to Mother St. Michel Gensoul, April 28, 1809. Translation of this letter in [Wolfe] *Ursulines in New Orleans,* 68-71.

51. Bishop John Cheverus writing to the Bishop of Quebec from Boston, June 16, 1810, says that they arrived at Philadelphia on June 8 and that there were twelve of them. Cf. AAQ., E.R., II, 15. The number twelve is certainly not correct.

52. [Wolfe] *Ursulines in New Orleans,* 71-72.

53. AUC., N.O., Private Archives, III, 130.

54. AUC., N.O., *Noms de toutes les Religieuses.* Olive Piet after her departure caused the community a great deal of trouble. She brought suit for remuneration for the time she had spent in the novitiate, although the community had paid all the expenses of her voyage from France and had provided for all her needs. She lost her case. AUC., N.O., Private Archives, III, 134.

Chapter 13

1. AUC., N.O., *Changement de la Règle de Paris*. This gives a full account of the episode. After the departure of the nuns for Havana in 1803, the few remaining choir religious found it particularly difficult to say the Divine Office as often as the Rule of Paris required. According to the Rule of Presentation of Our Lady, the religious were obliged to say the Divine Office only a few times a year.

2. AUC., N.O., Sr. Ste. Marie Olivier et al. to Abbé DuBourg, n.d. (copy).

3. *Ibid.*

4. AUC., N.O., Wm. DuBourg, January 16, 1813.

5. *Of. Let. Bks.*, V, 201, W.C.C. Claiborne to the Lady Abbess of the Ursuline Convent, April 4, 1811.

6. *Ibid.*, 203-204, W.C.C. Claiborne to the Honorable Mr. Gallatin, April 4, 18ll.

7. *Ibid.*, 260, W.C.C. Claiborne to the Lady Abbess of the Ursuline Convent, June 3, 18ll.

8. *Ibid.*, VI, l, W.C.C. Claiborne to Henry Clay, December 11, 1811.

9. Petition to Congress by Physicians and Surgeons of New Orleans (House of Representatives Files: 12 Cong., 3 sess., document signed Nov. 19, 1811) in Clarence Edwin Carter, *Territorial Papers of the U.S.*, Vol. IX, 955-956.

10. *Of. Let. Bks.*, VI 59, W.C.C. Claiborne to the Lady Abbess of the Ursuline Convent, February 19, 1812; *Debates and Proceedings in the Congress of the U.S.*, (Washington: Gales and Seaton, 1853), 12 Cong., 1 sess., (Feb. 26, 1812), 1105.

11. AUC., N.O., J. Dawson to the Ursuline Religious, April 20, 1812; *Debates and Proceedings*, 12 Cong., 1 sess., (Feb. 26, 1812), 1105.

12. Act approved April 23, 1812, 5 Stat., 107; *Debates and Proceedings* 12 Cong., 1 sess., 2272-2273.

13. Shea, *Catholic Church in the U.S.*, 671; Roger Baudier, *Catholic Church in Louisiana*, 266.

14. The statue, which was brought to America by Mother St.

Michel and which was usually kept in the choir of the religious, was placed above the main altar. [Wolfe] *Ursulines in New Orleans*, 74.

15. Originally this Mass was sung on some Sunday in January, but in 1851 Pius IX granted the privilege of having it on January 8.

16. The boarders and the orphans had been sent away December 13,1814, (AUC., N.O.., Private Archives, III, 140), the day that the British appeared at Villere's plantation a few miles below New Orleans.

17. *Ibid.*, 138-140. In view of the services rendered to the American forces at this time the Louisiana State Legislature passed an act, January 28, 1818, exempting the Ursulines of New Orleans from appearing in court thereafter. When their testimony would be essential for any case it would be taken at the Convent of the Ursulines. Cf. *Ibid.*, 142-153; Moreau l'Islet to Mother St. Michel Gensoul, January 27, 1818.

18. [Wolfe] *Ursulines in New Orleans*, 75. Sister Ste. Angèle Johnston, a native of Baltimore and a convert, was highly esteemed by Archbishop Carroll, who had received her into the Church. When she was leaving for New Orleans, her father said to Bishop DuBourg, "Monseigneur, I place my daughter in your hands. Take good care of her, and remember that I shall demand an account of you before the judgment seat of God." AUC., N.O., Biographical Sketches of a Number of Our Mothers.

19. AUC., N.O., Biographical Sketches of a Number of Our Mothers.

20. John Spencer Bassett (ed.) *Correspondence of Andrew Jackson* (7 vols.; Washington: Carnegie Institute of Washington, 1926-1935), II, 150.

21. AUC., N.O., *Notes sur la visite du Général Jackson au Couvent des Ursuline*. When Jackson returned to New Orleans in 1828 to assist at the celebration of the 13th anniversary of the Battle of New Orleans, he came to the convent accompanied by some officers and several of the most distinguished ladies and gentlemen of the city. All entered into the cloister with him saying, "General, we follow you everywhere." *Ibid.*

22. Father Olivier died August 9, 1817.

23. AUC., N.O., Sr. Ste. Marie Olivier and Sr. St. Michel Gensoul to Pius VII, May 2, 1815 (Copy).

24. AUC., N.O., Pope Pius VII to Sister Ste. Marie Olivier, October 16, 1815. Translation in [Wolfe] *Ursulines in New Orleans*, 81-82.

25. Roger Baudier, *Catholic Church in Louisiana,* 268.

26. AUC., N.O., *Lettres Circulaires.*

27. In 1831, Sister Marthe went to France to procure volunteers to help in the school of St. Claude. As the school was on the verge of closing, Bishop De Neckère asked the Ursulines to send some sisters to teach there. From 1831 to 1838 eight different Ursulines worked there for varying period of time. They were withdrawn only because the number of boarders at the convent had become so large that more teachers were imperative. At first the Ursulines thought of securing Religious of St. Joseph to continue the work; but Mother St. Thérèse and a companion of the Third Order of Mount Carmel had been at Bayou Lafourche since their arrival in 1834. Bishop Blanc asked them to take over the school of St. Claude and they accepted. Cf. AUC., N.O., *Une page de l'histoire de Mont-Carmel et des Ursulines en Louisiane; Notes au sujet du commencement de la maison appelée aujourd'hui Mont-Carmel.*

28. During a long period she filled two offices at the same time.

29. AUC., N.O., *Lettres Circulaires,* 307; [Wolfe] *Ursulines in New Orleans,* 92-97.

30. Shea, *Catholic Church in the U.S., III.,* 359.

31. AASL., Bishop DuBourg to Cardinal Dugnani, Lyons, April 6, 1816 (copy); Same to same, Bordeaux, June 24, 1816, SLCHR., I (January, 1919), 142-144; Shea, *Catholic Church in the U.S.,* III, 362-363.

32. *Ibid.*

33. *Annales de l'Association de la Propagation de la Foi* (Lyons, 1826), II, 336-339. Translation in RACHS., XIV (1903), 142-143: 203-204.

34. Roger Baudier, *Catholic Church in Louisiana,* 273.

35. Louise Callan, *The Society of the Sacred Heart in North America* (New York: Longmans, Green and Co., 1937), 43-44.

36. Marjory Erskine, *Mother Philippine Duchesne* (New York: Longmans, Green and Co., 1926), 135-136.

37. *Ibid.,* 135.

38. Mother Duchesne to Mother Thérèse, June 3, 1818. Quoted in Erskine, *Ibid.,* 135-136.

39. *Ibid.,* 139-141.

40. *Ibid.,* 142. Mother Duchesne had written that if they could

send a sister from France to help in the garden she should have leather stockings and gloves to keep off the mosquitoes.

41. *Ibid.,* 142-143.

42. *Ibid.,* 143-146.

43. *Ibid.,* 146.

44. *Ibid.,* 153.

45. *Ibid.,* April 29, 1819.

46. Perhaps she would have been more surprised had she known that at least one of the foundresses had a sincere devotion to Jesus under the title of the Sacred Heart. When the *Gironde* encountered a storm and the ship seemed about to founder, Mother St. François Xavier Mahieu prayed to the Sacred Heart. She promised to have three Masses of thanksgiving celebrated on the altar of the Sacred Heart in the convent at le Havre if they were delivered from danger. "No sooner was the promise made than it seemed Jesus Christ commanded the seas and the winds, for they became calm and tranquil." Cf. AUC., N.O., *Extraits des annales de la communauté du Havre de Grace.*

47. Quoted in [Wolfe] *Ursulines in New Orleans,* 83. The painting alluded to commemorates an extraordinary dream or vision vouchsafed to Mother St. Michel Gensoul, who beheld the Sacred Heart of Jesus inflamed with love for mankind and adored by angels. Overhead appeared the Eternal Father under the form of a venerable old man. Before the removal to the present convent this picture hung above the archbishop's throne in the convent chapel. Today it has a place of honor on the stair leading to the Ursuline Museum, New Orleans.

48. Erskine, *Mother Philippine Duchesne,* 152.

49. AMUQ., *Annales de ce monastère de Ste. Ursule de Québec,* II, 12: *Annales de l'Association de la Propagation de la foi,* I, 74. The Ursulines bought this property in 1818 as the site for a new convent.

Chapter 14

1. AUC., N.O., Sr. Ste. Marie Olivier and Sr. St. Michel Gensoul to Archbishop Carroll, October 16, 1815 (copy); Private Archives, III,

142.

2. NAUS., W.D., Letters Received J-257 (8), Sr. Ste Marie Olivier to Andrew Jackson, April 4, 1815.

3. AUC., N.O., A.J. Dallas to Maj. Gen. Gaines et al., June 19, 1815 (copy). The report of these proceedings could not be found in the files of the War Office at that time. *Ibid.*

4. AUC., N.O., Gallien Préval to Madame la Supérieure, June 7, 1815.

5. AUC., N.O., A.J. Dallas to Mother St. Marie Olivier, June 17, 1815.

6. Maj. Gen. Gaines or other Commanding Officer at New Orleans, P.B. Duplessis, collector of the Port of New Orleans, and Benjamin Morgan, respectable wholesale merchant. Cf. *Ibid.* and A.J. Dallas to Maj. Gen. Gaines et al., June 19, 1815.

7. Messieurs Livaudais, Colonel Foucher, and J. Bonneval, engineer. AUC., N.O., Sr. St. Michel Gensoul to James Madison, May 23, 1816 (copy).

8. *Ibid.*

9. NAUS., W.D., Letters Received J-257 (8), Sr. Ste. Marie Olivier to General Jackson, April 4, 1815.

10. AUC., N.O., Sr. St. Michel Gensoul to James Madison, May 23, 1816 (copy).

11. AUC., N.O., Sr. Ste. Marie Olivier and Sr. St. Michel Gensoul to Archbishop Carroll, October 16, 1815 (copy).

12. AUC., N.O., A. Maréchal to Abbé Sibourd, January 12, 1816. At that time, Father Maréchal was president of St. Mary's College, Baltimore. He was consecrated Archbishop of Baltimore in November, 1817.

13. In the meantime, Dallas had become Sec. of Treasury and Wm. H. Crawford, Sec. of War. The letter was forwarded to Sec. Crawford.

14. AUC., N.O., Carlos Trudeau to Madame de St. Xavier Farjon, July ll, 1800. He says also that there were no papers in his office relative to transactions before the fire of 1788. "These papers were entirely lost by this unfortunate accident."

15. AGI., S.D., 2645 (87-2-26), 418. On November 14, 1805, the members of the House of Representatives of the Territory of Orleans in a petition to the U.S. Congress said "that in consequence of repeated casualties by fire, and owing to the loss of papers and records consequent

upon the frequent political changes to which this country has been subjected, the title papers of numerous claims have been lost or entirely destroyed . . . That the claimants who have suffered most in the loss of papers are generally those who have remained long in peaceable possession, and who will be able to prove an acknowledged right not disputed for a succession of years. Cf. Clarence Edwin Carter, *Territorial Papers of the U.S.*, IX, 529-530.

16. See pp. 257-260, *supra.*

17. AGI., S.D., 2645 (87-2-26): 405, Sister Thérèse de St. Xavier Farjon to Charles IV, April 27, 1800.

18. AUC., N.O., Sor. Margarita de Sn. Ignacio Duliepure to Dr. Dn. Theodoro Henriquez, March 25, 1793; Dr. Henriquez before Quiñones, March 26, 1793; Sor Margarita de Sn. Ignacio Duliepure to Baron de Carondelet, March 26, 1793 (copy).

19. All this evidence has been assembled in a document of 165 pages, AUC., N.O., *Cahier renfermant toutes les pièces relatives aux réclamations du fiscal pour le domaine royal du roi d'Espagne.*

20. *Debates and Proceedings in the Congress of the United States,* 15 Cong., 1 sess., 2588.

21. AUC., N.O., H.M. Brackenridge to _____, April 25, 1820.

22. The Ursulines originally claimed all four squares bounded by Royal, Barracks, Levee, and Ursulines. Only the two squares facing Ursulines Street were indicated as "destined for the Religious" on Broutin's map of New Orleans, May 15, 1728, LSML.

23. AUC., N.O., H.M. Brackenridge to President Monroe, March 7, 1820 (copy).

24. AUC., N.O., H.M. Brackenridge to _____, April 25, 1820.

25. *Ibid.*

26. January 3 to July 9, 1821.

27. AUC., N.O., P.F. DuBourg to Madame de St. Joseph Laclotte, September 17, 1823.

28. AUC., N.O., Unsigned copy of a letter addressed to President Monroe, February 19, 1821.

29. Bishop DuBourg to the Cardinal Prefect of Propaganda, March 29, 1823, *SLCHR.*, III, (January - April, 1921), 131.

30. AUC., N.O., Private Archives, III, 209-210.

31. AUC., N.O., Notarial Act relative to lots 7, 8, 9, corner

Hospital and Decatur. The U.S. patents were registered at the Conveyance Office, New Orleans, by Edgar Grima, January 13, 1914, I, 7-11. The original patents are annexed to the act of registration.

32. AUC., N.O., Private Archives, III, 210.

33. As early as 1815 the city officials had tried to oblige the Ursulines to cede the ground needed for the opening of Conde. Cf. AUC., N.O., Sr. Ste. Marie Olivier to Archbishop Carroll, October 16, 1815 (copy).

34. ACNO., Concile de Ville, III, bk. 2, 51.

35. ACNO., N.O., Aug. Macarty to Madame la Supérieure, May 18, 1819.

36. ACNO., Concile de Ville, III, bk. 2, 70-71.

37. AUC., N.O., Note appended to Macarty to Madame la Supérieure, May 18, 1819.

38. ACNO., Concile de Ville, III, bk. 3, 34-35.

39. *Ibid.*

40. *Ibid..*, 137-138.

41. *Ibid.*, 142.

42. The convent records say only: "In 1821 they opened the streets through our garden." Cf. Private Archives, III, 217.

43. Bishop DuBourg to the Card. Prefect of Propaganda, March 29, 1823, *SLCHR.*, III (Jan. - April), 132.

44. AUC., N.O., Wm. H. Crawford to Rev. Louis W. DuBourg, November 22, 1822.

45. AUC., N.O., Copy of Wm. Wirt to James Monroe, April 11, 1820, enclosed in Wm. H. Crawford to Rev. Louis W. DuBourg, November 22, 1822.

46. AUC., N.O., *Pièce concernant l'hôpital,* September 24, 1822.

47. AUC., N.O., Ibid.; P.F. DuBourg to Madame de St. Joseph Laclotte, September 17, 1823; same to Mc Lanahan and Harper, September 25, 1823; J.J. Mc Lanahan to P.F. DuBourg, January 28, 1824.

48. NANA., G.R. Stringer, February 17, 1824. Certified copy in AUC., N.O.

49. These lots are numbered 13 to 18 on a plan made by Thomas Freeman and Gabriel Winter, Surveyor and Deputy Surveyor of the U.S., dated May 15, 1819. A copy by Joseph Pilié is annexed to above act and another by the same is in AUC., N.O.

50. Lots 1 - 6 on above plan.

51. AUC., N.O., H.M. Brackenridge to President Monroe, March 7, 1820 (copy).

Chapter 15

1. AUC., N.O., *Actes de prise d'habit.*

2. This number does not include Sister Ste. Marthe, Hospitalière, who lived and worked with the Ursulines from 1817 to 1823. She then left to work at a school for Negro girls on St. Claude Street.

3. In *Actes de prise d'habit*, 109 (AUC., N.O.), the date of writing is given as 1820. This seems to be an error as all other sources give 1821.

4. Mother St. Michel sent the letter, or letters by a Mr. Roland who was returning to Trois-Rivières from New Orleans. It is not clear whether a duplicate letter for Quebec was included in that to the religious of Trois-Rivières, or whether the superior of Trois-Rivières forwarded the letter she had received to Quebec. In the Archives of the Ursuline Monastery of Quebec there is a letter in Mother St. Michel's handwriting to "*Mes très Révérendes Mères,*" dated June 8, 1821. The same letter is quoted in full in *Les Ursulines des Trois-Rivières* (3 vols.; Trois-Rivières: P.V. Ayotte, 1892), II, 172-175, and is addressed to "Ma Révérand Mère". In the *Annales de ce Monastère de Ste. Ursule de Québec*, II, 1, it says: "*La mère St. Pierre, Supérieure des Ursulines des Trois-Rivières, avant reçu une lettre de la Mère St. Michel, Supérieure des Ursulines de la Nouvelle Orléans, demandant des sujets pour sa communauté, la lettre fut envoyée à notre Rev. Mère ainsi qu'une circulaire du 8 mai 1815, adressée pour les mêmes fins aux Ursulines de France.*"

5. *Ibid.*

6. To do so they were obliged to borrow $1200 from the bank at nine per cent. Cf. AUC., N.O., Private Archives, III, 213-214.

7. Half of them were already dead or had withdrawn before making profession.

8. AAQ., E.U., I, 104, L. Guil., Ev. De la Louisiane. *A Mgr.*

Plessis, archeveque de Québec, 17 juillet 1821. Contemporary copy in AMUQ. Translation in *RACHS*, XIX (1908), 190-191. This letter bears the date July 17 at the beginning and July 27 at the end.

9. AMUQ., *Annales de ce Monastère*, II, 2.

10. AAQ., Reg. 10:265, J [oseph] O [ctave] Ev., de Québec, to Rev. Mother St. Pierre . September 25, 1821.

11. AAQ., E.U., I, 105. L. Guil. Ev. de la Louisiane, to Monseigneur Plessis, February 4, 1822; AMUQ., contemporary copy. Translation of letter in *RACHS.*, XIX (1908), 193.

12. All three left before making profession. Little is known of them except the brief notes in AMUQ., *Annales de ce Monastère*, II, 4-5: "They are educated women, formed to virtue and the interior life by Father Richard, for many years a missionary at Detroit. He had intended to found a teaching congregation. Miss Lyons is English . . . These young ladies have taught at Detroit for fifteen years." Cf. also *Les Ursulines de Québec*, IV, 521.

13. AAQ., E.U., I, 106, L. Wm. Ev. de la Nouvelle Orléans to Monseigneur J.O. Plessis, March 19, 1822. Translation in *RACHS.*, XIX (1908), 204-205.

14. *Les Ursulines de Québec IV, 527.*

15. AMUQ., *Annales de ce Monastère*, II 4. However, in a letter to Bishop Plessis, dated at Detroit, April 20, Father Janvier said that he would leave Detroit by boat about May 10 and be in Montreal ten or fifteen days later. CF. AAQ, E.U., I, 108.

16. AAQ., E.U., I, 110, Bishop Dubourg to Monseigneur J.O. Plessis, July 29, 1822. Translation in *RACHS.*, XIX (1908), 204-205.

17. AAQ., Reg. I (1822-1825), *Commission donnée à M. Maguire Pitre de conduire des Religieuses Ursulines à New York, le 3 october 1822.* Father Maguire was made chaplain of the Ursuline Monastery in Quebec in 1832 and became known as "*notre Providence visible aux temps perilleux et le second Fondateur de notre maison.*" His career as administrator and educator was remarkable. CF. *Les Ursulines de Quebéc*, IV, 713-730.

18. AAQ., E.U., I, 115, P. Janvier to Monseigneur Plessis, September 16, 1822.

19. AMUQ., P.F. Janvier to Rev. Mother Superior, September 26, 1822.

20. Her name is sometimes given as Normanville. both forms

appear in the convent records. Cf. AUC., N.O., *Acte de prise d'habit*, 190; *Noms de toutes les religieuses.*

21. AAQ., E.U., I, 114-115. Translation in *RACHS.*, (1908), 205-206. This letter is dated at New York, September 12, 1822. Obviously, this is an error on the part of the writer and should read October 12.

22. AAQ., E.U., I, 113, Louis Willcocks to Rev. P. Janvier, September 11, 1822, writes: "The passage money for the Steamboat is $100 per person, and the accommodations I understand are not very good. The vessel also stops 3 or 4 days at the Havana. There is a line of Packets sailing from this part for New Orleans the 1st and 15th of each month. The next one that sails will be on the 1st Oct., a fine brig, with excellent accommodations and the price of the passage is $75 each person, and you are found in everything except wine and Porter. They furnish bed and bedding and a—& a."

23. AMUQ., *Annales de ce Monastère*, II, 11.

24. AMUQ., Sr. St. Etienne To Mother Superior, November 14, 1822.

25. She was elected superior, February 6, 1822. Although the election should have taken place within the octave of the feast of St. Ursula (October 21), it was postponed until the return of Bishop DuBourg and also in the hope that Mother St. Michel, who was seriously ill might recover. Cf. AUC., N.O., *Resultat des électiones triennales*, Private Archives, IV.

26. AMUQ., P. Janvier to Rev. Mother St. Henri, Donaldsonville, December 13, 1822.

27. AMUQ., E.U., I, 123, Sr. Ste. Hélene et al. to Monseigneur J.O. Plessis, April 3, 1823. Translation in *RACHS.*, XIX (1908), 110-211.

28. AUC., N.O., Private Archives, III, 214-215.

29. AUC., N.O., Private Archives, III. 216-217. The color of the underskirt was important. Since the habits were long enough to touch the floor, the religious ordinarily wore them hooked up in front and back, except in chapel. This permitted a large part of the underskirt to be seen.

30. AUC., N.O., *Actes de prise d'habit*, 109.

31. AAQ., E.U., I, 122, Sr. St. Joseph Laclotte to Archbishop Plessis, March 6, 1823. Translation in *RACHS.*, XIX (1908), 209-210.

32. AUC., N.O., Private Archives, III, 215-216.

33. AMUQ., Sr. St. Charles to Madame St. Joseph, August 17, 1823. Twenty two made their First Communion on the second Sunday after Easter. Sister St. Charles continued to give individual instruction to others until August 1. Cf. *Ibid.*

34. AMUQ., September 14, 1823.

35. Bishop DuBourg gave her the following letter of obedience: "The health of this good religious since her arrival is so affected by the change of climate that not only is she unable to perform her duties, but also according to the opinion of the doctor her life itself would be endangered by a prolonged stay in this country. I have deemed it necessary to advise her to return into her native country, and into her community of Trois-Rivières, certifying to her ecclesiastical and regular superiors that she has always conducted herself as an excellent religious." Quoted in *Les Ursulines des Trois-Rivières*, II, 184-185.

36. AAQ., E.U., I, 123, Sr. Ste. Hélène et al. to Monseigneur J.O. Plessis, April 3, 1823.

Chapter 16

1. AUC., N.O., Chain of Title to Convent Tract. It is noteworthy that this land is part of the plantation granted by the French government to M. de Coustillas by two concessions, one dated January, 1722, and the other February, 1724. In the long list of possessors before 1818 appear such prominent names as Pierre Marigny and Joseph Xavier de Pontalba.

2. NANO., Acts: Narcisse Broutin, N.P., (Nov. 26, 1818), 388, AUC., N.O., Transfer (1821) of property purchased by Mr. Kennedy (1818) to Ursulines, before G.R. Stringer, N.P., Oct. 26, 1827; COB., N.O., 2:7, Oct. 3, 1827. Kennedy gave three promissory notes: one for the sum of $10,000 payable four months after date; one for $11,880 payable one year after date; and one for $12,760 payable two years after date. As each note came due Mr. Kennedy received the money needed to pay it from the Ursulines. Cf. *Ibid.*

3. [Wolfe] *Ursulines in New Orleans*, 87.

4. Shea, *Catholic Church in the U.S.*, III, 370-371.

5. AUC., N.O., *Remise des intérêts et affairs de la communauté entre les mains de Msgr. DuBourg,* April 2, 1822.

6. Bishop DuBourg to the Card. Prefect of Propaganda, March 29, 1823, *SLCHR.,* III (January - April, 1921), 131.

7. Translation of this contract in *LHQ.,* XXIX (July, 1946), 651-659.

8. An undated and unsigned plan preserved in AUC., N.O. is undoubtedly that of this structure.

9. Originally they had expected to have only twenty-four. Cf. AUC., N.O., *Remise des intérêts . . .entre les mains de Mgr. DuBourg,* April 2, 1822.

10. "The foundations shall have one foot of depth, established at thirty inches thick . . . reduced to twenty-six inches at the level of the ground." The masonry was laid on cypress planks three inches thick.

11. This responsibility did not "extend to damage of any nature which shall be caused by acts of God."

12. July 30, 1825, Messrs. Gurlie and Guillot credited the Ursulines with $621.50 for the rent of these two slaves. The record does not indicate how long they worked. Cf. AUC., N.O., *Compte de MM. Gurlie et Guillot. Solde le 30 juillet 1825—Suivant quittance faite pardevant m. Lafitte Notaire le dit jour.*

13. AUC., N.O., *Contrat de M. Bradley avec les Dames Religieuses, 25 février 1822.* Quoted in full in *LHQ.,* XXIX (July, 1946), 649-651.

14. We conclude this from the fact that the nuns were to pay one half the cost of each kiln of bricks as soon as it was delivered. The first two kilns amounted to 140,792 bricks. The second payment was made May 14, 1823. Cf. AUC., N.O., Memorandum on back of Contract of Mr. Bradley.

15. They paid Bradley a total of $681.47 (sic) for 22,592 bricks. Cf. *Ibid.*

16. AUC., N.O., *Remise des intérêts . . . entre les mains de Msgr. DuBourg,* April 2, 1822.

17. AUC., N.O., *Devise d'une bâtisse en brique que nous obligeons de construire pour les dames Religieuses sur leur habitation formant l'aile Gauche de la Bâtisse, 12 september 1823.* This wing was 104 feet 4 inches long by 20 feet 8 inches wide, with a gallery 8 1/2 feet wide on three

sides.

18. AUC., N.O., *Compte de MM. Gurlie et Guillot. Solde le 30 juillet 1825.*

19. AMUQ., Sr. St. Joseph Laclotte to Mother St. Henri, May 20, 1824.

20. AUC., N.O., Private Archives, III, 217-220. This is an account of the transfer by one of the participants.

21. *Ibid.,* 218-219.

22. *Ibid.,* [Wolfe] *Ursulines in New Orleans,* 88, Very probably this was the chapel used by Father Martial while he had his school for boys on the Ursulines' plantation.

23. Roger Baudier, *Catholic Church in Louisiana,* 373.

24. AUC., N.O., Private Archives III, 220; *Compte de MM. Gurlie and Guillot. Solde le 30 juillet 1825.* The ceiling was made of cypress boards at a cost of $1800.

25. *Ibid.*

26. Samuel Wilson, Jr., "An Architectural History", 634.

27. AUC., N.O., *Compte de MM. Gurlie et Guillot. Solde le 30 juillet 1825.*

28. Since there is no record of the number of men employed, nor of the actual time during which Mr. Bradley and his men worked, there is no way of estimating the cost of the food and the lodging provided for them.

29. AUC., N.O., *Compte de MM. Gurlie et Guillot. Solde le 30 juillet 1825.*

30. This plantation was on the right bank of the river and about three miles above New Orleans. One part of this plantation, 16 *arpents* frontage on the river by 40 *arpents* of depth was purchased from Jacques Larchevêque in 1736; a second depth of 40 *arpents* was granted by Governor Miro in 1789; a contiguous strip of land of 4 2/3 *arpents* frontage was purchased from Robin de Logny in 1810. Cf. AUC., N.O., *Délibérations du Conseil,* I, 66; SLO., B.R., *Jacques Larchevêque aux Dames Religieuses Ursulines de la Nlle. Orléans, au 8 fèvrier 1736;* Concession by Miró, Dec. 2, 1789 (Translation).

31. SLO., B.R., *Vente d'Habitation par les Dames Religieuses á M. Pierre St. Pé.* Forty-two slaves were sold with the plantation; 27 males between the ages of 12 and 60, of whom 21 were less than 35 years

old; 10 females between the ages of 18 and 39; and 5 children varying in age from 6 months to 7 years.

32. AUC., N.O., *Vendu à l'encan par F. Dutillet, le 1 mars 1824.* The auctioneer received a commission of two per cent. Four lots fronting on Ursulines and Chartres were sold, January 4, 1825. CF. NANO., Acts: Marc Lafitte, No. 20 (January - June, 1825), 1.

33. AUC., N.O., *L'Acte de donation de l'archevéché.* This act was probably drawn up in the latter part of 1822 or early part of 1823 as Bishop DuBourg says in a letter dated March 29, 1823 that the nuns received word that he had succeeded in persuading the authorities at Washington to recognize their claim to the property on Chartres Street that the Ursulines in gratitude "spontaneously made donation to me and my successors in the See of New Orleans, of the buildings which they now occupy." *SLCHR.,* III (January -April, 1921), 131. The act was "ratified and confirmed" and signed April 1, 1826, by the twelve choir religious who had made their perpetual vows. Bishop DuBourg "by special commission of Our Holy Father the Pope" accepted the donation for himself and his successors. It was only in 1920 that the Ursulines surrendered the titles to this property to the Roman Catholic Church of the Diocese of New Orleans. CF. AUC., N.O., Edgar Grima to Rev. Mother Superior, April 4, 1920; COB., N.O., 318: 588.

34. In 1822 more than three hundred Negresses attended the instructions given by the Ursulines. Cf. *Annales . . . de la propagation de la foi,* I, 29.

35. *Ibid.,* III, 542. Cf also Bishop DuBourg to Father P. Borgna, C.M., Feb. 27, 1823, *SLCHR.,* III, (January - April, 1921), 124.

36. *Annales . . . de la propagation de la foi,* I, 46-47; *RACHS.,* XIV (1903), 158.

37. Bishop DuBourg to Abbé Lespinasse (n.d.) in *Annales . . . de la propagation de la foi,* II, 407: *RACHS.,* XIV (1903), 165.

38. Rev. Joseph Rosati to Abbé Perreau, June 7, 1827 in *Annales,* II, 411: *RACHS.,* XIV (1903), 199. Although the bishopric of New Orleans was established by the Spanish government, it had never been endowed. In a letter to Father Borgna,C.M. February 17, 1823, Bishop DuBourg wrote: ". . . you know that the Bishop has absolutely nothing, save what our good Ursuline Nuns are pleased to give him—a most precarious pittance, utterly insufficient for his pressing needs and his

manifold burdens." *SLCHR.*, III (January -April, 1921), 126.

39. AUC., N.O., *Compte de MM. Gurlie et Guillot. Sold le 30 juillet 1825.*

40. *Annales,* III, 542-543. The repairs amounted to 15,000 francs and the furniture for the college cost another 15,000 francs. Cf. *Ibid.,* II, 411-412; *RACHS,*, XIV (1903), 199.

41. Father Portier paid annual rent of 6000 francs. Cf. *Annales,* II, 411; *RACHS.*, XIV (1903) , 199, 200. Father Portier was the first Bishop of Mobile. He was consecrated Nov. 5, 1826. After more than 32 years of service, he died May 14, 1859.

42. In July, 1826, the school had over 200 students. For several months the house remained idle; then Bishop Rosati rented it to the public school authorities for 6000 francs a year. Cf. *Annales,* II, 412, 416; *RACHS.*, XIV (1903), 199-202; Roger Baudier, *Catholic Church in Louisiana,* 294, 306, 312.

43. The Bishop had neither robbed the Ursulines of their property nor prevailed upon them to give it to him. He had intended to ask them to give it to him when they moved to their new convent, but "they anticipated this petition. I have just received the Act of donation signed by every one of the nuns having the right to vote." Bishop DuBourg to Father P. Borgna, February 27, 1823, *SLCHR.*, III (January - April, 1921) 121.

44. AUC., N.O., *Rapport rendu du couvent des Ursulines de la Nouvelle-Orléans, avant la translation,* 1824, in Private Archives, IV, 167.

45. ACNO., March 30, 1825.

46. AUC., N.O., Private Archives, III, 220-221.

47. AUC., N.O., *Concile de Ville,* III, 357-359.

48. *Ibid.,* 360-362.

49. *Ibid.,* 357-361.

50. This orphanage was under the direction of the Sisters of Charity from 1830 to 1836. In 1836 the founder of the asylum, Julian Poydras died, and the institution passed completely into the hands of the Presbyterians.

51. AMUQ., Sr. St. Louis de Gonzague to Mother St. Henri, February, 1825.

52. AUC., N.O., *Rapport rendu du couvent* . . . 1824 in Private Archives, IV, 166.

53. AUC., N.O., Private Archives, III, 221. In April 1827, there were 68 boarders and 10 half-boarders. By the beginning of January, 1828, the number of boarders had increased to 80. CF. AMUQ., Mother St. Charles to Mother St. Joseph, April 30, 1827; Sister St. Etienne to Abbé S.J. DesJardins, January 8, 1828.

54. The plate used for engraving the card inserted in the books awarded as premiums to the students bore the following inscription: "*Prix de Bonne Conduite: Esprit de Piété, Lecture, Récitation, Ecriture, Calcul, Grammaire, Exercices, Géographie, Propreté, Application à tous les devoirs.*" This plate, preserved in AUC., N.O., was in use before 1824.

55. There is no record of the rates charted in 1824, but in AUC., N.O., there is a bill for a certain Mlle Celin Alvarez, dated March 17, 1832.

Pour neuf mois de pension alimentaire commencé le 10 mai échu l2 10 février	$144.00
Pour le blanchissage	24.00
Le maître de Piano	69.87
Le maître de Dessin	6.50
L'accord du Piano	6.50

Very probably the last three items are for 6 months or less as this girl was sick at the convent for three months. The bill was made out after her death.

56. AMUQ., Sister St. Charles to Mother St. Catherine, April 11, 1825.

57. AUC., N.O., Private Archives, III, 227-228.

58. *Ibid.*, 228.

59. AMUQ., Sr. St. Joseph Laclotte to Mother St. Henri, January 25, 1826.

60. AMUQ., Sr. St. Louis de Gonzague Bougie to Mother St. Henri, June 1, 1826.

61. Father Joseph Rosati, C.M., a Neopolitan priest, volunteered for the Louisiana Mission and sailed for America, June 12, 1816. He was one of the mainstays of the Seminary of the Barrens.

62. "Diary of Bishop Rosati," *SLCHR.*, III, (October, 1921).

63. *Ibid.*, IV, (January - April, 1922). 96-98.

64. [Wolfe] *Ursulines in New Orleans*, 88-89.

65. AMUQ., Sister St. Joseph Laclotte to Mother St. Henri, July

8, 1826.

66. In 1833, he was elevated to the rank of Archbishop of Besançon, and in the same year he died. Had he lived a little longer he would have been created a cardinal.

67. "Diary of Bishop Rosati", *SLCHR.*, IV (October, 1922, 253-263.

68. Roger Baudier, *Catholic Church in Louisiana,* 307.

69. AMUQ., Sr. St. Louis de Gonzague to Mother St. Henri, ____, 1827.

70. *Ibid.*, Bishop DuBourg had never made a visitation of the community. He said it was useless, since he knew perfectly the personnel and spirit of the community. CF. AUC., N.O., Private Archives, III, 222.

71. AUC., N.O., *Visite Pastorale de Msgr. Rosati, 1827,* in Private Archives, IV, 145-152.

72. *Ibid,* 147.

73. *Ibid.*, 146-148; CAA., N.D., *Approbation: Donné à la Nouvelle-Orléans, le 31e jour de mai 1827.* Signed: *Joseph, Ev de St. Louis et Admin. de la Nouv. Orléans.*

74. At this time the Nuns began to have the classes preceded by an hour of study.

75. French was taught in the morning and English in the afternoon. Three times a week *"un bon Irlandais"* came to give special instruction in English which pleased the parents very much. Cf. AMUQ., Sr. St. Etienne to Abbé S.J. Desjardins, January 8, 1828.

76. AMUQ., Sister St. Etienne to Abbé S.J. Desjardins, January 8, 1828. Bishop Rosati preached their annual retreat that year.

77. AMUQ., Sr. St. Louis de Gonzague to Mother St. Henri, ____, 1827.

78. [Wolfe] *Ursulines in New Orleans,* 89, and Roger Baudier, *Catholic Church in Louisiana,* 311, both say that Bishop Rosati officiated; but it is certain that Bishop Rosati was not in New Orleans at the time.

79. AUC., N.O., Private Archives, III, 222.

80. *Ibid.*, 223.

81. [Wolfe] *Ursulines in New Orleans,* 89.

82. The Capuchin school for boys did not last a decade. The Spanish school, Father Martial's school, and Father Portier's school were all shortlived.

Bibliography

I

ARCHIVAL MATERIAL

I. Baltimore, Maryland: *Baltimore Cathedral Archives.*

No correspondence between Archbishop Carroll and the Ursulines is to be found in this repository. One letter, Father Wm. DuBourg to Archbishop Carroll, County of Acadia, La., July 2, 1814 was used.

II. Baton Rouge, Louisiana: *State Land Office.*

Among the records transferred by the Surveyor General of Louisiana to the State Land Office there are several that pertain to property of the Ursulines. These include a record of purchase of land from Jacques Larchevêque in 1736, as well as the grant from Governor Miró, December 2, 1789. These documents and other papers and surveys are found in a bundle marked "Various Claims, Notices and Plats, Various Dates. Opelousas."

III. Bordeaux, France: *Archives of the Archbishopric.*

Out of all the correspondence that must have been exchanged concerning the Ursulines of New Orleans only three papers remain.

1. A letter written to the Archbishop of Bordeaux by Father Olivier, chaplain of the Ursulines, May 17, 1804, explaining the need of the religious for more subjects.

2. A list of books and articles of clothing needed by those who would come, signed by Mother St. Xavier Farjon, May 19, 1804.

3. A letter signed by all the members of the community, May 19, 1804, treating in much greater detail the matter outlined in Father Olivier's letter. This letter is countersigned by Father Patricio Walsh.

IV. Chicago, Illinois: *Newberry Library,* Ayer Collection.

Relation de la Louisiane. "Relat de Kened." appears on the back of this bound manuscript of 265 pages. Although there is no date, it is probably 1735.

V. Havana, Cuba:

A. *Archives of the Archbishopric.*

Rev. Dr. Venancio Novo, in behalf of the writer, instituted a search for documents in the Archbishop's office relative to this dissertation, but found none. However, Dr. Novo did not conclude that there are no documents on this subject in these archives, for he wrote (Dec. 12, 1946): "At the Archbishop's office there are many documents that have not been catalogued." These archives are not open to the research student.

B. *Colegio de las Ursulinas.*

Climate and book worms have wrought havoc with many of the early documents preserved in these archives. Some are so mutilated and faded as to be no longer decipherable. The writer found the following the most helpful.

1. A folio without cover title. It is divided into three parts. The first, "*Fundacion del Convento de Ursulinas en la nueva Orleans: y venida de 16 religiosas de el a la Ciudad de la Habana y motivo que lo osaciono,*" is a copy of the "*Libro de Fundación.*" The second part, "*Copia literal del libro de defunciónes de las Religiosas Ursulinas de la Habana,*" is a series of biographical sketches. The third part, "*Copia de un legajo que se encuentra en al Archivo de esta Comunidad de Ursulinas de la Habana,*" consists of transcripts of important letters and legal papers. Among these is Someruelos acknowledgement of Mother St. Monica's letter (Oct. 21, 1802) requesting that her petition to go to Havana or Mexico be forwarded to the King of Spain. The originals are no longer extant.

2. *Legajo* No. 2. This *legajo* consists of two parts: 1) Certifications given by the Ursulines who remained in New Orleans to those who went to Havana. 2) Letters and other documents relative to a piece of land in New Orleans given (March 6, 1801) to Jacob, a Negro, by Mother St. Monica Ramos.

3. *Legajo* No. 11. A thick bundle of the numerous papers required by the Spanish authorities before a young woman could make profession in a religious community. Mother St. Monica and her companions took these with them when they went to Havana in 1803.

VI. New Orleans, Louisiana, U.S.A.

A. *Archives of the Archbishopric.*

Practically all the documents which have a bearing on this dissertation and which were formerly in this repository are now in the Catholic Archives of America, Notre Dame University. Among the very few papers that remain is one letter from the Ursulines to Bishop DuBourg, a copy of the act of donation of the old convent to the Bishop of New Orleans, and a *"Plan du nouvel hôpital servant de Caserme en 1797."*

Addendum: When the writer was doing research for this dissertation she used the relevant documents at Notre Dame. Since then photostats of these documents have been sent to New Orleans where they have been catalogued and are available to the research student.

B. *Cathedral Archives.*

Several of the early registers were examined and a number of entries copied.

C. *Archives of the City of New Orleans.*

1. *Concile de Ville.* Minutes of the session of the City Council of New Orleans. During the sessions April 17, 1819 to October 18, 1820 the Council discussed the opening of the streets through the convent property; from October 9 to November 4, 1824, the removal of the orphans from the care of the Ursulines was considered.

2. Records and Deliberations of the Cabildo, Book I, August 18, 1769 to August 27, 1779.

D. *Conveyance Office.*

Many transactions can be found in the *Conveyance Office Books* to which the Ursulines were a party. These are especially useful in instances where the notarial records have been destroyed.

E. *Historic New Orleans Collection* (formerly in the Howard-Tilton Library, Tulane University).

1. Bouligny-Baldwin Papers. There are four letters from Sister Marie Madelaine de Jésus during the years 1788 to 1792. Nos. 49a, 52, 57, 58.

2. Documents in Spanish and French relating to Padre Antonio de Sedella and his ecclesiastical differences with Vicar-General Patricio Walsh of the St. Louis Cathedral in New Orleans, 1778-1807. This collection contains several references to the Ursulines.

3. Plan of the convent of the Rev. Ursuline Mothers (1793). Photostat copy in Spanish. Explanation of the plan by L.P. Barbin (in English) included in the folder.

F. *Louisiana State Museum Library* and *Louisiana Historical Society.*

The materials belonging to the Louisiana Historical Society are housed jointly with those of the Louisiana State Museum and no distinction is made between them.

1. Records of the Superior Council of Louisiana (1717-

1769). These documents (11,748 pieces) comprise all that remain of the transactions before the Superior Council. A typewritten calendar of these records is available. Very many of the papers have been briefed in the *Louisiana Historical Quarterly.* I, (1917) and following issues. The Ursulines are first mentioned in these documents, Feb. 15, 1728, in a petition made by Madame Manade seeking temporary refuge in the convent. Other papers concerning orphans, financial transactions, slaves, petitions, etc., relate to the Ursulines.

2. *Concessions.* A bound volume of transcripts from AC, G l, 465.

3. *Louisiane-Recensements.* A bound volume of transcripts from AC, G 1, 464.

4. *French MSS., Mississippi Valley, 1679-1769.* This volume was printed in *Publications* of the Louisiana Historical Society, IV (1908), 4-120.

5. *Notes and Documents Historique Louisiane, 1673-1803.* Compiled by J. Magns from the Archives of the *Ministère de la Marine et des Colonies à Paris.*

6. *Sommaires et Index des Documents sur l'histoire de la Louisiane contenus aux Archives du Ministère de la Marine à Paris.* Three bound volumes of transcripts, extracts, and summaries made under the direction of Margry. The compiler completely changed the meaning of the statement regarding the Ursulines in the letter of Bienville and Salmon, March 8, 1733.

7. Plan: *Nouvelle-Orléans, avec les noms des concessionnaires, par Broutin, ingénieur—le 15 mai 1728.* This plan shows the location of the first residence of the Ursulines.

G. *Office of Notarial Records.*

Shortly after the Civil War, Andrew Hero, a prominent notary at that time, led a movement to create a central office for the keeping of all notarial records of deceased and resigned notaries of the Parish of Orleans. That office was created by an act of the State Legislature in 1867. The old notarial records that form a part of this office are full of information concerning the early history and legal transactions of New Orleans and go back as far as the year 1739. There are many references to the Ursulines in the records of Garic, Pedesclaux, Broutin, Quiñones, and others. The many bound and carefully written indices are helpful in searching for documents of a past era.

H. *Archives of the Ursuline Convent.*

This was the richest source of information. The documents in this repository are carefully preserved in a fire-proof vault. The oldest original manuscript is the account of the organization of the community of New Orleans at Hennebont, January 1, 1727. Some of the early documents are remarkably well preserved, e.g., the original grant (1727) of the plantation at Pointe St. Antoine. For certain periods and on some subjects there is copious material. On the other hand, there are many lacunae in the records. The ordinary daily life of the religious and their pupils is almost a blank page. No register of pupils for the years 1727 to 1827 is extant. Undoubtedly many records were destroyed in the process of moving, since the Ursulines of New Orleans have lived in five different convents counting the Kolly house and the two convents on Chartres Street. Many of the records have been kept in manuscript volumes.

1. *Actes de Prise d'Habit et de Professions. Lettres Circulaires.* (Private Archives, II). This is a folio volume containing the records of receptions of novices and professions with the names of the ecclesiastical witnesses. The last part contains the obituary letters which are a valuable source of biographical data.

2. Biographical Sketches of Number of Our Mothers. These accounts include some interesting episodes not recorded in the obituary letters.

3. *Cahier renfermant toutes les pièces relatives aux réclamations du fiscal pour le domaine royal du Roi D'Espagne: entre autres pièces curieuses se trouvent trois plans des terrains et bâtisses des casernes de l'hôpital et du couvent en ville.* A volume of certified copies of the original documents made at the time that the Ursulines were attempting to establish their claim to the property on which the convent and the hospital stood. The documents are practically all in Spanish and are dated between 1797 and 1801.

4. *Délibérations du Conseil,* I. (Private Archives, V). A folio volume covering the period 1727 to 1902. This is an invaluable source of information. Here are recorded very many important decisions made by the community as well as the results of triennial elections. Near the end of this volume is a lengthy description of the procession from the Kolly house to the first convent on Chartres Street (1734) written

by one of the participants, and an historical sketch of the first eight years in New Orleans written by Mother St. André Melotte, probably in 1735. At certain periods the minutes of the council meetings are either not kept or were recorded elsewhere and have been destroyed.

5. *Journal depuis 1727 jusqu'en 1853*. This small manuscript volume is the work of several annalists. The part treating of the early years is obviously a compilation or a transcription from an earlier copy.

6. *Les Ursulines de la Nouvelle-Orléans depuis leur établissement, jusqu'à nos jours*. Cited as Ursuline Annals. This is a manuscript history of the convent compiled about 1881 by Rev. Charles Bournigalle while he was chaplain at the convent. Much of the material is taken from secondary sources, but the compiler had at his disposal practically all the manuscripts and documents in the convent archives.

7. *Livre ou sont les noms et les années de la naissance des nègres et négresses qui sont venus au couvent sur Notre Habitation le 2 octobre 1824*.

8. *Premier Registre de la Congrégation des Dames Enfants de Marie. Le 28 mai 1730*.

9. Private Archives, III. A volume of transcripts of documents from the archives interspersed with accounts of contemporary events. There is a copy of Mother St. Augustin Tranchepain's "*Relation*" and a French translation of Bishop Echevarria's letter to the King of Spain (1774).

10. Private Archives, IV. This small volume includes transcripts of many important documents from the archives. Some of the originals are no longer extant. The lists of officials of the convent and of members of the community have been brought down to date.

11. Miscellaneous documents. There is a vast number of loose manuscripts in French, Spanish and English filed in folders according to subject treated or nature of the document. They include letters from bishops, French and Spanish officials, presidents of the United States, and other important personages, as well as copies of important letters written by the Ursulines. There are many papers relative to admission of pupils, the cloister, departure of the sixteen religious for Havana in 1803, appearance in court, opening of the streets through the convent property, burial privileges, old bills, contracts, specifications for the convent erected on the plantation below New Orleans, places of honor in the

convent chapel, a few old account books, etc.

12. Pastoral letter published by Father Patricio Walsh, V.G., March 27, 1805.

13. Plans. There are several plans showing the location of buildings and the division into lots of the four squares bounded by Ursulines, Royal, Barracks and Decatur Streets. An unsigned and undated floor plan is probably that of the main convent building erected in 1823-1824.

14. A packet of letters received by Mother Colomba Fitzwilliam, O.S.U., (1940) from the Ursuline Convents in France that sent religious to New Orleans between 1727 and 1827. These letters contain some precious notes, but for the most part they indicate that nearly all records of these early missionaries were lost either during the French Revolution or after the enactment of the law of July 7, 1804, when the Ursulines were expelled from their convents.

VII. Paris, France: Cf. Library of Congress.

VIII. Quebec, Canada.

A. *Archives of the Archbishopric.*

Carefully prepared card indices facilitate the use of the various registers and manuscripts.

1. *Etats-Unis.* Several letters from volumes I, II, and VI were used. The correspondence in vol. I gives a comparatively detailed account of the preparations for the trip to New Orleans in 1822, the journey, and the response of the religious to their new field of labor.

2. *Lettres.* Items from volumes II and X in this series were useful.

3. *Registres de l'Evêché de Québec.* In Registers 10, H., and I, there are several letters and other papers relative to the Ursulines of Quebec and of Trois Rivières who went to New Orleans in 1822.

4. *Vicaires Généraux.* Four volumes (III, IV. VI, and VIII) of this series proved to be useful for this dissertation. The letters drawn from volumes III., IV, and VI were sent by Abbé de l'Isle Dieu and Abbé de Villars to the Bishop of Quebec during the years 1746 to 1783. The letters selected from volume VIII treat the same subjects as those in the *Registres* noted above. Many of the letters from various registers were printed in *Records* of the American Catholic Historical Society, XIX (1908), 185-213.

B. *Monastère des Ursulines.*

By a very special favor the writer was given access to the documents in the secret archives that have any bearing on this dissertation.

1. *Annales de Monastère, II.* Secret archives. These annals have been well and faithfully kept. They include not only a record of events but also copies of letters, etc.

2. Miscellaneous letters from bishops, priests and nuns that contain information on the Ursulines in New Orleans.

3. Transcripts of many letters found in the Archives of the Archbishopric of Quebec.

4. *Les Constitutions des Religieuses de Sainte Ursule de la Congrégation de Paris.* Paris: Gilles Blaizor, 1646. One of the very rare copies of this edition still in existence.

C. *Archives du Seminaire,* Laval University.

Only two items were found in this repository:

1. L'Evêque de Pontbriand to Abbé de l'Isle Dieu, Oct. 30, 1757. A transcript of the original at Ottawa, *Archives Nationales.*

2. *Mémoire de Monseigneur L'Evêque de Québec sur le don que son altesse Royal feu Monseigneur Le Duc d'Orleans à fait pour les pauvres communautés du diocese de Québec.* (n.d.)

IX. St. Louis, Missouri, U.S.A.: *Archives of the Archdiocese.*

Among the DuBourg papers there are a few letters and papers relative to this dissertation. There is also a eulogy of Mother St. Michel Gensoul (d. 1822) and of Mother St. Joseph Laclotte (d. 1827).

X. Santiago, Cuba: *Archives of the Archbishopric.*

Since New Orleans was under the jurisdiction of the Bishop of Santiago de Cuba from 1772 to 1787 one might justifiably expect to find letters and other documents in this repository. A diligent search of the archives of the archbishopric and of the cathedral under the direction of Archbishop Valentin Zubizarretto failed to uncover a single document.

XI. Seville, Spain: *Archivo General de Indias.*

(Cf. Washington, D.C.) Of the documents in this repository the majority were studied from transcripts or photostats in the Library of Congress, Washington, D.C., where the bulk of the material dealing with the United States history in the Spanish Archives is now available. Transcripts of some documents not found in Washington were obtained from Seville. They were all from the *Papeles procedentes de Cuba.*

1. *Legajo* 14. 1787-1788. Correspondence between Sister Antonia de Santa Monica Ramos and Governor Miró concerning the orphans at the convent. 8 letters.

2. *Legajo* 15. 1789-1790. Correspondence between Sister Antonia de Santa Monica Ramos and Governor Miró concerning the orphans and also relative to a proposed cloister wall on the side of the river. 10 letters.

3. *Legajo* 174. Although both the catalogue of the Archives at Seville and Hill, *Descriptive Catalogue of the Documents . . . in the Papeles Procedentes de Cuba* indicates that there are several papers in this *legajo* relative to the Ursulines in New Orleans (1771-1773), they were not there nor could they be located when the research was being done for this dissertation.

4. *Legajo* 538B 1795-1803. Several papers relative to the pensions paid to the Ursulines (1770-1803) and to the Poor Clares at the Ursulines Convent (1795-1796) by the Spanish government.

5. *Legajo* 612C 1802-1803. Correspondence between Sister St. Monica Ramos and the Intendant Morales on various subjects including the orphans, payments due the Ursulines, dowry of a novice, and withdrawal to the Spanish dominions after the retrocession of Louisiana to France. 9 letters.

XII. South Bend, Indiana, U.S.A.: *Catholic Archives of America,* Notre Dame University.

This unique collection at the University of Notre Dame was the life-work of Professor James Farnham Edwards of that institution. Edwards, fully aware of the neglect shown for the documents of the past, made a tour through the United States begging for these historical materials. He must have possessed rare eloquence for he obtained a vast amount of documents, among them practically all the early archives of the Archdiocese of New Orleans. In the *Catholic Archives of America* the papers are filed in chronological order and indexed according to subject. In many instances all the papers relating to one subject are found together as they were tied and numbered when the matter was closed.

1. 1781-1793. *Testimonios de las Exploraciones de las Novicias del Monasterior de Ursulinas de Esta Ciudad de la Nueva Orleans.*

2. 1786-1787. Seven letters concerning the three French Ursulines, Mother St. Xavier Farjon and companions.

3. 1792-1795. Twelve letters and other papers relative to the honors due Almonester, Vidal, and Henriquez in the chapel of the Ursulines.

4. 1793. *Diligencias obradas sobre los requisitos que deben acompanar a las Educandas pa. ser admitidas en la Clausura de Religs. Ursulinas.* (53 folio pages)

5. 1795. General proceedings of the visit of the diocese of Louisiana and in particular of New Orleans by Don Luis Peñalver y Cárdenas, its first bishop, and the notary, Dr. José Maria de Rivas, his private and official secretary. (64 folio pages)

6. 1798-1804. No. 84. *Diligencias obradas pa. indagar la existencia de un negro nombrado Maturin, Esclavo de las Religiosas Ursulinas, qe. se supuso ahogado el ano se 1776 y bajo de su meurte se permitio a su consorte Teresa pasar a otras nupcias.*

7. 1803. No. 157. Document referring to transfer of Louisiana and Florida to France and calling for a declaration of intention by Fathers of the territory. Declaration of intention of several having Irish names.

8. 1803. No. 165. *Correspondencia con la Me. Superiora de Ursulinas de esta Ciudad sobre su ida con quinze Monjas a la Havana.* 10 letters.

9. 1803. No. 166. *Correspondencia con el Govor. de estas Provincias y el Marques de Casa Calvo sobre ida de la R. Me. Sor Antonia de Sta. Monica Ramos Superiora de Religiosas Ursulinas conquinze Monjas para la Ciudad de la Havana.* 10 letters.

10. 1790-1825. Scattered through these years are several papers that relate to various subjects—Poor Clares, orphans, withdrawal to Cuba, repair of buildings, slaves, financial matters, etc.

XIII. Washington D.C., U.S.A.

A. *The Library of Congress.*

After the Archives of the Ursuline Convent, New Orleans, this was the writer's most fruitful source of information. Three letters from the Jefferson papers were used. Extensive study was made of the transcripts, photostats, and photofilms which now render available the bulk of the documents dealing with United States history in the Archives of Paris and of Seville.

I. The Jefferson Papers

1. 1804, June 13. Petition from Sr. Thérèse de St. Xavier and Nuns of the Order of St. Ursula in New Orleans to secure the property of the order by formal confirmation of title. (141:2447-2448).

2. 1804, June 15. W.C.C. Claiborne to Jefferson enclosing the above petition. (141:24464).

3. 1804, July 13. Jefferson to Sr. Thérèse de St. Xavier and Nuns of the Order of St. Ursula, assuring them that their property would be protected. (polygraph copy, 142:24602).

II. Paris

a. Archives des Colonies

1. Series B. The dispatches of the Ministers of the Marine and of the Colonies are gathered in this series. Volumes 55, 57, 61, 63, 83, 85, 87 contain letters from Maurepas concerning the Ursulines.

2. Series C11A. *Correspondance Générale, Canada.* This series corresponds to C13A for Louisiana, but after 1740 it is also very important for religious history in Louisiana. Several letters for the years 1746 to 1757 were found in volumes 86, 89, 92, 95, 96, 98, 99, 100, and 102. In some instances these letters, especially those written by Abbé de l'Isle Dieu, give extracts or summaries of letters that are no longer extant.

3. Series C13A. *Correspondance Générale, Louisiane.* This series yielded much information. Here are to be found ten letters written by Mother St. Augustin Tranchepain, nine of them to Abbé Raguet, and four from Abbé Raguet to Mother St. Augustin. Extracts from the minutes of the meetings of the Directors of the Company of the Indies during which the choice of Ursulines for the hospital was discussed and two drafts of the contract of 1726 are given. Data for the years 1726 to 1770 was drawn from volumes 10 to 29, 31, to 40, 43, 44, 46, 47, 49, and 50. The last reference to the Ursulines, August 13, 1804 (vol. 53) acknowledges work done by the orphans for the French Republic and records a gift in return. Although the architect's plans for the first convent (1733) are numbered as an integral part of this series, they are filed separately in the Library of Congress.

4. Series D 2d, 10. Lists of missionaries in Louisiana. This series is not folioed. The report of December 1, 1744 is important for the Ursulines.

5. Series F 1, 94. May 13, 1747. M. de maurepas to Bishop Pontbriand.

6. Series G 1, 412. Transcripts of the parochial registers of New Orleans.

7. Series G 1, 464. Passengers to Louisiana and census.

8. Series G 1, 465. Land grants.

b. Bibliothéque Nationale

1. *Fonds Français, nouvelle acquisitions, n. 2551. f. 40.* Lists Ursulines among the religious at Martinique. ff, 146-147. Letters patent for the establishment of a community of religious at Cap Français.

III. Seville: Archivo general de Indias

After the insurrection of 1768 Louisiana was included in the captaincy-general of Havana and subjected in judicial concerns to the *audiencia* at Santo Domingo until 1795 and after that date to the *audiencia* at Havana. Hence the two series, *Audiencia de Santo Domingo* and *Papeles procedentes de Cuba*, contain many documents valuable for this dissertation. Most of these documents were studied from transcripts or photostats in the Library of Congress. Cf. XI. Seville.

1. *Audiencia de Santo Domingo.* References to the Ursulines were found in letters and reports of various Spanish officials among others Miró, Carondelet, O'Reilly and Morales. There are several papers relative to the orphans, property, salary of the religious, a cloister wall, withdrawal to Cuba in 1803, aid given to the Ursulines by Don Almonester and the honors due him in their chapel etc. Material was drawn from *legajos* 2531, 2533, 2544, 2551, 2552, 2554, 2576, 2579, 2585, 2588, 2589, 2590, 2594, 2599, 2640, 2645, 2672, 2673, and 2678. The typewritten calendar, "Introductory Pages to the *legajos* in the Audiencia de Santo Domingo series in the Archivo General de Indias, Seville, of which the Library of Congress has reproductions, was indispensable in locating the various papers.

2. *Papeles procedents de Cuba.* In this series is found correspondence relative to the proposed transfer of the Ursulines to Havana (1773-1777) and the actual withdrawal of sixteen in 1803. *Legajos* 102, 155B, 180, 593, 1400, 1572, in addition to those listed in XI, Seville, contained useful material.

B. *National Archives of the United States.*

Several papers relative to this dissertation were found among the records transferred from the various departments.

I. Department of the Interior

1. Private land claim dockets nos. 2224 LA., 4445 La., and 5098 La. The official plats of survey of the lands involved in these claims are also available in this office.

II. Department of State

1. 1804, January 14. Bishop Carroll to Secretary of State Madison. Enclosure, a letter from the Ursulines to Bishop Carroll, is missing.

2. 1804, July 20. James Madison to Bishop Carroll, acknowledging the above letter.

III. War Department

1. 1815, May 27. Andrew Jackson to the Secretary of War, enclosing two letters from the Ursuline Nuns.

2. 1815, Nov. 26 A.J. Dallas to the Secretary of War, enclosing a letter from A. Maréchal (with ground plan of the convent) and the reply of the Secretary of the Treasury to Maréchal.

3. 1815, June 17. Secretary of War to General Edmund P. Gaines, relating to exchange of property between the United States and the Ursulines and Secretary of War to Madame Olivier, June 17, 1815, on the same subject.

II

BIBLIOGRAPHICAL AIDS

Brymer, Douglas (arch.). *Report on Canadian Archives (1884-1887).* 4 vols.; Ottawa: Maclean, Roger and Co., 1885-1888.

"Guide to Depositories of Manuscript Collections in Louisiana." Prepared by the Works Projects Administration, *Louisiana Historical Quarterly,* XXIV (April, 1941), 305-353.

Hill, Roscoe R. *Descriptive Catalogue of the Documents Relating to the History of the United States in the Papeles Procedentes de Cuba Deposited in the Archivo General de Indias at Seville.* Washington: Carnegie Institution of Washington, 1916.

Leland, Waldo G. *Guide to the Archives of the Government of the U.S. in Washington.* 2nd ed.; Washington: Carnegie Institution of Washington, 1907.

_____. *Guide to Materials for American History in the Libraries and Archives of Paris.* Washington: Carnegie Institution of Washington, 1932.

Parker, David W. *Guide to the Materials for United States History in Canadian Archives.* Washington: Carnegie Institution of Washington, 1913.

Phillips, Phillip L. *A List of Geographical Atlases in the Library of Congress with Bibliographical Notes.*

Robertson, James A. *A List of Documents in Spanish Archives Relating to the History of the United States Which Have Been Printed or of Which Transcripts Are Preserved in American Libraries.* Washington: Carnegie Institution of Washington, 1910.

Shepherd, Wm. R. *Guide to Materials for the History of the United States in Spanish Archives, Simancas, the Archivo Historico Nacional, and Seville.* Washington: Carnegie Institution of Washington, 1907.

Surrey, Nancy M. Miller. *Calendar of Manuscripts in Paris Archives and Libraries Relating to the History of the Mississippi Valley to 1803.* 2 vols.; Washington: Carnegie Institution of Washington, 1928-1929.

III

PRINTED SOURCES

Acts of Congress Relative to Land Claims in the Territory of Orleans. New Orleans: Bradford and Anderson, 1807.

American State Papers, Class VIII, *Public Lands*, II. Gales and Seaton, 1834.

Annales de l'Association de la Propagation de la Foi. Lyon: Rusand, 1827-1828. I - III.

Bassett, John Spencer (ed.). *Correspondence of Andrew Jackson.* 7 vols.; Washington: Carnegie Institution of Washington, 1929-1935. II.

Bellin, S. *Le Petit Atlas Maritime recueil de cartes et plans des quatre parties du Monde en cinq volumes.* Paris, 1764, I.

Carter, Edwin (ed.). *Territorial Papers of the United States.* Vol. IX, *The Territory of Orleans, 1803-1812.* Washington: U.S. Government Printing Office, 1940.

Casgrain, H.T. (ed.). *Extraits des Archives des Ministères de la Marien et de la Guerre*, Canada, 1755-1760. Québec: L.J. Demers et Frère, 1890.

Courrier de la Louisiane, 1824, 1824, 1827.

Debates and Proceedings in the Congress of the United States. Washington: Gales and Seaton, 1854.

Edits, Ordonnances Royaux, Déclarations et Arrêts du Conseil d'Etat du Roi Concernant le Canada. 7 vols.; Québec: E.R. Frechette, 1854.

French, B.F. *Historical Collections of Louisiana.* 5 parts; New York: Wiley & Putnams, 1846-1875, III.

Hachard, Madeleine. *Relation du Voyage des Dames Religieuses Ursulines.* Paris: Maisonneuve et Cie., 1872.

"Letters Concerning Some Missions of the Mississippi Valley, A.D. 1818-1827," *Records* of the American Catholic Historical Society, XIV (1903), 141-216.

Louisiana Gazette, June 12, 1812; Jan. 3 to July 8, 1821.

Moniteur de la Louisiana, 1804, 1807.

Pease, T.C. and Jenison, E. (eds.). *Illinois on the Eve of the Seven Years' War, 1745-1755. (Collections of the Illinois State Historical Library,* XXIX). Springfield, 1940.

Receuil des Lettres des Evêques et des Missionaires des Missions des Deux Mondes. Louvain: Vailinthout et Vandenzande, 1825.

Revised Laws of Louisiana, 1897. Comp. and annot. by Solomon Wolff. New Orleans: F.F. Hansell & Bro., 1897.

Rowland, Dunbar (ed.). *Official Letter Books of W.C.C. Claiborne, 1801-1816.* 7 vols.: Jackson, Miss.: State Department of Archives and History, 1917.

Rowland, Dunbar and Sanders, A.G. (eds.): *Mississippi Provincial Archives, French Dominion, 1701-1729.* Jackson Miss.: Miss. Dept. of Archives and History, 1929.

Serrano y Sanz, Manuel. *Documentos Historicos de las Florida y la Luisiana siglos XVI al XVIII.* Madrid: *Libreria General de Victoriano Suarez,* 1912.

"Some Correspondence Relating to the Dioceses of New Orleans and St. Louis (1818-1843)," *Records* of the American Catholic Historical Society, XIX (1908), 185-213.

Tranchepain, Mère St. Augustin de. *Relation du voyage des premières Ursulines à la Nouvelle-Orléans et de leur établissement en cette ville.* New York: Cramoisy Press, 1859.

Tranchepain, Sr. Mary of St. Augustin. "Account of the Voyage of the Ursulines to New Orleans in 1827." *U.S. Catholic Historical Magazine,* I (1887), 28-41.

IV

SECONDARY WORKS

A. Books

Annales de l'Ordre de Ste-Ursule formant la continuation de l'Histoire Générale du même institut depuis la Révolution Française jusqu'à nos jours. 2 vols.; Clermont-Ferrand; Ferdinand Thibaud, 1857.

Arthur, Stanley C. *Old New Orleans.* New Orleans: Harmanson, 1937.

Baudier, Roger. *The Catholic Church in Louisiana.* New Orleans: 1939; reprinted: Louisiana Library Association, 1972.

Baunard, L'Abbé. *Histoire de Mme Duchesne.* Paris: Poussielgue Frères, 1878.

Berquin-Duvallon. *Vue de la Colonie Espagnole du Mississippi oude Louisiane et Florida Occidentale en l'année 1802.* Paris: A L'Imprimerie Expeditive, 1803.

Burson, Caroline M. *The Stewardship of Don Esteban Miró, 1789-1792.* New Orleans: American Printing Co., 1940.

Callan, Louise. *The Society of the Sacred Heart in North America.* New York: Longmans, Green & Co., 1937.

Campbell, Thomas J. *The Jesuits, 1534-1921.* New York: Encyclopedia Press, 1921.

Castaneda, Carlos E. *The Mission Era: The End of the Spanish Regime, 1780-1810,* Vol. V of *Our Catholic Heritage in Texas, 1519-1936.* 7 vols.; Austin: Von Boeckmann-Jones Co., 1942.

Castellanos, Henry C. *New Orleans as It Was.* New York: L. Graham and Son, 1896.

Caughey, John Walton. *Bernardo de Galvez in Louisiana, 1776-1783.* Berkeley: University of California Press, 1934.

Chambers, Henry E. *Mississippi Valley Beginnings.* New York: Putnam, 1922.

Chambon, Rev. C.M. *In and Around the Old St. Louis Cathedral of New Orleans.* New Orleans: Philippe's Printery, 1908.

Channing, Edward. *A History of the United States.* 6 vols.; New York: Macmillan Co., 1909, I.

Charlevoix, Pierre F. X. de. *Histoire et description générale de la Nouvelle France, avec le Journal historique d'un voyage fait par ordre du roi dans l'Amérique Septentrionnale.* 6 vols.; Paris: Ganexu, 1744.

Colby, Charles Wm. *Founder of New France.* Toronto: Glassgow, Brook & Co., 1935.

Les Constitutiones des Religieuses de Sainte Ursule de la Congrégation de Paris. Paris: Gilles Blaizor, 1646.

Davis, Matthew L. *Memoirs of Aaron Burr, with Miscellaneous Selections from His Correspondence.* New York: Harper & Brothers, 1837.

De Courcy, Henry. *The Catholic Church in the United States.* New York: Edward Dunigan & Brother, 1857.

Dehey, Elinor T. *Religious Orders of Women in the United States.* Hammond, Ind.: W.B. Conkey, 1930).

Delanglez, Jean, S.J. *The French Jesuits in Lower Louisiana* (1700-1763). Washington: The Catholic University of America, 1935.

De Villaumbrosia, D. Pedre G. *Historia Chronológica y General de la Orden de Sata Ursula.* 4 vols.; Zaragoza: Jose Bedera, 1866.

Duncan, Rev. Herman C. *The Diocese of Louisiana.* New Orleans: A.W. Hyatt, 1888.

Easterly, Rev. Frederick J. *The Life of Right Reverend Joseph Rosati.* C.M. Washington: Catholic University of America, 1942Erskine, Marjory.

Mother Philippine Duchesne. New York: Longmans, Green & Co., 1926.

Fortier, Alcée. *A History of Louisiana.* 4 vols.; New York: Manzi, Joyant & Co., 1904.

Gayarré, Charles. *History of Louisiana.* 3rd ed., 4 vols.; Armand Hawkings, 1885.

Geschichte de hl. Angela Merici und des von ihr gestifteten Ordens der Ursulinen. Innsbruck, 1893.

Goebel, Edmund J. *A Study of Catholic Secondary Education During the Colonial Period up to the First Plenary Council of Baltimore, 1852.* Washington: Catholic University of America, 1937.

Gosselin, Auguste H. *L'Eglise du Canada depuis Monseigneur de Laval jusqu'à la Conquête,* Quebec: Laflamme & Proulx, 1911-1914.

_____. *L'Eglise du Canada après la Conquête.* Quebec: Laflamme, 1916.

_____. *Mgr. de Saint-Vallier et son temps.* Evreux: Eure, 1898.

Guilday, Peter. *The Life and Times of John Carroll.* 2 vols.; New York: Encyclopedia Press, 1922.

Heinrich, Pierre. *La Louisiane sous la Compagnie des Indes.* 1717-1731.

Paris: Maissoneuve Frères, 1908.

Hogan, Rev. J.A. *The Pilgrimage of Our Lady of Prompt Succor: An Historical Sketch.* New Orleans: J.G. Hauser, 1907.

Hubert-Robert, Régine. *L'Histoire Merveilleuse de la Louisiane Française, Chronique des XVIIe et XVIIIe siècles et de la Cession aux Etats-Unis.* New York: Maison Française, 1941.

King, Grace. *Jean Baptiste Le Moyne, Sieur de Bienville.* New York: Dodd, Mead and Co., 1893.

Laurent, Laval. *Québec et l'Eglise aux Etats-Unis sous Mgr. Briand et Mgr. Plessis.* Washington: Catholic University of America.

Lauvrière, Emile. *Histoire de la Louisiane Française (1673-1939).* University, La.: Louisiana State University Press, 1940.

Le Page Du Pratz. *Histoire de la Louisiane.* 3 vols.; Paris: De Bure, 1758.

Lettres de la Vénérable Mère Marie de l'Incarnation, Première Supérieure des Ursulines de la Nouvelle-France. Paris: Antoine Vuarin, 1684.

McCaleb, Walter Flavius. *The Aaron Burr Conspiracy.* New York: Wilson-Erickson, 1936.

Maria Alma, Sister. *Standard Bearers.* New York: P.J. Kennedy & Sons, 1928.

Martin, François-Xavier. *The History of Louisiana, from the Earliest Period.* 2 vols.; New Orleans: Lyman and Beardslee, 1827-1829.

Martin, Mère Marie de St. Jean, O.S.U., *L'Esprit de Ste. Angèle Merici.* Brescia: Morcelliana, 1947.

_____. *Ursuline Method of Education.* Rahway, N.J.: Quinn & Boden Co., 1946.

Monica, Sister M. *Angela Merici and Her Teaching Idea.* New York: Longmans, Green and Co., 1927.

Norman, Benjamin M. *Norman's New Orleans and Environs.* New Orleans, 1845.

O'Brien, J.J. *The Louisiana and Mississippi Martyrs.* New York: Paulist Press, 1928

O'Reilly, Rev. Bernard. *St. Angela Merici and the Ursulines.* New York: Pollard & Moss, 1880.

Orsenigo, Rev. Cesare. *Life of St. Charles Borromeo.* St. Louis: B. Herder, 1945.

Pastor, Ludwig. *The History of the Popes.* St. Louis: B. Herder, 1923, VI.

Postel, Abbé V. *Histoire de Sainte Angèle Mérici et de tout l'Ordre des Ursulines.* 2 vols.; Paris: Poussielque Frères, 1878.

Règlements des Religieuses Ursulines de la Congrégation de Paris; divisez en trois livres. Paris: Louis Josse, 1705.

Règles et Constitutions pour les Religieuses Ursulines de la Présentation Notre-Dame, de l'ordre de St. Augustin. Lyon: M.P. Rusand, 1829.

Rochemonteix, Camille de. *Les Jesuites et la Nouvelle France acc XVIIIe siecle.* 3 vols.; Paris: Letouzely et Ané, 1895-96.

Rose, Stewart. *Ignatius Loyola and the Early Jesuits.* London: Burns and Oates, 1891.

Rothenstenier, Rev. John. *History of the Archdiocese of St. Louis in Its Various Stages of Development from A.D. 1673 to 1927.* 2 vols; St. Louis: Blackwell Wielandy Co., 1928.

Ruskowski, Leo F. *French Emigré Priests in the United States.* Washington: Catholic University of America, 1940.

Schlarman, J.H. *From Quebec to New Orleans.* Belleville: Buechler Publishing Co., 1929.

Seebold, Herman de B. *Old Plantation Homes and Family Trees.* 2 vols.; New Orleans: Pelican Press, 1941.

Semple, Henry Churchill. see [Wolfe, Mother Thérèse].

Shea, John Gilmary. *History of the Catholic Church in the United States.* 4 vols.; New York: John G. Shea, 1886-1892.

[Thibaut, Mère Marie de Chantal]. *Sainte Angèle Mérici et l'Ordre des Ursulines.* 2 vols.; Paris: J. De Gigord, 1922.

Thwaites, Reuben G. (ed.). *Jesuit Relations and Allied Documents.* 72 vols.; Cleveland: The Burrows Brothers, 1900.

Les Ursulines de Québec depuis leur établissement jusqu'à nos jours. 4 vols.; Québec: C. Dareau, 1864.

Les Ursulines des Trois-Rivières depuis leur établissement jusqu'à nos jours. 3 vols.; Trois-Rivières: P.V. Ayotte, 1886.

The Ursulines in Louisiana, 1727-1824. New Orleans: Hyman Smith, 1886.

Villiers, Le Baron Marc de. *Histoire de la Fondation de la Nouvelle-Orléans (1717-1722).* Paris: Imprimerie Nationale, 1917.

Vogel, Claude L. *The Capuchins in French Louisiana (1722-1766).* Washington: Catholic University of America, 1928.

[Wolfe, Mother Thérèse], ed. Semple, Henry Churchill. *The Ursulines in New Orleans and Our Lady of Prompt Succor. A Record of Two Centuries, 1727-1925.* New York: P.J. Kenedy & Sons, 1925.

b. Periodical Articles

Adams, Reed Mc.C.E. "New Orleans and the War of 1812," *Louisiana Historical Quarterly,* XVII (Jan. - July, 1934), 167-182; 349-363; 502-523.

Baudier, Roger. "Pioneer Shrine of Our Lady of Prompt Succor," *Messenger of Our Lady of Prompt Succor,* (January, 1940), 11-22.

Bispham, Clarence W. "Contest for Ecclesiastical Supremacy in the Valley of the Mississippi, 1763-1803," *Louisiana Historical Quarterly,* I (January, 1918), 154-189.

———. "Fray Antonio de Sedella," *Louisiana Historical Quarterly,* II (January-October, 1919), 24-37; 369-392.

Bjork, David K. (ed.). "Documents Relating to the Establishment of Schools in Louisiana, 1771," *Mississippi Valley Historical Review,* XI (March, 1925), 561-569.

Briede, Kathryn C. "A History of the City of Lafayette," *Louisiana Historical Quarterly,* XX October, 1937), 895-964.

Carroll, M.A. "Education in Louisiana in French Colonial Days," *American Catholic Quarterly Review,* XI (1886), 396-417.

———, "Education in New Orleans in Spanish Colonial Days," *American Catholic Quarterly Review,* XII, (April, 1887), 253-417.

Corrigan, O.B. "Episcopal Succession in the United States. The Province of New Orleans," *Catholic Historical Review,* II (1916-1917), 127-130.

Cruzat, Heloise Hulse. "*Les Ursulines de la Louisiane,*" *Bulletin de la Société de Géographie de Québec,* XVI (November-December, 1922), 281-294.

———. "New Orleans Under Bienville," *Louisiana Historical Quarterly,* I (January, 1918), 5-23.

———, "Sidelights on Louisiana History, Church Education in New Orleans," *Louisiana Historical Quarterly,* I (January, 1918), 55-86.

———. "The Ursulines of Louisiana," *Louisiana Historical Quarterly,* XX (July, 1937), 578-589.

Dart, Henry P. "Documents Concerning Bienville's Lands in Louisiana,"

Louisiana Historical Quarterly, X (1917), 5-24; 161-184; 364-380; 538;561; XI (1928), 87-110; 209-232; 463-465.

Delanglez, John, S.J. "The Natchez Massacre and Governor Périer," *Louisiana Historical Quarterly,* XVII (October, 1934), 641.

Devron, Dr. G. *"Deux lettres inédites du Rev. Père N.I. de Beaubois, S.J. (1726-1727), fondateur de la mission des Jesuites en Louisiane et premier directeur des Ursulines de la Nouvelle-Orléans,"* Comptes-Rendus de L'Athénée Louisianais, I, 1 septembre 1897, 142-149.

Dimitry, Chas. "The Oldest House in the Mississippi Valley, *The Southern Bivouac,* II (January, 1887), 457-460.

Faye, Stanley. "The Schism of 1805 in New Orleans," *Louisiana Historical Quarterly,* XXII (January, 1939), 98-141.

Fossier, A.E. "The Charity Hospital of Louisiana," *New Orleans Medical and Surgical Journal,* (May-October, 1923).

Guay, Chas. *"La Nouvelle-Orléans et les Religieuses Ursulines,"* La Semaine Religieuse de Québec, XIX (11 mai - 27 mai 1907), 615-618; 631-635; 649-653.

Hughes, William M. "An American Shrine: Our Lady of Louisiana," *Donahoe's Magazine,* LI (February, 1904), 157-164.

Kendall, John S. "Old New Orleans Houses," *Louisiana Historical Quarterly,* XVII (October, 1934), 680-705. Very inaccurate.

Kenny, Laurence J., S.J. "The First American Nun in This Country," *Illinois Catholic Historical Review,* I (April, 1919), 495-499.

King, Grace. "Notes on the Life and Services of Bienville," *Louisiana Historical Quarterly,* I (January, 1918), 39-53.

Lafarque, André. "The French Governors of Louisiana," *Mississippi Valley Historical Review,* XIV (1927), 156-167.

_____. "Pierre Clement de Laussat," *Louisiana Historical Quarterly,* (January, 1941), 5-8.

Lenhart, John M. "The Double Jurisdiction in French Louisiana (1722-1766)", *Franciscan Studies,* VII (September, 1947), 344-347.

"Lettre de Bienville," *La Revue Canadienne,* October, 1881, 596-599.

Miller, Rev. N. "Pioneer Capuchin Missionaries," *Historical Records and Studies,* XXI (1932), 170-234.

Mobley, James Wm. "The Academy Movement in Louisiana," *Louisiana Historical Quarterly,* XXX (July, 1947), 738-978.

Munroe, W.B. "The Office of Intendant in New France, a Study of

French Colonial Policy," *American Historical Review*, XII (1906), 15-38.

O'Brien, J.J. "Sketch of the Expulsion of the Society of Jesus from Colonial Louisiana," *Publications* of the Louisiana Historical Society, IX (1916) 9-24.

O'Callaghan, M.T. "Echoes of Gallicanism in New France," *Catholic Historical Review*, VI n.s. (1926), 16-58.

"Our Convents, The Ursulines," *Metropolitan Magazine*, IV (1856), 24-32.

Porter, Betty. "The History of Negro Education in Louisiana," *Louisiana Historical Quarterly*, XXV (July, 1942), 728-821.

Renshaw, Henry. "The Louisiana Ursulines," *Publications* of the Louisiana Historical Society, II (December, 1901), 25-42.

Richardson, Caroline F. "A Note on the Organization of the Oldest School for Girls in the Mississippi Valley," *Proceedings* of the Mississippi Valley Historical Association, VIII (1914-1915), 201-209.

Riley, Martin Luther. "The Development of Education in Louisiana Prior to Statehood," *Louisiana Historical Quarterly*, XIX, (July, 1936), 595-634.

Rothensteiner, John. "Historical Sketch of Catholic New Madrid." *St. Louis Catholic Historical Review*, IV (July, 1922, 113-129.

Roy, Regis. "*Monseigneur François de Mornay, Troisième Evêque de Québec,*" *Bulletin des Recherches Historiques*, X (1904), 20-22.

St. Charles, Mother. "The First American Born Nun," *Illinois Catholic Historical Review*, I (Oct. 1918), 173-175.

Santis, F.L.R. and Souvay, Chas. L. "Church of Lafayette, Louisiana (1821-1921)," *St. Louis Catholic Historical Review*, III (1921) 247-248.

Soniat, Meloncy C. "The Faubourgs Forming the Upper Section of the City of New Orleans," *Louisiana Historical Quarterly*, XX (January, 1937), 192-211.

Souvay, Rev. C.M. "Episcopal Visitation of the Diocese of New Orleans, 1827-1828," *St. Louis Catholic Historical Review*, I (July-October, 1919), 215-230.

Steck, Francis Borgia. "Interesting Incidents in the Catholic History of the Southwest," *Fortnightly Review*, XL (June, 1933), 121-122.

Styles, William A. "Pioneer American Nuns," *Avé Marie*, LV, n.s. (February 7, 1942), 167-170.

Sulte, Benjamin, "*Les Gouverneurs des Trois-Rivières*," *Bulletin des Recherches Historiques*, II (1896), 66-72.

Surrey, N.H. "The Development of Industries in Louisiana during the French Regime, 1673-1763)," *Mississippi Valley Historical Review*, IX (1922) 227-235.

Têtu, Mgr. Henri. "Mgr. Duplessis de Mornay,", *Bulletin des Recherches Historiques*, IV (August, 1898), 258-265.

Théard, D.J. "The Founding of New Orleans," *Louisiana Historical Quarterly*, III (1920), 68-70.

"Ursulines of New Orleans. The Arrival of Postulants from France a Century Ago," *Records* of the American Catholic Historical Society, XXI (1910), 125-128.

Vogel, Ettie M. "The Ursuline Nuns in America," *Records* of the American Catholic Historical Society, I (1884-1886), 214-243.

Watrin, Philibert F., S.J. "Memoir on the Louisiana Missions," *Researches* of the American Catholic Historical Society, XVII (July, 1900), 89-92.

_____. "*Mémoire abrégé sur les missions de la colonie nommée Louisiane*," *Magazine of Western History*, I (1885), 263-266.

Wilson, Samuel, Jr. "An Architectural History of the Royal Hospital and the Ursuline Convent of New Orleans," *Louisiana Historical Quarterly*, XXIX (July, 1946), 559-659.

_____. "Early Aids to Navigation at the Mouth of the Mississippi River," *United States Naval Institute Proceedings*, LXX (March, 1944), 279-290.

Winston, James E. "The Cause and Results of the Revolution in Louisiana," *Louisiana Historical Quarterly*, XV (April, 1932), 181-213.

Supplementary Reading

For an updated bibliography of early Louisiana Catholicism, see Charles E. Nolan, "Louisiana Catholic Historiography" in the 1993 archdiocesan bicentennial volume, *Cross, Crozier, and Crucible.*

Baudier, Roger. *Through Portals of the Past: The Story of the Old Ursuline Convent of New Orleans.* New Orleans, 1955.

Callan, Louise, R.S.C.J. *Rose Philippine Duchesne: Frontier Missionary of the Sacred Heart.* Westminster: Newman Press, 1957.

Caraman, Philip. *St. Angela — The Life of Angela Merici Foundress of the Ursulines,* London: Longmans, Green and Co., Ltd., 1963.

Conrad, Glenn R. *A selected Bibliography on Scholarly Literature on Colonial Louisiana and New France.* Lafayette, LA.: Center for Louisiana Studies, 1982.

Conrad, Glenn R., ed. *A Directory of Louisiana Biography.* Lafayette, LA.: Louisiana Historical Association in cooperation with the Center for Louisiana Studies, 1988.

Davis, Edwin Adams. *Louisiana, A Narrative History.* Baton Rouge, LA.: Claitor's Publishing Division, 1971.

Ellis, John Tracy. *Catholics in Colonial America.* Baltimore, MD.: Helicon Press, Inc., 1963.

Farnsworth , Jean M. and Masson, Ann M., eds. *The Architecture of Colonial Louisiana, Collected Essays of Samuel Wilson, Jr., F.A.I.A.* Lafayette, LA: The Center for Louisiana Studies, University of Southwestern Louisiana, 1987.

Goodspeed Publishing Co., ed. *Biographical and Historical Memoirs of Louisiana...in Three Volumes, Illustrated.* Chicago, 1892. Louisiana Classic Series Reprint. Baton Rouge: Claitor's Publishing Division, 1975, 3 Vols.

Hachard, Marie-Madeleine, OSU. *Letters of Marie-Madeleine Hachard, Ursuline of New Orleans,* 1727-28. Translated by Myldred Masson Costa. New Orleans, LA, 1974.

Howard, Janice M. *Angela.* St. Lynheham, Australia: Australian Province of Ursulines, 1989.

Ledochowska, Teresa. *Angela Merici and the Company of St. Ursula.* 2 Vols., Milan: Ancora, 1968.

McAvoy, Thomas T., C.S.C., *A History of the Catholic Church in the United States.* Notre Dame, Indiana: University of Notre Dame Press, 1969.

Mahoney, Irene, O.S.U. *St. Angela Merici, Foundress of the Ursulines.* New Rochelle, New York, 1985.

Mariani, L., Tarolli, E., Seynaeve, M. *Angelo Merici, Contributo Per Una Biografia,* Milan: Ancora, 1986.

Martin, Marie de St. Jean, OSU. *The Spirit of St. Angela.* Translated from the French. Southward, England, 1950.

Moran, Mary Yvonne, OSU. *Angela: God's Magnet.* Great Neck, N.Y., 1988.

Myers, Francis d'Assisi, OSU. *St. Angela of the Ursulines.* Milwaukee, 1952.

Reeves, Sally Kittredge. *Legacy of a Century.* New Orleans, LA., 1987.

Reidy, Mary. *The First Ursuline: The Story of St. Angela Merici.* Westminster, Md., 1961.

Taylor, Joe Gray. *Louisiana, A History.* New York: W.W. Norton & Co., 1976.

Toledano, Roulhac, Evans, Sally Kittredge, and Christovich, Mary Louise. *New Orleans Architecture Volume IV: The Creole Faubourgs.* Gretna, LA : Pelican Publishing Co., 1974.

Wall, Bennett H., ed. *Louisiana, A History.* 2nd. ed. Arlington Heights, Ill.: Forum Press, Inc., 1990.

Index